SPECTR

TEACHER'S EDITION **1**

A Communicative Course in English

Joan Dye
Nancy Frankfort

Donald R. H. Byrd *Project Director*

Anna Veltfort *Art Director*

Regents/Prentice Hall
Englewood Cliffs, NJ 07632

Publisher: Tina B. Carver
Development and Editing: (Student Book) Larry Anger, Mary Vaughn, Deborah Goldblatt, Deborah Brennan, Jeffrey Krum, Karen Davy, Stephanie Karras; (Teacher's Edition) Gerry Strei, Larry Anger, Karen Davy
Production and Manufacturing: Jan Sivertsen, Shari Toron, Ray Keating, Sylvia Moore, Lori Bulwin, Leslie Coward, David Riccardi
Composition: (Teacher's Edition) Don Williams
Cover Design: Roberto de Vicq
Interior Concept and Page-by-Page Design: Anna Veltfort
Audio Program Producer: Phyllis Dolgin

ACKNOWLEDGMENTS

Illustrations: Student Book pp. 1-4, 6 (bottom), 8-9, 15, 18-19, 28-29, 38-39, 52-53, 60, 64-65, 74-75, 85 (bottom), 88-89, 92-93, 100-101, 110-111, 120-121, 134-135, 144-145, 150, 152, 154-155, 157 (top, bottom), 160 by Anna Veltfort; pp. 7, 33 (map), 34, 37, 49, 55-57, 72, 81 (left), 82-83, 96, 123 (middle), 124 (top) by Chris Reed; pp. 5, 16-17, 31, 33 (except map), 51, 67-69, 95 (bottom), 97 (middle), 104-105, 127-129 by Gene Myers; pp. 6 (top), 21 (left), (original photo courtesy of Lan Chile), 22 (top), 24 (drawings), 50 (bottom), 62, 81 (right) by Jim Kinstrey; pp. 87, 113-115, 117, 119 by Ivor Parry; pp. 11 (left), 43 (top), 103, 106-107, 118, 125-126 (top), 153, 157 (middle) by Don Martinetti; pp. 36, 63 (bottom), 70 (top), 132 by Cathy Braffet; pp. 11 (right), 12, 14, 41, 45 (right), 133 by Silvio Redinger; pp. 26, 45 (left), 46-47, 50 (top), 59 by Denise Brunkus; pp. 140, 142 (bottom), 143 by Anne Burgess; pp. 141, 147-149 by Randy Jones; pp. 84, 116 by Susan Tomlingson; p. 48 by Arnie Ten; p. 28 (watermelon) by David Riccardi; p. 85 (middle) by Roberto de Vicq; p. 86 (top) by Ron Barrett; p. 94 by Daisy de Puthod.

Photos: pp. 4, 13, 20 (top row, bottom middle), 21-23, 26, 45-46, 61, 130 (bottom right) by Ken Karp; p. 5 (top left) by Barry Talesnick/Retna Ltd.; p. 5 (top right) by Chris Walter/Retna Ltd.; p. 5 (bottom left) courtesy of Kirarasha (Kinkara Music Publisher); p. 5 (bottom right) ©1990 CBS Records International, Inc.; p. 10 courtesy of Japan National Tourist Organization; p. 20 (bottom left) by Ed Lettau/Photo Researchers; p. 54 (top left, middle left, middle right, bottom left) by Laima Druskis; p. 54 (top right) City of New York Dept. of Sanitation; p. 66 courtesy of British Tourist Authority; p. 90 (top) by Richard Rodamar; pp. 90 (bottom three), 112 (fourth), 137-139, 153, 156 by Rhoda Sidney; pp. 91 (top and middle), 92 (bottom left and right), 102 courtesy of the Greater New Orleans Tourist and Convention Commission; pp. 91 (bottom), 93 courtesy of the Chamber of Commerce of the New Orleans Area; p. 32 (top) by the USDA; p. 32 (second) courtesy of the Rice Council; p. 32 (middle) United Fresh Fruit and Vegetable Association; p. 32 (bottom) the Massachusetts Horticultural Society; p. 122 Movie Star News; pp. 130 (top left), 146 New York Convention and Visitors Bureau; p. 130 (top right, bottom left) by Irene Springer; p. 156 (top right) United Nations.

Realia: pp. 10, 16, 20, 24, 27, 30, 40, 42-44, 54-57, 63, 66, 70-71, 73, 76, 86, 90, 95, 97-98, 102, 108, 123-124, 126, 131, 136, 142, 158 (bottom) by Roberto de Vicq; pp. 122, 143, 146, 153, 156, 158 (top), 159, 160 by Anna Veltfort.

Prentice Hall International (UK) Limited, *London*
Prentice Hall of Australia Pty. Limited, *Sydney*
Prentice Hall Canada, Inc., *Toronto*
Prentice Hall Hispanoamericana, S.A., *Mexico*
Prentice Hall of India Private Limited, *New Delhi*
Prentice Hall of Japan, Inc., *Tokyo*
Simon & Schuster Asia Pte. Ltd., *Singapore*
Editora Prentice Hall do Brasil, Ltda., *Rio de Janeiro*

10 9 8 7 6 5 4 3 2 1

ISBN 0-13-829920-4

CONTENTS

UNIT		PAGES	THEMES	FUNCTIONS
1	**Lessons 1 – 7**	1–10	Greetings Introductions Self-identification	Introduce yourself Identify people Greet formally and informally Verify spelling
2	**Lessons 8 – 13**	11–20	Telephone calls	Make an informal telephone call Identify someone on the telephone Ask for someone's phone number Call Directory Assistance Thank someone Ask for change Apologize
3	**Lessons 14 – 19**	21–30	Cities and countries Socializing Addresses	Ask about the location of cities Ask where people are from Introduce people Offer something to drink Say good-bye after meeting someone Ask for someone's address
4	**Lessons 20 – 25**	31–40	Neighborhood locations Directions	Give locations in a neighborhood Give locations in an apartment building Give directions in a neighborhood
	Review of units 1 – 4	41–44	Review	Review
5	**Lessons 26 – 31**	45–54	Jobs and occupations Personal information	Talk about jobs and occupations Talk about your job Talk about where you live Exchange personal information

S E Q U E N C E

LANGUAGE	FORMS	SKILLS

Hello. Hi. I'm Kenji Sato.
  My name is William Stone. Nice to meet you.
Excuse me, are you Tom Cruise? Yes, I am. No, I'm not.
How are you? Fine. Not bad.
What's your name, please?
  Could you spell your last name?
  N-I-E-L-S-E-N? Yes, that's right.
	Present of *be*:
	• *am, is*
	• contractions
	• questions with *are*
	• short answers with *I*
	Alphabet
	Formula *Could you . . . ?*
		Listen for a spelling
		Listen to the intonation of short
		  statements
		Read a postcard
		Write a short postcard to a friend
		  (workbook)

Is Susan there? Yes, she is. Just a minute, please.
  No, she isn't.
Is this Bill? No, this is Carlos.
What's your phone number? It's 555-2012.
I'd like the number of Jane Schaeffer.
Thank you. You're welcome.
Do you have change for a dollar?
Yes, I do. Here you are. No, I don't.
I'm sorry. That's O.K.
	Present of *be*:
	• yes-no questions and short
	  answers with *is*
	Numbers 0–10
	Formula *I'd like . . .*
	Formulaic use of *do*
		Listen for a phone number
		Listen to the intonation of questions
		Read a short newspaper article
		Write an opinion about the telephone
		  (workbook)

Where's Tokyo? In Japan.
Where are you from? I'm from Brazil.
The Lopezes are from Mexico.
Tony, this is my friend Linda.
  Linda, this is Tony.
Do you want some coffee? Yes, please.
  No, thank you.
Good-bye. Nice meeting you.
What's Jim's address? It's 60 Bank Street.
	Present of *be*:
	• information questions
	• statements
	• yes-no questions
	• short answers
	Plural of names
	Formulaic use of *do*
	Numbers 11-100
	Possessive of names
		Listen for addresses
		Listen to a radio advertisement
		Listen to the intonation of statements
		  and questions
		Read a letter and an envelope
		Write a short friendly letter
		  (workbook)

Is the post office near here? Where's the post office,
  please? On Second Avenue./Between Main and
  High Streets./Across from the park./Next to the
  restaurant./On the corner of Second and High.
Where's the Brunis' apartment? On the first floor.
Walk to the corner. Go straight ahead for two blocks.
  Turn right/left.
	Prepositions of place
	Ordinal numbers 1st–10th
	Possessive of names
	Imperative
	Adverbs of location
		Listen for directions
		Listen to the pronunciation of
		  possessives of names
		Read a page from a tour guide
		Write directions for a walking tour
		  (workbook)

Review	Review	Review

Laura is an accountant. She works in an office.
  Accountants work in offices.
What do you do? I'm a doctor. Where do you work?
  I work at Memorial Hospital.
Do you live around here? Do you live in a house/an
  apartment? Where do you live?
  On Maple Street./At 25 Maple Street./
  On the second floor./In apartment 2B.
Are you married? No, I'm single.
	Formulaic use of third person
	  simple present in statements
	Articles *a* and *an*
	Plurals of nouns
	Simple present with *you* and *I*:
	• statements
	• questions
	• short answers
	Prepositions *in, on,* and *at*
		Listen for information about people
		Listen to consonant reduction and
		  blending in *do you, is he,* and *is she*
		Read a short newspaper article
		  on jobs
		Write about your job (workbook)

UNIT	PAGES	THEMES	FUNCTIONS
6 **Lessons 32 – 38**	55–66	Birthdays Family Languages Nationalities	Give day, month, and year Talk about birthdays and birth dates Give information about people Talk about family Talk about languages and nationalities Ask what something means Ask how to say something Ask for clarification Ask to borrow something
7 **Lessons 39 – 43**	67–76	Business calls Leisure plans	Make a business telephone call Leave a message Say hello and good-bye Talk about leisure plans
Review of units 5 – 7	77–80	Review	Review
8 **Lessons 44 – 50**	81–90	Clothing and personal belongings Colors	Talk about clothing and personal belongings Compliment someone Look for a lost item Ask where something is Give directions Talk about the past
9 **Lessons 51 – 57**	91–102	Suggestions Objections Time	Talk about what people are doing Talk about the weather Make a suggestion Object or agree Ask what time it is Find out hours Talk about movies Talk about likes and dislikes Talk about feelings

SEQUENCE

LANGUAGE	FORMS	SKILLS
What's the date next Sunday? When's your birthday? It's February twelfth (12th). What year were you born? In 1971. Christine lives at 27 Willow Street. She goes to high school and she works at Macy's. Samuel and Nancy are husband and wife. Do you have any brothers or sisters? What does your sister do? What language do they speak in Jamaica? Do you speak Portuguese? Are you Brazilian? What does *mucho gusto* mean? How do you say "thank you" in Korean? Excuse me? Could you speak a little slower, please? Could I use your pencil? Sure. Here.	Ordinal numbers 11th–31st Formulaic use of *was* and *were* with *born* Simple present: • affirmative statements • irregular verbs • third person singular pronunciation • questions • negative statements • short answers Formula *Could I . . . ?* Terminology for family relationships	Listen for dates Listen to consonant reduction and blending in *What does he/she . . . ?* Read an advertisement Write a short paragraph about yourself (workbook)
May I help you? May I speak to Richard Lightner, please? May I take a message? Could you ask him to call me? I'll give him the message. Good morning/afternoon/evening. Good-bye./Good night./Have a nice weekend./See you tomorrow. What are you going to do this weekend? I'm going to visit a friend. What is Rob going to do this evening/tomorrow night/next weekend/on Sunday?	Formula *May I . . . ?* Formula *I'll . . .* Object pronouns Formulaic use of future with *going to* Expressions of future time	Listen for names, days, and telephone numbers in phone conversations Listen for consonant reduction with pronouns *them, him,* and *her* Read a short article Write a phone message (workbook)
Review	Review	Review
What color are her gloves? That's a nice blouse. They're on the table. I don't have my keys! Is there a telephone near here? There's one upstairs. Where were you?	Colors Demonstrative pronouns: *that* and *those* *In, on, under,* and *behind* Possessive adjectives *There is* The past of *be*	Listen to descriptions of clothing and personal belongings Listen to the intonation of information questions Read a short newspaper article Write an opinion about TV (workbook)
He's reading a book. It's hot and sunny. Let's go to a museum. That's a good idea. / That's too boring. What time is it? What time do you open? What's playing this week? I don't really like old movies. I'm having a wonderful time.	The present continuous *Let's . . .* Weather Articles: *a, an,* and *the* Time Subject questions Placement of adjectives	Listen to a weather report Listen to suggestions and objections Listen for times Read a page from a tour guide Write a movie review (workbook)

S E Q U E N C E

INTRODUCTION

A complete course. The new edition of *Spectrum* is a six-level course designed for adolescent and adult learners of English. Levels 1 and 2 of *Spectrum* are appropriate for beginning students and "false beginners." Levels 3 and 4 are intended for intermediate classes. Levels 5 and 6 are for advanced learners. The student book, workbook, and audio cassette program for each level provide practice in all four communication skills, with a special focus on listening and speaking in levels 1 to 4, and on reading and writing in levels 5 and 6.

Real communication from the beginning. *Spectrum* is "a communicative course in English," and is based on the idea that communication—the exchange of information—is not merely the end-product of language study, but rather the very process through which a new language is acquired. To this end, *Spectrum* has three basic aims:

- to provide motivating materials that teach students to function in real-life situations;
- to teach only authentic English that stimulates natural conversation both in and outside the classroom; and
- to give students a feeling of success and achievement as they learn the language.

From the very beginning, students practice language that can be put to immediate use. For example, students learn to ask for information, make suggestions, and apologize. They learn the appropriate language for different situations, such as formal speech used with strangers and informal speech with friends. Most importantly, they are encouraged to express their own ideas and feelings, and to give their own opinions.

Language learning the natural way. *Spectrum* acknowledges that students can understand more English than they are able to produce. In other words, their ability to comprehend language (to listen or read) naturally precedes their ability to produce it (to

speak or write). To this end, *Spectrum* places great emphasis on comprehension. Students in the beginning and intermediate levels begin each unit by listening to and reading conversations that provide rich input for language learning. Many of the functions, grammatical structures, and vocabulary items in these conversations become "active" and are practiced in the lessons that follow. However, some of the functions and structures in these conversations are "receptive"—they are intended for comprehension only—and do not become productive until later units or levels.

At the advanced levels (levels 5-6), each unit begins with an authentic text for reading and discussion, and provides cultural and thematic input. In addition, a realistic conversation provides context for active practice in the pages that follow.

A carefully graded syllabus. As they engage in a variety of exercises that practice basic linguistic functions, students are guided toward the use of correct grammatical structures. Both the functions and the structures in the *Spectrum* syllabus are carefully graded according to simplicity and usefulness. Grammatical structures are presented in clear paradigms with informative usage notes.

Sometimes students encounter and use grammar and expressions that are not formally introduced until later units or levels—for example, when language items are needed to perform a given function appropriately. The goal is to provide students with a continuous stream of input that challenges their current knowledge of English, thereby allowing them to progress naturally to a higher level of competence. In the beginning level, for instance, students learn expressions such as "Could you spell your last name?" and "May I take a message?," although the modals *could* and *may* are not analyzed systematically until the intermediate level. In the advanced level, the same structures are expanded further. This system of preview-review works as follows:

- the structures are previewed—introduced formulaically.
- they are then analyzed—examined and practiced systematically.
- when appropriate, they are reviewed—recycled for further practice.

Changes in the new edition. Heeding the insights and suggestions of reviewers and long-time users of *Spectrum* around the world, significant changes have been made in the new edition of *Spectrum*.

- The first four levels of *Spectrum* are available in split editions—1A, 1B, 2A, 2B, 3A, 3B, 4A, and 4B—as well as full editions.
- Each student book contains a substantial amount of new material accompanied by color illustrations and photographs.
- At the beginning and intermediate levels, each unit begins with a summary of the language that is featured and practiced. In addition, there is a preview task on this page that relates the theme of the first lesson to the students' own experiences or prepares the students for the cultural material in the lesson.
- The student book is divided into self-contained one- and two-page lessons, each with its own thematic focus. The workbook is divided into corresponding one- and two-page lessons.
- A greater range of exercise types, including interviews, role-plays, and information-gap activities, has been included to challenge students.
- There is an increase in the number and variety of listening activities in the course.
- Reading selections at the end of each unit are more challenging. They are often longer and include pre-reading tasks as well as strategies for reading in English.

REVIEWERS AND CONSULTANTS

For the preparation of the new edition, Regents/Prentice Hall would like to thank the following long-time users of *Spectrum*: Motofumi Aramaki, *Sony Language Laboratory*, Tokyo, Japan; *Associacão Cultural Brasil-Estados Unidos (ACBEU)*, Salvador-Bahia, Brazil; *AUA Language Center*, Bangkok, Thailand, Thomas J. Kral and faculty; Pedro I. Cohen, Professor Emeritus of English, Linguistics, and Education, *Universidad de Panamá*; *ELSI Taiwan Language Schools*, Taipei, Taiwan, Kenneth Hou and faculty; James Hale, *Sundai ELS*, Tokyo, Japan; *Impact*, Santiago, Chile; *Instituto Brasil-Estados Unidos (IBEU)*, Rio de Janeiro, Brazil; *Instituto Brasil-Estados Unidos No Ceará (IBEU-CE)*, Fortaleza, Brazil; *Instituto Chileno Norteamericano de Cultura*, Santiago, Chile; *Instituto Cultural Argentino Norteamericano (ICANA)*, Buenos Aires, Argentina; Christopher M. Knott, *Chris English Masters Schools*, Kyoto, Japan; *The Language Training and Testing Center*, Taipei, Taiwan, Anthony Y.T. Wu and faculty; *Lutheran Language Institute*, Tokyo, Japan; *Network Cultura, Ensino e Livraria Ltda*, São Paulo, Brazil; *Seven Language and Culture*, São Paulo, Brazil.

Components of the beginning course

Flexible design. The new edition of *Spectrum* has been designed to be used in a variety of instructional programs and teaching situations.

- The full editions of student books 1 and 2 consist of fourteen units divided into one- or two-page lessons. The split editions contain seven units each. At this beginning level, there are review sections after every three or four units.
- The workbooks are divided into lessons and review sections which correspond to the lessons in the student books. The workbook lessons can be used in class or assigned as homework.
- There is an audio cassette program to accompany the student book and workbook at each level. The full edition has a six-cassette program. Each split edition has a three-cassette program.
- The teacher's editions provide a wide range of suggestions for using the various components of the course.
- A testing package includes a placement test for the six-level course and achievement tests for each level.

Variable course length. For classes using the full edition of the student book, each level of *Spectrum* contains approximately sixty hours of instructional material. Class time can be expanded to approximately ninety hours by using the optional activities in the teacher's edition and by using the workbook lessons as a regular classroom activity. Using sections of the audio cassette program for practice in the language laboratory can also increase the length of the instructional program.

Each split edition of the student book contains approximately thirty hours of classroom material. Class time can be expanded to approximately forty-five hours by using the optional activities in the teacher's edition and by incorporating the workbook lessons into the classroom program.

T H E   S T U D E N T   B O O K

Each unit of the student book begins with a preview page which gives an overview of the language in the unit and a preview of the conversations in the first lesson.

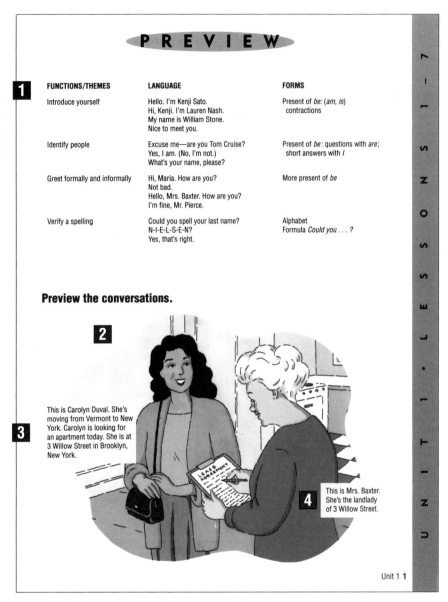

PREVIEW

1

FUNCTIONS/THEMES	LANGUAGE	FORMS
Introduce yourself	Hello. I'm Kenji Sato. Hi, Kenji. I'm Lauren Nash. My name is William Stone. Nice to meet you.	Present of *be*: (*am, is*) contractions
Identify people	Excuse me—are you Tom Cruise? Yes, I am. (No, I'm not.) What's your name, please?	Present of *be*: questions with *are*; short answers with *I*
Greet formally and informally	Hi, Maria. How are you? Not bad. Hello, Mrs. Baxter. How are you? I'm fine, Mr. Pierce.	More present of *be*
Verify a spelling	Could you spell your last name? N-I-E-L-S-E-N? Yes, that's right.	Alphabet Formula *Could you . . . ?*

Preview the conversations.

2

3 This is Carolyn Duval. She's moving from Vermont to New York. Carolyn is looking for an apartment today. She is at 3 Willow Street in Brooklyn, New York.

4 This is Mrs. Baxter. She's the landlady of 3 Willow Street.

UNIT 1 · LESSONS 1–7

Unit 1 **1**

---

1. Each preview page gives a concise summary of the functions, themes, language, and grammatical structures taught in the unit.

2. Illustrations and photographs introduce students to the theme and setting of the first lesson.

3. Discussion questions encourage students to think about the theme and relate it to their own lives. Students may discuss these questions in English or in their native language.

4. Illustration and discussion invite cross-cultural comparisons. Information about culture and context facilitate comprehension.

Each unit is divided into one- and two-page lessons. In the first lesson, opening conversations focus on comprehension.

1. Moving to a new city

Carolyn Duval finds a nice apartment.

A
Carolyn Duval Excuse me—are you Mrs. Baxter?
Woman No, I'm not.
Carolyn Sorry.

B
Carolyn Excuse me—are you Mrs. Baxter?
Mrs. Baxter Yes, I am.
Carolyn I'm Carolyn Duval.
Mrs. Baxter Nice to meet you, Ms. Duval.

C
Mrs. Baxter Let's see. . . . Carolyn . . . C-A-R-O-L-Y-N?
Carolyn Yes, that's right.
Mrs. Baxter Could you spell your last name, please?
Carolyn D-U-V-A-L.
Mrs. Baxter Sign here, please.

2 Unit 1

1. Opening—or presentation—conversations present natural language set in authentic situations students can relate to.

2. The context of the conversations is enhanced by full-color art which illustrates the story.

3. Conversations are recorded on cassette in natural spoken English. Sound effects help give the conversations authenticity. Recorded material is always indicated by the symbol ▄▄▄.

4. New functions and structures are introduced initially for recognition only as students listen to and read the conversations. Time is allowed for the new language to be absorbed—to "sink in"—before it is actively practiced. Most of the functions, structures, vocabulary, and expressions taught in *Spectrum* are systematically previewed in this way.

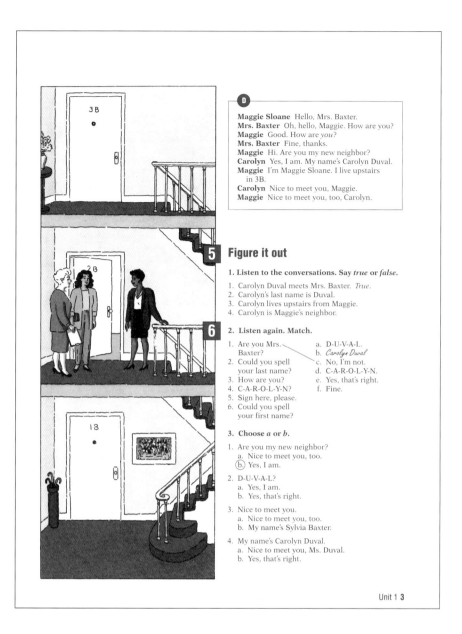

D

Maggie Sloane Hello, Mrs. Baxter.
Mrs. Baxter Oh, hello, Maggie. How are you?
Maggie Good. How are *you*?
Mrs. Baxter Fine, thanks.
Maggie Hi. Are you my new neighbor?
Carolyn Yes, I am. My name's Carolyn Duval.
Maggie I'm Maggie Sloane. I live upstairs in 3B.
Carolyn Nice to meet you, Maggie.
Maggie Nice to meet you, too, Carolyn.

Figure it out

1. Listen to the conversations. Say *true* or *false*.

1. Carolyn Duval meets Mrs. Baxter. *True*.
2. Carolyn's last name is Duval.
3. Carolyn lives upstairs from Maggie.
4. Carolyn is Maggie's neighbor.

2. Listen again. Match.

1. Are you Mrs. Baxter?
2. Could you spell your last name?
3. How are you?
4. C-A-R-O-L-Y-N?
5. Sign here, please.
6. Could you spell your first name?

   a. D-U-V-A-L.
   b. *Carolyn Duval*
   c. No, I'm not.
   d. C-A-R-O-L-Y-N.
   e. Yes, that's right.
   f. Fine.

3. Choose *a* or *b*.

1. Are you my new neighbor?
   a. Nice to meet you, too.
   b. Yes, I am.

2. D-U-V-A-L?
   a. Yes, I am.
   b. Yes, that's right.

3. Nice to meet you.
   a. Nice to meet you, too.
   b. My name's Sylvia Baxter.

4. My name's Carolyn Duval.
   a. Nice to meet you, Ms. Duval.
   b. Yes, that's right.

Unit 1 **3**

5. Students can listen to the conversations several times, each time focusing on different information. The exercises in the **Figure it out** section encourage recognition of the new language but do not require students to produce it.

6. Task-based exercises help students learn valuable skills, such as listening for the main idea, listening for specific details, and drawing inferences.

Next, several thematic lessons stress productive practice through real communication.

1 **2. Nice to meet you.**

INTRODUCE YOURSELF

3 ▶ Listen to the conversations below.
▶ Practice them with a partner. Use your own name.
▶ Introduce yourself to five classmates.

Kenji Hello. I'm Kenji Sato.
Lauren Hi, Kenji. I'm Lauren Nash.

William Hello. My name's William Stone.
Vicky I'm Vicky Martinez.
William Nice to meet you, Vicky.
Vicky Nice to meet you, too.

Hi is more informal than **hello.**

INTRODUCE YOURSELF • **PRESENT OF** *BE (AM, IS)*: **CONTRACTIONS**

2 ▶ Study the frames: Contractions

5

| I am | Maggie Sloane. | | I'm | Maggie Sloane. |
| It is | nice to meet you. | → | It's | nice to meet you. |

I'm and **It's** are contractions.
Nice to meet you = It's nice to meet you.

3 ▶ Practice the conversation using contractions.
▶ Practice it again, using your own name.

Maggie I am Maggie Sloane. *I'm Maggie Sloane.*
Carolyn My name is Carolyn Duval.
I am your new neighbor.
Maggie It is nice to meet you, Carolyn.
Carolyn It is nice to meet you, too.

4 Unit 1

1. A general theme serves to naturally group together important functions and structures in each one- or two-page lesson.

2. A clear and colorful design divides each lesson into major teaching points. Important functions and grammar points are clearly highlighted so the teacher and the student know the goals of each lesson.

3. Natural spoken models of the new language are recorded on cassette and provide aural input before students practice on their own.

4. Students practice new language in context, and examples of oral exchanges and conversations are always provided for reference.

5. After they are practiced in context, structures are analyzed formally. Special usage notes for grammatical structures, functions, and vocabulary are given when appropriate.

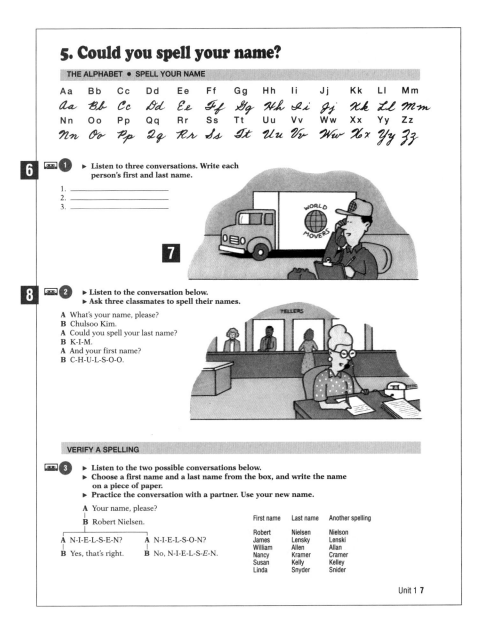

5. Could you spell your name?

THE ALPHABET • SPELL YOUR NAME

Aa	Bb	Cc	Dd	Ee	Ff	Gg	Hh	Ii	Jj	Kk	Ll	Mm

Nn	Oo	Pp	Qq	Rr	Ss	Tt	Uu	Vv	Ww	Xx	Yy	Zz

6

► Listen to three conversations. Write each person's first and last name.

1. _____
2. _____
3. _____

7

8

► Listen to the conversation below.
► Ask three classmates to spell their names.

A What's your name, please?
B Chulsoo Kim.
A Could you spell your last name?
B K-I-M.
A And your first name?
B C-H-U-L-S-O-O.

VERIFY A SPELLING

► Listen to the two possible conversations below.
► Choose a first name and a last name from the box, and write the name on a piece of paper.
► Practice the conversation with a partner. Use your new name.

A Your name, please?
B Robert Nielsen.

A N-I-E-L-S-E-N?   A N-I-E-L-S-O-N?
B Yes, that's right.   B No, N-I-E-L-S-*E*-N.

First name	Last name	Another spelling
Robert	Nielsen	Nielson
James	Lensky	Lenski
William	Allen	Allan
Nancy	Kramer	Cramer
Susan	Kelly	Kelley
Linda	Snyder	Snider

Unit 1 **7**

6. Task-based listening activities give students practice in hearing, understanding, and responding to spoken English.

7. Illustrations, photographs, and realia provide the context for meaningful language practice.

8. At least one exercise in each lesson is more open-ended and less controlled in nature. This type of exercise encourages students to use the language that they have learned to communicate important and relevant information about themselves and their experiences.

The thematic lessons are followed by a comprehension lesson, which offers more challenging input, listening practice, pronunciation hints, and a conversation task.

6. Welcome to Willow Street.

George Arno, owner of Arno's Coffee Shop, meets his new neighbor, Carolyn Duval.

1

2

3

4

1

George	Hi.
Carolyn	Hello.
George	Moving in?
Carolyn	Yes, I am.
George	Well then, we're neighbors. My name's George Arno and that's my coffee shop.
Carolyn	I'm Carolyn Duval. Nice to meet you.
George	Nice to meet you, too, Miss . . . uh . . . Laval?
Carolyn	No, *Du*val. But just call me Carolyn.
George	O.K., Carolyn. And you can call me George.
Loretta	GEORGE!
Jeff	Excuse me . . . uh . . . Mr. Arno, Mrs. Arno wants to . . .
Loretta	GEORGE!
George	Thanks, Jeff. COMING, LORETTA! Well, nice meeting you, Carolyn. Come in for coffee sometime.
Carolyn	Thank you. I will.

8 Unit 1

1. All dialogues are on cassette and have been recorded at normal conversational speed featuring authentic-sounding voices and sound effects.

2. A two-page illustration, rich in visual cues, encompasses the comprehension dialogue and the exercises that follow. The illustration can be used as a point of departure for additional practice.

3. A dialogue provides additional input by reinforcing language from the unit as well as previewing functions and structures from future units.

4. A storyline featuring recurring characters runs throughout the book and can be used to prompt class discussion about the characters and situations.

6 📼 **3. How to say it**

Listen to this conversation.

Maggie Hi, my name's Maggie Sloane.

Carolyn Nice to meet you.

I'm Carolyn Duval.

UNITED STATES
POST OFFICE

Pala

ACADEMY
WINNER

5 **2. Figure it out**

True or *False?*

1. Carolyn is moving to Willow Street.
2. Carolyn is George Arno's new neighbor.
3. Carolyn's last name is Laval.
4. Mrs. Arno's first name is Loretta.
5. "Arno's" is a coffee shop on Willow Street.

7 📼 **4. Listen in**

The man in the phone booth is making an appointment. Listen to the conversation. Spell the man's last name.

8 **5. Your turn**

Look at Maggie Sloane and her neighbor, John Pierce, above. Play the role of Maggie. Greet John.

Unit 1 **9**

5. **Figure it out**, an activity that usually follows the dialogue, tests listening comprehension.

6. **How to say it** uses sentences or short exchanges from the unit to teach intonation and pronunciation. Clues to the production of authentic conversational English include vowel reduction, consonant loss, and blending.

7. **Listen in** is a short, unscripted listening activity—for example, an "overheard" conversation, telephone recording, radio broadcast, or public announcement—which provides valuable additional listening practice.

8. **Your turn** features an open-ended conversation activity that allows students to use the language they have learned in imaginative ways. Students act out possible conversations for situations depicted in the illustration.

In the last lesson of each unit, reading activities provide practice in interpreting and understanding authentic models of written English.

7. Here I am in Kyoto!

1

Dear Susan,
Here I am in Kyoto! I really like it here. There are a lot of beautiful places, and the people are friendly, too. Japan is a very interesting country. I'll write again soon and tell you all about it.
Love,
Marilyn

2

Ms. Susan Laszlo
915 Shevlan Drive
El Cerrito, CA 92022
U. S. A.

3 1. **Read the postcard. Say** *True* **or** *False.*

1. Marilyn is in Japan.
2. Susan lives in Kyoto.
3. Marilyn likes Japan.
4. The people in Kyoto are nice.

4 2. **Find two reasons why Marilyn likes Kyoto.**

10 Unit 1

1. Students read real-life texts such as postcards, letters, magazine and newspaper articles, and advertisements.

2. Reading provides students with written language input. Previously learned functions and structures are reinforced while new items are previewed. These texts may be written at a level somewhat above the students' oral language ability in an attempt to provide challenge as well as to provide the rich language input that is a feature of *Spectrum*.

3. Certain exercises accompanying each text focus on general comprehension. Other exercises guide students through the selection with the intention of improving students' reading strategies in English.

4. The topics of the readings provide natural points of departure for open-ended communication such as discussion and sharing opinions.

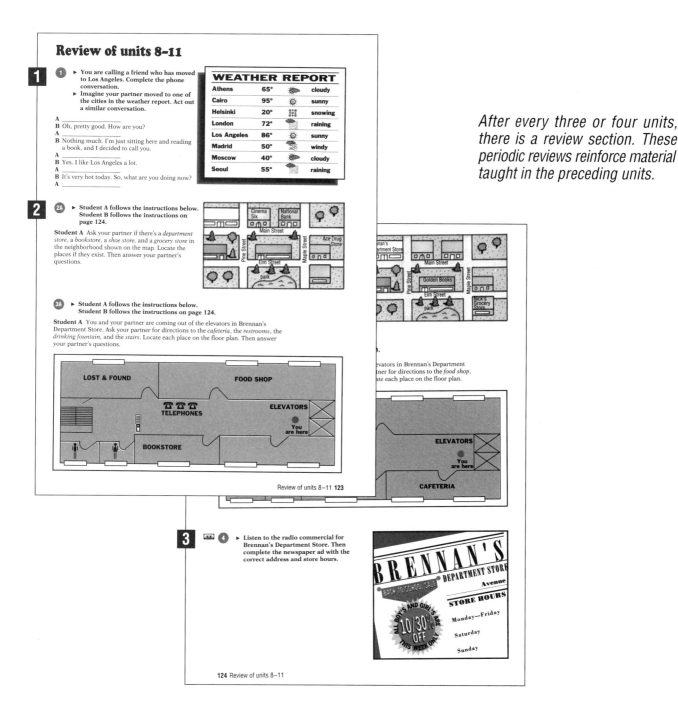

After every three or four units, there is a review section. These periodic reviews reinforce material taught in the preceding units.

1. Language is recombined in a variety of productive pair and group activities.

2. Information-gap activities are an important feature of the review sections. Each student in a pair refers to a different page for his or her instructions.

3. Listening tasks provide additional aural comprehension practice.

THE WORKBOOK

The workbook can be used independently by students at home or as additional work in class. It is divided into lessons which correspond to the lessons in the student book. There are also corresponding review sections.

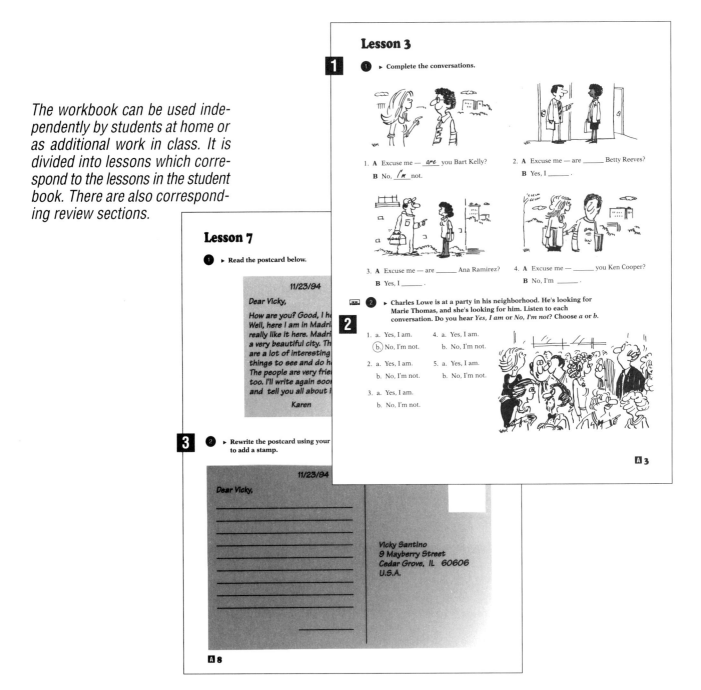

1. The workbook provides writing practice on the functions, grammatical structures, and vocabulary introduced in the student book.

2. It provides additional listening practice, including exercises that focus on stress, intonation, blending, and the pronunciation of particular sounds.

3. The last lesson of the workbook unit is either a guided composition or a free writing activity. The writing task is usually related to the theme of the reading in the last lesson of the student book unit.

THE TEACHER'S EDITION

The teacher's edition provides a wide range of suggestions for using the components of the course. The recommendations for teaching each exercise in the student book can be adapted to suit individual teaching styles and to meet the needs of particular students.

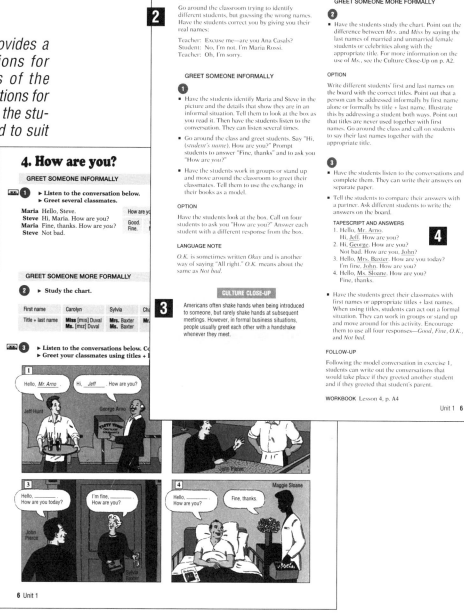

1. The teacher's edition features page-by-page instructions conveniently interleaved with duplicates of the student book pages. Also included are the scope and sequence chart, vocabulary lists, and guide to pronunciation symbols from the student book. The answer key for the workbook exercises and the scripts for the workbook listening activities are located at the back of the book.

2. Suggested warm-up exercises and optional activities are provided for each lesson and can be used when time is available.

3. Background information, including notes on language and culture, is given for conversations and readings as well as for certain exercises. Notes concerning methodology and pronunciation are also provided.

4. Included in the instructions are answer keys for exercises and scripts for the listening activities.

THE AUDIO CASSETTE PROGRAM

For each level, there is a set of audio cassettes that may be used with the student book and its accompanying workbook. Material that is recorded on cassette is preceded by the symbol 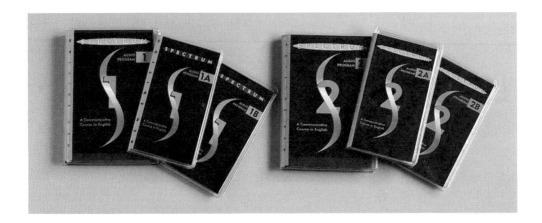.

1. Four cassettes (two cassettes for a split edition) in each set contain material from the student book and feature all the conversations, model dialogues, and listening activities, as well as a dramatization of the reading selection in each unit. These realistic recordings have been done by professional actors and include music and sound effects.

2. Two cassettes (one cassette for a split edition) in each set are to be used with the workbook and contain additional listening activities as well as exercises that focus on different aspects of pronunciation in English.

3. Complete scripts for the recorded material from the student book and workbook are located in the teacher's edition.

THE TESTING PACKAGE

A placement test for the six-level course and two achievement tests for each level are available to programs using *Spectrum*.

The placement test has been developed to allow teachers and administrators to place students in the appropriate level of *Spectrum*. The two achievement tests can serve as mid-term and final exams in programs that use the full editions of the student book. They can be used as final exams in programs using the split editions.

GENERAL TEACHING CONCEPTS

Although specific suggestions are given for each pair and group activity in the page-by-page teaching notes of this teacher's edition, some general teaching concepts are particularly applicable to the successful use of *Spectrum*. These include ways to stimulate classroom interaction through problem-solving, role-playing, and other communicative practice in groups and pairs. Also included are ideas for using games and songs, and evaluating students' progress.

Paired practice and group work. Students need to interact freely with others in order to achieve the communicative goals of the course. Many of the exercises in *Spectrum* have been specifically designed for practice in pairs or small groups, thus allowing all of the students to be actively involved at the same time. This type of practice gives students a chance to use new language without the pressure of performing in front of the class, thus encouraging a favorable attitude toward English and promoting a feeling of success and self-esteem.

- Before having the students work in pairs or groups, act out part of the exercise with a volunteer to demonstrate how to do the exercise.
- While your students are practicing, it is a good idea to move from pair to pair to offer assistance where necessary and to discourage students from using their native language.
- After acting out the conversation once, students should exchange roles and, if possible, choose new partners. Changing roles and partners is especially valuable in conversational exercises where students ask for personal information, because with each new partner the conversation will be slightly different, thus providing a new challenge.
- To conclude the practice, sets of students can volunteer to go through the exercise for the whole class.

It is possible to divide students into groups or pairs at random according to how they are seated in the classroom. Some teachers, however, find it effective to place students into groups based on their individual needs and abilities. At times it is better to put students of similar abilities together so that more proficient students can challenge each other and less proficient students can take the time they need to concentrate on difficult areas. In this way, all students can work at their own pace. At other times it is advantageous to have strong students work with students who are progressing more slowly in order to provide encouragement and serve as peer models.

For those class situations where it is difficult to have students work in groups or pairs, you can present an exercise by practicing it with several individual students. After the students are familiar with the exercise, call on pairs to practice it together. Each new pair of students should add new vocabulary or give personal information if appropriate.

Problem-solving and information-gap activities. Communication is most authentic when there is an actual exchange of information between students, with neither speaker knowing in advance what the other will say or how he or she will say it. Many of the activities in the new edition of *Spectrum* incorporate this element of unpredictability. Such tasks as locating places on a map, identifying people's occupations based on a series of clues, conducting interviews, or asking for directions require the students in a pair or group to seek information they do not have—to collaborate, examine alternatives and options, and exchange opinions.

Problem-solving and information-gap activities are extremely valuable. By focusing the students' attention on a problem to be solved, they are provided with an opportunity for real communication. More important than the actual completion of the task are the interaction skills the students use to reach their goal. During an activity, you should be prepared to:

- assist students in using functions necessary for pair or group interaction, such as asking for a meaning, interrupting politely, asking for and giving an opinion, and asking for clarification; and

- move from pair to pair or from group to group, noticing whether one or two students are dominating or whether someone is interrupting in an inappropriate manner.

By observing the process of communication, you can give the group suggestions on how to improve the interaction.

Role-playing and dramatization. Role-playing activities and dramatization of conversations and situations can make language come alive and can add variety, spontaneity, and fun to the classroom. These activities can be enhanced, whenever possible, by the use of real objects as suggested by the artwork in the text, such as items of clothing, currency, fruits and vegetables, theater tickets, and so forth. Such supplementary materials provide a multi-sensory experience for the student. To make a role-playing activity effective and useful, you should:

- encourage students to move about and respond physically in the roles they are playing. For example, positioning themselves in groups can make conversations seem more natural and feel more "real."
- have them use facial expressions and gestures that reinforce meaning. If a formal introduction is taking place, students should smile and shake hands. If a student is giving directions, he or she should point the way.
- encourage students to use vocal expression to convey meaning. For example, when saying "I'm tired," fatigue should be apparent in the voice.
- be sure they use voice quality to convey characterization. For example, a person acting out a phone call can be portrayed as a young child, as a teenager in trouble, or as an older person who has some wonderful—or terrible—news to tell.
- be sure they make the distinction between formal and informal language when appropriate.

- point out appropriate intonation and stress. For example, when correcting or verifying an item, heavy stress is on the part of the sentence being corrected:
  Student 1: Is this 2845?
  Student 2: No, it's 2835.
- point out different expressions that convey the same language function or meaning when appropriate. For example, in greeting someone, students can say *Hi*, *Hello*, *How do you do?* and *Good morning*. They can use an expression such as *O.K.* to mean *I agree*, *I feel fine*, *Yes*, or *I accept*.

Games. Games provide an enjoyable way to change the focus from language learning to language use. They heighten the learner's interest and can be used both for amusement and to stimulate learning. They create an environment in which students interact to reach a goal while following rules that limit and guide their behavior. The student book contains a number of problem-solving activities that can be made into games simply by designating groups as teams and setting rules and time limits.

You can devise your own games from ones you already know, such as Hangman, Tic–tac–toe, Bingo, and Twenty Questions. Twenty Questions, for example, can be used to encourage real communication. A student who is "it" chooses a well-known historical or popular personality and plays the role of that person. The other students ask up to twenty questions about the person's talents, abilities, place of residence, country of origin, or other facts, adapting language learned from the textbook. Students should ask only yes-no questions and must listen to all the questions and answers in order to guess the identity of the famous person. The student who guesses correctly is then "it."

Songs. Songs are an important aspect of culture, representing the history, folklore, and current idiom of a country. They have universal appeal and can provide enjoyment, relaxation, and a sense of community. Singing can build students' confidence by allowing them to enjoy a degree of fluency in English before they have achieved it in speaking. Songs can also serve as memory aids for learning vocabulary and internalizing stress and rhythm patterns. If an appropriate song cannot be found, you may wish to write new words for a familiar melody, using structures from the lesson. It is helpful to explain the context of a song before students listen to it or learn it.

Error correction. Making errors is an unavoidable part of the language-learning process. At the same time, most people agree that a fear of making errors can inhibit students from speaking and keep them from getting essential oral practice. It is important to correct students in a way that is supportive, yet clear, direct, and focused, so they will learn to monitor themselves and express themselves more appropriately.

Language errors fall into many different categories. There are errors of meaning, appropriateness, grammar, and pronunciation. Generally speaking, it is most important to correct errors that really affect communication and those that relate to the focus of an exercise or activity. If an exercise emphasizes a specific grammar point, errors related to that point should be corrected. If an exercise covers an aspect of pronunciation, the emphasis should be on pointing out the relevant pronunciation errors. If the students are engaged in more open-ended practice—such as a problem-solving or role-playing activity—grammar and pronunciation errors become less important than meaning and appropriateness.

- It is usually most effective to give students a chance to correct themselves first before you supply a correction. You can give a hint by saying what type of error has been made, such as "word order" or "tense."
- Students can also benefit from correcting their own and one another's errors in homework assignments. One or two students can write the homework on the board and the entire class can check it for errors, making corrections on their own papers.

- Develop a sense of timing when correcting errors or supplying needed structures and vocabulary. If a student is struggling to express an idea and is searching for a word, it may be best to assist him or her immediately so that the idea can be expressed. On the other hand, if a pair of students are engaged in free conversation and are communicating well except for a few errors, it could be distracting to interrupt them. During such practice you can note the errors that students have made frequently and point them out at the end of the activity.

Evaluation of students' progress. Tests and other methods of evaluation, such as carrying out a task or participating in a role-play activity, are an important part of the language-learning process. Students can see what areas they need more practice in, and teachers can use the results for planning future lessons. The review sections in the student book have been expressly designed for the purposes of evaluation and review. However, if you want to check your students' progress more often, you can prepare your own informal tests by designing items similar to those used in the textbook. The ideas suggested below show how various types of test items reflect the learning objectives of *recognition*, *recall*, *transfer*, and *creative use* of language.

- For testing *recognition*, students can demonstrate their understanding of information by:
  1. matching items, such as parts of conversations;
  2. selecting an item from three or four choices, such as choosing the appropriate answer to a question;
  3. organizing information, such as rearranging lines from a known dialogue, putting words into the correct order to form a sentence, and alphabetizing names; or
  4. listening to dialogue lines and identifying the speaker.

- For testing *recall*, students can demonstrate that they have acquired specific knowledge by:

1. filling in blanks with the appropriate response, such as the correct verb form, a word which describes a picture, or the words missing from a dialogue;
2. saying or writing the expected response after listening to a dialogue or piece of information;
3. writing sentences for pictures; or
4. writing sentences or paragraphs from dictation.

- For testing *transfer* of knowledge, students can show they are able to apply known information in different situations by:
  1. paraphrasing or summarizing a passage they have heard or read;
  2. editing a passage to change one tense to another;
  3. transforming a dialogue from a formal to an informal register;

4. providing expressions appropriate in a given situation, such as two people being introduced to each other; or
5. writing the missing words in a passage (the cloze method).

- For testing the *creative use* of English, students can show their proficiency by:
  1. relating an experience, either orally or in writing;
  2. answering questions about a reading passage;
  3. writing original sentences based on information that has been provided; or
  4. performing specific tasks, such as giving information about themselves, expressing opinions, asking questions, and creating dialogues.

PAGE-BY-PAGE TEACHING INSTRUCTIONS

PREVIEW

*The chart at the top of the **PREVIEW** page in the Student Book lists the "productive" language introduced in the unit—these are the language items that students will practice actively in the exercises following the opening conversation. In each unit there is a certain amount of "receptive" language as well—items intended for comprehension only. "Receptive" language is introduced mainly in the comprehension dialogues and readings but may appear in the opening conversations as well. Some examples of receptive language in Unit 1 are:*

Let's see…
Moving in?
We're neighbors.
Just call me Carolyn.
You can call me George.
Mrs. Arno wants to…
Nice meeting you.
Come in for coffee sometime.
Thank you. I will.

Before you begin teaching, go over the functions/themes, language, and forms in the chart. This will give you a preview of what you will encounter as you guide the students through each unit.

As you progress through the book, both you and the students can use the chart for reference or to review the language that has been practiced.

Preview the conversations.

This pre-listening activity provides background information to help students understand the opening conversations and relate them to their own experience. The activity in this unit supplies information about two of the storyline characters who appear in the conversations on pp. 2-3 and throughout Level 1. You can go over this section in English or in any language you and your students both speak.

- Have students examine the illustration. Point out Carolyn Duval and Sylvia Baxter. Use the information in the boxes to help get across the idea that Carolyn Duval is moving from her home in Vermont into an apartment in Brooklyn, New York, and that Mrs. Baxter will be her new landlady.

- Ask students if they or their parents have ever moved to a new city, rented an apartment, or signed a lease.

CULTURE CLOSE-UP

A lease agreement, as pictured in the illustration, is a formal contract between a tenant (someone renting an apartment) and a landlord or landlady (the person who owns the apartment). The lease details the length of time the tenant may stay, the responsibilities of both owner and tenant, the amount of rent to be paid each month, plus the amount of the security deposit (money that is refunded at the end of the lease).

Vermont is a state in the New England region of the United States and is about 200 miles (325 kilometers) north of New York City.

P R E V I E W

FUNCTIONS/THEMES	LANGUAGE	FORMS
Introduce yourself	Hello. I'm Kenji Sato. Hi, Kenji. I'm Lauren Nash. My name is William Stone. Nice to meet you.	Present of *be*: (*am, is*) contractions
Identify people	Excuse me—are you Tom Cruise? Yes, I am. (No, I'm not.) What's your name, please?	Present of *be*: questions with *are*; short answers with *I*
Greet formally and informally	Hi, Maria. How are you? Not bad. Hello, Mrs. Baxter. How are you? I'm fine, Mr. Pierce.	More present of *be*
Verify a spelling	Could you spell your last name? N-I-E-L-S-E-N? Yes, that's right.	Alphabet Formula *Could you . . . ?*

Preview the conversations.

This is Carolyn Duval. She's moving from Vermont to New York. Carolyn is looking for an apartment today. She is at 3 Willow Street in Brooklyn, New York.

This is Mrs. Baxter. She's the landlady of 3 Willow Street.

1. Moving to a new city

Carolyn Duval finds a nice apartment.

A

Carolyn Duval Excuse me—
are you Mrs. Baxter?
Woman No, I'm not.
Carolyn Sorry.

B

Carolyn Excuse me—are
you Mrs. Baxter?
Mrs. Baxter Yes, I am.
Carolyn I'm Carolyn Duval.
Mrs. Baxter Nice to meet
you, Ms. Duval.

C

Mrs. Baxter Let's see. . . .
Carolyn . . . C-A-R-O-L-Y-N?
Carolyn Yes, that's right.
Mrs. Baxter Could you spell
your last name, please?
Carolyn D-U-V-A-L.
Mrs. Baxter Sign here, please.

1. Moving to a new city

*The first lesson of every unit begins with a **conversation** that introduces the new language to be covered in the unit. Students focus on the receptive tasks of listening and reading so they can absorb new language items without feeling pressure to speak. The **Figure it out** exercises are designed to test and enhance comprehension without requiring students to use the new language actively. This does not mean that you should discourage students from speaking if they feel ready. It simply means that you should give them this time for the new language to "sink in" if they need it. Active practice begins on p. 4.*

WARM-UP

As the students arrive to class, greet them appropriately ("Good morning," "Good afternoon," "Good evening," "Hello"). Encourage them to return your greeting.

BACKGROUND

Carolyn Duval is moving from Vermont to an apartment in New York City. Today she meets her landlady, Sylvia Baxter, for the first time and signs a lease. She also meets her new neighbor, Maggie Sloane. Carolyn's apartment is in Brooklyn, New York, one of the five boroughs of New York City.

LANGUAGE

Excuse me. is a polite expression used to get someone's attention.

Could you...? is used to soften a request or make it more polite.

How are you? is a formulaic greeting and not actually a question about the other person's health. Typical responses are: "Fine," "Good," "O.K.," "Not bad," etc.

Nice to meet you. is short for *It's nice to meet you.*

PROCEDURE

- As students examine the illustrations, point out the people and situations by asking simple questions and making statements such as the following:

  Where is Carolyn Duval?
  Where is Mrs. Baxter?
  This is Maggie Sloane.
  Maggie is Carolyn's neighbor. She lives upstairs.

- Play the conversations on cassette or read them aloud. Students can follow along in their books as they listen. (If you are reading the conversations aloud, speak at a normal speed and perform each role as realistically as possible. Show the change in speakers by shifting your position or by pointing to the appropriate character in the illustrations.)

- Students can listen to the conversations as many times as they need to in order to understand the language introduced. Before they listen for the second time, have them go over the questions in exercise 1 of **Figure it out**. This will focus their attention on specific details of the conversations. They can go over exercise 2 before listening a third time.

METHODOLOGY NOTE

On the cassette, an optional pronunciation practice is provided for the conversations. A pause occurs after each line so that the students can repeat.

CULTURE CLOSE-UP

In Conversation B, since Carolyn Duval and Sylvia Baxter are meeting for the first time, they address one another using titles. Carolyn addresses Sylvia Baxter as Mrs. Baxter. From this we know that Sylvia is or was married to a person named Baxter. When women in the U.S. marry, they often take on their husband's last name. Many people then address them using *Mrs.* followed by the husband's last name.

Sylvia addresses Carolyn as Ms. Duval. The title *Ms.* can be used for both married or single women. It is becoming more and more common, especially in business situations. Also a woman nowadays often does not take her husband's name when she gets married and prefers to be addressed with *Ms.* followed by her own last name.

Sylvia and Carolyn do not shake hands when they introduce themselves. Many people in the U.S. reserve handshaking for business situations.

In Conversation D, even though Maggie Sloane knows Sylvia Baxter, she addresses her as Mrs. Baxter. This is in part because Sylvia Baxter is older than Maggie and in part because a landlord–tenant relationship tends to be rather formal.

Figure it out

1. Listen to the conversations. Say *true* or *false*.

- Have the students read the statements silently before they listen. This will give them a specific purpose for listening to the conversations.

- Play the conversations on the cassette or read them aloud. If they like, students can cover the dialogue boxes and look only at the pictures as they listen.

- Tell the students to read the statements again to figure out whether they are true or false. They can write their answers on separate paper.

- Read each statement aloud and call on students to say *True* or *False*. Students can point to the line in the conversation that gave them the answer.

ANSWERS
2. True
3. False
4. True

2. Listen again. Match.

- To give students a focus for this listening practice, have them read the exercise items before they listen.

- Have the students listen to the conversations again. To vary the practice, they can keep their books closed as they listen.

- Give the students enough time to figure out and write down the answers. Then read each item aloud and call on individual students to give the letter of the matching response or to say the response itself. Write the answers on the board.

ANSWERS
2. a
3. f
4. e
5. b
6. d

3. Choose *a* or *b*.

- Tell the students to read the sentences silently and choose the correct response. Students can write the numbers and letters or both sentences on separate paper.

- Read each item aloud and call on individual students to give the correct letter or to say the correct response. Model the exchanges for them.

ANSWERS
2. b
3. a
4. a

OPTION

Students can repeat each line of the conversations for pronunciation practice. The conversations are recorded twice on the cassette, the second time with a pause after each sentence to allow for repetition. If you read the conversations aloud, speak at a normal speed and leave time for students to repeat.

FOLLOW-UP

Students can write out the six two-line dialogues they matched in exercise 2 of the **Figure it out** section.

WORKBOOK Lesson 1, p. 1. *Upon completion of the Student Book lesson, assign the corresponding Workbook page or pages.*

Maggie Sloane Hello, Mrs. Baxter.
Mrs. Baxter Oh, hello, Maggie. How are you?
Maggie Good. How are *you*?
Mrs. Baxter Fine, thanks.
Maggie Hi. Are you my new neighbor?
Carolyn Yes, I am. My name's Carolyn Duval.
Maggie I'm Maggie Sloane. I live upstairs in 3B.
Carolyn Nice to meet you, Maggie.
Maggie Nice to meet you, too, Carolyn.

Figure it out

1. Listen to the conversations. Say *true* or *false*.

1. Carolyn Duval meets Mrs. Baxter. *True*.
2. Carolyn's last name is Duval.
3. Carolyn lives upstairs from Maggie.
4. Carolyn is Maggie's neighbor.

2. Listen again. Match.

1. Are you Mrs. Baxter?
2. Could you spell your last name?
3. How are you?
4. C-A-R-O-L-Y-N?
5. Sign here, please.
6. Could you spell your first name?

  a. D-U-V-A-L.
  b. *Carolyn Duval*
  c. No, I'm not.
  d. C-A-R-O-L-Y-N.
  e. Yes, that's right.
  f. Fine.

3. Choose *a* or *b*.

1. Are you my new neighbor?
   a. Nice to meet you, too.
   b. Yes, I am.

2. D-U-V-A-L?
   a. Yes, I am.
   b. Yes, that's right.

3. Nice to meet you.
   a. Nice to meet you, too.
   b. My name's Sylvia Baxter.

4. My name's Carolyn Duval.
   a. Nice to meet you, Ms. Duval.
   b. Yes, that's right.

2. Nice to meet you.

1
► Listen to the conversations below.
► Practice them with a partner. Use your own name.
► Introduce yourself to five classmates.

Kenji Hello. I'm Kenji Sato.
Lauren Hi, Kenji. I'm Lauren Nash.

William Hello. My name's William Stone.
Vicky I'm Vicky Martinez.
William Nice to meet you, Vicky.
Vicky Nice to meet you, too.

Hi is more informal than **hello**.

INTRODUCE YOURSELF ● PRESENT OF *BE* (*AM*, *IS*): CONTRACTIONS

2 ► Study the frames: Contractions

| **I am** | Maggie Sloane. | → | **I'm** | Maggie Sloane. |
| **It is** | nice to meet you. | | **It's** | nice to meet you. |

I'm and **it's** are contractions.
Nice to meet you = It's nice to meet you.

3 ► Practice the conversation using contractions.
► Practice it again, using your own name.

Maggie I am Maggie Sloane. *I'm Maggie Sloane*.
Carolyn My name is Carolyn Duval.
I am your new neighbor.
Maggie It is nice to meet you, Carolyn.
Carolyn It is nice to meet you, too.

2. Nice to meet you.

WARM-UP

Demonstrate greeting behavior in English. Smile and shake hands as you introduce yourself to several students: "Hello. My name's (*your name*)."

INTRODUCE YOURSELF

- Have the students examine the photographs. Ask them which conversation is informal and which is formal. Encourage them to look for such features as handshaking, formal clothes, and the use of *Nice to meet you* as indications of formality in the second conversation.

- Play the cassette or read the conversations aloud. The students can listen several times.

- Model the first conversation. Point to yourself and say "Hello. I'm (*your name*)." Introduce yourself to several students. Encourage students to introduce themselves to you in the same way. Respond "Hi, (*student's name*). I'm (*your name*)."

- Go over the second conversation in the same way. To show students that you are now acting out a more formal situation, pretend to adjust your tie, comb your hair, etc., before actually introducing yourself.

- Call on several pairs of students to introduce themselves to each other, first informally and then formally. You can also have the students work in pairs to practice introducing themselves to each other. Tell them to stand up straight and shake hands when introducing themselves formally.

- If possible, have the students introduce themselves to five classmates they do not actually know. Students can use informal language and stand up and walk around as they complete this task. Point out that *Nice to meet you* is appropriate for both formal and informal conversations.

INTRODUCE YOURSELF • PRESENT OF *BE* (*AM, IS*): CONTRACTIONS

- Have the students study the frames. Write the sentence *I am* (your name). on the board. Then erase *I am* and write *I'm* in its place. Point out that the apostrophe replaces the *a* in *am*. Read the new sentence aloud. Repeat the procedure to introduce the contractions *it's* and *name's*.

- Tell the students to work in pairs. Have them change roles so they can practice both sides of the exchange.

ANSWERS

Carolyn My <u>name's</u> Carolyn Duval. <u>I'm</u> your new neighbor.
Maggie <u>It's</u> nice to meet you, Carolyn.
Carolyn <u>It's</u> nice to meet you, too.

- Have the students use their own names and practice the conversation, first without and then with contractions. Go around the classroom and check their work.

OPTION

Have the students copy the conversation on a separate sheet of paper, using the appropriate contractions. Move around the room to verify spelling and punctuation.

FOLLOW-UP

Students can write out the conversation that would take place if they introduced themselves in a business situation.

WORKBOOK Lesson 2, p. 2

3. Are you Tom Cruise?

WARM-UP

For this activity, bring one or more balls to class. Have the students form a circle. Throw the ball to a student and initiate the following exchange:

Teacher: Hi. My name's (*your name*).
Student: Hello. I'm (*student's name*).
Teacher: Nice to meet you, (*student's name*).
Student: Nice to meet you, too.

The student then throws the ball to another student and initiates a similar exchange. If your class is large, you may want to form two or more circles for this activity.

IDENTIFY YOUR CLASSMATES

- Ask several students "Excuse me—are you (*a famous person's name*)?," modeling the correct intonation and stress. Then have a student ask you the same question. Answer "No, I'm not. I'm (*your name*)." Next call on pairs of students to take turns asking the same question and answering with their own names.

- Ask several students "Excuse me—are you (*that student's name*)?" Elicit the answer "Yes, I am." Then introduce yourself: "Hi. My name's (*your name*)." Encourage students to respond with "Nice to meet you, (*your name*)."

- Have the students write their full names on three slips of paper. Collect the names and put them in a box. Students choose three slips of paper at random. If a student draws his or her own name or the same name more than once, he or she should return the slip of paper and choose another one.

- Tell the students to find the three classmates and introduce themselves, using the model conversation as a guide.

OPTION

If the students already know each other's names, they can play the role of a famous person and write that person's name on three slips of paper instead.

IDENTIFY SOMEONE • PRESENT OF *BE* (*ARE*)

- Tell the students to study the frames as you read aloud the question and answers.

- Ask a student "Are you (*his or her name*)?" Write the question on the board and then the answer—*Yes, I am.*—below it. Point out the difference in word order between questions and statements in English.

- Ask another student "Are you (*famous person*)?" Write the answer — *No, I'm not.* — on the board. Point out that *I am* can be contracted in negative short answers but not in affirmative short answers.

- Have the students look at the photos and the illustrations. Then give them a few minutes to complete the conversations.

- Have the students practice the conversations in pairs. Tell them to change roles so that each student can practice both sides of the exchanges.

ANSWERS
2. Are you
   I'm not, I'm
3. Are you
   I am
4. Are you
   I'm not, I'm

OPTION

Divide the class into two groups. Have each group make a list of several famous people. A student from Group A acts out the identity of a famous person from his or her group's list. Students in Group B try to guess the name of the famous person by asking "Are you (*name*)?" The student from Group A answers "Yes, I am" or "No, I'm not." If Group B has difficulty guessing the identity of a famous person, students in Group A can give clues in their native language or in English. When Group B guesses the student's "identity," a student from Group B can then act out the identity of a famous person from that group's list.

FOLLOW-UP

Students can write out an ending for each conversation in exercise 3.

WORKBOOK Lesson 3, p. 3

3. Are you Tom Cruise?

IDENTIFY YOUR CLASSMATES

1 ▶ **Your teacher will give you the names of three classmates. Find them and introduce yourself.**

A Excuse me—are you _____ ?
B No, I'm not. I'm _____ .

A Excuse me—are you _____ ?
C Yes, I am.
A Hi. My name's _____ .
C Nice to meet you, _____ .
A Nice to meet you, too.

IDENTIFY SOMEONE • PRESENT OF *BE* (*ARE*)

2 ▶ **Study the frames: Present of *Be***

Yes-no questions	Short answers	Contraction	No contraction
Are you Tom Cruise?	Yes, **I am**.	No, **I'm not**.	Yes, **I am**.
	No, **I'm not**.		

3 ▶ **Look at the photos. Then complete the conversations with the correct forms of the verb *be*. (To find out more about these famous people, see p. 167.)**

1 Excuse me — *Are you* Tom Cruise?
Yes, _I am_ .

2 Excuse me — _____ Whitney Houston?
No, _____ . _____ Janet Jackson.

3 Excuse me — _____ Yumi Matsutoya?
Yes, _____ . Nice to meet you.

4 Excuse me — _____ Julio Iglesias?
No, _____ . _____ Emmanuel.

4. How are you?

GREET SOMEONE INFORMALLY

1 ▶ **Listen to the conversation below.**
▶ **Greet several classmates.**

Maria	Hello, Steve.
Steve	Hi, Maria. How are you?
Maria	Fine, thanks. How are *you*?
Steve	Not bad.

How are you?

Good.	O.K.
Fine.	Not bad.

GREET SOMEONE MORE FORMALLY

2 ▶ **Study the chart.**

First name	Carolyn	Sylvia	Charles
Title + last name	**Miss** [mɪs] Duval **Ms.** [mɪz] Duval	**Mrs.** Baxter **Ms.** Baxter	**Mr.** Baxter

Use **Miss** or **Ms.** with single women.
Use **Mrs.** or **Ms.** with married women.

3 ▶ **Listen to the conversations below. Complete them with first names or titles + last names.**
▶ **Greet your classmates using titles + last names.**

4. How are you?

WARM-UP

Go around the classroom trying to identify different students, but guessing the wrong names. Have the students correct you by giving you their real names:

Teacher: Excuse me—are you Ana Casals?
Student: No, I'm not. I'm Maria Rossi.
Teacher: Oh, I'm sorry.

GREET SOMEONE INFORMALLY

- Have the students identify Maria and Steve in the picture and the details that show they are in an informal situation. Tell them to look at the box as you read it. Then have the students listen to the conversation. They can listen several times.

- Go around the class and greet students. Say "Hi, (*student's name*). How are you?" Prompt students to answer "Fine, thanks" and to ask you "How are *you*?"

- Have the students work in groups or stand up and move around the classroom to greet their classmates. Tell them to use the exchange in their books as a model.

OPTION

Have the students look at the box. Call on four students to ask you "How are you?" Answer each student with a different response from the box.

LANGUAGE NOTE

O.K. is sometimes written *Okay* and is another way of saying "All right." *O.K.* means about the same as *Not bad.*

CULTURE CLOSE-UP

Americans often shake hands when being introduced to someone, but rarely shake hands at subsequent meetings. However, in formal business situations, people usually greet each other with a handshake whenever they meet.

GREET SOMEONE MORE FORMALLY

- Have the students study the chart. Point out the difference between *Mrs.* and *Miss* by saying the last names of married and unmarried female students or celebrities along with the appropriate title. For more information on the use of *Ms.*, see the Culture Close-Up on p. 2.

OPTION

Write different students' first and last names on the board with the correct titles. Point out that a person can be addressed informally by first name alone or formally by title + last name. Illustrate this by addressing a student both ways. Point out that titles are never used together with first names. Go around the class and call on students to say their last names together with the appropriate title.

- Have the students listen to the conversations and complete them. They can write their answers on separate paper.

- Tell the students to compare their answers with a partner. Ask different students to write the answers on the board.

TAPESCRIPT AND ANSWERS
1. Hello, <u>Mr. Arno</u>.
   Hi, <u>Jeff</u>. How are you?
2. Hi, <u>George</u>. How are you?
   Not bad. How are you, <u>John</u>?
3. Hello, <u>Mrs. Baxter</u>. How are you today?
   I'm fine, <u>John</u>. How are you?
4. Hello, <u>Ms. Sloane</u>. How are you?
   Fine, thanks.

- Have the students greet their classmates with first names or appropriate titles + last names. When using titles, students can act out a formal situation. They can work in groups or stand up and move around for this activity. Encourage them to use all four responses—*Good, Fine, O.K.,* and *Not bad.*

FOLLOW-UP

Following the model conversation in exercise 1, students can write out the conversations that would take place if they greeted another student and if they greeted that student's parent.

WORKBOOK Lesson 4, p. 4

5. Could you spell your name?

WARM-UP

Form a circle. As in the warm-up activity to Lesson 3, throw a ball to a student and initiate the following exchange:

Teacher: Hello, (*student's name*).
Student: Hi, (*your name*). How are you?
Teacher: Fine, thanks. How are you?
Student: Not bad.

The student then throws the ball to a classmate and initiates a similar exchange. Continue the practice.

THE ALPHABET • SPELL YOUR NAME

- Read the alphabet aloud once as the students listen, following along in their books. Then have them repeat the letters after you. For additional practice, call on individual students to say the letters in succession, or write the alphabet on the board and point to different letters at random for students to pronounce.

- Have the students listen to the three conversations. Play the conversations on cassette or read them aloud. Have students listen to each conversation twice. First they listen without writing. Then they listen again and write down each person's first and last name.

TAPESCRIPT AND ANSWERS
1. **A** What's your name, please?
   B <u>Pedro Diaz</u>.
   A P-E-D-R-O?
   B Yes, that's right.
   A And could you spell your last name?
   B D-I-A-Z.

2. **A** Your name, please?
   B <u>Deborah Jones</u>.
   A Deborah? Is that D-E-B-R-A?
   B No, it's D-E-B-O-R-A-H.

3. **A** What's your name, please?
   B <u>Anne Bernstein</u>.
   A Is that A-N-N or A-N-N-E?
   B A-N-N-E.
   A And could you spell your last name, Ms. Bernstein?
   B B-E-R-N-S-T-E-I-N.

- Play the cassette or read the conversation aloud. Tell the students to follow along in their books. Then take the role of B and use your own information as you have a student take the role of A and ask you the questions.

- Have the students move around the classroom and ask three classmates their names. Tell them to use the conversation in their books as a model. Have them write down each name and show it to the classmate to verify that the spelling is correct.

OPTION

The students can practice the conversation in pairs, using their own names. Tell them to take turns playing the role of A and B.

VERIFY A SPELLING

- As the students follow along in their books, play the cassette or read the tapescript aloud with a student. In addition, you can have the students practice the two possible conversations in pairs.

- Tell the students to choose a first and a last name from the box and write it on a piece of paper.

- Have students work in pairs to practice the conversation using their "new" names. Tell the partners to take turns playing the role of B. Partners can show each other their papers to verify the spellings.

TAPESCRIPT
A Your name, please?
B Robert Nielsen.
A N-I-E-L-S-E-N?
B Yes, that's right.

A Your name, please?
B Robert Nielsen.
A N-I-E-L-S-O-N?
B No, N-I-E-L-S-*E*-N.

FOLLOW-UP

Students can write out one of the conversations they had with other classmates in exercise 2.

WORKBOOK Lesson 5, pp. 5-6

5. Could you spell your name?

THE ALPHABET ● SPELL YOUR NAME

Aa	Bb	Cc	Dd	Ee	Ff	Gg	Hh	Ii	Jj	Kk	Ll	Mm

Aa Bb Cc Dd Ee Ff Gg Hh Ii Jj Kk Ll Mm

Nn	Oo	Pp	Qq	Rr	Ss	Tt	Uu	Vv	Ww	Xx	Yy	Zz

Nn Oo Pp Qq Rr Ss Tt Uu Vv Ww Xx Yy Zz

 1

▶ **Listen to three conversations. Write each person's first and last name.**

1. _____
2. _____
3. _____

 2

▶ **Listen to the conversation below.**
▶ **Ask three classmates to spell their names.**

A What's your name, please?
B Chulsoo Kim.
A Could you spell your last name?
B K-I-M.
A And your first name?
B C-H-U-L-S-O-O.

VERIFY A SPELLING

3

▶ **Listen to the two possible conversations below.**
▶ **Choose a first name and a last name from the box, and write the name on a piece of paper.**
▶ **Practice the conversation with a partner. Use your new name.**

A Your name, please?

B Robert Nielsen.

A N-I-E-L-S-E-N?   **A** N-I-E-L-S-O-N?

B Yes, that's right.   **B** No, N-I-E-L-S-*E*-N.

First name	Last name	Another spelling
Robert	Nielsen	Nielson
James	Lensky	Lenski
William	Allen	Allan
Nancy	Kramer	Cramer
Susan	Kelly	Kelley
Linda	Snyder	Snider

6. Welcome to Willow Street.

George Arno, owner of Arno's Coffee Shop, meets his new neighbor, Carolyn Duval.

1

George	Hi.
Carolyn	Hello.
George	Moving in?
Carolyn	Yes, I am.
George	Well then, we're neighbors. My name's George Arno and that's my coffee shop.
Carolyn	I'm Carolyn Duval. Nice to meet you.
George	Nice to meet you, too, Miss . . . uh . . . Laval?
Carolyn	No, *Du*val. But just call me Carolyn.
George	O.K., Carolyn. And you can call me George.
Loretta	GEORGE!
Jeff	Excuse me . . . uh . . . Mr. Arno, Mrs. Arno wants to . . .
Loretta	GEORGE!
George	Thanks, Jeff. COMING, LORETTA! Well, nice meeting you, Carolyn. Come in for coffee sometime.
Carolyn	Thank you. I will.

6. Welcome to Willow Street.

These two "comprehension pages" in each unit help students build their receptive knowledge of English vocabulary, structures, and pronunciation.

*Students first listen to a **comprehension dialogue** that integrates language introduced in the unit with items that won't be presented formally until later units or levels. The goal is to allow students to familiarize themselves with English before asking them to use it actively. Comprehension is checked by means of a **Figure it out** exercise which does not require students to use any of the language productively.*

*The **How to say it** section provides practice in pronunciation. Emphasis is placed on stress and intonation, reduction, consonant loss, and blending in sentences spoken at normal conversational speed. In the appendix, there are examples of three basic stress and intonation patterns in English sentences: affirmative statements, yes-no questions, and information questions. The appendix also includes a chart of the phonetic symbols used in the* Spectrum *series.*

*The **Listen in** activity gives students the opportunity to "overhear" an authentic conversation in English. Because they have no text to refer to as they listen, the activity helps prepare them for real-life listening experiences. The illustrations set a context for the overheard conversation.*

*The **Your turn** activity rounds out the lesson with productive practice of some of the functions and structures introduced in the unit.*

WARM-UP

Call on volunteers to spell aloud the first and last names of another student. The rest of the class points to the person whose name is being spelled.

1. Conversation

BACKGROUND

George Arno, the owner of Arno's Coffee Shop, meets Carolyn Duval, who is moving in next door. A coffee shop is an inexpensive restaurant that may serve anything from coffee and cake to complete dinners. The conversation is interrupted by Jeff Hunt. Jeff works at Arno's with George and George's wife, Loretta.

LANGUAGE

Moving in? is short for *Are you moving in?*

Just call me… and *You can call me…* are ways of telling someone that he or she can address you by your first name.

Coming… is short for *I'm coming.*

PROCEDURE

- Have the students examine the illustrations as you point out the people and the situations. Ask questions and make statements like these:

  Where is Carolyn Duval?
  Where is George Arno?
  This is Carolyn's apartment building.
  This is Arno's Coffee Shop.

- Have the students listen to the conversation as you play it on cassette or read it aloud. You can have the students listen as many times as they need to in order to understand the conversation.

2. Figure it out

True or *False*?

- Have the students read over the five statements. Then play the conversation again or read it aloud and have students answer *True* or *False* for each statement. Students can write their answers on separate paper.

- Have the students check their answers in pairs before listening to the conversation again. Then write the answers on the board as you go over them with the class.

  ANSWERS
  1. True
  2. True
  3. False
  4. True
  5. True

3. How to say it

- Read the conversation aloud or play it on cassette. Then present it again and have the students repeat each line.

- Refer the students to their books and point out the lines used to show rising and falling intonation and the inverted triangles to indicate syllables with the strongest stress. You can write the exchanges and the intonation lines on the board and trace them with your finger as you read the sentences aloud for the students to repeat.

- Practice the conversation with another student in front of the class. Then have the students practice in pairs. Move around the room and check their work, giving help where needed.

- Finally, call on pairs of students to read the conversation. If necessary, repeat each line with the correct syllable stress and the appropriate intonation.

4. Listen in

- Read the instructions aloud as the students follow in their books. Point out the man in the phone booth in the illustration. Remind the students that their task is merely to spell the man's last name.

- Play the conversation on cassette or read the conversation below, shifting your position to indicate a change in speakers. You may wish to play the cassette or read the tapescript several times before calling on a student to say the answer.

  TAPESCRIPT AND ANSWER
  A Your name, please?
  B Jim <u>Kowalski</u>.
  A Could you spell your last name?
  B K-O-W-A-L-S-K-I.
  A K-O-W-A-L-S-K-Y?
  B No, S-K-I.

5. Your turn

- Read the instructions aloud as the students follow in their books. Have the students find Maggie Sloane and John Pierce in the illustration.

- Divide the class into pairs. Have the pairs figure out what Maggie and John might be saying in this situation. Tell them to create a dialogue. They may write down their dialogues if they find it helpful. Then have the pairs practice their conversations, changing roles so that each student can practice both sides of the exchange.

- Call on a pair to act out their conversation for the class. Write it on the board.

  POSSIBLE CONVERSATION
  Maggie Hi, John.
  John Hi, Maggie. How are you?
  Maggie Fine, thanks. How are you?
  John Not bad.

  FOLLOW-UP

  Students can write out their conversations from the **Your turn** section.

  WORKBOOK Lesson 6, p. 7

Listen to this conversation.

Maggie Hi, my name's Maggie Sloane.

Carolyn Nice to meet you.

I'm Carolyn Duval.

2. Figure it out

True or *False*?

1. Carolyn is moving to Willow Street.
2. Carolyn is George Arno's new neighbor.
3. Carolyn's last name is Laval.
4. Mrs. Arno's first name is Loretta.
5. "Arno's" is a coffee shop on Willow Street.

■ 4. Listen in

The man in the phone booth is making an appointment. Listen to the conversation. Spell the man's last name.

5. Your turn

Look at Maggie Sloane and her neighbor, John Pierce, above. Play the role of Maggie. Greet John.

7. Here I am in Kyoto!

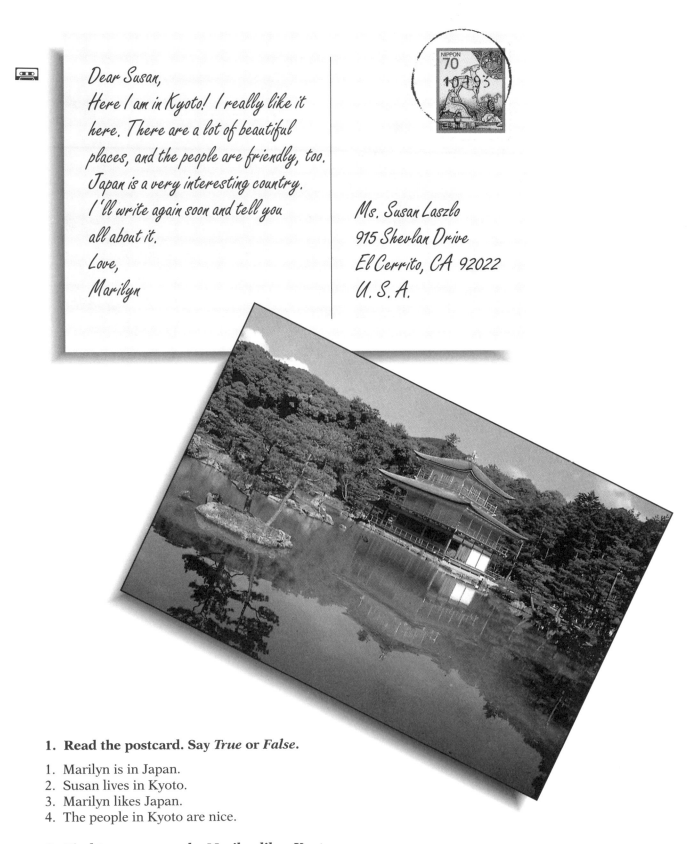

Dear Susan,

Here I am in Kyoto! I really like it here. There are a lot of beautiful places, and the people are friendly, too. Japan is a very interesting country. I'll write again soon and tell you all about it.

Love,
Marilyn

Ms. Susan Laszlo
915 Shevlan Drive
El Cerrito, CA 92022
U.S.A.

1. Read the postcard. Say *True* or *False*.

1. Marilyn is in Japan.
2. Susan lives in Kyoto.
3. Marilyn likes Japan.
4. The people in Kyoto are nice.

2. Find two reasons why Marilyn likes Kyoto.

7. Here I am in Kyoto!

Each unit ends with an authentic document that provides students with additional input in English. The accompanying exercises focus on reading comprehension and the development of reading skills in English.

The corresponding workbook lesson includes a writing task which is usually related to the reading. As an alternative, you may assign the writing task suggested in the Follow-Up activity.

BACKGROUND

A woman named Marilyn is in Kyoto, Japan. She writes a postcard to her friend Susan, who lives in El Cerrito, California. The postcard shows the Golden Pavilion in Kyoto, which was built in 1397. Conventions for writing addresses in the U.S. will be covered in Unit 3.

PROCEDURE

- Have the students look at the picture and guess where the postcard is from. Make sure they understand the meaning of the word *postcard*.

1. Read the postcard. Say *True* or *False*.

- Have the students read the postcard silently. Then play the cassette or read the postcard. Tell the students to answer *True* or *False* on separate paper.

- Have the students compare and discuss their answers with a partner. Call on different students to read their answers aloud. Have a student write the answers on the board.

ANSWERS
1. True
2. False
3. True
4. True

2. Find two reasons why Marilyn likes Kyoto.

- Tell the students to scan the postcard to find the two reasons. They can write down their answers and compare them in pairs. Call on a pair of students to write the answers on the board.

ANSWERS
There are a lot of beautiful places.
The people are friendly.

OPTION

Have the students read over the postcard again. Tell them to underline or write down on separate paper any words they don't understand. Answer any questions they have. If possible, use gestures, pictures, and realia to teach the meanings of new words such as *like, beautiful, friendly,* and *interesting*.

CULTURE CLOSE-UP

While the closing *Love* is common in correspondence between female friends and among family members, male friends are more likely to use closings such as *Best regards*.

The *CA* in Susan's address is the standard postal abbreviation for *California*.

FOLLOW-UP

Students can rewrite Marilyn's postcard changing *Kyoto* and *Japan* to a city and country of their choice. They can change the word *interesting* to *exciting* or *beautiful*.

WORKBOOK Lesson 7, p. 8. Point out the punctuation (commas, question mark, and periods) in the postcard. Also, tell the students to capitalize the first word of each sentence, the word *I*, and all names of people and places.

PREVIEW

Before you begin teaching, go over the functions/themes, language, and forms in the chart. This will give you a preview of what you will encounter as you guide the students through the unit.

Preview the conversations.

This activity focuses on the use of public telephones and the problems people have using them.

- Have the students examine the first set of illustrations. If possible, show them actual bills, coins, and a credit card. Discuss the questions. You may also want to talk about the differences between pay phones and home or office telephones.

- Discuss the questions under the picture on the right. If necessary, explain what "out of order" means.

CULTURE CLOSE-UP

Many public telephones in the U.S. still operate with coins. A quarter is usually needed for a local call. Additional coins are needed for a long-distance call. Because public pay phones take coins, they are often out of order due to vandalism, especially in large cities. Pay telephones of the future will accept only credit or billing cards. This is already true in many countries around the world.

Note that throughout the Student Book, telephone numbers begin with 555. It should not be assumed that all telephone numbers in the U.S. begin this way. The telephone company has reserved the 555 exchange for use in books, movies, and television programs.

PREVIEW

FUNCTIONS/THEMES	LANGUAGE	FORMS
Make an informal telephone call	Is Susan there?	Present of *be: is* in yes-no questions and short answers
Identify someone on the phone	Yes, she is. Just a minute, please. (No, she isn't.)	
	Is this Bill?	
	No, this is Carlos.	
Ask for someone's phone number	What's your phone number?	Numbers 0–10
Call Directory Assistance	It's 555-2012.	Formula *I'd like . . .*
Thank someone	I'd like the number of Jane Schaefer.	
	Thank you.	
	You're welcome.	
Ask for change	Excuse me—do you have change for a dollar?	Formulaic use of *do*
	Yes, I do. Here you are. (No, I don't.)	
Apologize	I'm sorry.	
	That's O.K.	

Preview the conversations.

a bill

a coin

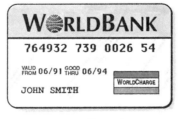

a credit card

What do you need to use this telephone? A bill? A coin? A credit card? What about in your country?

What's the problem with this telephone? Does this ever happen to you?

8. Out of order

Bill is in town for the day, and he's trying to call his friend Susan.

A

Bill Excuse me, miss—do you have change for a dollar?
Woman Let's see. . . . No, I'm sorry, I don't.

B

Bill Sir? Do you have change for a dollar?
Man Uh . . . Let's see. . . . Ah, yes, I do. Here you are.
Bill Thank you.
Man You're welcome.

C

Operator Directory Assistance. May I help you?
Bill Yes. I'd like the number of Susan Chang, please— C-H-A-N-G.
Operator The number is 555-1037.
Bill 555-1037. Thank you.

D

Woman Hello?
Bill Hello, is Susan there?
Woman I'm sorry, you have the wrong number.
Bill Oh . . . is this 555-1037?
Woman No, it isn't.
Bill I'm sorry.
Woman That's O.K.

E

Susan's sister Hello?
Bill Hello, is Susan there?
Susan's sister No, I'm sorry, Susan isn't here right now. She's at work.

F

Susan's sister Hello?
Bill Hello, is Susan there?
Susan's sister Yes, she is. Just a minute, please.
Susan Hello?
Bill Hello, Susan? This is Bill.
Susan Bill?
Bill Bill Mitchell.
Susan Oh, hi, Bill! How . . . (*click!*)
Bill Hello?. . . Hello?

Uh . . . ma'am? Do you have change for a dollar?

8. Out of order

With a coin or bill in hand, go around the classroom and ask different students for change. Prompt them to reply with "Yes, I do" or "No, I don't" and to act out the situation—for example, you might ask students who have change to produce it.

BACKGROUND

Bill is in the town where his friend Susan lives. He is trying to call her on a public telephone. He gets change to use the phone from a passerby and calls Directory Assistance to obtain Susan's number. After some difficulty, he finally reaches Susan only to be cut off while talking to her. Obviously, it's not a good day for Bill.

LANGUAGE

Phone is short for *telephone*.

I'm sorry. is a polite expression of regret.

Let's see. (*Let us see.*) is said when a person pauses to think about or check something.

Here you are. is said when handing something to someone.

You're welcome. is a polite response to *thank you*.

That's O.K. is a typical response to *I'm sorry*.

Just a minute. is a way of asking someone to wait for a short time.

Click! indicates a disconnected telephone communication.

PROCEDURE

- Explain that Bill wants to make a phone call but that he needs change first. Point out the people and the situations in the pictures as the students look at them. Ask simple questions like these:

  (Point to illustration B.)
  Does Bill have a dollar?
  Is Bill happy?
  (Point to illustration C.)
  Is Bill at a pay phone?
  (Point to illustration D.)
  Is Bill angry?
  (Point to illustration F.)
  Is it day or night?

- Have students listen to the conversations with their books open. Answer any questions they have about vocabulary or structures.

OPTION

Use currency and coins to practice making change. For example, if you have access to U.S. money, give some students more than a dollar's worth of change and others less. Ask students "Do you have change for a dollar?" Tell students to respond by giving you the correct change and saying "Here you are," or by saying "No, I'm sorry, I don't."

CULTURE CLOSE-UP

In the United States, personal calls are usually made after 8:00 a.m. and before 11:00 p.m., except in an emergency. Business calls are usually made between 9:00 a.m. and 5:00 p.m.

Figure it out

1. Listen to the conversations. Say *true* or *false*.

- Have the students read the statements silently. Then play the cassette or read the conversations aloud.

- Have the students read the statements again and answer *True* or *False* on separate paper.

- So that students can check their answers, read the statements aloud and call on different students to say *True* or *False*.

  ### ANSWERS
  1. False
  2. True
  3. False

OPTION

Here are some additional true/false items you can use:

1. The woman has change for a dollar. (False)
2. The man gives Bill change for five dollars. (False)

2. Listen again. Put the events in order.

- Have the students read the sentences to themselves before they listen.

- Play the cassette or read the conversations again. You can have the students close their books as they listen.

- Ask the students to put the events in order. They can write the numbers or the sentences on separate paper.

- Students can work in pairs to compare and correct their answers. Have different students write the answers on the board.

  ### ANSWERS
  1 — Bill wants change for a dollar.
  2 — Bill calls Directory Assistance.
  3 — Bill calls the wrong number.
  4 — Susan is at work.
  5 — Susan is there.

3. Match.

- Have students work in pairs to match the columns.

- Read each numbered item aloud and call on individual students to give the correct letter or to say the correct response.

  ### ANSWERS
  1. b
  2. e
  3. c
  4. a
  5. d

4. Look at the picture below. Choose *a* or *b*.

- Have the students study the photograph at the bottom of the page. Read the amounts aloud as sentences. For example, say "A quarter equals twenty-five cents. A dime equals ten cents." Also say "A dollar equals one hundred cents."

- Have the students work in pairs on this problem-solving activity. So that the pairs can correct their answers, read each item aloud and call on students to give the correct letter or to say the correct amounts.

  ### ANSWERS
  1. b
  2. a

FOLLOW-UP

Students can write out the five two-line exchanges they matched in exercise 3.

WORKBOOK Lesson 8, p. 9

Figure it out

1. Listen to the conversations. Say *true* or *false*.

1. Susan calls Bill.
2. Susan's number is 555-1037.
3. Bill is lucky today.

2. Listen again. Put the events in order.

___ Bill calls the wrong number.
___ Susan is there.
___ Susan is at work.
_1_ Bill wants change for a dollar.
___ Bill calls Directory Assistance.

3. Match.

1. Thank you.   a. No, it isn't.
2. Here you are.   b. You're welcome.
3. I'm sorry.   c. That's O.K.
4. Is this 555-6696?   d. No, I don't.
5. Do you have change   e. Thank you.
   for a dollar?

4. Look at the picture below. Choose *a* or *b*.

1. Change for a dollar is _____ .
   a. 8 dimes and 2 nickels
   b. 4 quarters

2. Change for a quarter is _____ .
   a. 2 dimes and 1 nickel
   b. 4 nickels

a quarter 25 cents
a dime 10 cents
a nickel 5 cents
a penny 1 cent

9. Phone calls

 1 ▶ Complete the phone conversations below with *a*, *b*, or *c*.
▶ Listen to the conversations to check your answers.
▶ Practice them with a partner.

a. No, she isn't here right now. She's at work.
b. This is Susan.
c. Yes, she is. Just a minute, please.

MAKE A CALL • PRESENT OF *BE* (*IS*)

2 ▶ Study the frames.
▶ Practice the conversations in exercise 1 again. This time ask for Bill.

Yes-no questions			Short answers			Negative statements			Affirmative statements		
Is	Bill	there?	Yes,	he	**is.**	He	**isn't**	here.	He	**'s**	at work.
	Susan		No,	she	**isn't**.	She			She		

's = is
isn't = is not

You may say:
he isn't or **he's not**.
she isn't or **she's not**.

CALL YOUR CLASSMATES

3 ▶ Act out this conversation in groups of three using your own names.

A (*Dials number*) *Rrring, rrring*
B Hello?
A Hello, is _____ there?
B Yes, he (she) is. Just a minute, please.
C Hello?
A Hello, _____ ? This is _____ .
C Oh, hi, _____ . How are you?
A Fine, thanks. How are you?
C Not bad.

9. Phone calls

WARM-UP

Act out making an informal phone call. Pretend you are dialing a phone. With an imaginary handset in hand, say "Hello, is Susan there?" Then move around the class and repeat the process, this time substituting students' names for *Susan*. Have students pretend they have their own handsets in hand as they reply "Yes, he/she is" or "No, he/she isn't."

MAKE AN INFORMAL CALL

- Have students choose *a*, *b*, or *c* to complete each of the phone conversations.

- Play the cassette or read the conversations aloud as students check their answers.

   ANSWERS
   1. b
   2. c
   3. a

- Have the students work in pairs to practice the exchanges.

MAKE A CALL • PRESENT OF *BE* (*IS*)

- Have students study the patterns in the frames. Then read aloud the questions and answers from the frames. Answer any questions students may have.

- Demonstrate the difference between short affirmative and negative answers by modeling a question and explaining that there are three possible ways to answer. Write the following patterns on the board:

   A: Is Susan there?
   B: 1. Yes, she is.
         (We never say "Yes, she's.")
      2. No, she isn't.
      3. No, she's not.

Practice with the students. Have them provide the three possible answers. Then practice the exchange again with *Bill/he*.

- Have the students work in pairs to practice the conversations in exercise 1 again. Tell them to ask for Bill this time.

OPTION

Ask different students about the presence or absence of classmates or famous persons in the classroom. Write the two ways of answering in the negative on the board and encourage them to practice with both forms. For example:

S1: Is Tom Cruise here?
S2: No, he isn't. OR No, he's not.

CALL YOUR CLASSMATES

- Divide the class into groups of three. Students can refer to their books as they act out the conversation. To give the illusion of a phone conversation, have them pretend they are using telephones and have Student A sit with his or her back to the other two.

- Call on groups of students to present the conversation in front of the class.

OPTION

Read the conversation aloud to demonstrate that rising intonation occurs at the end of yes-no questions and that falling intonation occurs at the end of statements. Have the students close their books. Then write *1 .* and *2 ?* on the board. As you read the conversation again, have the students write down or call out the number for the punctuation mark that goes at the end of each sentence. Check their work.

IDENTIFY SOMEONE ON THE TELEPHONE AND IN PERSON

- Have students study the frames as you read the questions and answers aloud. Ask them which question is used on the telephone. Go over the note to the right. Provide additional examples such as *It is (It's) a telephone. It is (It's) out of order.* Point out that the use of *it* in *No, it's Carlos.* is an exception to the usual rule of using *it* only to refer to a thing.

- Tell students to read the conversations to themselves. Then have them complete the exercise on separate paper. Call on four students to read the completed conversations aloud so that the other students can check their work.

    ### ANSWERS
    1. **Phil** This is
       Phil Is this
       George This is

    2. **Jeff** I am
       Carolyn I'm OR My name is
       Jeff he isn't OR he's not

OPTION

Have students work in pairs to substitute their own names for the characters and practice the conversations. Encourage them to dramatize the exchanges by using the correct intonation and appropriate gestures. Call on pairs to present their conversations to the class.

UNSCRAMBLE THESE PHONE CALLS

- Have students unscramble the lines in each conversation. They can copy the unscrambled versions on separate paper.

- Read the conversations aloud in their correct form or play the cassette. Have students listen and correct their answers.

ANSWERS
1. 1 — Hello?
   2 — Hello, Susan? This is Bill.
   3 — Bill?
   4 — Is this Susan Chang?
   5 — No. You have the wrong number.
   6 — I'm sorry.
   7 — That's O.K.

2. 1 — Hello?
   2 — Hello, is this Susan?
   3 — No, it isn't. This is Jane.
   4 — Hi, Jane. This is Bill.
       Is Susan there?
   5 — No, she isn't here right now.
       She's at work.

3. 1 — Hello?
   2 — Hello, is this Susan?
   3 — Yes, it is.
   4 — Hi, Susan. This is Bill.
   5 — Bill! How are you?
   6 — Great.

- Students can erase the names in their written versions of the unscrambled conversations and substitute their own. Have them refer to their written versions of the conversations as they act them out.

METHODOLOGY NOTE

Working in small groups of three to six students is beneficial for language practice. In such small groups, each student has more opportunity to use the language. This is especially beneficial for students who are uncomfortable speaking in front of the entire class. Monitor the small groups' activities by circulating throughout the classroom. You can note pronunciation and intonation errors. After the small groups have completed the activity, you may select one or more students to act out the conversations with you in front of the entire class.

FOLLOW-UP

Students can write out the conversation in exercise 3.

WORKBOOK Lesson 9, pp. 10-11

4 ▶ **Study the frames.**

👤👤	Are you Bill?	Yes, I am.
		No, I'm Carlos.
☎	Is this Bill?	Yes, it is.
		No, this is Carlos.
		No, it's Carlos.

It usually refers to a thing and takes the same form of the verb as *he* and *she*:

Is your number 555-1037?   Yes, **it is**.
Is your number 555-1032?   No, **it isn't**. **It's** 555-1037.

5 ▶ **Complete the conversations.**

1. **George** Hello?
   Phil Hello, is George there?
   George ___*This is*___ George.
   Phil Hi, George. _____ Phil Wang.
   George Phil Wang?
   Phil _____ George Dobbs?
   George No. _____ George Arno.

2. **Carolyn** ___*Are you*___ Jeff Hunt?
   Jeff Yes, _____ .
   Carolyn Nice to meet you, Jeff. _____ Carolyn Duval. Is George Arno here?
   Jeff No, _____ .

📼 **6** ▶ **Put the lines of the conversations below in order.**
   ▶ **Listen to the conversations to check your work.**
   ▶ **Act out the conversations using your own names.**

1. ___ Bill?
   ___ That's O.K.
   _1_ Hello?
   _2_ Hello, Susan? This is Bill.
   ___ I'm sorry.
   ___ Is this Susan Chang?
   ___ No. You have the wrong number.

2. _2_ Hello, is this Susan?
   _4_ Hi, Jane. This is Bill. Is Susan there?
   _1_ Hello?
   _3_ No, it isn't. This is Jane.
   _5_ No, she isn't here right now. She's at work.

3. ___ Hi, Susan. This is Bill.
   ___ Hello?
   ___ Yes, it is.
   ___ Bill! How are you?
   ___ Hello, is this Susan?
   ___ Great.

10. Numbers

NUMBERS: 0-10

0	1	2	3	4	5	6	7	8	9	10
zero	one	two	three	four	five	six	seven	eight	nine	ten

 1 ▶ **Listen to these phone numbers. Then say them.**

1. 555-4481   3. 555-9444   5. 555-1038   7. 555-0384
2. 555-7023   4. 555-4917   6. 555-3394   8. 555-4901

> Zero is pronounced "oh" when saying a phone number.

2 ▶ **Practice saying the numbers on the passports and credit card.**

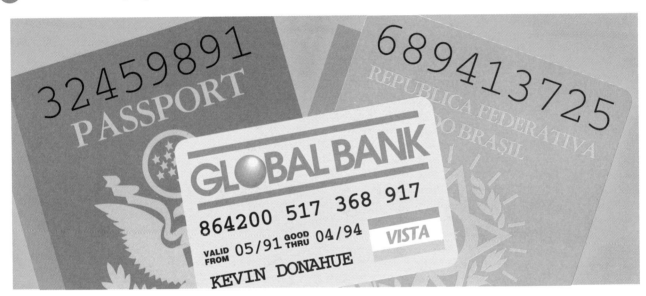

ASK FOR SOMEONE'S PHONE NUMBER

 3 ▶ **Marco is taking orders for pizzas. Listen to the conversations and write down the phone numbers.**

1. _____
2. _____
3. _____
4. _____

4 ▶ **Listen to the conversation below.**
▶ **Ask three classmates for their phone numbers. Write down the numbers and confirm them.**

A What's your phone number?
B It's 555-2012.
A 555-2102?
B No. It's 555-2012.
A 555-2012.
B That's right.

10. Numbers

WARM-UP

Have the students follow along in their books as you read aloud the numbers 0-10 at the top of the page. Then have the students repeat them after you. Next point to different numbers and have the class say them. Point again and call on individual students to respond.

NUMBERS: 0-10

- Play the cassette or read the phone numbers aloud. Then point out the note to the right and read aloud the information about the pronunciation of *zero*. To provide an example, read aloud item 2 in the exercise.

- After students listen to and repeat the phone numbers, call on individual students to say the numbers.

OPTION

With books closed, students can write the phone numbers on separate paper as you read them aloud or play them on cassette. They can check their answers by looking in their books. Students can also take turns dictating the different phone numbers to you as you write them on the board, or they can work in pairs and take turns dictating the numbers to each other.

- Call on different students to read the numbers on the passports and credit card aloud.

OPTION

Have students work in pairs. They can use identification numbers of their own—from driver's licenses, passports, and so on—and practice saying them aloud by dictating them to their partners. Finally, they should check each other's work.

- Play the cassette or read the tapescript aloud as the students listen and write down the phone numbers they hear.

- Have the students listen again and check their work as different students write the answers on the board.

TAPESCRIPT AND ANSWERS

1. **A** What's your name, please?
   B Maria Nunes.
   A What's your phone number?
   B 555-0642.

2. **A** Your name, please?
   B Donna Washington.
   A And your phone number?
   B 555-3985.

3. **A** Your name, please?
   B Midori Tanaka.
   A And what's your phone number?
   B 555-2683.

4. **A** What's your name?
   B Boris Petrov.
   A What's your phone number?
   B 555-3354.

- Play the cassette or read the conversation aloud as the students listen. Then have two students practice it in front of the class. Tell them to use their own telephone numbers.

- The students can work in groups of four or move around the classroom to find out three classmates' phone numbers. Have them write down the numbers and then confirm them with their classmates.

FOLLOW-UP

Students can listen to the conversations in exercise 3 and write them out.

WORKBOOK Lesson 10, p. 12

11. Phone frustrations

WARM-UP

Have students write their names on slips of paper. Collect the slips and then distribute them randomly. Call on students to spell aloud the name they received.

CALL DIRECTORY ASSISTANCE

- Play the cassette or read the conversation aloud. Then have two students read it aloud.

- Have students work in pairs to take turns playing the role of Student A and Student B. (See Methodology Note below.) Tell them to model their exchanges on the conversation they've just heard.

METHODOLOGY NOTE

Ensure that role-playing activities are information-gap activities whenever possible. For example, in the activity above, tell students who are playing the role of Student A to cover the numbers on the list in their books. In this way, an "information gap" exists as in real life when asking for a number you don't have in front of you.

ASK FOR CHANGE

- After playing the cassette or reading the conversations aloud, choose different students to join you in reading each conversation in front of the class. Point out the note on the informality of the word *thanks*.

- Have the students move around the classroom to ask for change from their classmates. Tell them to use the conversation as a guide.

APOLOGIZE FOR A WRONG NUMBER

- Have the students work in small groups of three or four. Tell them to take turns saying each part in the exchange. They can use their own names and numbers or those from the list in exercise 1. Go around the classroom and check group work. Call on one or more groups to present their exchanges to the class.

FOLLOW-UP

Students can write out the conversation in exercise 3.

WORKBOOK Lesson 11, pp. 13-14

11. Phone frustrations

CALL DIRECTORY ASSISTANCE

 1 ▶ **Listen to the conversation below.**

A (*Dials number*) *Rrring, rrring*
B Directory Assistance.
A I'd like the number of Jane Schaefer.
A Could you spell the last name, please?
B S-C-H-A-E-F-E-R.
A The number is 555-5275.
B Thank you.
A You're welcome.

▶ **Play these roles:**

Student A You need to call someone in the list, but you don't have the phone number. Call Directory Assistance.

Student B Play the role of the operator. Use the information in the list.

Sanchez Pedro 315 Washington ...555-9821
Sato Aki 915 River Avenue 555-3004
Schaefer Jane 201 W 23 St............555-5275
Scott John R 910 Union St 555-3003
Scotto Julia 1785 Park Road..........555-0403
Shafer L A 111 W 48 St 555-8707
Shaw Anne 915 River Avenue 555-3924
Shaw James 425 Adams St...........555-0862
Shin Young 202 E 28 St 555-1343
Silva Paul 522 California 555-4508
Silver Frank 647 Second Ave.........555-3473
Simmons J B 2665 Lake Road 555-1159
Small Carolyn 407 Lincoln St 555-2683
Smith Carl 809 River Avenue.........555-6182
Smith David 505 E 32 St 555-7396
Smith Nancy 10 Wilson St............555-6936
Smith Robert 924 Third Avenue....555-3254
Stavros Tony 812 Union St 555-4829
Sullivan Jean 21 E 19 St 555-9821

ASK FOR CHANGE

 2 ▶ **You need change to make a phone call. Listen to the two conversations below.**
▶ **Find a classmate who can give you change.**

A Excuse me—do you have change for a dollar?
B Let's see. . . . No, I'm sorry, I don't.

A Excuse me—do you have change for a dollar?
C Yes, I do. Here you are.
A Thanks.
C You're welcome.

> **Thank you** is more formal than **thanks**.

APOLOGIZE FOR A WRONG NUMBER

3 ▶ **Work in small groups. Sit with your back to the group and call someone in it. If you get a wrong number, call again.**

A (*Dials number*) *Rrring, rrring*
B Hello?
A Hello, is _____ there?
B No, you have the wrong number.
A Is this _(number)_ ?
B No, it isn't.
A I'm sorry.
B That's O.K.
A (*Dials again*) *Rrring, rrring*

12. Arno's Coffee Shop

 John Pierce stops in to have a cup of coffee at Arno's.

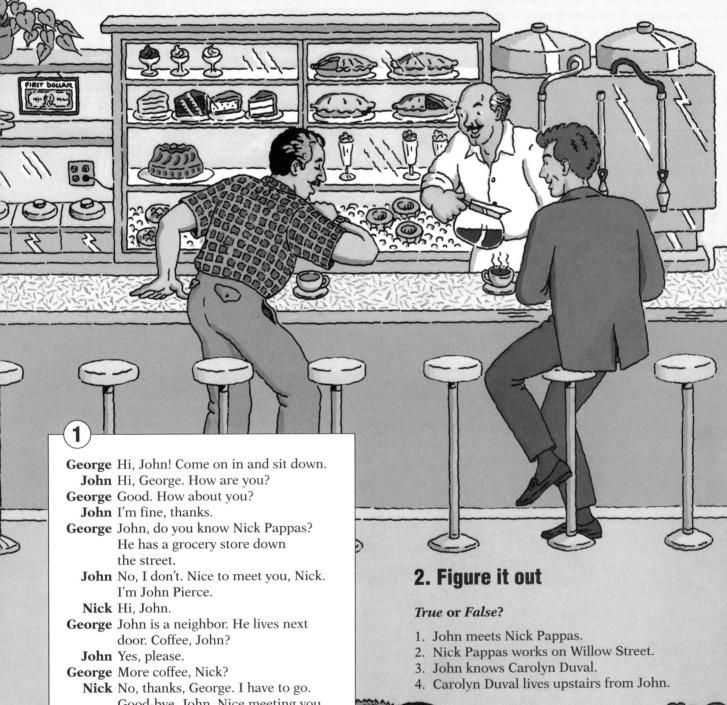

1

George Hi, John! Come on in and sit down.
John Hi, George. How are you?
George Good. How about you?
John I'm fine, thanks.
George John, do you know Nick Pappas? He has a grocery store down the street.
John No, I don't. Nice to meet you, Nick. I'm John Pierce.
Nick Hi, John.
George John is a neighbor. He lives next door. Coffee, John?
John Yes, please.
George More coffee, Nick?
Nick No, thanks, George. I have to go. Good-bye, John. Nice meeting you.
John Bye, Nick.
George See you, Nick. (*To John*) So, John, how's your new neighbor?
John My new neighbor?
George Yes—Carolyn Duval. She just moved into your building.
John Oh, yeah—into the apartment upstairs. . . . I don't know her.
George Oh, she's very nice. . . .

2. Figure it out

True or *False*?

1. John meets Nick Pappas.
2. Nick Pappas works on Willow Street.
3. John knows Carolyn Duval.
4. Carolyn Duval lives upstairs from John.

12. Arno's Coffee Shop

WARM-UP

Dictate five telephone numbers to the students. Say each number twice. The first time you say a number, the students are to listen only. The second time they should write the number down. Call on students to read back the numbers they have written.

1. Conversation

BACKGROUND

John Pierce, one of George Arno's neighbors, stops in to have coffee at Arno's Coffee Shop. George introduces John to his friend Nick Pappas. Then he asks John about John's new neighbor, Carolyn Duval.

LANGUAGE

Come on in. is an informal way of welcoming someone.

How about you? is another way of saying "And you?"

...down the street refers to a location that is a short distance away on the same street.

...have to (do something) indicates obligation.

How's...? is short for *How is...?*

...yeah is a very casual way of saying "yes."

PROCEDURE

- Have students examine the illustrations. Point out the people and situations depicted by asking questions and making statements like these:

  Where's Nick Pappas?
  This is John Pierce.
  This is a cup of coffee.
  Is John drinking coffee?
  Where's George Arno?

- Allow students to listen to the conversation as many times as they need to in order to understand it.

2. Figure it out

True or *False*?

- Have students read over the four statements on p. 18. Then have them listen to the conversation and answer *True* or *False* on separate paper.

- Have students check their answers in pairs before listening to the conversation again. Then go over the answers with the class.

  ANSWERS
  1. True
  2. True
  3. False
  4. True

3. Listen in

- Read the instructions aloud as the students follow along in their books. Point out the man on the phone in the illustration. Remind the students that their task is to write down the friend's new telephone number.

- Play the conversation on cassette or read the tapescript as the students listen. If you read the conversation aloud, shift your position to indicate a change in speakers.

- Have the students listen to the conversation again as a student writes the answer on the board.

TAPESCRIPT AND ANSWER

Operator The number you have reached, 555-3362, has been changed. The new number is <u>555-3457</u>. Please make a note of it. 555-3362 has been changed. The new number is 555-3457.

4. Your turn

- Read the instructions aloud as the students follow along in their books. Divide the class into pairs and tell them to take turns acting out the different parts in the conversation.

- Call on different pairs to present their conversations to the class. Check their work. You might write one of the conversations on the board.

POSSIBLE CONVERSATION

Woman *(Dials number.) Rrring, rring*
   Man Hello?
Woman Hello, is Mary there?
   Man I'm sorry, you have the wrong number.
Woman Is this 555-9907?
   Man No, it's 555-9904.
Woman Oh, I'm sorry.
   Man That's O.K.

5. How to say it

- Follow the basic procedure for **How to say it** in Unit 1 on p. 9.

PRONUNCIATION NOTE

The telephone greeting *Hello?* has the rising intonation pattern of a yes-no question. The person who answers the phone is actually asking a question to find out who is calling. Other examples of rising intonation are *Susan?*, *Hello, is Susan there?* and *Is this 555-1032?* The intonation of *Susan?* rises on the stressed syllable just as it does with *Hello?* Short answers, such as *No, it isn't*, have the same rising-falling intonation as statements.

OPTION

Ask students to indicate the intonation pattern as you read additional examples of rising or rising-falling intonation patterns. The students can point upward for rising and downward for rising-falling. You can use questions and short statements that the students have already practiced. For example:

Coffee, John? (rising)
My new neighbor? (rising)
Is this Bill? (rising)
I'm sorry. (rising-falling)
No, I don't. (rising-falling)

6. Your turn

- Have students follow in their books as you read the instructions. Point out the man and Loretta Arno.

- Have students act out the conversation in pairs. They may want to write it down. You can ask for volunteers to act out the conversation for the class.

OPTION

Have the class create the conversation while you write it on the board. Then you can ask a student to act out the conversation with you.

FOLLOW-UP

Students can write out the conversation in exercise 4.

WORKBOOK Lesson 12, p. 15

3. Listen in

The man below is trying to call a friend, but the number has been changed. Listen and write down the friend's new telephone number.

5. How to say it

Listen to this conversation.

A Hello?

B Hello, is Susan there?

A Susan?

B Is this 555-1032?

A No, it isn't.

6. Your turn

The man below needs some change. Act out his conversation with Loretta Arno.

4. Your turn

The woman above is calling a friend and gets the wrong number. Act out a possible conversation.

Woman *(Dials number.) Rrring, rrring*
Man Hello?
Woman _____?
Man I'm sorry, you have the wrong number.
Woman _____?
Man No, it's 555-9904.
Woman _____.
Man That's O.K.

13. Is the telephone your friend or your enemy?

Lisa Daoud
High School Student

The telephone is my
friend! I love to talk to
my friends on the
telephone.

Louis Sanchez
Architect

It's my _enemy_! People
call me with bad news
and more work!

Ashok Gupta
Retired Doctor

Oh, it's my _____ .
A telephone is very
important in an
emergency.

Arthur Shawcross
Construction Worker

The telephone is
definitely my _____!
It's expensive and my
telephone is often out
of order.

Evelyn Pollack
Housewife

The telephone is my
good _____! I have
six children and I need
a telephone. Believe
me!

Rika Ito
Potter

Oh, it's not my _____ .
It's my _____ .
People always call
when I'm in the shower
or asleep.

1. **Read the article. Then fill in each blank with "friend" or "enemy."**

2. **What's your opinion? Is the telephone your friend or your enemy?**

13. Is the telephone your friend or your enemy?

BACKGROUND

This survey is probably from a magazine or newspaper. People are asked their opinions about telephones.

PROCEDURE

1. Read the article. Then fill in each blank with "friend" or "enemy."

- Explain that this is an opinion survey. Then tell the students to read the first two entries silently. Check for understanding of the words *friend* and *enemy*.

- Have the students read the rest of the survey silently and then fill in each blank with *friend* or *enemy*. They can compare their answers in pairs.

- Play the cassette or read the text aloud so that the students can check their answers. Have a student write the answers on the board.

  ANSWERS
  friend
  enemy
  friend
  friend, enemy

2. What's your opinion? Is the telephone your friend or your enemy?

- Have the students write their opinions in response to the question. You may ask them to share their answers in pairs or with the class.

OPTION 1

Divide the class into pairs. Have students survey their partners and write down their partner's answer to the question. Ask students to share their answers in small groups or with the class.

OPTION 2

Ask students to interview a friend or relative, using the same question: *What's your opinion? Is the telephone your friend or your enemy?* Have them bring their answers to class to share with their classmates. On the board, write the heading *Telephone Survey* and draw two columns with the headings *friend* and *enemy*. Record the number of responses from the students' surveys under the appropriate column. Conclude by asking the students if most of the people surveyed consider the telephone their friend or their enemy.

FOLLOW-UP

Students can write why they think the telephone is their friend or enemy, using the opinions as a model.

WORKBOOK Lesson 13, p. 16. Before assigning the writing task, review general capitalization and punctuation rules with the students.

PREVIEW

Before you begin teaching, go over the functions/themes, language, and forms in the chart. This will give you a preview of what you will encounter as you guide the students through the unit.

Preview the conversations.

- Have the students examine the first photograph. Point out Carlos and the airplane. See if the students can figure out where Carlos is from. If necessary, point out the tail section with the airline's logo.

- As the students examine the second photograph, discuss the sentences under it. Have the students talk about visiting someone in their country.

CULTURE CLOSE-UP

As a sign of hospitality in the U.S., it is customary to offer a drink to a friend who is visiting one's home. Coffee, tea, soda, water, etc., may be offered. Especially in informal situations, the kitchen may be the place where a drink or snack is offered.

PREVIEW

FUNCTIONS/THEMES	LANGUAGE	FORMS
Ask about the location of cities Ask where people are from	Where's Tokyo? In Japan. Where are you from? I'm from Brazil. The Lopezes are from Mexico.	Present of *be*: information questions; statements; yes-no questions and short answers Plural of names
Introduce people	Tony, this is my friend, Linda. Linda, this is Tony.	
Offer something to drink	Do you want some coffee? Yes, please. (No, thank you.)	Formulaic use of *do*
Say good-bye after meeting someone	Good-bye. Nice meeting you.	
Ask for someone's address	What's Jim's address? It's 60 Bank Street. Sixty or sixteen? Sixty—six-oh	Numbers 11–100 Possessive of names

Preview the conversations.

Carlos is flying to New York. Where is he from?

Carlos is at a friend's house in New York. His friend is offering him something to drink. What is it? What do you normally offer your friends?

14. Where are you from?

🔊 Carlos Gomez is going to New York to visit his friends Betty and Jim Fox.

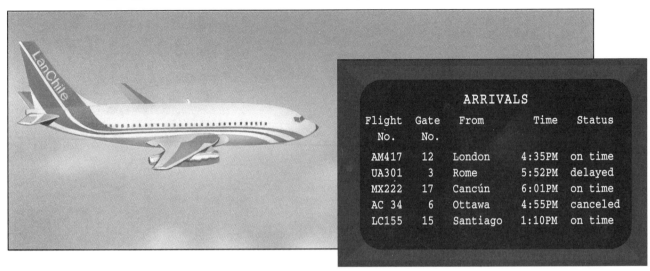

ARRIVALS				
Flight No.	Gate No.	From	Time	Status
AM417	12	London	4:35PM	on time
UA301	3	Rome	5:52PM	delayed
MX222	17	Cancún	6:01PM	on time
AC 34	6	Ottawa	4:55PM	canceled
LC155	15	Santiago	1:10PM	on time

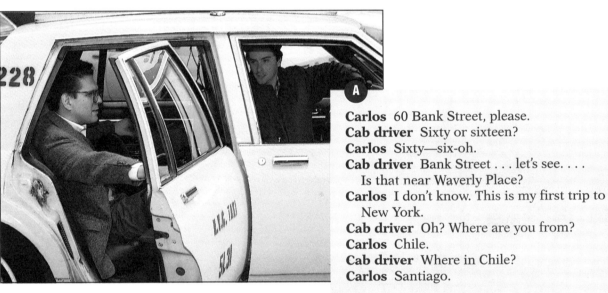

A

Carlos 60 Bank Street, please.
Cab driver Sixty or sixteen?
Carlos Sixty—six-oh.
Cab driver Bank Street . . . let's see. . . .
Is that near Waverly Place?
Carlos I don't know. This is my first trip to
New York.
Cab driver Oh? Where are you from?
Carlos Chile.
Cab driver Where in Chile?
Carlos Santiago.

B

Betty Carlos! You're here!
Carlos Betty! Jim! How are you?
Jim We're fine. How about you?
Carlos Great! It's good to be here finally.

14. Where are you from?

Show the students a world map or a globe. Point out Santiago, Chile and New York City and have the students repeat the names after you. Continue the practice by pointing to other major cities.

BACKGROUND

Carlos Gomez travels to New York from Chile to visit his friends Betty and Jim Fox. Carlos and Jim are old friends from school. While visiting the Foxes, Carlos meets Jim's sister, Karen.

LANGUAGE

Where in…(Chile)? is used to ask for a specific location within a larger area—in this case, *Which city/place (in Chile)?*

Great! indicates that the speaker feels very good.

Nice meeting you. is often said when departing. It's short for *It was nice meeting you.*

PROCEDURE

- Point out and say the names of the different characters in the pictures. Make statements and ask simple questions about what's going on in the pictures. For example:

  In the first picture, Carlos is in an airplane.
  He's on his way to New York.
  Where's Carlos in the next picture?
  (In a taxi. In New York.)

- Play the cassette or read the conversations aloud as the students listen with their books closed. Have them listen again as they follow along in their books. Answer any questions they have about vocabulary or structures.

OPTION 1

If possible, have different students read the conversations with you. Indicate appropriate stress, intonation, and gestures. For example, shrug your shoulders to indicate "I don't know" and wave as you say "Good-bye, everyone."

Have the students act out the conversations in pairs or small groups. Have them shake hands as they are introduced in Conversation C. Call on different pairs or groups to present their conversations to the class.

OPTION 2

If a globe or map of the world is available, have the students locate London, Rome, Cancún, Ottawa, Santiago, and New York. Then have them point out their own countries and cities and practice the English pronunciation of the places they point to.

Figure it out

1. Listen to the conversations. What city is Carlos from?

- Read the question aloud to the students. Then have them listen to the conversations and answer the question. Call on a student to say the answer.

  ANSWER
  Santiago

2. Listen again. Say *true* or *false*.

- Have the students read the statements to themselves before they listen.

- Read the conversations aloud or play them on cassette. Tell the students to cover the dialogue boxes and to look only at the pictures as they listen. Have the students answer *True* or *False* on separate paper.

- Tell the students to compare and discuss their answers with a partner. Then call on different students to read the statements and their answers aloud. Have a student write the answers on the board.

  ANSWERS
  1. False
  2. True
  3. True
  4. False
  5. True

OPTION 1

You can ask students additional true/false items:

1. Jim and Betty's address is 16 Bank Street. (False)
2. Santiago is in Chile. (True)
3. Carlos is an old friend of Jim's from school. (True)
4. Carlos wants cream and sugar in his coffee. (False)

OPTION 2

Have the students work in groups. Tell them to write *True* on one piece of paper and *False* on another. Then with their books closed, have them listen to the conversation again. Next read each of the true/false statements (including the ones from OPTION 1) aloud. After reading each statement, give the groups time to work cooperatively and decide on the answer. Tell them to hold up their answers.

METHODOLOGY NOTE

Group work of the type mentioned above is a form of cooperative learning. In cooperative learning, students help each other to reach specific goals. When students work in groups, it is often advantageous to have a range of English proficiency levels represented in each group so that students at higher levels of proficiency can assist those at lower levels. If all groups have a balance of proficiency levels, a more equal opportunity to excel will exist. You can determine students' proficiency levels by using test scores, homework assignment scores, and/or classroom observation.

3. Choose *a* or *b*.

- Have the students read the sentences and choose the correct responses. Students can work in pairs to compare their answers and practice the exchanges.

- Call on different pairs to read the exchanges aloud. Ask a student to write the answers on the board.

  ANSWERS
  1. a
  2. a
  3. a
  4. b

FOLLOW-UP

Students can write out the exchanges from exercise 3.

WORKBOOK Lesson 14, p. 17

Jim Carlos, this is my sister, Karen. Karen, this is Carlos— an old friend from school.
Carlos Hi, Karen.
Karen Nice to meet you, Carlos.

Jim Do you want some coffee, Carlos?
Carlos Yes, please.
Jim Cream and sugar?
Carlos No, thanks.

Karen Good-bye, everyone.
Betty, Jim, Carlos Bye.
Karen Nice meeting you, Carlos.
Carlos Nice meeting you, too.

Figure it out

1. Listen to the conversations. What city is Carlos from?

2. Listen again. Say *true* or *false*.

1. Jim and Betty live in Santiago.
2. Jim and Betty live on Bank Street.
3. Betty is Jim's wife.
4. Carlos is Karen's friend from school.
5. Karen is Jim's sister.

3. Choose *a* or *b*.

1. We're fine. How about you?
   a. Great.
   b. You're here!

2. Good-bye.
   a. Nice meeting you.
   b. Nice to meet you, too.

3. Karen, this is Carlos. Carlos, Karen.
   a. Nice to meet you.
   b. Nice meeting you.

4. Cream and sugar?
   a. Do you want some coffee?
   b. Yes, please.

15. The Silvas are from Brazil.

CITIES AND COUNTRIES

See p. 166 for a complete list of countries.

1 ▶ **Ask and answer questions about the location of the cities below.**

A Where's Tokyo?
B In Japan.

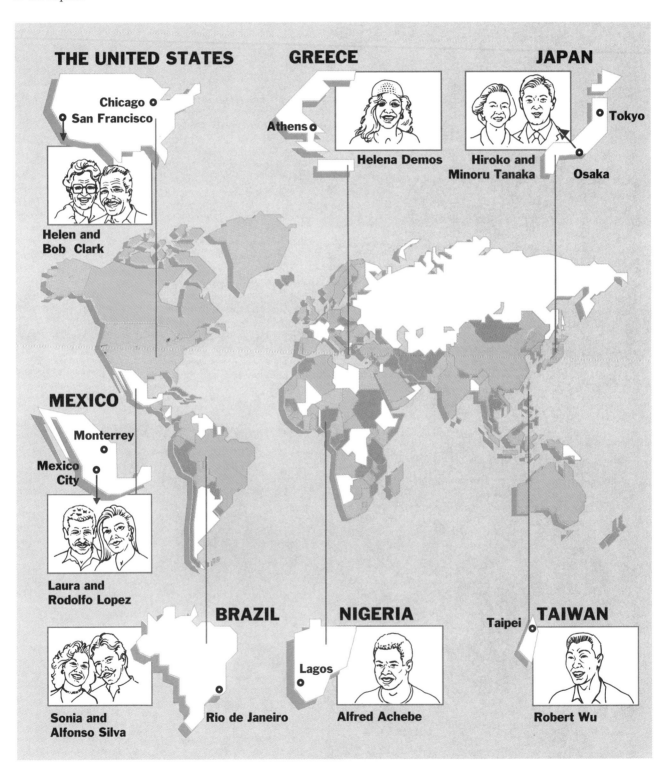

THE UNITED STATES

Chicago o
o San Francisco

Helen and
Bob Clark

GREECE

Athens o

Helena Demos

JAPAN

o Tokyo

Hiroko and
Minoru Tanaka

Osaka

MEXICO

Monterrey
o

Mexico
City o

Laura and
Rodolfo Lopez

BRAZIL

Sonia and
Alfonso Silva

Rio de Janeiro

NIGERIA

Lagos
o

Alfred Achebe

TAIWAN

Taipei o

Robert Wu

15. The Silvas are from Brazil.

WARM-UP

Go around the classroom and ask individual students where they are from. If all or most of the students are from the same place, tell them to pretend they're from different cities and countries. You may wish to refer students to the list of countries on p. 166.

CITIES AND COUNTRIES

- Hold up your book and say the names of the cities and the countries as you point them out. Have the students repeat after you.

- Call on a student and ask the example question:

  A Where's Tokyo?
  B In Japan.

  Then go around the room and ask about the other cities. You might have the students hold up their books and point to the location as they respond. You can have the students start at the top of the page and move from left to right. For example:

  A Where's Chicago?
  B In the United States.

  A Where's Athens?
  B In Greece.

  A Where's Tokyo?
  B In Japan.

  A Where's San Francisco?
  B In the United States.

OPTION

Divide the class into two teams—Team A and Team B. Be sure a world map or globe is available to each team. Assign each team member a different major city from the countries listed on p. 166. Then begin the game. Have a member from Team A say the name of a city. Then have Team B try to locate the city on the map or globe and say the name of the country in which the city is located. Then it's Team B's turn. You may wish to keep score, giving one point for each correct answer.

SAY WHAT COUNTRY PEOPLE ARE FROM

- Have the students look at the box as you play the cassette or read the names aloud. Then have them repeat the names and the endings after you.

- On the board, write names that end in the letters listed at the bottom of the box. For example:

Frank and Marilyn Chur**ch**—the Churches
Sylvia and John Ca**sh**—the Cashes
Nel and Sam Nes**s**—the Nesses
Roberto and Maria Sanche**z**—the Sanchezes
Laura and Michael Tra**x**—the Traxes

Have the students repeat the names after you. Replace the plural names on the board with blanks. Call on different students to write the last names in the blanks and say them. Then have the class repeat the plural names after you.

- Read aloud the instructions for the second part of the exercise. Tell the students to look at the map on p. 24. Point to Sonia and Alfonso Silva and say "The Silvas are from Brazil." Call on different students to tell you where the other people are from. For example:

T: Where are Helen and Bob Clark from?
S: The Clarks are from the United States.
T: Where is Helena Demos from?
S: Helena Demos is from Greece.

- Have the students practice in pairs. Tell them to take turns asking each other which country each person or couple on the map on p. 24 is from.

OPTION

Have each student come to the board to write down and then say the plural form of his or her name. Check for correct spelling and pronunciation of the endings.

PRONUNCIATION NOTE

The regular plural (as well as the possessive and the third person singular present tense) has three pronunciations: [ɪz] (*Lopezes*), [z] (*Silvas*), and [s] (*Clarks*). The sound [ɪz] occurs after the sounds [s], [z], [ʃ], [ʒ], [tʃ], and [dʒ]. The sound [z] occurs after all other voiced sounds (vowels and consonants). The sound [s] occurs after the voiceless consonant sounds [p], [t], [k], [f], and [θ].

ASK WHAT CITY AND COUNTRY PEOPLE ARE FROM • PRESENT OF *BE*

- Tell the students to study the frames. Make sure

they understand the headings at the top of the frames.

- Explain that *we're not* and *they're not* are acceptable variants for *we aren't* and *they aren't*. Answer any questions students have about the frames.

OPTION

Ask a student "Where are you from?" and prompt him or her to answer "I'm from… ." Then ask another student about the student's answer— "Where is he (she) from?" Prompt the answer— "He (She)'s from… ." Continue the practice with other students. Include yourself to practice *we*. To practice *they*, ask two students who are from the same city or country.

- Tell the students to look at the conversation and listen while you play the cassette or read the conversation aloud. Then, as they listen again, have them locate on the map the characters from the conversation and the places where they live.

- Explain the role-play instructions. Have the students work in pairs to take turns playing the roles of A and B. To help them get started, write the first exchange on the board:

A: Where is Robert Wu from?
B: He's from Taiwan.

Call on different pairs to present their exchanges to the class.

FIND OUT WHERE YOUR CLASSMATES ARE FROM

- Tell the students to fill in the blanks with the correct city or country while you play the cassette or read the conversations. Then ask two students to write the answers on the board.

ANSWERS
1. **B** Japan
   A Taiwan
2. **B** Mexico City
   A Mexico City

- Divide the students into small groups. Tell them to fill in the blanks again, using personal information. If they all come from the same country, they can name their cities or neighborhoods instead. Ask them to practice the new dialogues aloud.

WORKBOOK Lesson 15, pp. 18-20

2 ► Listen to the pronunciation of the plural names in the box.

► Say what countries the people on the map on p. 24 are from. For married couples, use the plural form of their names.

The Silvas are from Brazil.

Helen and Bob Clark	→ the Clark**s**	[s]
Sonia and Alfonso Silva	→ the Silva**s**	[z]
Laura and Rodolfo Lopez	→ the Lopez**es**	[ɪz]

ch, **sh**, **s**, **z**, **x**: Add -**es**.

3 ► Study the frames: Present of *Be*

Information questions				Statements				Yes-no questions				Short answers		
		you		I	**'m**				you			Yes,	I	**am.**
	are	they		We	**'re**	from Japan.		**Are**	they		from Tokyo?	No,		**'m not.**
Where			from?	They					he			Yes,	we	**are.**
		he						**Is**	she			No,	they	**aren't.**
	is	she		He	**'s**							Yes,	he	**is.**
				She								No,	she	**isn't.**

You may say:

we aren't or **we're not**.
they aren't or **they're not**.

 4 ► The people on the map are on vacation together. Listen to the conversation below.

Robert Wu Sonia, where are you and Alfonso from?
Sonia Silva We're from Brazil.
Robert Wu Oh, are you from Rio?
Sonia Silva Yes, we are.
Robert Wu And the Lopezes—are they from Brazil, too?
Sonia Silva No, they aren't. They're from Mexico.

► Play these roles:

Student A Ask where the people below are from. Don't look at the map.
Student B Use the information on the map to answer Student A's questions.

Robert Wu	Sonia and Alfonso Silva	Laura and Rodolfo Lopez
Hiroko and Minoru Tanaka	Helena Demos	Helen and Bob Clark

 5 ► Listen to the conversations below. Fill in the blanks with the correct city or country.
► Practice the conversations in small groups. Use personal information.

1. **A** Where are you from?
   B I'm from _____ . How about you?
   A I'm from _____ .

2. **A** Where are you from?
   B I'm from _____ .
   A Oh, I'm from _____ , too.

16. Socializing

🔲 ① ► The people in the picture above are at a party. Listen to the conversations.
► Imagine you're at a party with students from your school. Greet a friend.
► Introduce another student to your friend.
► Introduce yourself to someone you don't know.

OFFER SOMETHING TO DRINK

🔲 ② ► Listen to the two possible conversations below.
► Offer another student something to drink.

> **A** Do you want some coffee?
>
> **B** Yes, please.
> **B** No, thanks.
> **A** How about some tea?
> **B** O.K. Thanks.

coffee   tea   water   milk   soda

SAY GOOD-BYE AFTER MEETING SOMEONE

③ ► **Say good-bye to the classmates you met today.**

Linda Good-bye, Tony. Nice meeting you.
Tony Bye, Linda. Nice meeting you, too.

> When you first meet someone, say "Nice to meet you."
> When you say good-bye, say "Nice meeting you."

16. Socializing

Greet students by saying "Hi, (*the student's name*)! How are you?" Encourage them to answer. Accept answers such as "Fine. And you?" or "Fine, thank you." Following the pattern on p. 26, introduce some students to each other.

GREETINGS AND INTRODUCTIONS

- Tell the students to look at frames 1, 2, and 3. Explain that the people in the pictures are at a party. Play the cassette or read the conversations aloud.

- If possible, divide the students into groups of four. Have them pretend they're at a party. Tell them to take turns playing the roles of the characters in the three frames. Tell them to use their own names. Move around the classroom to check their work.

- Call on different groups to present the scenes to the class.

OFFER SOMETHING TO DRINK

- Play the cassette or read the conversations as the students read along in their books. You can read the conversations a second time with two students. Have each student say the different B responses.

- Tell the students to work in pairs and to take turns offering, accepting, and refusing something to drink. Have them model their exchanges on the sample conversations. Suggest that they use the items in the picture in their questions.

OPTION

Bring all or some of the following realia to class— a coffee pot, tea pot, cup, saucer, glass, milk container, soda can or bottle, and sugar. Demonstrate the conversations using the realia. Then have small groups use the realia and practice the conversations.

METHODOLOGY NOTE

Realia includes items from real life such as dishes, utensils, and clothes. It also includes facsimiles, such as toy cars, paper hats, or play money. The use of realia is recommended, especially for students at beginning levels of language acquisition. By using actual objects or facsimiles, students can make meaningful associations and therefore more readily recall new words and related structures. The use of realia is advised in many current second-language approaches and methodologies including the Natural Approach and Total Physical Response (TPR).

SAY GOOD-BYE AFTER MEETING SOMEONE

- Read the sample conversation aloud with another student as the students follow along in their books.

- Point out that *Nice to meet you* is used when someone is first introduced and *Nice meeting you* is used when saying good-bye.

- Have the students work in the same groups as in exercise 1. Tell them to say good-bye to their classmates using the sample exchange as a model. Go around the classroom and check their work.

OPTION

Divide the students into groups of four or five. Have one student act as the host or hostess at a party, introducing the guests and offering them drinks. Use realia if possible. Have students say good-bye to one another at the end of the party.

WORKBOOK Lesson 16, p. 21

17. Addresses

WARM-UP

Have the students follow along in their books as you read aloud the numbers at the top of the page or play the cassette. Then have the students repeat the numbers after you. Next point to different numbers and have the class say them. Point again and call on individual students to respond.

NUMBERS: 11-100

- Tell the students to listen carefully to the pronunciation of the numbers as you play the cassette or read the tapescript. Before you begin, slightly exaggerate the difference in pronunciation between -ty and -teen.

- As you play the cassette or read the tapescript a second time, have the students circle the correct answer or write the number they hear on separate paper. Have them listen as many times as necessary. Tell a student to write the answers on the board.

TAPESCRIPT AND ANSWERS

1. 13	3. 90	5. 15	7. 17
2. 60	4. 14	6. 80	8. 12

ASK FOR SOMEONE'S ADDRESS

- Go over the information in the blue boxes with the students. Have them repeat the examples of the possessive of names after you. Also have them repeat after you—"one-fourteen, one-fifteen, six-nineteen, six-twenty," etc.

- Point out the mailing labels and then play the cassette or read the addresses aloud.

- Read the sample exchange aloud with a student or play the cassette. Then have the students work in pairs. Have them practice asking for addresses, using the information on the address labels. Tell them to use the sample conversation as a guide.

- Call on different pairs to say their exchanges for the class so you can check their work.

ANSWERS

A What's Roberta's address?
B It's 17 Hyde Park Street.
A Seventeen or seventy?
B Seventeen—one-seven.

A What's Gary's address?
B It's 30 Bryan Road.

A Thirty or thirteen?
B Thirty—three-oh.

A What's Ann's address?
B It's 114 Lakeland Street.
A One fourteen or one forty?
B One fourteen—one-one-four.

A What's Tim's address?
B It's 619 King Avenue.
A Six nineteen or six ninety?
B Six nineteen—six-one-nine.

OPTION

Have each student make up an address. Tell them they can use the list on p. 17 for ideas. Ask them to write the addresses on separate paper and read them aloud. Check their work.

ADD SOMEONE TO YOUR ADDRESS BOOK

- Play the cassette or read the conversation aloud with a student while the students follow along in their books.

- Read aloud the instructions and the questions in the box. Answer any questions students have about structures or vocabulary—for example, make sure they understand the meaning of *address book*.

- Tell the students to use separate paper as a sample address book page and to move around the classroom and write down the full names, addresses, and phone numbers of three classmates. Have them use the questions in the box to ask for the information.

- Tell students to verify the addresses by showing them to their classmates, reading them aloud, and asking "Is this right?" Go around the classroom and check their work.

OPTION

Read aloud Nestor's and Helen's addresses. Then you can have students work in pairs—one student can be Nestor and the other Helen. Tell them to use the conversation as a guide and to ask about each other's addresses. Finally, have them use their own names and ask for each other's addresses.

PRONUNCIATION NOTE

Four-digit numbers in addresses are pronounced as separate units of two digits each. For example, for 1430 Langdon Street, we say "Fourteen-thirty... ."

WORKBOOK Lesson 17, p. 22

17. Addresses

NUMBERS: 11–100

11	12	13	14	15	16	17	18	19	20
eleven	twelve	thirteen	fourteen	fifteen	sixteen	seventeen	eighteen	nineteen	twenty

21	30	40	50	60	70	80	90	100
twenty-one	thirty	forty	fifty	sixty	seventy	eighty	ninety	one hundred

 1 ▶ **Which number do you hear? Choose *a* or *b*.**

1. a. 13 b. 30   3. a. 19 b. 90   5. a. 15 b. 50   7. a. 17 b. 70
2. a. 16 b. 60   4. b. 14 b. 40   6. a. 18 b. 80   8. a. 12 b. 20

ASK FOR SOMEONE'S ADDRESS

 2 ▶ **Listen to the addresses on the mailing labels.**
▶ **Practice conversations like the one below, using the addresses on the labels.**

A What's Jim's address?
B It's 60 Bank Street.
A Sixty or sixteen?
B Sixty—six-oh.

Possessives of names are
pronounced like plurals of names:

Pat**'s** address   [s]
John**'s** address   [z]
Liz**'s** address   [ɪz]

114 is said
"one-fourteen."

Mr. Jim Fox
60 Bank Street
New York, NY 10014
U.S.A.

Ms. Roberta Tudhope
17 Hyde Park Street
Toronto, Ont.   M65 1M5
CANADA

Mr. Gary Cooke
30 Bryan Road
London W7H 7F8
ENGLAND

Ms. Ann O'Reilly
114 Lakeland Street
Kilmacud, Blackrock
County Dublin Ireland

Mr. Tim Rogers   2011
619 King Avenue
New South Wales
AUSTRALIA

ADD SOMEONE TO YOUR ADDRESS BOOK

 3 ▶ **Listen to the conversation below.**

A What's your address, Carol?
B 1430 Langdon Street. L-A-N-G-D-O-N.
A And what's your phone number?
B 555-8214.
A And your last name is Merrill?
B Right. M-E-R-R-I-L-L.
A Thanks.

▶ **Using the questions below, find out the full names, addresses, and phone numbers of three students. Write them in your address book.**
▶ **Verify that your information is correct.**

Carol Merrill
1430 Langdon Street
Los Angeles, CA 90063   U.S.A.
213-555-8214

Nestor Morales
Cerro del Borrego 135
Copilco, D.F. 31245   MEXICO
52-5-555-6528

Helen Murata
872 Lake Road
Willowdale, Ont. M2C 2H8
CANADA
615-555-7778

What's your address?
What's your phone number?
What's your last name?
Could you spell that?
What's the number again?
Is this right?

18. Laundromat

Loretta Arno runs into Stella Pappas, Nick's wife, in the laundromat.

25¢ – 5 min.
Quarters only

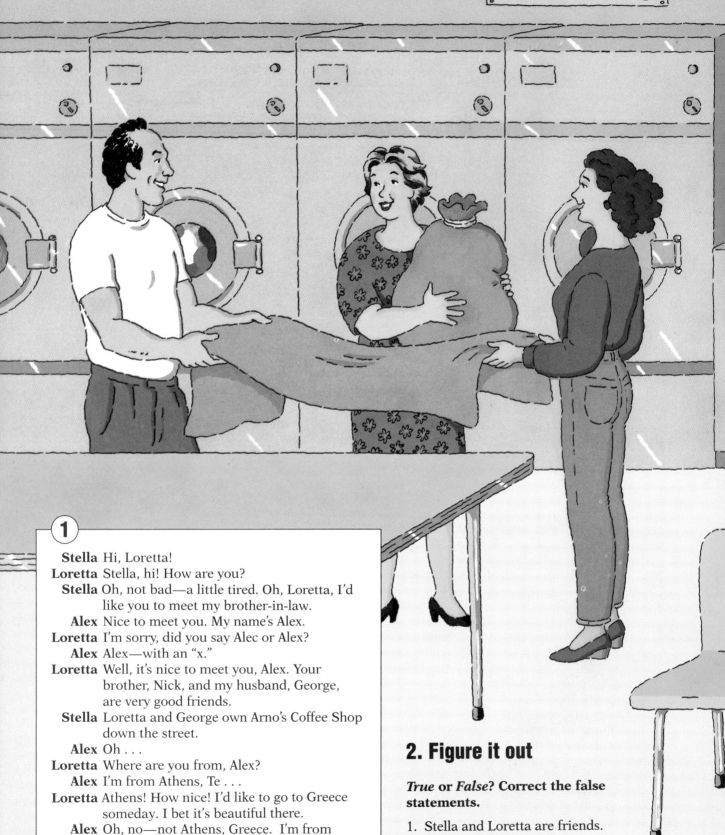

1

Stella Hi, Loretta!

Loretta Stella, hi! How are you?

Stella Oh, not bad—a little tired. Oh, Loretta, I'd like you to meet my brother-in-law.

Alex Nice to meet you. My name's Alex.

Loretta I'm sorry, did you say Alec or Alex?

Alex Alex—with an "x."

Loretta Well, it's nice to meet you, Alex. Your brother, Nick, and my husband, George, are very good friends.

Stella Loretta and George own Arno's Coffee Shop down the street.

Alex Oh . . .

Loretta Where are you from, Alex?

Alex I'm from Athens, Te . . .

Loretta Athens! How nice! I'd like to go to Greece someday. I bet it's beautiful there.

Alex Oh, no—not Athens, Greece. I'm from Athens, Texas.

2. Figure it out

True or *False*? Correct the false statements.

1. Stella and Loretta are friends.
2. Nick is Stella's husband.
3. Alex is Stella's brother.
4. Alex is from Athens, Greece.

18. Laundromat

Review the possessive of names. Point to a student's book and say "(*Student's name*)'s book." Go around the classroom and point to objects which belong to different students. Prompt the class to respond with the possessive.

1. Conversation

BACKGROUND

The conversation takes place at a laundromat, a place where people go to wash their clothes if they don't have a washing machine or dryer at home. Loretta Arno runs into Stella Pappas there. Stella introduces Loretta to her brother-in-law, Alex.

LANGUAGE

How nice! is an informal way of saying that something is agreeable and pleasing.

I bet... is an informal way of saying "I imagine that... ."

I'm sorry... is used here not so much to express regret as to ask for the repetition or clarification of information.

PROCEDURE

- As the students look at the picture, point out the people, their relationships, and the situations. As in previous units, make comments and ask questions about what's going on.

- Play the cassette or read the conversation aloud. Tell the students to follow along in their books. If you read, be sure to speak at a normal speed and perform each role as realistically as possible. Answer any questions students have about vocabulary or structures.

OPTION

Divide the students into groups of three. Tell them to practice reading the conversation. They can take turns reading the different parts.

CULTURE CLOSE-UP

There are laundromats in most cities and towns throughout the U.S. In large cities, some are open twenty-four hours a day. Washing machines and dryers are coin-operated. Most laundromats have vending machines where you can usually buy laundry detergent. Frequently laundromats also have bulletin boards to display lists of items for sale, community notices, and other information.

2. Figure it out

True or *False*? **Correct the false statements.**

- Have the students read the statements to themselves before they listen. Check for comprehension of vocabulary items such as *friends*, *husband*, *brother*, and *brother-in-law*.

- Play the cassette or read the conversation. Then tell the students to use separate paper to answer *True* or *False* and to correct the false statements. You may have to provide an example of a corrected false statement.

- Call on different students to say their answers aloud. Have a student write the answers on the board.

ANSWERS
1. True
2. True
3. False. Alex is Nick's brother. OR Alex is Stella's brother-in-law.
4. False. Alex is from Athens, Texas.

3. Listen in

- Read the instructions aloud as the students follow along in their books. Point out the young man in the illustration. Tell the students to read over the exercise items. Answer any questions they have about the instructions and the exercise items.

- Play the advertisement on cassette or read the tapescript as the students listen. Have them choose the correct answers. Play or read the advertisement again while students check their answers. Call on a student to read the answers aloud.

TAPESCRIPT

A Mmmm. This coffee is good.
B It's from the International Food Shop.
A The International Food Shop?
B You can buy coffee and tea from all over the world at the International Food Shop. 350 Pine Street, near Fulton Street in Brooklyn.

ANSWERS
1. a
2. b

4. How to say it

- Follow the basic procedure for **How to say it** in Unit 1 on p. 9.

PRONUNCIATION NOTE

Information questions have the same final rising-falling intonation as statements.

OPTION

Make two flashcards—one showing the rising-falling pattern of wh- information questions and statements and the other the rising intonation pattern of yes-no questions. Read the sentences from the conversation aloud and have the students point to the correct flashcard. You can also have the students copy the flashcards onto slips of paper and then hold up the appropriate one as you read the sentences aloud.

5. Your turn

1.
- Have the students follow along in their books as you read the instructions. Point out Liz, Jane, and Jenny in the illustration.

- Have the students act out the conversation in groups of three. Refer them to frame 2 of the pictures at the top of p. 26 as a guide in making up their conversations.

- Call on different groups to present their conversations to the class. You might also write a sample conversation (or one of the groups') on the board. For example:

> Jane: Liz, this is my friend Jenny. Jenny, this is Liz. Jenny is from San Francisco.
> Liz: Nice to meet you, Jenny.
> Jenny: Nice to meet you, too.

2.
- Point out the man in the picture who is asking for change. Refer the students to p. 12 or model a possible exchange for them to follow. For example:

> Man: Excuse me, ladies—do you have change for a dollar?
> Liz: Let's see… . No, I'm sorry, I don't.
> Jane: Hmmm…I don't think so… . No, I don't.
> Jenny: Uh…Let's see… . Ah, yes, I do. Here you are.

- Have the students act out their own conversations in groups of four. Call on different groups to present their conversations to the class.

OPTION

Have the students use their own names and role-play the first conversation. Encourage them to add some information about the student who is being introduced, as in the sample above—"Jenny is from San Francisco."

WORKBOOK Lesson 18, p. 23

▭ 4. How to say it

Listen to this conversation.

A Where are you from?

B Chicago. How about you?

A I'm from Brazil.

B Are you from Rio?

A Yes, I am.

▭ 3. Listen in

The young man is listening to an advertisement on the radio. Read the statements below. Then listen to the ad and choose *a, b,* or *c.*

1. The International Food Shop is at _____ .
   a. 350 Pine Street
   b. 315 Pine Street
   c. 350 Fulton Street

2. At the shop you can buy _____ .
   a. bread and cheese
   b. coffee and tea
   c. cream and sugar

5. Your turn

1. Look at Liz, Jane, and Jenny above. Jane is introducing Liz to her friend Jenny, who is from San Francisco. Act out the conversation.

2. A man is asking Liz, Jane, and Jenny for change. Act out the conversation.

19. My new address and phone number are . . .

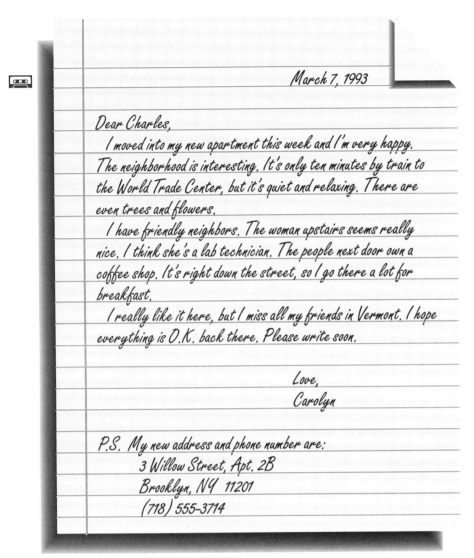

March 7, 1993

Dear Charles,

I moved into my new apartment this week and I'm very happy. The neighborhood is interesting. It's only ten minutes by train to the World Trade Center, but it's quiet and relaxing. There are even trees and flowers.

I have friendly neighbors. The woman upstairs seems really nice. I think she's a lab technician. The people next door own a coffee shop. It's right down the street, so I go there a lot for breakfast.

I really like it here, but I miss all my friends in Vermont. I hope everything is O.K. back there. Please write soon.

Love,
Carolyn

P.S. My new address and phone number are:
3 Willow Street, Apt. 2B
Brooklyn, NY 11201
(718) 555-3714

1. Read the letter. Who do you think Carolyn is talking about? (To check your answers, listen to the conversations again on pp. 3 and 8.)

1. Who's the woman upstairs?
2. Who are the people next door?

2. *True or False?*

1. Carolyn's neighborhood is quiet and relaxing.
2. The World Trade Center is in her neighborhood.
3. There's a coffee shop down the street from Carolyn's apartment.
4. Charles is a friend from Vermont.

3. Look at the envelope. What do these abbreviations stand for?

1. NY *New York*   3. Apt.
2. VT   4. S.

4. Compare the envelope to a properly addressed envelope in your country.

Include the apartment number.

Is it Street, Avenue, Drive, Road, Place, or Boulevard?

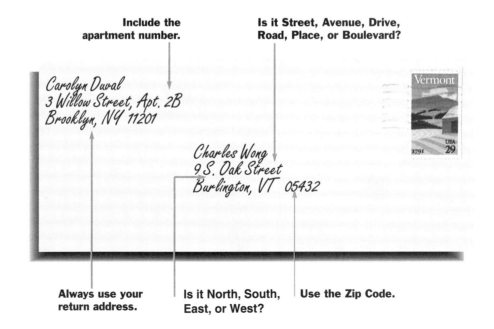

Carolyn Duval
3 Willow Street, Apt. 2B
Brooklyn, NY 11201

Charles Wong
9 S. Oak Street
Burlington, VT 05432

Always use your return address.

Is it North, South, East, or West?

Use the Zip Code.

19. My new address and phone number are...

Carolyn Duval writes a letter to her friend Charles Wong in Vermont. Carolyn tells Charles about her new apartment and her neighbors. She gives him her new address and phone number.

PROCEDURE

1. Read the letter.

- Read aloud the instructions and the questions. Have students read the letter and answer the questions on separate paper.

- Play the cassette or read the conversations from pp. 3 and 8 so the students can check their answers. They can follow along in their books as they listen. You may also want to have the students listen to the letter as well. Have a student write the answers on the board.

  ANSWERS
  1. Maggie Sloane
  2. George and Loretta Arno

2. *True* or *False*?

- Tell the students to read the statements and to answer *True* or *False* on separate paper. Call on different students to read the statements and their answers aloud. Check their work.

  ANSWERS
  1. True
  2. False
  3. True
  4. True

OPTION

Have the students read over the letter again. Tell them to underline or write down on separate paper any words they don't understand. Answer any questions they have. If possible, use gestures, pictures, and realia to teach the meanings of new words such as *interesting, quiet, upstairs, lab technician, back there*, etc.

3. Look at the envelope.

- Tell the students to look at the envelope. Point out the apartment number, the return address, etc. Read aloud the sentences surrounding the envelope. Ask different students the questions.

- Write the first abbreviation and the answer on the board. Then write the remaining abbreviations on the board and ask students to tell you what each stands for. Call on different students to write the answers next to the abbreviations.

  ANSWERS
  2. Vermont
  3. Apartment
  4. South

OPTION

Make four flashcards with an abbreviation on one side (*NY, VT, Apt.,* and *S*) and the corresponding word on the other side (*New York, Vermont, Apartment,* and *South*). Show one side to the class and have them say or write the word or abbreviation from the other side.

4. Compare the envelope to a properly addressed envelope in your country.

- Have students address an envelope as they would in their home country. Discuss with them the similarities and differences between an envelope addressed in the U.S. and one addressed in their country.

FOLLOW-UP

Students can work in pairs to address envelopes to each other. Have them include their return addresses.

WORKBOOK Lesson 19, p. 24. You may want to review capitalization and punctuation rules in English before assigning the writing tasks. Point out the indentation used for the two paragraphs in the postcards.

PREVIEW

Before you begin teaching, go over the functions/themes, language, and forms in the chart. This will give you a preview of what you will encounter as you guide the students through the unit.

Preview the conversations.

- Have the students examine the first illustration. See if they can figure out what Bill is looking for. If necessary, point out Bill, the package in his hand, and the man he's talking to.

- Have the students examine the second illustration. See if they can figure out Bill's situation—that he's had bad luck trying to mail the package. If necessary, point out the "Closed" sign and explain what it means.

CULTURE CLOSE-UP

In the U.S., public services such as post offices are usually open Monday through Friday from 8:30 a.m. to 5:00 p.m. Some post offices are also open on Saturday mornings. Like most public and private businesses in the U.S., post offices adhere very strictly to their posted business hours. Even if you arrive just at the moment the entrance is being locked and ask to get in, you are usually turned away.

PREVIEW

FUNCTIONS/THEMES	LANGUAGE	FORMS
Give locations in a neighborhood	Excuse me—is the post office near here? Where's the post office, please? On Second Avenue./Between Main and High Streets./Across from the park./ Next to the restaurant./On the corner of Second and High.	Prepositions of place
Give locations in an apartment building	Where's the Brunis' apartment? On the first floor.	Ordinal numbers 1st–10th Possessive of names
Give directions in a neighborhood	Walk to the corner. Go straight ahead for two blocks. Turn right/left.	Imperative Adverbs of location

Preview the conversations.

Bill Hinko is looking for something. What is it?

What's Bill's problem? Does this ever happen to you?

20. Where's the post office?

Bill Hinko has just moved to Greenville and is trying to find the post office.

A

Bill Excuse me—where's the post office, please?
Woman Hmm . . . I think it's that way. Or is it that way? I'm not sure.

B

Bill Excuse me—where's the post office?
Man That way.
Woman No, dear, it's that way.
Man Honey, you're wrong. The post office is on Second Avenue, next to Fred's Restaurant.
Woman No, it's not, dear. It's on the corner of State and Fifth.
Man No, dear . . .

C

Bill Excuse me—is the post office near here?
Man I'm sorry, I don't know.
Bill Thanks anyway.

20. Where's the post office?

On the board, write *Excuse me, where's* _____? Write the name of a familiar place in the blank. Have a student ask you the question. Say the answer and write it on the board. (Keep the answer simple—for example, say "It's on (*name of the street*).") Then go around the classroom asking students other locations. You can also have them work in pairs and ask each other.

BACKGROUND

A man named Bill Hinko is trying to find the post office in the town where he has just moved. He asks several local people for directions. When he finally gets there, the post office is closed. This is not one of Bill's lucky days!

LANGUAGE

Hmmm... indicates that the person making the sound is thinking or wondering about something.

Dear and *honey* are terms of endearment.

Thanks anyway. is like saying "Although you weren't able to help, thanks for trying."

Sir is used to get the attention of a man whose name is not known.

Just... is another way of saying "simply."

...between Main and High is short for "between Main Street and High Street."

PROCEDURE

- As the students look over the illustrations, point out the people and the situations by making statements and asking simple questions like these:

  This is Bill Hinko.
  Where's Bill? Is he in school?
  This is the post office.
  Is this Bill's first trip to the post office?

  To help explain the situations, you can point to and imitate the gestures and body language of the characters in the illustrations.

- Have the students listen to the conversation twice, first with their books closed, then with them open. Go over any vocabulary and structures the students have questions about. You can use the map to reinforce meaning, especially with expressions such as *next to, on the corner, near, turn left, straight ahead, on the right,* and *across from*.

Read aloud the directions the man gives in Conversation D as you hold up your book and with your index finger trace the route Bill takes on the map. Then have the students work in pairs. One student can read the directions aloud while the other traces them on the map. Then they can switch roles.

Figure it out

1. Read the sentences below. Then listen to the conversations and complete the sentences.

- Have the students read the sentences silently. You can remind them that this will help them focus on what to listen for. Then tell the students to close their books. Play the cassette or read the conversations aloud.

- Have the students listen to the conversations again, this time with their books open. Give them enough time to write the missing words in the exercise blanks or on separate paper.

- Call on individual students to read their completed sentences aloud so students can check their work. Have a student write the answers on the board.

ANSWERS
1. Second
2. Main, High
3. five

2. Follow your teacher's commands.

- Model the commands by saying them and then carrying them out. Next choose one or two students to follow the commands as you read them aloud. Finally, call on individual students to follow different commands from the exercise.

OPTION

You can have all the students follow the commands as you say them aloud. Depending on how your classroom is arranged, you may have to modify or omit commands 3, 4, and 5.

METHODOLOGY NOTE

Exercise 2 above is an example of Total Physical Response, or TPR, as it is commonly known. TPR is an excellent way to provide students at beginning levels with comprehensible input to help increase their receptive vocabulary and improve their listening comprehension. There are many opportunities to use TPR with your students throughout the beginning levels of the

Spectrum series. The basic TPR procedure consists of the following steps:

1. The teacher models the actions for the commands he or she says.
2. One or two student volunteers come to the front of the class and the teacher gives them the same commands to act out.
3. The teacher gives the commands for individual students or for the entire class to act out.

3. Using the map of Greenville above, complete these sentences.

- Read the instructions aloud. Then point to Fred's Restaurant and to the post office on the map as you read the first exercise item aloud.

- Have the students silently read over the exercise items. Answer any questions they have about vocabulary. You can use the map and appropriate gestures to help the students understand the terms *next to, across from, on the corner of, on,* and *between*.

- Tell the students to complete the sentences by writing the answers on separate paper. You can have them work with a partner to compare and discuss their answers. Call on different students to read the completed sentences aloud.

ANSWERS
2. the park
3. Greenville Hospital
4. Greenville Hospital
5. the State Street Hotel
6. Second, Norwood, State

CULTURE CLOSE-UP

Most cities and towns in the U.S. are planned on a grid pattern like the one in the map on p. 33. Older cities, however, are often structured differently. Washington, D.C. and Detroit, for example, are laid out in a star pattern.

FOLLOW-UP

Students can write out the sentences in exercise 1. Then they can write four more sentences like items 1 and 2 by referring to different buildings and their locations on the map.

WORKBOOK Lesson 20, p. 25

Bill Excuse me, sir—where's the post office, please?

Man Just walk to the corner and turn left. That's Second Avenue. Go straight ahead for two blocks, and it's on the right.

Bill Let's see—left at the corner and straight for two blocks.

Man That's right. It's across from the park, between Main and High.

Bill Thank you very much.

Man You're welcome. But hurry! It closes at five.

Figure it out

1. Read the sentences below. Then listen to the conversations and complete the sentences.

1. The post office is on _____ Avenue.
2. It's between _____ Street and _____ Street.
3. It closes at _____ o'clock.

2. Follow your teacher's commands.

1. Stand up.
2. Turn right.
3. Walk straight ahead.
4. Go to the door.
5. Go to the board.
6. Turn left.
7. Go to your seat.
8. Sit down.

3. Using the map of Greenville above, complete these sentences.

1. Fred's Restaurant is next to _the post office_ .
2. The post office is across from _____ .
3. The fire department is across from _____ .
4. _____ is on the corner of State and Fifth.
5. Fox's Books is next to _____ .
6. Frank's Grocery is on _____ Avenue, between _____ Street and _____ Street .

21. Locations and directions

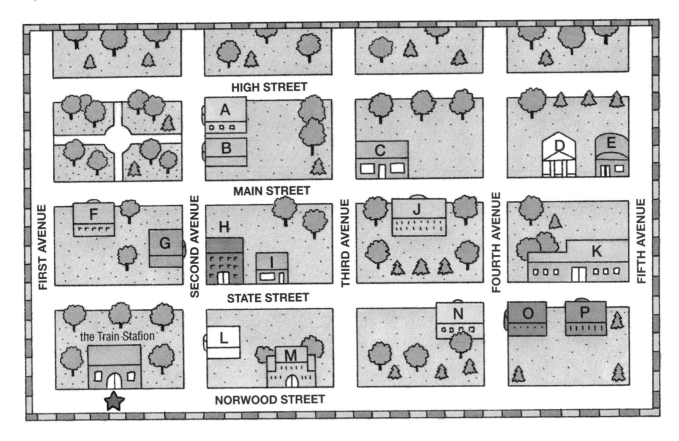

HIGH STREET

MAIN STREET

STATE STREET

NORWOOD STREET

FIRST AVENUE

SECOND AVENUE

THIRD AVENUE

FOURTH AVENUE

FIFTH AVENUE

the Train Station

TALK ABOUT LOCATION ● PREPOSITIONS OF PLACE

1 ▸ **Look at the map above. Then study the frame. Find the post office and Fred's Restaurant on the map.**

> The post office is **on** Second Avenue.
> It's on Second **between** Main and High.
> It's **across from** the park.
> It's **next to** Fred's Restaurant.
> Fred's Restaurant is **on the corner of** Second and High.

 2 ▸ **Listen to the conversation below.**

A Where's the post office, please?
B It's on Second Avenue, between Main and High.
A (*Repeats*) Second Avenue between Main and High.
B That's right.
A Thank you very much.

▸ **Play these roles:**

Student A Ask where the places in the box are located.
Then find them on the map above.

Student B Using the map on p. 33, answer Student A's questions.

> Some places
>
> the post office
> the First City Bank
> Greenville High School
> the Circle Theater
> the fire department
> the Third National Bank
> Fox's Books
> Winkle's Department Store
> Greenville Hospital
> the library

21. Locations and directions

WARM-UP

On the board, write *Where's* _____? Ask and
answer the question about the location of a piece
of furniture in the classroom. For example, say
"Where's Juan's desk? It's next to Maria's desk."
Then ask students the location of different pieces
of furniture or objects in the classroom.

TALK ABOUT LOCATION • PREPOSITIONS OF PLACE

- Tell the students to examine the map and study
  the frame. Have them work in pairs to locate the
  post office and Fred's Restaurant. Call on a
  student to point out the two locations on the map.

OPTION

You can conclude the exercise by asking students
"What is building A?" and "What is building B?"
(Building A is Fred's Restaurant. Building B is the
post office.)

- Play the cassette or read the conversation aloud.
  Then have two students read it aloud.

- Have the students work in pairs to take turns
  playing the roles of Student A and Student B.
  Tell them to model their exchanges on the
  conversation they've just heard. Call on different
  pairs to present their conversations to the class.

OPTION

You can ask different students the location of
familiar buildings or landmarks in your
immediate vicinity. Prompt them to reply with *on,
between, across from, next to,* and *on the corner.*
Then have them work in pairs to take turns asking
each other about the location of additional
familiar places.

ASK FOR AND GIVE DIRECTIONS • THE IMPERATIVE

- Tell the students to study the frame. Explain that when we use the imperative, *You* (singular or plural) is understood but not stated.

- Read the instructions aloud as the students read along with you. Hold up your book and with your index finger, trace the directions to the State Street Hotel as you play them on the cassette or read them aloud.

- Tell the students to find each location as they listen to the conversations. After each conversation, students should write down the appropriate letter. They can listen as many times as necessary.

- Students can work in pairs to compare and discuss their answers. Tell them to check their answers by looking at the map on p. 33.

TAPESCRIPT

1. **A** Excuse me—where's the State Street Hotel, please?
   B Oh, it's right near here. Walk to the corner and turn left on Second Avenue. Go straight for one block and turn right on State Street. The State Street Hotel is on the corner.
   A Let's see…it's on the corner of Second and State.
   B Yes, that's right.
   A Thanks a lot.
2. **A** Excuse me—is Frank's Grocery near here?
   B Yes, it is. It's just around the corner on Second Avenue. Walk to the corner and turn left. Frank's Grocery is on your right.
   A Thanks.
3. **A** Excuse me, sir—where's the police station?
   B It's very easy. Go straight ahead for two blocks and turn left on Third Avenue. Walk two more blocks and turn right on Main Street. The police station is on your right, between Third and Fourth.
   A Let's see…it's on Main between Third and Fourth.
   B Yes, that's right.
   A Thank you very much.
   B You're welcome.
4. **A** Excuse me—is the Capital Theater near here?
   B Yes, it is. Go straight ahead for four blocks and turn left on Fifth Avenue. Walk two more blocks to Main Street. The theater is on the corner of Main and Fifth, next to the Third National Bank.
   A Thanks a lot.
   B You're welcome.

ANSWERS
2. L   3. J   4. E

- Read the instructions aloud and answer any questions students may have about what they're supposed to do.

- Play the cassette or read the conversation aloud as many times as necessary as the students write down their answers. Then ask a student to write the answers on the board.

ANSWERS
B corner, right, State, two, left

- Explain that this time students have to trace backwards on the map to find out where the tourist is when she asks for directions. Have them use their completed conversations to locate the tourist. Tell them to check their answers on p. 33.

ANSWER
On Third Avenue.

- Read the instructions aloud. Have students work in pairs to take turns asking for and giving directions. Explain that the locations listed in the exercise are the starting places for the student asking for directions and that this same student must choose a place on the map where he or she wants to go. Go around the classroom and check students' work.

- Call on different pairs to give their directions to the class. Tell the class to check the directions by tracing the routes on the map.

ORDINAL NUMBERS: 1ST-10TH • POSSESSIVES OF NAMES

- Have the students look at the numbers as you say them aloud. Say the numbers again as you point to chairs in a row or students in their desks.

- As the students study the frames, say the words, slightly exaggerating the pronunciation of the final possessive sounds. Say them again and have the students repeat.

- Read the instructions aloud. Then read the sample exchange aloud with another student.

- Have students work in pairs to take turns asking and answering the questions about the location of different people's apartments noted in the box. Tell them to use the sample exchange as a model. Go around the class to check their work.

FOLLOW-UP

Students can write out the directions to four different places on the map from the locations specified in exercise 6.

WORKBOOK Lesson 21, pp. 26-28

ASK FOR AND GIVE DIRECTIONS • THE IMPERATIVE

 3 ▶ **Study the frame: The Imperative**

Walk to the corner of Second and State.
Go straight ahead for two blocks.
Turn right (left).

 4 ▶ **Four people are at the train station and are asking directions to the places below.**
Look at the map on p. 34 as you listen to the conversations. Then find each place on the map.
▶ **Look at the map on p. 33 to check your answers.**

1. _H_ the State Street Hotel 3. ___ the police station
2. ___ Frank's Grocery 4. ___ the Capital Theater

 5 ▶ **A tourist is asking directions to Greenville Hospital. As you listen to the conversation below, fill in the blanks.**
▶ **Where's the tourist? Check your answer on p. 33.**

A Excuse me—is Greenville Hospital near here?
B Yes, it is. Walk to the _____ and turn _____ on _____ .
Go straight ahead for _____ blocks. The hospital is on the _____ .
A Thank you very much.
B You're welcome.

 6 ▶ **Ask a classmate directions to a place on the map. Start at the following locations:**

1. the post office 2. Winkle's Department Store 3. the library 4. the park

ORDINAL NUMBERS: 1ST – 10TH • POSSESSIVES OF NAMES

 7 ▶ **Study the numbers. Then study the frames below: Possessives of Names**

1st	**2nd**	**3rd**	**4th**	**5th**	**6th**	**7th**	**8th**	**9th**	**10th**
first	second	third	fourth	fifth	sixth	seventh	eighth	ninth	tenth

Singular	Philip Tate**'s**	[s] apartment	Ann Bruni**'s**	[z] apartment	Doris Fox**'s**	[ɪz] apartment
Plural	the Tate**s'**		the Bruni**s'**		the Fox**es'**	

8 ▶ **Find the State Street Apartments on the corner of State and Fourth. Then ask and answer questions like this:**

A Where's the Brunis' apartment?
B It's on the fourth floor. Apartment 4F.

Ann and Jack Bruni	4F
Rosa Cela	9D
the Chungs	10C
Carmen Contreras	3B
Peter Dodge	2C
Bill and Doris Fox	7A
Nancy Frank	6B
John Hong	8E
the McCoys	1D
Philip and Jane Tate	1A

22. What's in the neighborhood?

 ▶ How many of these places are in the neighborhood near your school? Make a chart, like the one on the right, and write down the names of the places. Do not fill in the locations.

PLACE	LOCATION
1. the Taj Mahal Restaurant	
2. the Good Food Grocery	
3. Mel's Hardware	
4. Sunnyview Park	
5. Paradise Disco	

a hotel

a hardware store

a clothing store

a theater

a park

a record store

a grocery store

a good restaurant

▶ Exchange charts with another student, and find a classmate who can give you directions to each place. Write down the locations.

▶ Share the information with other students or with the whole class.

A Excuse me — is _____ near here?
B I'm sorry, I don't know.
A Thanks anyway. . . .

A Excuse me—is _____ near here?
C Yes, it is. Just _____ . _____ is on the _____ .
A Let's see. . . . It's on _____ Street.
C That's right.
A Thanks a lot.

a discotheque

22. What's in the neighborhood?

WARM-UP

Give the students directions to one or two places in the neighborhood of the school. Then have them work in pairs to ask each other for directions to other places nearby.

GIVE DIRECTIONS TO PLACES IN THE NEIGHBORHOOD

- Have students examine the illustrations and the chart. Ask them for the names of some similar places in the neighborhood.

- Tell the students to use separate paper to make a chart with the names of five local places. They can refer to the chart in their books as a guide. Remind them to leave the locations blank.

- Write the sample exchange on the board and work with the students to fill in the blanks with information relevant to the surrounding neighborhood. Call on two students to read the sample exchange aloud with you in front of the class.

- Have the students exchange charts with a partner and then find a classmate to give them directions to each place. Refer students to the sample exchange as a guide in asking for and giving the directions. Then refer students to A's middle line in the sample exchange—"... It's on _____ Street." Tell them that's the kind of location information they should write on their charts.

- Have the students share the information from their charts by reading it aloud in small groups or for the entire class.

OPTION

Have students pretend that each aisle in the classroom is a street and that each chair equals one block. Have one student give another student directions. For example:

S1: Go straight ahead for three blocks.
S2: (Walks past three chairs.)
S1: Turn right.
S2: (Turns left.)
S1: No, turn right, please.
S2: (Turns right.)

Call on other pairs of students to give each other directions.

CULTURE CLOSE-UP

Neighborhoods in large U.S. cities usually consist mostly of houses and apartment buildings. Stores are generally found in the downtown area or in shopping malls or plazas spread throughout the city. One exception to this is New York City, which has many ethnic neighborhoods with their own stores, restaurants, etc.

FOLLOW-UP

Students can write out the conversation from the sample exchange.

WORKBOOK Lesson 22, p. 29

23. Map mystery

Draw a simple street map on the board, similar to the one on p. 37. Include three buildings labeled A, B, and C. Write a large *X* at some location on the map. Place your finger on the *X* and trace the way to each of the buildings as you say the directions for how to get there. Call on different students to try it.

SOLVE A PUZZLE

- Read the instructions aloud. Have the students work in groups of three or four on this problem-solving activity. Begin by working on two or three clues with the entire class.

- Have the groups begin the activity. Tell them not to look at the answers at the bottom of the page until they have finished writing their own answers on separate paper.

OPTION

You can draw the map from p. 37 on the board. You need not include the actual buildings or trees, only the letters and the numbers. Tell the students to copy your drawing of the map on their own separate paper. Then tell them to write the names of the buildings and the streets on their maps as they discover the locations from reading the clues. For example, they should write *Oak Street Theater* next to the letter *C*.

FOLLOW-UP

On the board, write *Where is the* _____? Tell the students to use the pattern on the board to write down five questions about familiar places in their community. Then they can exchange papers and write answers, using the expressions of location they have learned.

WORKBOOK Lesson 23, p. 30

23. Map mystery

SOLVE A PUZZLE

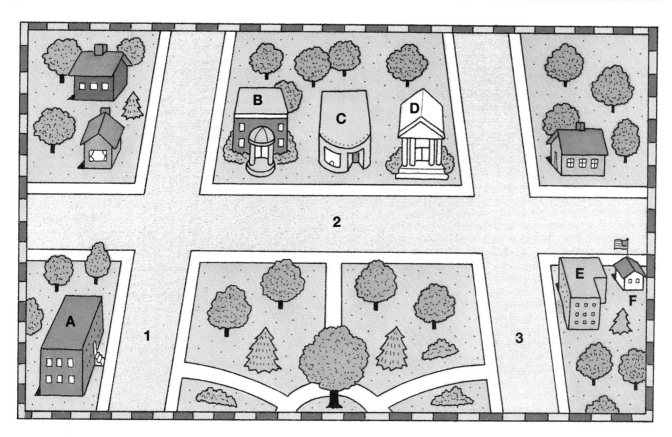

 ▶ **Find the buildings and streets on the map of Glenwood above. The buildings are labeled A, B, C, D, E, and F, and the streets are numbered 1, 2, and 3. Use the clues below.**

Clues:

1. The Oak Street Theater is not on a corner.
   Hint: *The Oak Street Theater is A, C, or F.*
2. The Oak Street Theater is across from the park.
3. The Oak Street Theater is between the Glenwood Savings Bank and the library.
4. The police station is across from the park.
5. The post office is next to the police station.
6. You're at the post office. Turn left, walk to the corner, and turn left. You're on Walnut.
7. The library is not on the corner of Oak and Walnut.
8. You're at the Oak Street Theater. Turn right and walk to the corner. Turn left on Elm. The hospital is on your right.

Buildings	Streets
the Oak Street Theater	Oak Street
the Glenwood Savings Bank	Walnut Street
the library	Elm Street
the police station	
the post office	
the hospital	

Answers to Exercise 1

A. the hospital   1. Elm Street
B. the library   2. Oak Street
C. the Oak Street Theater   3. Walnut Street
D. the Glenwood Savings Bank
E. the police station
F. the post office

24. Traffic jam

John Pierce offers Maggie Sloane a ride to the bank, but Maggie finds out that sometimes it's faster to walk.

1

John	Maggie!
Maggie	Oh, John . . . hi, how are you? Listen, I'm in a terrible hurry. The bank closes in fifteen minutes.
John	Is your bank near here?
Maggie	Yes, it's only three blocks away—on Fulton Street.
John	Well, get in. I'll take you.
Maggie	Are you sure? It's not out of your way?
John	No, not at all.
Maggie	This is so nice of you, John. Thank you.
John	Don't mention it.
Maggie	Say, this is a nice car!
John	Yeah, it's my brother's. He's away for a month.

2

John	Now let's see. . . . Fulton Street is that way . . .
Maggie	Yes, just turn right at the next corner.
John	That's a one-way street.
Maggie	Oh, you're right. Well, turn right at this corner.
John	I'm in the wrong lane. Well, let's see. . . . Maybe I can . . .
Cab driver	What are you doing? Are you crazy or something?
John	Oh, this traffic is terrible!
Maggie	You know what? I think I'll walk. But thanks anyway.

24. Traffic jam

WARM-UP

On the board, write:

Where's the post office?
It's (three blocks from here).

Ask students how far away other familiar buildings are from the school. Have them write their answers on separate paper. Ask the questions again and call on different students to read their answers aloud to see if they agree.

1. & 2. Conversation

BACKGROUND

These two pages show a busy street in downtown Brooklyn. John Pierce offers Maggie Sloane a ride to the bank, and they get caught in heavy traffic.

LANGUAGE

...in a terrible hurry is used when someone needs to get somewhere very quickly.

...(three blocks) away expresses distance from the speaker.

...out of your way indicates that some location is not in the same direction as the one you are going (and is therefore inconvenient).

...not at all is used to emphasize *No*.

Don't mention it. is a polite response to *Thank you*. It's a casual way of saying "You're welcome."

You know what? is short for *Do you know what?* and is used to get someone's attention.

PROCEDURE

■ Have the students examine the illustrations. Ask a student to point out Maggie Sloane. Point out the other characters—John Pierce and the cab driver—and ask questions and make statements about the situation. For example:

This is a busy street.
Is John in a car?
Where's the cab driver?

■ Have students listen to the conversation. Explain any unknown words with gestures, realia, or translation. Answer any questions about sentence structures.

OPTION

Model the conversation with appropriate motions—for example, put your hands on an imaginary steering wheel and shake your fist as you say the cab driver's lines. Also use appropriate gestures and intonation. Set the scene by arranging chairs to simulate the seats in John's car and in the taxi cab. Then act out the conversation with two students. Finally, have the students work in groups of three to act out the conversation.

3. Figure it out

True or ***False?***

- Have the students read over the five statements. Then have them cover the dialogue boxes and look only at the picture as they listen to the conversation and answer *True* or *False*. They can write their responses on separate paper.

- Have the students discuss their answers with a partner before listening to the conversation again. Tell them to uncover the conversation and check their answers. Then write the answers on the board as you go over them with the class.

ANSWERS
1. False
2. True
3. False
4. True
5. True

4. How to say it

- Preview the conversation by talking about the situation—Speaker A is at Arno's Coffee Shop and is calling for a taxi but dials the wrong number.

- Have students listen to and repeat the pronunciation of the three possessives several times. Then have them listen to the conversation.

- Have the students practice the conversation in pairs. Move around the room and give help when needed. Check students' pronunciation of the possessives. You can call on a pair of students to read the conversation for the class.

OPTION

Students can practice the pronunciation of the possessives with their own names. On the board, make three columns and write a student's name at the top of each column—one for each of the three pronunciations. For example:

Pablo's [z]   Alex's [ɪz]   Pravit's [s]

Have the three students say their own names in the possessive. Then have the other students go to the board and write their own names in the appropriate column. Have each student pronounce the possessive of his or her own name. To give the possessives context, ask the students to make up and say a sentence using a classmate's name. For example, Maria says "That's Pablo's book."

5. Your turn

- Read the instructions aloud as the students follow along in their books. Point out the man in the blue car talking to the man on the street. Say the line of the man in the car and then call on a student to volunteer a possible answer.

- Have the students work in pairs to act out the exchange. Go around the classroom and check their work. Call on pairs to say their exchanges for the class.

POSSIBLE ANSWER
Go straight ahead. It's on the next block on your left, next to Sophia Video.

6. Listen in

- Read over the instructions with the students. Point out the characters in the illustration.

- Tell the students to read over the directions (a, b, and c) in the exercise. Explain that they will hear a conversation between the man and the woman and that they should listen for the correct directions to the hospital.

- Have the students listen to the conversation as many times as necessary and choose a, b, or c. Call on a student to read the correct answer aloud.

TAPESCRIPT
A Where's the nearest hospital, please?
B Hmm...let's see...That would be Brooklyn Hospital. Go straight ahead for seven blocks. That's Ashland Place. Turn right on Ashland. The hospital will be on your left.

ANSWER
b

FOLLOW-UP

Students can write out the conversation they practiced in **Your turn**.

WORKBOOK Lesson 24, p. 31

3. Figure it out

1. *True* or *False*?

1. Maggie is not in a hurry.
2. Maggie's bank is on Fulton Street.
3. The car is John's.
4. John is in the wrong lane to turn right.
5. Maggie walks to the bank.

4. How to say it

Listen to the pronounciation of the words below. Then listen to the conversation.

Arno's	Mitch's	Pat's
[z]	[ɪz]	[s]

A I'd like a taxi at Arno's Coffee Shop.
B A taxi?
A Is this 555-3822?
B Yes, it is.
A And it's not Mitch's Taxi?
B No, it's not. It's Pat's Restaurant.

5. Your turn

The man in the car wants to go to the post office on Montague Street. Find the post office in the picture. Then act out his conversation with the other man.

Excuse me—where's the post office, please? . . .

6. Listen in

The man on the motorcycle is asking for directions. Read the statements below. Then listen and choose the right directions.

a. Go straight ahead for seven blocks and turn right. The hospital is on your right.
b. Go straight ahead for seven blocks and turn right. The hospital is on your left.
c. Go straight ahead for seven blocks and turn left. The hospital is on your left.

25. **Can You Read a Map?** Try this Test of Buenos Aires.

Imagine you're in Buenos Aires for the first time. It's the city of the tango and home to 10 million Argentines. You have your map and you're ready to go, but how are your map-reading skills? Can you follow directions, or do you get lost easily? Try this little test. As you read the descriptions below, find the places on the map.

1 Plaza de Mayo (May Plaza) This plaza or square is over 400 years old, and it is in the eastern part of the city near the river. Several important buildings are on this plaza including the Cabildo (the town hall) and the presidential palace, called the Casa Rosada (Pink House).

2 Avenida Florida (Florida Avenue) This street is only one block west of the Cabildo. It's probably the most popular shopping street in the city. There are over 600 shops here, and it is a pedestrian area. That means that people, not cars, travel up and down this street.

3 Avenida 9 de Julio (9th of July Avenue) Five blocks west of Florida is another famous Argentine street, Avenida 9 de Julio. It is one of the widest boulevards in the world. There are many interesting places here, including the obelisk and the 9 de Julio fountain.

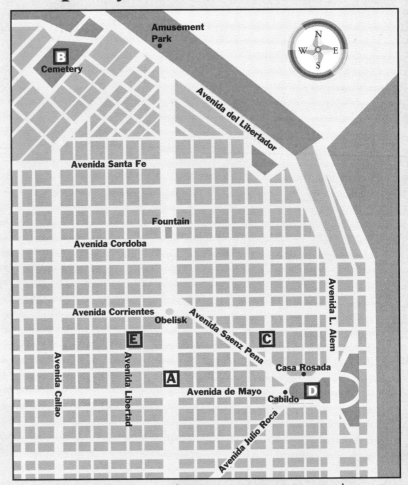

4 Teatro Colón (Columbus Theater) Two more blocks west of the obelisk is Avenida Libertad (Liberty Avenue) and the Teatro Colón, a famous opera house. Some of the best performers in the world sing here.

5 La Recoleta La Recoleta, about 15 blocks north from Teatro Colón, is a popular attraction for tourists. This historic neighborhood is famous for its cemetery. Many important Argentines are buried here, including Eva Perón. There are also many fashionable restaurants here and some of the most beautiful homes in Buenos Aires.

Solution
1. D
2. C
3. A
4. E
5. B

Imagine you and your friends have one day to see Buenos Aires. Working in groups of four, do the following:

1. Choose four places to visit.
2. Decide where to go first, second, third, and last.
3. Indicate your route on the map.

25. Can You Read a Map?

BACKGROUND

The map of Buenos Aires, Argentina, is accompanied by a little test to see if the reader can locate five different points of interest in the city by following written directions.

PROCEDURE

Imagine you're in Buenos Aires for the first time.

- Read the instructions aloud. Give the students a few minutes to examine the map and read over the surrounding text. Then play the cassette or read the text aloud.

- Have the students work in pairs to take turns reading over the test items and tracing out the locations on the map. Tell them not to turn their books upside down for the answers until they've found all five places. Go around the classroom and check their work, giving help where needed.

Imagine you and your friends have one day to see Buenos Aires.

- Have students work in groups of four on this cooperative learning exercise. Tell each group member to pick a different place on the map to visit and to write it down on separate paper. Have each group decide where to start from and where to go first, second, third, and last. They can write this information down as well. For example:

Let's start at the obelisk. First, let's go to the 9 de Julio fountain. Second,... etc.

They can indicate the route by tracing it out on the map.

- Call on groups to report on the places and routes they chose by having them read aloud what they've written down.

OPTION 1

Have the students underline or write down on separate paper any words that they don't understand. Use gestures, realia, pictures, or words the students already know to help them with the meanings of new words such as *imagine, ready to go, get lost easily*, etc. Give only very basic and simple explanations of new structures at this time.

OPTION 2

Have the students work in small groups. If possible, give each group a local map. Tell them to imagine they have a day off. Have them choose four places to visit.

CULTURE CLOSE-UP

People who live in the U.S. tend to be very "map-conscious" and "map-oriented." Detailed city and country maps are readily available and are often a great help in finding one's way around. Some expensive models of new automobiles provide a map on a small TV screen to help the driver find his or her way around large cities. A computer controls the map, which actually shows the driver 1) where he or she is at any given moment and 2) the best route to take to where he or she wants to go.

FOLLOW-UP

Students can write out the directions from one place on the map (A, B, C, D, or E) to another.

WORKBOOK Lesson 25, p. 32. Remind students to begin each sentence of their directions with a verb like in **Listen in** on p. 39 of the Student Book.

Review of units 1-4

- Read the instructions aloud to the students. Take the part of Alfredo and act out the conversation with a student.

- Have the students work in pairs to act out the conversation. Go around the classroom and check their work.

- Go over the remaining instructions with the students. Tell them to work in groups of four and to write the four names on separate slips of paper. Tell them to mix up the slips. Have each group member draw a slip. Write the four names on the board and have the group members find the other three people and then introduce themselves.

- Call on a group to act out their introductions. Write a sample exchange on the board.

  POSSIBLE ANSWERS
  Yes, I am.
  Nice to meet you.

- Read the first set of instructions aloud. Tell the students to read over the incomplete conversation. Then have them work individually to complete it. Have them also complete the ending. Call on three students to act out the conversation. Check their work.

- Have the students work in groups of three. Tell them to act out the conversation using their own names and personal information. Encourage them to continue the conversation with additional information.

- Tell the groups to end the conversation according to the pattern in their books. Finally, call on different groups to present their conversations to the class.

  POSSIBLE ANSWERS
  Fine, thanks. How are you?
  Nice to meet you.
  Where are you from?

  Bye.
  Nice meeting you, too.

- Read the instructions and the information on the forms aloud as the students follow along in their books.

- Tell the students you will play the cassette or read the tapescript so they can complete Cathy's registration form. Have them listen as many times as necessary. Call on a student to write the answer on the board.

  TAPESCRIPT AND ANSWERS
  Man Your name, please?
  Cathy Cathy Marceau. M-A-R-C-E-A-U.
  Man Is that Cathy with a "K" or a "C"?
  Cathy With a "C."
  Man What's your address, please?
  Cathy 64 Cluny Street. Ottawa, Canada, K1G 0K2.
  Man Now let's see…Cluny. C-L-U-N-Y?
  Cathy Yes, that's right.
  Man Ottawa. O-T-T-A-W-A, Canada, K1G 0K2.
  Cathy Thank you very much.

- Have the students work in pairs to take turns filling out the last registration form for each other. Tell them to ask each other questions like those that were asked about Cathy. Go around the classroom and check their work.

- Call on a pair of students to say their exchanges aloud as they write each other's registration information on the board.

OPTION

Collect the registration forms from the students, mix them up, and randomly pass them out. Call on pairs of students. Have one student dictate the information on his or her card while the other student writes the information on the board. Have the student whose name and address appear on the board verify the information.

Review of units 1-4

1 ▶ Keiko Kurosawa is trying to find Alfredo Rivera at the International Business Association (IBA) conference in Honolulu. Complete their conversation.

Keiko Excuse me—are you Alfredo Rivera?
Alfredo _____ .
Keiko Hello, Mr. Rivera. I'm Keiko Kurosawa from Electronic Office News here in Honolulu.
Alfredo _____ .

▶ Working in groups of four, write the names on the right on four pieces of paper. Choose one piece of paper, but don't tell the group your name.
▶ Imagine you're at the IBA conference. Find the other three people and introduce yourself.

IBA CONFERENCE Keiko Kurosawa Electronic News	**IBA CONFERENCE** Mark Harper King Wire Service
IBA CONFERENCE Alfredo Rivera Global Computer	**IBA CONFERENCE** Cathy Marceau World Press

2 ▶ Mark Harper introduces Keiko to his friend Cathy Marceau. Complete Keiko's side of the conversation.
▶ In groups of three, act out the conversation using your own names and information.

Mark Hi, Keiko. How are you?
Keiko _____ . _____ ?
Mark Fine. Keiko, this is my friend Cathy.
Keiko _____ .
Cathy Nice to meet you, too.
Keiko _____ ?
Cathy I'm from Ottawa, Canada.

▶ Say good-bye and end the conversation.

Cathy Good-bye, everyone.
Mark, Keiko _____ .
Cathy Nice meeting you, Keiko.
Keiko _____ .

 3 ▶ Listen to the conversation and complete Cathy's registration form below.
▶ Complete the last registration form for a classmate.

International Business Association	International Business Association	International Business Association
Name Keiko Kurosawa **Address** 658 Kolopua Street Honolulu, HI 96819 U.S.A.	**Name** Cathy Marceau **Address** _____	**Name** _____ **Address** _____

4 ▶ Review the pronunciation of numbers. Practice the conversation using the addresses in the box.

A What's your address?
B 113 First Avenue.
A One thirty or one thirteen?
B One thirteen.

113 First Avenue
770 Fifth Street
214 Third Street
1550 Tenth Avenue
319 Seventh Street

5 ▶ Work in groups of three. Play these roles:

Student A You're at the IBA conference and are trying to reach one of the people on the notepad. Make the two phone calls below.

Student B You answer the phone in conversation 1.

Student C You're the operator in conversation 2. Give Student A the correct phone numbers.

1. **A** (*Dials number*) *Rrring, rrring*
   B Hello?
   A _____ ?
   B I'm sorry. You have the wrong number.
   A _____ ?
   B Yes, it is, but I'm not Mary Harrison.
   A _____ .
   B That's O.K.

Harrison, Mary   555-3789
Herrera, Tomas   555-1739
Ho, Dae Jin   555-5433
Howell, Louise   555-9078
Hua, Lin   555-2861
Hunter, Susan   555-6652

2. **A** (*Dials number*) *Rrring, rrring*
   C Directory Assistance. May I help you?
   A _____ .
   C Is it in Honolulu?
   A _____ .
   C The number is _____ .
   A _____ .
   C You're welcome.

Haleamau, Loke 555-8920
Han, Chan Hee. 555-1641
Hanohano, Kaniela. 555-6651
Harrison, Mary. 555-3689
Herrera, Tomas. 555-1730
Ho, Dae Jin. 555-6433
Horbieta, Maria. 555-4358
Horvath, James. 555-1896
Howell, Louise. 555-9088
Hua, Lin. 555-2869
Hunter, Susan. 555-6651
Hutton, Joseph. 555-0444

6 ▶ Act out the conversation in groups of three. Use your own information.

A Hello?
B _____ ?
A Yes, he (she) is. Just a minute, please.
C _____ ?
A Hi, _____ . This is _____ .
C _____ ?
A Not bad. And you?
C _____ .

7 ▶ Mark, Cathy, and Keiko are being interviewed on the evening news. Fill in the blanks with the correct forms of *be*. Use contractions if possible.

Interviewer We _____ at the International Business Association conference here in Honolulu, and people _____ here from many countries. Where _____ you from? The United States?

Mark No, we _____ . We _____ from Ottawa, Canada. I _____ Mark Harper, and this _____ my colleague, Cathy Marceau.

Interviewer It _____ very nice to meet you. (*Turning to Keiko*) And you? Where _____ you from? _____ you from Canada, too?

Keiko Me? No, I _____ from Canada. I _____ from right here, Honolulu.

- Have the students look over the instructions and exercise information. Read the exchange aloud with another student. Then say the addresses in the box and have the students repeat after you.

- Write the following pairs on the board and have the students repeat them after you:

  thirty 30 — thirteen 13
  seventy 70 — seventeen 17
  forty 40 — fourteen 14
  fifty 50 — fifteen 15
  ninety 90 — nineteen 19

- Tell the students to work in pairs to take turns asking and answering the questions about the addresses in the box. Call on different pairs to share their exchanges with the class.

- Take the part of Student A. Read the instructions (about yourself) aloud. Call on two students to play the roles of B and C and read their instructions aloud. Then have all the students read over the incomplete conversations. Act out the conversations with the two students.

- Have the students work in groups of three. Tell them to take turns playing the roles of A, B, and C. Have them use the names and phone numbers from the two lists in their books. Call on different groups to present their conversations to the class.

POSSIBLE ANSWERS
1. Is this Mary Harrison?
   Is this 555-3789?
   I'm sorry.

2. **A** I'd like the number of Loke Haleamau.
   A Yes, it is.
   C 555-8920
   A Thank you.

- Tell the students to read over the instructions and the incomplete conversation. If the level of the class is such that a model conversation is needed, you can call on two students to act out the conversation with you for the rest of the class.

- Have the students work in groups of three to act out the conversation. Tell them to simulate a real telephone conversation.

- Call on different groups to act out their conversations for the class. Write one or more of the conversations on the board.

POSSIBLE ANSWERS
B Is Mary there?
C Hello?
A Mary, Tomas
C Tomas! How are you?
C Great.

- Read the instructions aloud to the students. Have them silently read the incomplete conversation. Answer any questions they have about vocabulary or structures.

- Tell the students to do the exercise individually. Then have them work in groups of three to check their work and practice the conversation. Call on a group to act out the conversation for the class. Have another group write the answers on the board.

ANSWERS
Interviewer 're, are, are
Mark 're not/aren't, 're, 'm, is
Interviewer 's, are, Are
Keiko 'm not, 'm

OPTION

Tell the groups to act out the conversation, using personal information. Call on different groups to present their interviews to the class.

8

- Read aloud the instructions and the questions in the box. Depending on the level of the class, you may want to model the conversation by acting it out with a small group of students.

- Tell the students to work in small groups to take turns offering to buy their group members something. Refer them to the illustrations and the questions in the box.

- Call on different groups to act out their conversations for the class. Have them simulate a snack bar environment.

9

- Read aloud the instructions and the questions for exercise 9A on p. 43 and 9B on p. 44. Divide the class into pairs. So the pairs have a model, call on a student and demonstrate asking for, giving, and following directions to one of the places on the map. For example:

  A Where is the Grand Hotel?
  B (Assuming the entrance to the City Convention Center is where Emory Street begins...) Go straight ahead on Emory Street for one block. Turn left and go one block. Cross Midvate Avenue. The Grand Hotel is on your right.

  As you present the model, the students can trace the route in their books.

- The students can take turns playing the roles of Student A and Student B. Tell them to assume the entrance to the Convention Center is where Emory Street begins.

- Call on different pairs of students to act out their conversations for the class. Check their work.

POSSIBLE 9A ANSWERS

A Where is the Holiday Disco?
B (As you leave the Convention Center...) take a right on Fairfield Avenue and go seven blocks to Forbes Avenue. Turn left and go two blocks to Young Street. Turn right. The Holiday Disco is on your left.

A Where is Brown's Record Store?
B Go straight ahead on Emory Street for five blocks to Cedar Avenue. Turn left on Cedar and go one block. Brown's Record Store is on your left, between Midvate Avenue and Clark Street.

A Where is the Town Library?
B Go straight ahead on Emory Street to Woodlawn Avenue. Turn left on Woodlawn and go straight ahead to Clark Street. Turn right on Clark Street. The Town Library is on your left, between Woodlawn and Harrison Avenues.

A Where is Sam's Drugstore?
B Go right on Fairfield Avenue for four blocks and turn left on Ridgedale Avenue. Go straight ahead for five blocks to Jerome Avenue. Turn right and go two blocks. Sam's Drugstore is on your left.

8 ▶ **Work in small groups. Imagine that you and your classmates are in a snack bar. Offer to buy something for your classmates, using the questions in the box below.**

Do you want some _____?
How about some _____?
Do you have change for _____?

coffee

soda

gum

candy

popcorn

9A ▶ **Student A follows the instructions below.**
Student B follows the instructions on p. 44.

Student A You're at the telephone at the City Convention Center. Ask your partner for directions to the places in the box. Locate each building on the map below. Then use the map to give directions to the places your partner asks about.

Where is . . . ?

the Grand Hotel
the Holiday Disco
Brown's Record Store
the Town Library
Sam's Drugstore

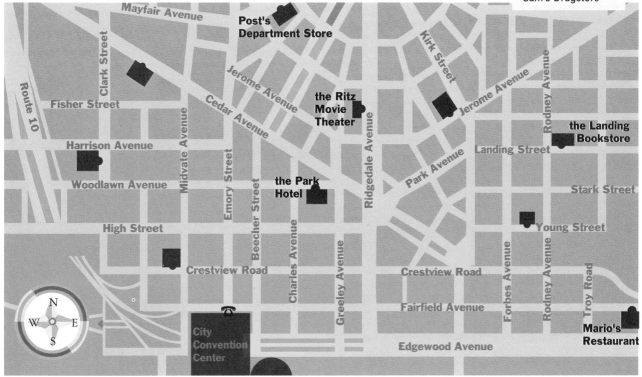

9B ▶ **Student B follows the instructions below.**
Student A follows the instructions on p. 43.

Student B You're at the telephone at the City Convention Center. Use the map below to give directions to the places your partner asks about. Then ask your partner for directions to the places in the box. Locate each building on the map.

> Where is . . . ?
>
> Mario's Restaurant
> the Park Hotel
> Post's Department Store
> the Landing Bookstore
> the Ritz Movie Theater

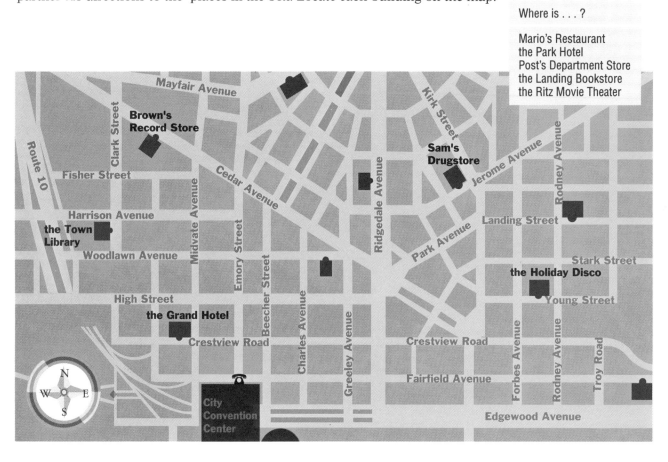

10 ▶ **What does 's mean? Change 's to is if possible in the conversation below.**

A What**'s** the conference at the Park Hotel?
B It**'s** the International Business Association conference—a conference for businessmen and women from around the world.
A Oh! Alfredo**'s** friend Nancy is at that conference.
B No, she**'s** in Italy on vacation, but Nancy**'s** boss is here in Honolulu for the conference.

11 ▶ **Write interview questions for each of the answers below, using the correct forms of be.**

1. **A** _____ ?
   B No, I'm not. I'm Toshi Tanaka.

2. **A** _____ ?
   B I'm from Hawaii.

3. **A** _____ ?
   B No, I'm not. I'm from Wailuku.

4. **A** Please give me your address and phone number. But first, _____ again?
   B My last name is Tanaka.

5. **A** _____ ?
   B My address is 213 Mailani Street.

6. **A** And _____ ?
   B My phone number at work is 555-3294.

▶ **Imagine you're meeting your partner for the first time. Using your interview questions, interview your partner and write down his or her answers.**
▶ **Tell another classmate about your partner.**

POSSIBLE 9B ANSWERS

A Where is Mario's Restaurant?

B (As you leave the Convention Center...) turn right and go nine blocks on Fairfield Avenue. Mario's Restaurant is on your right.

A Where is the Park Hotel?

B Go straight ahead for three blocks on Emory Street. Turn right on Woodlawn Avenue and go two blocks. The Park Hotel is on your right, between Charles and Greeley Avenues.

A Where is Post's Department Store?

B Go straight ahead for seven blocks on Emory Street to Mayfair Avenue. Turn right and go one block. Post's Department Store is on your right.

A Where is the Landing Bookstore?

B Go right on Fairfield Avenue eight blocks to Rodney Avenue. Turn left and go four blocks. The Landing Bookstore is on your right, at the corner of Rodney Avenue and Landing Street.

A Where is the Ritz Movie Theater?

B Go right on Fairfield Avenue four blocks to Ridgedale Avenue. Turn left and go straight ahead for four blocks. The Ritz Movie Theater is on your left.

■ Review two meanings of *'s* with the students. Write the following sentences on the board and have the students repeat them after you:

That's right.
My name's (*your name*).

I know Mr. Silva's address.
He's from Brazil.

Call on different students to see if they can change *'s* to *is* in the appropriate sentences. (That is right. My name is... . He is from Brazil.) Have the students identify the possessive use of *'s* (Silva's).

■ Read the instructions aloud to the students. Have them work in pairs on the exercise. Tell them to practice the conversation with and then without the changes.

■ Call on a pair of students to read aloud the conversation in both forms. Write the answers on the board.

ANSWERS
What is...
It is...
...she is...

■ Read the instructions aloud. Tell the students to silently read over the incomplete conversations. In front of the class, practice the first exchange with a student.

■ Tell the students to do the exercise individually. Then have them work in pairs to compare their answers and to practice the exchanges.

SAMPLE ANSWERS
1. Are you Akiro Abe?
2. Where are you from?
3. Are you from Honolulu?
4. ...what's your last name...?
5. What's your address?
6. ...what's your phone number at work?

■ Call on two different pairs to write their interviews on the board and act them out for the class. Check their work.

■ Read the second set of instructions aloud. Tell the partners to use the interview questions to interview each other and to write down what they find out on separate paper.

■ Tell the students to find a different partner to report their findings to. Tell them to use the information they've written down. To help them get started, you might write the following examples on the board:

My partner is (*student's name*).
He (She)'s from (*student's country*).
He (She)'s from (*student's city*).

Go around the classroom and check students' work.

WORKBOOK Review of units 1-4, pp. 33-34

Before you begin teaching, go over the functions/themes, language, and forms in the chart. This will give you a preview of what you will encounter as you guide the students through the unit.

Preview the conversations.

- Have the students examine the first illustration. Talk about Kate and Linda's casual meeting at a bus stop. Discuss the questions under the picture.

- Tell the students to look at the illustrations to the right. Mimic each greeting as you read aloud the accompanying statement—bow as you say "They're bowing," etc. Discuss the difference between friends and acquaintances and between formal and informal ways of greeting. Have the students talk about ways of greeting people in their country.

CULTURE CLOSE-UP

Many foreigners think Americans are impolite or "cold" because they make very little fuss when they greet one another. The most common way for Americans to greet one another is simply to stand, smile, and say "Hello." In business circles, shaking hands is the most common greeting gesture, but it is unusual for friends to shake hands when they meet. Although kissing and hugging are becoming more common, these forms of greetings are usually practiced only among family members and very close friends. It is very unusual for men to greet one another with a kiss.

FUNCTIONS/THEMES

Talk about jobs and
    occupations

Talk about your job

Talk about where you live

Exchange personal
    information

LANGUAGE

Laura is an accountant.
She works in an office.
Accountants work in offices.

What do you do?
I'm a doctor.
Where do you work?
I work at Memorial Hospital.

Do you live around here?
Do you live in an apartment/a house?
Where do you live?
On Maple Street./At 25 Maple Street./On
    the second floor./In apartment 2B.

Are you married?
No, I'm single.

FORMS

Formulaic use of the third person
    simple present: statements
Articles *a* and *an*
Plurals of nouns

Simple present with *you* and *I*:
    statements; questions and
    short answers

Prepositions *in*, *on*, and *at*

Preview the conversations.

Linda!

Kate! How are you?

Kate sees Linda at a bus stop.
How do they greet each other?
Are they friends or acquaintances?

They're bowing.

They're shaking hands.

They're kissing.

They're hugging.

Here are some different ways of greeting people. How do
you greet friends? Acquaintances? Family members? Do
you bow, shake hands, kiss, hug, or just say "hello"?

26. Bus stop

Kate runs into Linda, an old acquaintance, at a bus stop.

A

Kate Linda!
Linda Kate! How are you? Do you work around here?
Kate Yes, I work in that building across the street.
Linda Really? What do you do?
Kate I'm a lawyer.
Linda Oh, that's interesting.
Kate What about you? What do *you* do?
Linda I work at Memorial Hospital.
Kate Oh . . . are you a doctor?
Linda No, I'm a biologist. I do research.

B

Linda Here's my bus.
Kate That's my bus too.
Linda Oh, where do you live?
Kate On Grand Avenue.
Linda Really? Where on Grand?
Kate At 356.
Linda You're kidding! We're neighbors. I live on the next block.

26. Bus stop

WARM-UP

As you greet students, ask several of them where they live. Next, to review expressions of location, ask "Is that near _____?" or "Is that across from _____?" or "Is that next to _____?" Then have students ask each other the same types of questions.

BACKGROUND

It's the end of the workday and Kate is waiting for the bus. She sees an old acquaintance, Linda, and starts a conversation with her.

LANGUAGE

...around here refers to the immediate vicinity.

Really? is used to express mild surprise and enthusiasm about what the other person is saying.

What do you do? is another way of saying "What kind of work do you do?"

Oh is used to express mild surprise and interest in what the other person is saying.

You're kidding! is used to express mild doubt or surprise.

Congratulations! is a way to extend best wishes to someone about an important occasion in that person's life.

PROCEDURE

- Follow a procedure similar to that indicated for the opening conversations in the previous units.

- Have students listen to the conversation as they follow along in their books. If you read the conversation aloud, be sure to use appropriate stress, intonation, and gestures.

OPTION

Have the students repeat each line from the conversation after you. Then use questions from the conversation to ask students about their personal lives—for example, "Do you work around here? What do you do? Where do you live?" You can also write the questions on the board and have the students work in pairs to take turns asking and answering them.

CULTURE CLOSE-UP

It is acceptable in the United States to ask what people do for a living, but it is usually not appropriate to ask how much money they earn.

Figure it out

1. Listen to the conversation. What do Kate and Linda do?

■ Have the students read the instructions and the exercise items to themselves before they listen to the conversation again. Tell them to listen with their books closed and to then open their books and complete the sentences in their books or on separate paper.

■ Have the students read or listen to the conversation again to check their answers. Ask two students to read their completed sentences aloud as another student writes them on the board.

ANSWERS
1. lawyer
2. biologist

2. Listen again. Say *true* or *false*.

■ Tell the students to read over the statements before they listen. Then have them listen to the conversation again.

■ Call on individual students to say *True* or *False* for the statements. Have a student write the answers on the board.

ANSWERS
1. True
2. False
3. False
4. True

3. Match.

■ Tell the students to read over the sentences in the two columns. Answer any questions they have about vocabulary or structures. Then have the students work in pairs to match the sentences in the columns.

■ Call on pairs to read the matching sentences aloud so you can check their work. Ask a student to write the answers on the board.

ANSWERS
1. c
2. d
3. a
4. e
5. b

FOLLOW-UP

Have students use separate paper to write down the five two-line exchanges they matched in exercise 3.

WORKBOOK Lesson 26, p. 35

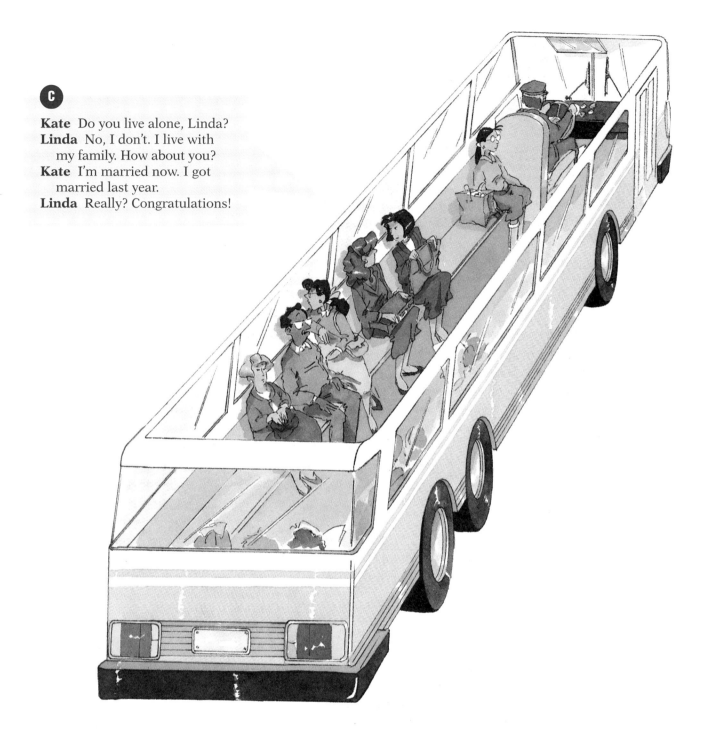

C

Kate Do you live alone, Linda?
Linda No, I don't. I live with
my family. How about you?
Kate I'm married now. I got
married last year.
Linda Really? Congratulations!

Figure it out

1. Listen to the conversation. What do Kate and Linda do?

1. Kate is a _____ .
2. Linda is a _____ .

2. Listen again. Say *true* or *false*.

1. Kate and Linda live on Grand Avenue.
2. Kate and Linda live at 356 Grand Avenue.
3. Linda lives alone.
4. Kate is married.

3. Match.

1. What do you do?
2. Do you live around here?
3. Do you live alone?
4. I'm married now.
5. Where do you work?

a. No, I'm married.
b. I work across the street.
c. I'm a biologist.
d. No, I don't. I live on State Street.
e. Congratulations!

27. Jobs and occupations

1. David
   teacher

2. Bill
   mechanic

3. Pedro
   doctor

hospital

garage

4. Pravit
   cook

10. Noriko
    banker

restaurant

office

9. Laura
   accountant

school

bank

5. Jean
   nurse

8. Barbara
   secretary

7. Tom
   waiter
   (waitress: F)

6. Ana
   lawyer

1 ▶ **What are the occupations of the people above? Where do they work?**

David is a teacher. He works in a school.

| I | work | Use **a** before a consonant sound: He's **a** teacher. |
| He/She | work**s** | Use **an** before a vowel sound: She's **an** accountant. |

48 Unit 5

27. Jobs and occupations

Tell the students to look at the pictures on p. 48. Say two sentences about each of the people—for example, "Jean is a nurse. She works in a hospital." Then see if students can identify Jean and the hospital.

NAMES OF OCCUPATIONS • *A* AND *AN*

- Read the instructions to the students. Then have them look at the pictures and the corresponding words. Answer any questions they have about the meanings of the occupation words.

- Have the students study the frames. Read aloud the words and sentences in them. Then point to yourself as you say "I work." Say "He works" as you point to a male student. Say "She works" as you point to a female student.

- Explain to the students that *a* is used before consonant sounds and *an* is used before vowel sounds. Answer any questions students have about the frames.

- Have the students work in pairs to match the people with the places they work. Tell them to ask and answer questions similar to those in the instructions. Write a sample exchange on the board for them to follow:

A: What's Bill's occupation?
B: He's a mechanic.
A: Where does he work?
B: He works in a garage.

- As you point to each picture, call on a different pair of students to present the corresponding exchange. Ask different students to write the responses on the board.

ANSWERS

1. David is a teacher. He works in a school.
2. Bill is a mechanic. He works in a garage.
3. Pedro is a doctor. He works in a hospital.
4. Pravit is a cook. He works in a restaurant.
5. Jean is a nurse. She works in a hospital.
6. Ana is a lawyer. She works in an office.
7. Tom is a waiter. He works in a restaurant.
8. Barbara is a secretary. She works in an office.
9. Laura is an accountant. She works in an office.
10. Noriko is a banker. She works in a bank.

OPTION

Say "a" or "an" with each occupation name and have the students repeat after you. Write on the board and say "I'm a teacher. I work in a school. Laura is an accountant. She works in an office." Have the students repeat each sentence after you. Then have them repeat just the underlined parts. Next you may want to make two columns on the board, one with *a* at the top and the other with *an*. Call on different students to write the occupations from p. 48 in the appropriate column. Then have them repeat each indefinite article + occupation after you.

ASK ABOUT PEOPLE'S JOBS • TALK ABOUT YOUR OWN JOB

- Before you have them listen to the conversation, tell the students to read the instructions and the incomplete exchanges on p. 49.

- Play the cassette or read the conversation aloud. Then tell the students to listen again and to complete the conversation in their books or on separate paper.

- Tell the students to identify A and B from the characters pictured on p. 48. Then have them work in pairs to compare their answers and practice the conversation.

- Call on a pair to present the conversation to the class and to name the two people.

  ### ANSWERS
  B a banker
  B At the First National Bank
  A a teacher

  A is David.
  B is Noriko.

- Divide the class into small groups. Direct them to talk about what they do. Tell them to use the conversation as a guide. They can use personal information or choose an occupation from p. 48. You may need to help by giving words for occupations and places not included on p. 48.

- Read over the instructions and the incomplete conversation with the students. Divide them into groups of three and tell them to take turns saying the parts of A, B, and C. Tell them to use the information from exercise 2. If necessary, provide an example by introducing one student to another.

- Have a pair of students read aloud the question and answers in the box. Say other examples aloud such as "In a school. At Meadowbrook School."

LANGUAGE NOTE

One rule for the use of *in* and *at* is to use *in* with an indefinite place and *at* with a definite or specified place.

TALK ABOUT PEOPLE'S JOBS • PLURALS OF NOUNS

- Tell the students to study each frame. Model the pronunciation of the singular and plural form of

each word. Have the class repeat each pair after you.

- Demonstrate the rules for writing the plurals of words that end in *y* and *ch, sh, s, z, x*. On the board, write:

  secretar~~y~~ + es = secretaries
  (with *i* above the crossed-out *y*)
  waitress + es = waitresses
  -ch, -sh, -z, -x + es = watches (for example)

- Read the general statement aloud and have the class repeat after you. Call on different students to make general statements about the remaining occupations on p. 48. Ask different students to write the answers on the board.

  ### POSSIBLE ANSWERS
  2. Mechanics work in garages.
  3. Doctors work in hospitals/doctors' offices.
  4. Cooks work in restaurants.
  5. Nurses work in hospitals.
  6. Lawyers work in offices.
  7. Waiters/Waitresses work in restaurants.
  8. Secretaries work in offices/banks.
  9. Accountants work in offices/banks.
  10. Bankers work in banks.

OPTION

Make three columns on the board with [s], [z], and [ɪz] as headings. Tell the students to copy the columns on separate paper. Then have them repeat the pronunciation of the plural forms of the occupations on p. 48 after you. As they repeat each occupation, have them write the word in the appropriate column. Call on different students to read aloud their column entries as you write the words in the appropriate column on the board.

WHO'S WHO?

- Have the students examine the illustrations. Read the instructions aloud and go over the example with the class.

- Have the students work in pairs. Tell them to use the jobs listed in the box in their answers. Call on different pairs to read aloud the clues and their answers. Have a pair of students write the answers on the board.

  ### ANSWERS
  Gloria is a secretary.
  Carlos is a teacher.
  Martin is an accountant.
  Ann is a lawyer.
  Mark is a doctor.

WORKBOOK Lesson 27, pp. 36-37

2 ▶ Two of the people on p. 48 are talking. As you listen to their conversation, complete it below.

▶ Who are the two people? Identify A and B.

A What do you do?
B I'm _____ .
A Oh, really? Where do you work?
B _____ . How about you? What do you do?
A I'm _____ .

▶ Work in small groups and talk about what you do. Use personal information or choose an occupation from p. 48.

3 ▶ Using the information from exercise 2, introduce a student in your group to another classmate.

A _____ , this is _____ . _____ works at _____ .
B Oh, really? What do you do there?
C I'm _____ .

> Where do you work?
>
> **In** a hospital.
> **At** Memorial Hospital.

4 ▶ Study the frames: Plurals of Nouns

accountant	accountant**s**	[s]

waiter	waiter**s**	[z]
secretary	secretarie**s**	

y: Change to *i*. Add *-es*.

nurse	nurs**es**	[ɪz]
waitress	waitress**es**	

ch, sh, s, z, x: Add *-es.*

▶ Make a general statement about each occupation on p. 48.

Teachers work in schools.

5 ▶ Look at the three married couples. What are their jobs? Use the clues below.

Maria works in a hospital, but she's not a doctor.
Maria is a nurse.
Gloria works in a law office, but she's not a lawyer.
The nurse's husband works in a school.
The secretary is married to an accountant.
Ann works in an office, but it's not a doctor's office.
Mark works in an office, but it's not a law office.

doctor	nurse	teacher
accountant	secretary	lawyer

Carlos and Maria Madera

Mark and Ann Gardner

Martin and Gloria Jacobson

28. Where do you live?

1
- ▶ **Complete the conversations below with appropriate questions from the box.**
- ▶ **Listen to check your answers.**
- ▶ **Practice the conversations with a partner, using personal information.**

> Where do you live?   Do you live around here?   How about you?
> What floor?   Where on Maple Street?

1. **A** _____ ?
   B In Tokyo.
   _____ ?
   A I live in Bangkok.

2. **A** _____ ?
   B Yes, I live on Maple Street.
   A Really? _____ ?
   B At 25—between Main and Ridge.
   A Oh, we're neighbors! I live on
   the same block.

3. **A** _____ ?
   B Two, please.

in Bangkok   **on** Maple Street   **at** 25 Maple Street
in Apartment 2B   **on** the second floor

2
- ▶ **Look at the picture below and think about the situation.**
- ▶ **Working in groups of six, find out where your classmates live.**
- ▶ **Two classmates have cars. Decide who will go home in each of the two cars.**

28. Where do you live?

WARM-UP

Refer the students to p. 24. Ask the class where the different people in the illustration live. Say "Where does (*the person's name*) live?" Prompt the class to reply with short answers. For example:

T: Where does Helena Demos live?
C: In Athens.

TALK ABOUT WHERE YOU LIVE

- Tell the students to silently read over the instructions, the questions in the box, and the incomplete conversations. Answer any questions they have.

- Have the students work in pairs to complete each conversation. Tell them to select the most appropriate question for each blank from the box.

- Tell the pairs to listen to check their answers as you play the cassette or read the conversations aloud. Have a student write the answers on the board. Then have the pairs practice reading the completed conversations aloud.

ANSWERS
1. **A** Where do you live?
   B How about you?
2. **A** Do you live around here?
   A Where on Maple Street?
3. **A** What floor?

- Tell the pairs to practice the conversations, using personal information. Go around the classroom and check their work.

- Tell the students to study the blue box. Point out the use of *in*, *on*, and *at* with specific locations. You can have the students repeat the phrases in the box after you.

OPTION

Have the students work in small groups. Have each group member write a sentence about themselves, using one or more of the prepositions *in*, *on*, and *at*. Provide an example such as "I live *at* 691 Avenida Santa Fe *in* Apartment 803A." Go around the classroom and check their progress. Call on groups to read their sentences aloud. Check their work.

- Tell the class to look at the illustration and to think about the situation. Read aloud the instructions and the dialogue lines in the picture. Ask students the two questions.

- Divide the class into groups of six. Tell the groups to pretend they're leaving a party and to find out where their classmates live by asking "Where do you live?" and/or "What street do you live on?" Have each group appoint a "secretary" to write down the information.

- Tell the class that only two students in each group have cars and they must decide who will ride in each of the two cars. Go around the classroom and check their work. Choose the group with the most fluent conversation and have them present it to the class.

METHODOLOGY NOTE

Exercise 2 is a fairly unstructured task and allows for a certain amount of free conversation. Since this is probably a new experience for beginning students, it may be a good idea to model a sample conversation. Work with a small group of more proficient students and help rehearse the scene and corresponding conversation before presenting it to the class. After the presentation, assign each group member to a different practice group.

For group work involving free conversation or discussion, it is also a good idea to assign roles to certain students—for example, the "captain" to ensure that each group member participates; the "noise monitor" to make sure that the group does not disturb other students; the "secretary" to write down the group's conclusions or findings; and the "reporter" to report the group's work or findings to the class.

WORKBOOK Lesson 28, p. 38

29. How about you?

WARM-UP

On the board, write some facts about yourself. For example:

I'm single.
I live with three friends.
I live in a large house.

Ask the students to come up with two or three facts about themselves to say to the class. Alternatively, they can pretend they're famous persons and make up the information.

EXCHANGE PERSONAL INFORMATION • SIMPLE PRESENT WITH *I* AND *YOU*

- Tell the students to study the frames. Ask them to follow along in their books as you read the contents of each frame to them. Answer any questions they have about the structures.

OPTION

After the students have studied the frames, have them close their books. On one side of the board, write scrambled versions of each of the possible questions from the frames. Across from the questions, write the answers in correct, unscrambled form. For example:

Scrambled	Unscrambled
do where ? you live	I live on Maple Street.
? married you are	Yes, I am.

Leave a space beneath each question and answer. Call on volunteers to unscramble the questions and write the correct versions in the appropriate spaces on the board. Remind them to capitalize the first word in each question. Check their work. Then erase the answers and write them in scrambled form. Continue the practice.

- Tell the students to examine the illustrations as you and a student read aloud the exchanges at the bottom of each illustration.

- Have the students read over the first set of instructions and the six exercise responses. Answer any questions they have about vocabulary or structures.

- Divide the class into small groups. Tell the members to work together to write interview questions for the six responses. Tell them the previous two lessons may be helpful. Make sure all group members write the questions on separate paper.

- Call on different pairs of students to read the exchanges aloud. Have a student write the interview questions on the board.

POSSIBLE ANSWERS
1. Do you live around here?
2. Do you live in an apartment?
3. Do you live alone?
4. Are you married?
5. What do you do?
6. Where do you work?

- Tell the students to use their questions to interview four classmates. Have them move around the classroom and write down their findings on separate paper.

- Call on different students to act out one of their interviews with the students they interviewed. This can be done in front of the entire class or in groups. Check their work.

OPTION

Divide the class into two teams—A and B. On slips of paper, write information and yes-no questions from the lesson. Write one question for each member of Team A. On other slips, write answers to the questions. Use any answers from Lesson 29 and previous lessons that match the questions. Fold the slips of paper. Randomly distribute the answer slips to Team B members and the questions to Team A. Call on Team A members to ask their questions. Tell Team B members to raise their hands if they have appropriate answers. Call on them to read their answers aloud. You can then reverse the process and give the answers to Team A and the questions to Team B. You may wish to keep score, giving one point for each correct match.

You can also have one team scramble the order of the words in the questions while the other team scrambles the answers. Then the teams exchange slips for unscrambling. After you check their work, they can play the game again.

WORKBOOK Lesson 29, pp. 39-40

29. How about you?

EXCHANGE PERSONAL INFORMATION • SIMPLE PRESENT WITH *I* AND *YOU*

1 ▶ **Study the frames: Simple Present with *I* and *You***

Information questions

| Where | **do** | you | **live**? | | | | |
| | | | **work**? | |

Affirmative statements

	live		
I		on Maple Street.
	work	

Negative statements

		live	around here.
I	**don't**		
		have	a job.

Yes-no questions

| **Do** | you | **live** | around here? |
| | | **work** | |

Short answers

Yes,		**do**.
	I	
No,		**don't**.

Compare the present of *be* and the simple present:

Are you married?   Yes, I **am**.
Do you **live** around here?   Yes, I **do**.

2 ▶ **Working in small groups, write interview questions for each of the answers below.**

1. _____ ?
   Yes, I live on this block.

2. _____ ?
   No, I live in a house.

3. _____ ?
   No, I don't. I live with my family.

4. _____ ?
   No, I'm single.

5. _____ ?
   I'm an accountant.

6. _____ ?
   I work at the Playful Toy Company on Main Street.

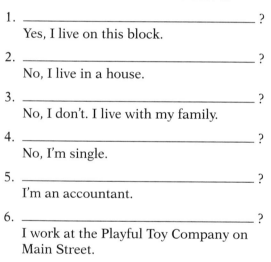

Do you live alone?
No, I'm married.

Do you live in an apartment?
Yes, I do.

Do you live alone?
Yes, I'm single.

▶ Using your interview questions, interview four classmates. Write down their answers.
▶ Act out one of your interviews for other classmates.

30. Cafeteria

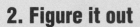 Carolyn runs into Maggie in a cafeteria. Maggie is on her lunch hour.

1

Carolyn	Hi, Maggie!
Maggie	Carolyn! Nice to see you. Have a seat.
Carolyn	Thanks.
Maggie	How are you doing?
Carolyn	Fine. How about you?
Maggie	Oh, I'm fine, thanks.
Carolyn	Do you work around here?
Maggie	Yes, I work at Brooklyn Hospital.
Carolyn	Oh, what kind of work do you do?
Maggie	I'm a lab technician.
Carolyn	Hmm . . . that sounds interesting.
Maggie	Yes, it's a good job. What do *you* do?
Carolyn	Me? Oh, I'm an actress.
Maggie	Really? How exciting!
Carolyn	Well . . . I'm out of work.
Maggie	Oh, that's not so exciting.
Carolyn	No, it isn't. Right now, I'm looking for an office job.
Maggie	Well, I hope you find something. Anyway . . . speaking of work, I've got to get back to the hospital. See you later.
Carolyn	Bye.

2. Figure it out

1. *True* or *False*? Correct the false statements.

1. Maggie works in a hospital.
2. Maggie is a doctor.
3. Carolyn is an actress.
4. Maggie has a good job.
5. Carolyn has a good job.

2. Find another way to say it.

1. How are you? *How are you doing?*
2. I don't have a job.
3. Do you work in the neighborhood?
4. Sit down.
5. What do you do?

30. Cafeteria

WARM-UP

On the board, write the following endings to greetings:

...to meet you.
...are you?
...about you?
...meeting you.

See if students can come up with the missing words. Write them on the board:

How... ?   Nice... .

Have the students complete the four sentences. Work with them to use the sentences in a complete conversation. Write it on the board and practice it with different students in front of the class.

1. Conversation

BACKGROUND

Maggie Sloane is having lunch in a cafeteria near her job. Carolyn Duval runs into her and Maggie asks Carolyn to join her.

LANGUAGE

Have a seat. is an informal way of saying "Please sit down."

How are you doing? is similar to *How are you?* or *How are things going (with you)?*

...that sounds interesting. is used to express interest in what the other person has just said.

I'm out of work. is an informal way of saying "I'm unemployed."

See you later. is short for *I'll see you later.*

PROCEDURE

- Point out the people and the situations in the pictures as the students look at them. Make simple statements and ask simple questions like these:

  This is a cafeteria.
  Where are Maggie and Carolyn?

- Have the students silently read over the conversation. Answer any questions they have about vocabulary or structures.

- As the students follow along in their books, play the cassette or read the conversation aloud.

2. Figure it out

1. *True* or *False*? Correct the false statements.

- Read over the instructions and the statements with the students. Then have them listen to the conversation again and answer *True* or *False* on separate paper. Tell them to correct the false statements.

- Have the students work in pairs to compare answers. Call on different students to read their answers aloud. Ask a student to write the answers on the board.

  ANSWERS
  1. True
  2. False. Maggie is a lab technician.
  3. True
  4. True
  5. False. Carolyn is out of work.

2. Find another way to say it.

- Go over the instructions and the first exercise item with the students. Have them work in pairs to write down their answers. To help them find the answers, suggest that they look through Carolyn and Maggie's conversation.

- Call on pairs to read their answers aloud and to write them on the board. Check their work.

  ANSWERS
  2. I'm out of work.
  3. Do you work around here?
  4. Have a seat.
  5. What kind of work do you do?

3. Listen in

- Read the instructions to the students as they follow along in their books. Tell them to read over the exercise items before they listen to the conversation.

- Play the cassette or read the tapescript aloud. Tell the students to choose *a*, *b*, or *c*. Have them listen as many times as necessary.

- Call on two students to read their completed statements aloud. Write the answers on the board.

TAPESCRIPT

Irma Joe! What a surprise!

Joe Irma! How are you? Do you work around here?

Irma No, but I live around the corner now.

Joe Really?

Irma Yes—Remember my friend Bill Evans...the lawyer?

Joe Yeah, sure.

Irma Well, we got married last June.

Joe Hey, congratulations! That's great.

Irma So, what's new with you? Do you still live near here?

Joe Yes, I do. On Henry Street.

Irma Well, come up and see us sometime.

Joe Thanks. I will.

ANSWERS

1. c
2. b

4. How to say it

- Have the students read over the questions in their books. Tell them to pay close attention to the pronunciation of the underlined words as you play the cassette or read the questions aloud. If you read them aloud, be sure to blend the sounds as indicated by the phonetic transcriptions.

PRONUNCIATION NOTE

The phonetic transcriptions in brackets [ ] demonstrate how the sounds of the underlined words are reduced and blended into what sounds like one word in normal conversational speech.

OPTION

Have the students repeat the questions after you. Use a rising-falling hand gesture to indicate the intonation of the wh- information questions and a rising hand gesture for the yes-no questions. Then go around the classroom and ask different students the questions. For items 3 and 4, ask students the questions about other students.

5. Your turn

- Read the instructions to the students. Tell them to read over the incomplete conversation.

- Have the students work in pairs to complete the conversation. Tell them that answers will vary.

- Have the pairs act out the conversation. The partners can take turns playing the two roles. Finally, call on different pairs to present their versions to the class.

SAMPLE ANSWERS

Do you work near here?
I work at Winkle's Department Store on Main Street.
I'm an accountant.
I live at 25 Maple Street.

CULTURE CLOSE-UP

A cafeteria is a type of restaurant where the customers serve themselves. They pick up their own food at a counter, pay the bill, and then find a seat at a table. The advantages of eating at a cafeteria are that the prices are usually lower than in a regular restaurant and supposedly there is less waiting time. Since the advent of fast-food chains in the U.S., cafeterias seem to be on a decline. However, they are still popular in institutions such as hospitals and schools.

WORKBOOK Lesson 30, p. 41

📼 3. Listen in

Irma, the woman on the left, runs into an old acquaintance, Joe. Read the statements. Then listen to the conversation and choose *a*, *b*, or *c*.

1. _____ is a lawyer.
   a. Irma
   b. Joe
   c. Bill Evans

2. Irma _____ .
   a. lives alone
   b. lives with Bill
   c. lives with a friend

📼 4. How to say it

Listen to these questions about jobs.

1. <u>Where do you</u> work? [ˈwerdəyu]
2. <u>What do you</u> do? [ˈwədəyu]
3. <u>Is he</u> a doctor? [ˈɪzi]
4. <u>Is she</u> a lawyer? [ˈɪʃi]

5. Your turn

Sam, the man on the left, is having lunch with an old acquaintance, Judy. What do you think he is saying? Complete Sam's part of the conversation. Then act out the conversation with a partner.

Sam So, how's everything?
Judy Good. How are things with you?
Sam Not bad. _____ ?
Judy Yes, I work down the street. How about you? Where do you work?
Sam _____ .
Judy Really? What do you do there?
Sam _____ .
Judy Oh, that's interesting. Do you live near here, too?
Sam _____ .
Judy You're kidding! My sister lives across the street from you.

31. How do you like your job?

Richard Daniels, clown
I really enjoy my job. I like to laugh and I love people, especially children. I can also travel a lot.

Pete Bennett, sanitation worker
I don't really like my job, but what else can I do? I have a family, and we need the money.

Sandy Jackson, park ranger
I love my job. I work outside most of the day. I like the outdoors a lot, so I feel I'm very lucky. I do a job I enjoy.

Eloida Jaico, accountant
Well, it's a job that I do well. It pays well too, but sometimes I think I'd like to do something a little more exciting.

Manuel Rivas, veterinarian's assistant
I like my job just fine. It's only a part-time job now, but I'd like to get more experience and make it a full-time job.

Clifford Hall, police officer
Sometimes I like my job, and other times I hate it. My wife doesn't like it at all. She thinks it's dangerous. But the work is important.

Read the article. Then answer the questions.

1. Which people like their jobs?
2. Which people aren't sure that they like their jobs?
3. Which people don't like their jobs?
4. Who is married, according to the article?
5. Who likes children, according to the article?

31. How do you like your job?

This survey asks six people how they like their jobs. It's a good example of an opinion survey one might find in a newspaper or magazine.

PROCEDURE

- Have the students read over the questions at the bottom of the page. After making sure students understand the questions, have them read the survey. Then play the cassette or read the text aloud as the students follow along in their books.

- Tell the students to answer the questions and then to work with a partner to compare and discuss their answers. Call on pairs to say their answers aloud. Ask two students to write the answers on the board.

  ### ANSWERS
  1. Richard Daniels, Sandy Jackson, and Manuel Rivas
  2. Eloida Jaico and Clifford Hall
  3. Pete Bennett and sometimes Clifford Hall
  4. Pete Bennett (implied) and Clifford Hall
  5. Richard Daniels

- Point out the pictures and talk about them. Have the students repeat the names and occupations after you.

OPTION 1

Depending on the level of the students, you might ask them to give reasons for their answers. For example, for item 1, call on different students and ask:

Why do you think Richard Daniels, Sandy Jackson, and Manuel Rivas like their jobs?

OPTION 2

Have the students interview three classmates to find out how they like their jobs. If students don't have jobs, tell them to make up jobs for themselves. They can use p. 48 as a guide. Call on students to report their findings to the class.

FOLLOW-UP

Students can write down why the different people in the survey like or dislike their jobs.

WORKBOOK Lesson 31, p. 42. Before assigning the writing task, draw students' attention to some of the writing conventions that appear in the sample. Point out, for example, the commas before the conjunctions *and* and *but* in the last two sentences.

PREVIEW

Before you begin teaching, go over the functions/themes, language, and forms in the chart. This will give you a preview of what you will encounter as you guide the students through the unit.

Preview the conversations.

- Have the students examine the illustration and the corresponding sentences as you read the sentences aloud. If students have never been on a plane, talk about train or bus travel.

- Discuss the sentences and the immigration form with the students. Ask them to describe what visitors to their country have to do when they arrive. If possible, tell the class about an experience of your own when you passed through Immigration.

CULTURE CLOSE-UP

People in the United States often engage in conversations with strangers while traveling long distances on planes, trains, or buses. However, when riding on public transportation within a city, people usually do not talk to strangers.

PREVIEW

FUNCTIONS/THEMES	LANGUAGE	FORMS

Give day, month, and year
Talk about birthdays and
  birth dates
	What's the date next Sunday?
	It's February twelfth (12th).
	When's your birthday?
	It's January thirty-first (31st).
	What year were you born?
	In nineteen seventy-one (1971).
		Ordinal numbers 11th–31st
		Formulaic use of *was* and *were*
		  with *born*

Give information about
  people
	Christine Pappas lives at 27 Willow
	  Street. She goes to high school and
	  she works at Macy's.
		Simple present: affirmative
		  statements; irregular verbs; third
		  person singular pronunciation

Talk about family	Samuel and Nancy are husband
	  and wife.
	Do you have any brothers or sisters?
	What does your sister do?
		Terminology for family relationships
		Summary of simple present:
		  questions, statements, and short
		  answers

Talk about languages and nationalities	What language do they speak in Jamaica? Do you speak Portuguese? Are you Brazilian?	More simple present
Ask what something means Ask how to say something Ask for clarification	What does *mucho gusto* mean? It means "Nice to meet you." How do you say "thank you" in Korean? Excuse me? Could you speak a little slower, please?	More simple present
Ask to borrow something	Could I use your pencil? Sure, here.	Formula *Could I . . . ?*

Preview the conversations.

Ellen and Lisa don't know each other, but they are talking together on the plane. Do you like to talk to strangers on planes?

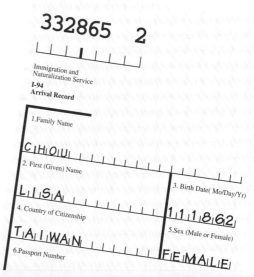

Visitors to the United States fill out this form when they arrive. What do visitors to your country have to do?

32. Vacation

Lisa Chou meets Ellen Stone on a flight from Taipei to New York.

Flight attendant Take this form, fill it out, and keep it with your passport. You'll need it to pass through Immigration.

Lisa I'm sorry, could you speak a little slower, please?

Flight attendant Oh, sure. Fill out this form and keep it with your passport. *(To Lisa's husband)* Here's one for you, too.

Lisa He doesn't speak English.

Flight attendant Could you help him?

Lisa Sure.

The form reads:

332865 2

Immigration and Naturalization Service
I-94
Arrival Record

1. Family Name — C H O U
2. First (Given) Name — L I S A
3. Birth Date (Mo/Day/Yr) — 1 1 1 8 6 2
4. Country of Citizenship — T A I W A N
5. Sex (Male or Female) — F E M A L E
6. Passport Number — 1 3 8 7 9 2 4 7
7. Airline and Flight Number — U A 8 2 5
8. Country Where You Live — T A I W A N
9. City Where You Boarded — T A I P E I
10. City Where Visa Was Issued — T A I P E I
11. Date Issued (Mo/Day/Yr) — 0 5 2 3 9 0
2. Address While in the United States (Number and Street) — 2 3 L E X I N G T O N A V E.
3. City State — N E W Y O R K, N E W Y O R K

Lisa Excuse me—what does "city where you boarded" mean?

Ellen It means the city where you got on the plane.

Lisa Thanks. And one more thing—what does "birth date" mean?

Ellen It's the month, day, and year you were born.

Lisa Oh, I see. Thank you.

32. Vacation

WARM-UP

On the board, write *Do you like… ?* Go around the classroom and ask students questions with this pattern. For example:

Do you like to travel?
Do you like your job?

Have the students open their books to p. 43 and look at the snack bar items. Use the same pattern to ask about the items—for example, "Do you like coffee?" Elicit the short answers: "Yes, I do." and "No, I don't."

BACKGROUND

Lisa Chou and her husband are traveling from Taipei to New York. The flight attendant talks to Lisa about the immigration forms. Lisa asks Ellen Stone, who is sitting next to her, for help with the form. Lisa and Ellen strike up a friendly conversation.

LANGUAGE

To pass through immigration means to go through immigration—to complete the necessary immigration steps.

Oh, sure. is a casual way of saying "Of course" or "Certainly."

I see. is another way of saying "I understand."

What about you? is another way of saying "How about you?"

PROCEDURE

- Point out Lisa, her husband, Ellen, and the flight attendant. Talk about the situation they are in. Point out the immigration form and talk about its purpose.

- Tell the students to follow along in their books as you play the cassette or read the conversations aloud. Answer any questions students have about vocabulary or structures.

OPTION 1

Talk about the purpose of the immigration form as it directly relates to the conversation. You might begin by holding up your book and pointing to the form and then to Lisa Chou, her husband, and Ellen Stone as you say "Lisa Chou and her husband have to fill out this form, but Ellen Stone doesn't." See if any students can explain why this is the case. To provide a confirmed explanation, you can point to the appropriate characters in the first picture and say "Lisa and her husband have to fill out the form because they're not from the United States. They're visiting the United States. They're from Taipei. They're Chinese. Ellen doesn't have to fill it out because she's from the United States."

OPTION 2

Tell the students to pretend they are aboard an international flight. Have them work in groups of four and simulate a scene inside an airplane—for example, tell them to sit in rows and pretend they're on a flight to New York. One student in each group should be the flight attendant. Have them act out the conversations on pp. 56-57. Encourage the groups to expand on the conversations as well—for example, have Lisa's husband say something. Go around the room and select the best performance for presentation in front of the class.

Figure it out

1. Listen to the conversations and answer the questions.

- Have the students read the questions silently. Then play the cassette or read the conversations aloud.

- Tell the students to write down their answers. Call on pairs of students to ask and answer the questions aloud. Ask a student to write the answers on the board.

  ### ANSWERS
  1. Taipei, Taiwan
  2. New York

2. Listen again. Say *true, false,* or *it doesn't say.*

- Tell the students to read over the instructions and the statements. Explain that *it doesn't say* means the information isn't in the conversations. Then have the students listen to the conversations again and answer *True, False,* or *It doesn't say.*

- Read the statements aloud and call on different students to say their answers. Have a student write the correct answers on the board.

  ### ANSWERS
  1. False
  2. True
  3. False
  4. It doesn't say.
  5. It doesn't say.

OPTION

Make up additional statements for the conversations and have the students respond with *True, False,* or *It doesn't say.* You may want students to correct the false statements. For example:

1. T: "Birth date" means the city where you were born.
   S: False. It means the month, day, and year you were born.

2. T: Ellen has one brother.
   S: True

3. T: Lisa's brother is an artist.
   S: It doesn't say.

3. Match the items on the Arrival Record on p. 56.

- Tell the students to draw a line from the item in the numbered column to the appropriate item in the lettered column or to write the answers on separate paper.

- Have the students work in pairs to compare answers. Then have a student write the answers on the board.

  ### ANSWERS
  2. c
  3. e
  4. g
  5. d
  6. f
  7. a

OPTION

Create a blank form similar to the one filled out on p. 56 and make copies for the students. Tell them to work with a partner to fill in the information. Go around the classroom and check their work.

FOLLOW-UP

Students can write out the questions and complete-sentence answers for exercise 1.

WORKBOOK Lesson 32, p. 43

C

Ellen This pen is out of ink. Could I use your pen?
Lisa Excuse me?
Ellen Could I use your pen?
Lisa Oh, sure.

D

Ellen Are you Chinese?
Lisa Yes, I was born in Taipei, but my family is is originally from Shanghai. What about you? Are you from New York?
Ellen Yes. I'm going home to visit my family.
Lisa Oh, how nice. Do you have a large family?
Ellen No, just one brother. Here. Let me show you some pictures.

E

Ellen These are my parents, and this is my brother, David.
Lisa Who's that?
Ellen That's my cousin Dan. He's 22.
Lisa He's very good-looking. What does he do?
Ellen He's an artist, but he works as a waiter at night.

Figure it out

1. Listen to the conversations and answer the questions.

1. Where is Lisa from?
2. Where is Ellen from?

2. Listen again. Say *true*, *false*, or *it doesn't say*.

1. Lisa's husband speaks English.
2. Ellen's family lives in New York.
3. Ellen's cousin is a cook.
4. Lisa and her husband have friends in New York.
5. Ellen is a student.

3. Match the items on the Arrival Record on p. 56.

1. Family name   a. 23 Lexington
2. First name   Avenue
3. Sex   b. Chou
4. Date issued   c. Lisa
5. Country of   d. Taiwan
    citizenship   e. female
6. City where you boarded   f. Taipei
7. Address while in   g. May 23, 1990
    the United States

33. When's your birthday?

11th eleventh	**12th** twelfth	**13th** thirteenth	**14th** fourteenth	**20th** twentieth	**21st** twenty-first
22nd twenty-second	**23rd** twenty-third	**24th** twenty-fourth	**25th** twenty-fifth	**30th** thirtieth	**31st** thirty-first

1 ▶ **Say the dates in blue on the calendar. What day is it? What's the date?**

It's Thursday,
January 11th.

S=Sunday
M=Monday
T=Tuesday
W=Wednesday
T=Thursday
F=Friday
S=Saturday

```
           JANUARY              FEBRUARY               MARCH                 APRIL
    S  M  T  W  T  F  S    S  M  T  W  T  F  S    S  M  T  W  T  F  S    S  M  T  W  T  F  S
       1  2  3  4  5  6                1  2  3                1  2  3    1  2  3  4  5  6  7
    7  8  9 10 11 12 13    4  5  6  7  8  9 10    4  5  6  7  8  9 10    8  9 10 11 12 13 14
   14 15 16 17 18 19 20   11 12 13 14 15 16 17   11 12 13 14 15 16 17   15 16 17 18 19 20 21
   21 22 23 24 25 26 27   18 19 20 21 22 23 24   18 19 20 21 22 23 24   22 23 24 25 26 27 28
   28 29 30 31            25 26 27 28            25 26 27 28 29 30 31   29 30

             MAY                  JUNE                  JULY                 AUGUST
    S  M  T  W  T  F  S    S  M  T  W  T  F  S    S  M  T  W  T  F  S    S  M  T  W  T  F  S
       1  2  3  4  5                   1  2    1  2  3  4  5  6  7                1  2  3  4
    6  7  8  9 10 11 12    3  4  5  6  7  8  9    8  9 10 11 12 13 14    5  6  7  8  9 10 11
   13 14 15 16 17 18 19   10 11 12 13 14 15 16   15 16 17 18 19 20 21   12 13 14 15 16 17 18
   20 21 22 23 24 25 26   17 18 19 20 21 22 23   22 23 24 25 26 27 28   19 20 21 22 23 24 25
   27 28 29 30 31         24 25 26 27 28 29 30   29 30 31               26 27 28 29 30 31

          SEPTEMBER              OCTOBER              NOVEMBER              DECEMBER
    S  M  T  W  T  F  S    S  M  T  W  T  F  S    S  M  T  W  T  F  S    S  M  T  W  T  F  S
                      1       1  2  3  4  5  6                1  2  3                      1
    2  3  4  5  6  7  8    7  8  9 10 11 12 13    4  5  6  7  8  9 10    2  3  4  5  6  7  8
    9 10 11 12 13 14 15   14 15 16 17 18 19 20   11 12 13 14 15 16 17    9 10 11 12 13 14 15
   16 17 18 19 20 21 22   21 22 23 24 25 26 27   18 19 20 21 22 23 24   16 17 18 19 20 21 22
   23/30 24 25 26 27 28 29  28 29 30 31          25 26 27 28 29 30      23/30 24/31 25 26 27 28 29
```

DATES

 2 ▶ **Listen to the dates on the notepad. Then say them.**

1/31/71 is said
"January thirty-first,
nineteen seventy-one."

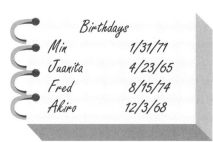

Birthdays

Min	1/31/71
Juanita	4/23/65
Fred	8/15/74
Akiro	12/3/68

▶ **Write down the dates you hear. Then write them in short form.**

1. *December 4, 1982 (12/4/82)*
2. _____
3. _____
4. _____
5. _____

3 ▶ **Ask a partner questions like these. He or she will answer using a calendar.**

1. What's today's date? *January 11th.*
2. What day is today? *Thursday.*

3. What's the date tomorrow?
4. What's the date next Sunday?

TALK ABOUT BIRTHDAYS

 4 ▶ **Listen to the conversation and complete it.**

A When's your birthday?
B _____ .
A What year were you born?
B _____ .

▶ **Try to find another student who . . .**

1. . . . was born the same month as you.
2. . . . was born the same day of the week as you.
3. . . . has the same birthday as you.
4. . . . was born the same year as you.
5. . . . has the same birth date as you.

33. When's your birthday?

WARM-UP

Call on different students to count from 1 to 10 and to say their phone numbers aloud. Call on others to say the ordinal numbers—*first* through *tenth*. Use the ordinals in context—for example, point to a row of desks and say "This is the first desk, and this is the second desk." Have the students continue.

Have the students follow along in their books as you read aloud the ordinal numbers 11th–31st at the top of the page. After you read the ordinals again with the students repeating after you, point to different numbers and have the class say them. Point again and call on individual students to respond.

ORDINAL NUMBERS: 11TH - 31ST • THE MONTHS OF THE YEAR • THE DAYS OF THE WEEK

- Read the instructions aloud as the students follow along in their books. Write the words *day* and *date* on the board. Help students understand the difference by pointing to *day* and saying "Monday." Then point to *date* and say "January first." On the board, write *Monday* under *day* and *January 1st* under *date*.

- Point out the days of the week in the box on the left and have the students repeat them after you. Model the exercise activity by pointing to January 11th on the calendar and asking "What day is it?" Answer "It's Thursday." Then ask "What's the date?" and answer "January eleventh. It's Thursday, January eleventh." Ask students the days and dates of the other blue numbers on the calendar. Then have them work in pairs to ask each other.

DATES

- Point out the notepad and have the students repeat the words *birthday/birthdays*. Check to see if they know the meaning.

- Point to the blue note and read it aloud. Then tell the students to listen to the dates on the notepad as you play the cassette or read the tapescript aloud. Have them listen several times. Then have the class say the dates aloud.

- Read the second set of instructions. Point out the example. Play the cassette or read the tapescript aloud as the students write down the dates.

- Tell the students to look at the dates they wrote

down and to write them again in short form: month/day/year (as in item 1—12/4/82).

- Tell the students to work in pairs to compare their answers. Ask a student to write the answers on the board.

TAPESCRIPT AND ANSWERS
2. June fifth, nineteen thirty-five.
   June 5, 1935 (6/5/35)
3. May sixth, nineteen forty-nine.
   May 6, 1949 (5/6/49)
4. July second, nineteen nineteen.
   July 2, 1919 (7/2/19)
5. January thirty-first, nineteen ninety.
   January 31, 1990 (1/31/90)

- Divide the students into pairs. Make sure they have access to a current calendar. Read the instructions aloud. Tell the students to ask their partners questions like the ones in the exercise. Go around the class and check their work. Call on different pairs to share their exchanges with the class.

TALK ABOUT BIRTHDAYS

- Tell the students to listen with their books closed while you play the cassette or read the tapescript aloud. Then have the students open their books and complete the conversation as they listen again.

- Have the students work in pairs. Tell them to check their answers as they listen to the conversation again. Write the answers on the board. Have the pairs practice the conversation aloud.

TAPESCRIPT AND ANSWERS
A When's your birthday?
B <u>September 15th</u>.
A What year were you born?
B <u>1970</u>.

- Point out the second set of instructions. Refer the students to item 1 and write the question for it on the board—*What year were you born?*

- Tell the students to write down questions for the other items and to use them as they survey their classmates. You can have the students write the questions on the board for you to check before they begin their surveys.

- Call on students to report their findings to the class.

WORKBOOK Lesson 33, p. 44

34. Family tree

WARM-UP

Go around the classroom and ask the students family-related questions such as "Are you married?" and "Do you have a large family?" You might want to begin by writing the questions on the board. Prompt different students to ask you the same questions.

FAMILY MEMBERS

- Read aloud the instructions and the sample statement. Explain what a family tree is. If necessary, use translation.

- Give the students sufficient time to study the family tree and the pictures. Then have them repeat the words surrounding the pictures.

- Hold up your book and point to picture 1 and say the sample statement again. Tell the students to work in pairs to take turns saying how the other people are related. Have them write their answers on separate paper.

- Call on different students to read their answers aloud. Check their work and have other students write the sentences on the board.

ANSWERS

2. Nancy and Barbara are mother and daughter.
3. Tim and Jack are father and son.
4. Tim and Rick are uncle and nephew.
5. Nancy and Judy are aunt and niece.
6. Charles and Jack are grandfather and grandson.
7. Lily and Judy are grandmother and granddaughter.
8. Lynn and Samuel are sister and brother.
9. Judy and Barbara are cousins.

OPTION

Divide the class into two teams. Tell the teams to look at the pictures and find other relationships in the Butler family. Give them an example— "Charles and Lily are husband and wife." Explain that the team that finds the most additional relationships first wins.

- Read the instructions and the first item aloud. Answer any questions students have about the exercise procedure.

- Have the students complete the exercise on their own and then check their answers with a partner. Call on different students to read the

completed statements aloud. Have a student write the answers on the board.

ANSWERS

2. daughter   5. brother   8. grandmother
3. husband   6. father   9. uncle
4. wife   7. aunt   10. niece

- Point out Barbara in the Butlers' family tree. Read the instructions aloud. Tell the students they will listen to some descriptions and then write down the speaker's name. Depending on the level of the students, you may wish to do the first exercise item with the class.

- Play the cassette or read the tapescript. If you read, be sure to allow sufficient time between speakers so that the students can do the exercise and write down their answers. Have them listen as many times as necessary.

- Have the students compare their answers with a partner. Then have them listen again as they check their answers. Write the answers on the board.

TAPESCRIPT

1. My mother and father are Samuel and Nancy Butler. I have a brother named Rick.
2. Samuel and I have two children, Barbara and Rick.
3. My sister Judy is 20 years old. I'm 22.
4. My sister, Lynn, lives in Chicago.
5. Charles and I have four grandchildren.
6. My wife, Lynn, and I are very happy. We have two wonderful children.

ANSWERS

1. Barbara   3. Jack   5. Lily
2. Nancy   4. Samuel   6. Tim

- Read the instructions aloud. Have the students draw their own family trees on separate paper. (If this activity is done as homework, students may wish to add photographs to their family trees.)

- Go around the class and check students' work. Ask questions and make comments about the students' family trees.

OPTION

Have the students work in pairs. Tell the partners to take turns asking questions about each other's family tree. For example, Student A points to a person in Student B's tree and asks "Who's this?" Then A would point to another person in B's tree and ask "How is he/she related to this person?"

WORKBOOK Lesson 34, p. 45

34. Family tree

1 ▶ **Look at Barbara Butler's family tree and the pictures below. Say how the people in the pictures are related.**

Samuel and Nancy are husband and wife.

The Butler Family

1. husband   wife

2. mother   daughter

3. father   son

4. uncle   nephew

5. aunt   niece

6. grandfather   grandson

7. grandmother   granddaughter

8. sister   brother

9. cousins

2 ▶ **Fill in the blanks with the correct words.**

1. Charles' wife is Samuel's _mother_ .
2. Jack's sister is Tim's _____ .
3. Lynn's father is Lily's _____ .
4. Judy's mother is Tim's _____ .
5. Nancy's son is Barbara's _____ .

6. Rick's grandfather is Samuel's _____ .
7. Tim's wife is Rick's _____ .
8. Samuel's mother is Barbara's _____ .
9. Judy's father is Barbara's _____ .
10. Lynn's daughter is Samuel's _____ .

3 ▶ **Who's talking? Listen to some members of Barbara's family describe themselves. Identify the speakers.**

1. _____
3. _____
5. _____

2. _____
4. _____
6. _____

4 ▶ **Draw your own family tree. Use Barbara Butler's tree as a model.**

35. Who's that?

GIVE INFORMATION ABOUT PEOPLE

Christine Pappas

Jeff Hunt

George Arno

Maggie Sloane

I live with my parents at 27 Willow Street. I go to high school, and I have a job, too. I work at Macy's Department Store in the evenings. My parents own a grocery store.

I live with my parents at 93 Pineapple Street. I work at Arno's Coffee Shop. My parents teach at Brooklyn College. My mother teaches biology, and my father teaches English.

I live at 5 Willow Street. I own Arno's Coffee Shop with my wife, Loretta. I work there all day and I really enjoy my work. I meet many interesting people there.

I live at 3 Willow Street. I live alone and I really like my apartment. I'm a lab technician at Brooklyn Hospital.

  1 ▶ **Listen to the information above about some people at Arno's Coffee Shop.**
▶ **Say where each person lives and works.**

A Who's that?
B Oh, that's Christine Pappas. She lives at 27 Willow Street.
A Where does she work?
B She works at Macy's.

> I live
> He/She live**s**

TALK ABOUT THE PEOPLE AT ARNO'S ● SIMPLE PRESENT: AFFIRMATIVE STATEMENTS

  2 ▶ **Study the frames: Simple Present**

Regular verbs			Pronunciation		Irregular verbs	
I You We They	work live teach		work**s**	[s]	I **have** a sister. We **go** to school. They **do** homework.	He **has** a sister. She **goes** to school. He **does** homework.
		in Brooklyn.	live**s**	[z]		
He She	work**s** live**s** teach**es**		teach**es**	[ɪz]		

▶ **Listen to the sentences in the frame that begin with *he* and *she*. Notice the pronunciation of the third person forms of the verbs.**

3 ▶ **Work in groups of four. Choose one of the people above and study carefully the information under the picture.**
▶ **Tell the classmates in your group everything you can remember about the person. (Try not to look in your book.)**

Christine Pappas lives with her parents at 27 Willow Street.
She goes to high school and . . .

> he → his
> she → her

35. Who's that?

WARM-UP

Have the students look at the first picture on p. 56. Hold up your book, point to the different characters in the picture, and ask different students "Who's that?" Then point to different students in the class and ask others who they are.

GIVE INFORMATION ABOUT PEOPLE

- Tell the students to read over the information about the people in the pictures. Answer any questions they have about vocabulary or structures.

- Have the students listen to the information about the people at Arno's Coffee Shop. Then read the model conversation aloud with another student or play the cassette. Point out and read aloud the information in the box.

- Have the students work in pairs to take turns asking each other about the people in the pictures. Tell them to use the questions from the model conversation.

- Call on different pairs to say the exchanges to the class and to write them on the board. Check their work.

ANSWERS

A Who's that?
B Oh, that's Jeff Hunt. He lives at 93 Pineapple Street.
A Where does he work?
B He works at Arno's Coffee Shop.

A Who's that?
B Oh, that's George Arno. He lives at 5 Willow Street.
A Where does he work?
B He works at Arno's Coffee Shop.

A Who's that?
B Oh, that's Maggie Sloane. She lives at 3 Willow Street.
A Where does she work?
B She works at Brooklyn Hospital.

TALK ABOUT THE PEOPLE AT ARNO'S •
SIMPLE PRESENT: AFFIRMATIVE STATEMENTS

- Tell the students to study the frame entitled *Regular verbs*. Read the possible sentences aloud.

Point out the pronunciation note and have the students repeat the verbs after you. Then have them repeat the possible sentences after you.

- Tell the students to look at the frame entitled *Irregular verbs*. Read the sentences aloud and have the students repeat them after you.

- Have the students locate the sentences that begin with *he* and *she*. Tell them to pay particular attention to the pronunciation of the verbs as you play the cassette or read the sentences.

- Introduce the forms in the box—*he/his, she/her*. Demonstrate their use by pointing to a male student and saying "That's (*student's name*). He has his book here today." Do the same with a female student.

- Divide the students into groups of four. Have each member in a group choose a different person from the top of p. 60 and study the information about that person.

- Have the students close their books and take turns telling their groups as much information as they can remember about the person they chose. Point out the sample about Christine Pappas at the bottom of the page.

- Finally, have the class open their books. Call on different students to close their books and tell the class everything they can remember about the people they chose. Have the class fill in any missing information.

OPTION

Have the students work in groups. Assign a different character from the book to each group. Tell the groups to write a short paragraph about their characters. Tell them to write paragraphs similar to those on p. 60, but to use the third person—*He/She lives...*, etc. Call on a student from each group to read the group's paragraph to the class. Have another group member write the paragraph on the board.

You can assign the following characters and refer the students to the corresponding pages:

Carolyn Duval (pp. 1-3 and 52)
Loretta Arno (pp. 8 and 28)
Nick Pappas (p. 18)
Survey characters (p. 54)

TALK ABOUT THE PEOPLE AT ARNO'S • SIMPLE PRESENT: SUMMARY

- Have the students study the frames as you read aloud the headings and possible sentences. Answer any questions they have.

- Have the students work in pairs to take turns asking and answering the questions in the frames.

- Have the class work in pairs. Read the first set of instructions aloud. Tell the pairs to use the patterns in the frame to help them write the questions.

- Call on different pairs to read the exchanges aloud. Call on other students to write the questions on the board.

  POSSIBLE ANSWERS
  1. Where does Christine Pappas live?
  2. Does she live alone?
  3. Does Christine work?
  4. Where do her parents work?

- Read the second set of instructions aloud. Tell each partner to choose a different character from p. 60 and to write questions about that person on separate paper.

- Have the students close their books. Tell the partners to take turns asking each other the questions and responding from memory. When they finish, they can check the answers in their books. Go around the room and check students' work.

TALK ABOUT YOUR FAMILY AND FRIENDS

- Direct the students to look at the photo. Read the instructions aloud. Have the students listen as you play the cassette or read the conversation aloud with another student.

- Point out the words in the box used to describe a man, a woman, and a child. Answer any questions students have about these words and the words in the conversation.

- Ask the students to bring photos of family and friends to class. Bring to class photos of your own family and/or friends to show and talk about. Before the students begin to talk about their photos, you can model a description for them. Show your photos to the class and talk

about the people in them. Remember to use language similar to that in the lesson. For example:

This is my mother and father.
They live in Minneapolis, Minnesota.
My mother's a nurse, and my father's a cook at a local restaurant.

- Divide the class into pairs. Tell the partners to take turns telling each other about the people in their photos. Go around the classroom to check pair work. Ask questions about the people in the students' photos. Also encourage the partners to ask questions about each other's photos.

OPTION

To encourage the students to ask questions, show them a "mystery photo" of someone. Tell them to try to discover the identity of the person by asking you questions about the person.

- Tell the students to read over the questions. Point out the box and demonstrate the use of *they* and *their*, indicating two students and saying "They have their books today."

- Read the instructions aloud. Then tell the students to interview three classmates. Tell them to ask questions like the ones listed. Tell them to write down the responses.

- Call on each student to tell the class about one classmate and his or her family.

CULTURE CLOSE-UP

Among persons living in the U.S. since birth, it is not common to find extended families living in the same house. When sons and daughters reach adulthood, they often live apart from their parents, even before they marry. It is not uncommon for them to have their own jobs and to rent or own an apartment or house, etc. Grandparents and other close relatives also tend to live in separate dwellings.

WORKBOOK Lesson 35, pp. 46-47

4 ▶ **Study the frames: Simple Present**

Information questions			Statements		Yes-no questions			Short answers		
	do	you	I	**work**	**Do**	you		Yes,	I	**do.**
		they	We	**don't work**		they		No,	we they	**don't.**
Where			They				**work** here?			
		he		here.		he		Yes,	he	**does.**
	does	she	He	**works**	**Does**	she		No,	she	**doesn't.**
			She	**doesn't work**						

5 ▶ **Ask an appropriate question about Christine Pappas for each of the answers below.**
▶ **Ask similar questions about the other people on p. 60. Your partner will try to answer from memory.**

1. **A** _____ ?
   B She lives at 27 Willow Street.

2. **A** _____ ?
   B No, she doesn't. She lives with her parents.

3. **A** _____ ?
   B Yes, she does. She works at Macy's Department Store.

4. **A** _____ ?
   B They own a grocery store.

TALK ABOUT YOUR FAMILY AND FRIENDS

6 ▶ **Some friends are looking at photos. Listen to the conversation.**

A Who's that?
B Oh, that's my sister, Carla.
A She's very pretty. How old is she?
B Twenty-four.
A What does she do?
B She's an accountant. She works in a bank.

man: good-looking, handsome
woman: good-looking, pretty
child: good-looking, cute

▶ **Bring to class photos of family members and friends.**
▶ **Show your pictures to a partner and talk about the people in them.**

7 ▶ **Interview three classmates about their families and record their answers. Ask questions like the ones below.**
▶ **Tell the rest of the class about one classmate and his or her family.**

1. Do you live with your parents?
2. Do you have any brothers and sisters?
3. What are their names?
4. What do they do?   they → their
5. Do you have any nieces and nephews?

6. Are you married?
7. What does your husband/wife do?
8. Do you have any children? How old are they?
9. Do you have a lot of family (*cousins, aunts uncles*) in (*name of city*)?

36. Do you speak Chinese?

See p. 166 for a more complete list of languages, countries, and nationalities.

1 ► Look at the chart of some common languages and answer the questions.

1. What language do they speak in Jamaica?
2. What are two languages they speak in India?
3. What language do they speak in Chile?
4. What language do Brazilians speak?
5. Where do they speak Arabic?
6. Where do they speak Chinese?

Languages	Countries	Nationalities
Chinese	China	Chinese
English	the United Kingdom the United States Jamaica	British American Jamaican
Spanish	Spain Mexico Chile	Spanish Mexican Chilean
Hindi	India	Indian
Bengali	Bangladesh India	Bangladeshi Indian
Arabic	Morocco Jordan Saudi Arabia	Moroccan Jordanian Saudi Arabian
Japanese	Japan	Japanese
German	Germany Switzerland Austria	German Swiss Austrian
Portuguese	Portugal Brazil	Portuguese

 2 ► Complete the conversations below. Then listen to confirm your answers.

1. **A** Do you speak _____ ?
   B Yes, I do.
   A Are you British?
   B No, I'm _____ .

2. **A** Where are you from?
   B I'm from _____ .
   A Oh, do you speak Hindi?
   B No, I speak _____ .

3 ► Imagine that you're from one of the countries in the chart. Write down your new language and nationality on a piece of paper.
► Find out other students' new languages and nationalities. Find someone who . . .

1. . . . is Chinese and speaks Chinese.
2. . . . is Indian, but doesn't speak Bengali.
3. . . . speaks English, but isn't from the United States.
4. . . . speaks Portuguese, but isn't Brazilian.
5. . . . speaks Spanish, but isn't Spanish.
6. . . . is Japanese and speaks Japanese.
7. . . . speaks Arabic, but isn't from Jordan.
8. . . . speaks German, but isn't from Germany.

36. Do you speak Chinese?

WARM-UP

On the board, write *I'm _____. I'm from _____.* Point to your country on a map or globe as you say your nationality and country—"I'm (*nationality*). I'm from (*country*)." Call on a pair of students to point out their countries on the map or globe. Refer to the board and prompt them to say their nationalities and countries. Go around the classroom and have students say their nationalities and countries, giving help when needed. If all or most of the students are the same nationality and are from the same country, refer them to p. 166 and have them make statements such as the following:

Algerians are from Algeria.

LANGUAGES AND NATIONALITIES

- Read the instructions aloud and have the students look over the chart. Point out the headings and make sure the students understand what they mean. Have them repeat the words in the chart after you.

- Refer students to the chart as you identify the country, nationality, and language of a famous person the students know about. For example, say "Tom Cruise is from the United States. He's American. He speaks English."

- Have students work in pairs to ask and answer the questions. Encourage them to answer with complete sentences. Go around the class and check their work. Help them with their pronunciation of the languages and countries.

- Call on different pairs to ask and answer the questions. Ask a student to write the short form of the answers on the board.

ANSWERS
1. English
2. Hindi and Bengali
3. Spanish
4. Portuguese
5. In Morocco, Jordan, and Saudi Arabia
6. In China

OPTION

Have the pairs continue the exercise by asking each other about additional languages and places on the chart. Call on pairs to present their exchanges to the class.

- Read the instructions aloud. Then have the students look at the pictures and silently read over the incomplete conversations.

- Have the students complete the conversations as you play the cassette or read the conversations aloud. Then have them confirm their answers as they listen again. Ask a student to write the answers on the board.

ANSWERS
1. **A** English
   B Jamaican
2. **B** India
   B Bengali

- Have students work in pairs to practice the dialogues. Call on two different pairs to say the exchanges for the class.

- Tell the students to imagine that they are from one of the countries in the chart and to write down their new language and nationality on separate paper.

- Read the second set of instructions aloud. Tell the students to read over the exercise items. Explain that they are to move around the classroom to find out their classmates' new languages and nationalities. Help them get started by writing on the board sample questions they can ask. For example:

Where are you from?
What language do you speak?
Do you speak Spanish? Are you Spanish?

- Call on students to report their findings to the class. Check their pronunciation of nationalities, languages, and countries.

OPTION

On the board, write the countries from the chart in random order. Also write *In _____, they speak _____.* Point to different countries and prompt different students to complete the sentence you wrote on the board. For example:

T: (Points to Morocco)
S: In Morocco, they speak Arabic.

Tell the students to try not to refer to their books.

ASK WHAT SOMETHING MEANS • ASK HOW TO SAY SOMETHING

- Tell the students to look at the foreign expressions in the box. See if any students know the meanings and can pronounce the expressions.

- Ask a student to read the sample dialogue with you. Then have the students repeat the foreign expressions after you. (Note that the expressions are written in the Roman alphabet, which is not necessarily the alphabet of the languages listed. This has been done to standardize the pronunciation so that if a native speaker is not available to pronounce the words, you can at least simulate the pronunciation by sounding out the expressions as though they were English words.)

- Have the students work in pairs to find out what the expressions mean. Refer them to p. 167.

- Point out the English expressions in the box and have the students repeat them after you. Read the instructions aloud. Then read aloud the sample dialogue with another student.

- Have the students work in pairs. Tell them to take turns asking and answering the questions about how the English expressions are said in different languages. Refer them to the languages listed in the box on the left and to the answers on p. 167. Tell the students to model their conversations on the sample dialogue.

SAMPLE CONVERSATION
A Do you speak Greek?
B A little.
A How do you say "please" in Greek?
B *Parakalo*.

- Call on different pairs of students to present their conversations to the class.

ASK FOR CLARIFICATION

- Have the students read over the questions in the two columns. Answer any questions they have about vocabulary or structures.

- Tell the students to match each question in the left column with one in the right column that means the same. Read the example aloud or ask a student to read it.

- Have the students compare answers with a partner. Then call on students to read the matched sentences to the class. Ask a student to write the answers on the board.

ANSWERS
2. d
3. b
4. a
5. f
6. e

- Have the students examine the form. Talk about credit cards and credit card applications.

- Point out the *Date of Birth* on the form. Then read the conversation aloud with a student or play the cassette. If you read, remember to speak slowly when you say "September 15, 1965" the second time.

- Tell the students to copy a blank version of the form on separate paper. Then have them work in pairs to fill out each other's form. Tell them to use the conversation and the questions they matched above as a guide in asking for the information.

- Go around the classroom, giving help where needed. Then have the partners exchange forms and check the information that was filled in.

OPTION

Tell the students to close their books. On the board, write a question from one of the columns in the first part of the exercise. Call on one student to say it. Then see if another student can say it the other way. Continue the practice.

BORROW SOMETHING

- Point out the items in the box as you have the students repeat the names after you. Then have two students join you in reading the sample conversation aloud.

- Read the instructions aloud. Have the students work in groups of three. Tell them to take turns asking and answering questions like those in the sample conversation. Encourage them to use real objects and appropriate gestures as they act out the exchanges.

- Call on different groups to act out their conversations for the class. Check their work.

FOLLOW-UP

Students can write out personal information in response to the questions in exercise 6.

WORKBOOK Lesson 36, p. 48

4 ▶ **Look at the foreign expressions in the box below. Find out what they mean. (You can find the answers on p. 167.)**

A Do you speak Spanish?
B Yes, I do.
A What does *mucho gusto* mean?
B (It means) "Nice to meet you."

Some foreign expressions

Mucho gusto. (Spanish)   Do svidanye. (Russian)
Shukran. (Arabic)   Habari gani. (Swahili)
Parakalo. (Greek)   Arigato. (Japanese)
Obrigado. (Portuguese)   Pen yangai. (Thai)

5 ▶ **Find out how to say each English expression below in two languages.**

A Do you speak Korean?
B A little.
A How do you say "thank you" in Korean?
B *Kamsamida*.

Some English expressions

Thank you.   Good-bye.
Hello.   I love you.
Please.   How are you?

 6 ▶ **Match each question with another way to say it.**

1. What's your address?
2. What's your date of birth?
3. What's your place of birth?
4. What's your marital status?
5. What's your place of employment?
6. What's your business phone?

a. Are you married or single?
b. Where were you born?
c. Where do you live?
d. When were you born?
e. What's your phone number at work?
f. Where do you work?

 ▶ **Listen to the conversation below.**
▶ **Copy the form and fill it out for another student.**

A What's your date of birth?
B Excuse me?
A When were you born?
B September 15, 1965.
A Could you speak a little slower, please?
B Oh, sure. September 15, 1965.

GLOBAL BANK
VISTA CARD APPLICATION

Please fill out the form below to apply for your Global Bank Vista Card.

PERSONAL INFORMATION

Name
Ann Robards

Address
1422 Chadwick Drive, Dayton, Ohio 45406

Date of Birth   Place of Birth
0 9 1 5 6 5   *Lima, Peru*

Marital Status
Married

EMPLOYMENT INFORMATION

Place of Employment
Fairview High School

Address
16 Main Street, Dayton, Ohio

Business Phone
513-555-3331

 7 ▶ **Imagine you need one of the items in the picture to complete a form. Borrow it from another student.**

A Excuse me, do you have a pencil?
B No, I'm sorry, I don't.

A Excuse me, could I use your pencil?
C Sure, here.
A Thanks.

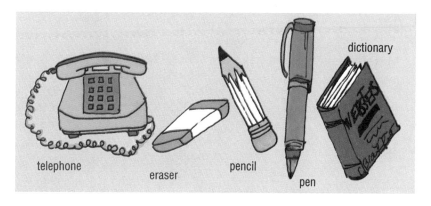

telephone   eraser   pencil   pen   dictionary

37. Take my advice.

John Pierce is watching TV one evening when Mrs. Baxter knocks at the door.

1

Mrs. Baxter	(*Knock, knock, knock!*)
John	Who is it?
Mrs. Baxter	It's Mrs. Baxter.
John	(*To himself*) Mrs. Baxter? (*Opening the door*) Mrs. Baxter! How are you this evening?
Mrs. Baxter	Good evening, Mr. Pierce. I'm sorry to bother you.
John	Oh, that's O.K. I was just watching television. Come in. Sit down. Would you like . . . uh . . . some tea? Or coffee?
Mrs. Baxter	Oh, no, please don't bother. I only have a few minutes. Uh, Mr. Pierce . . . it's the fourth of December.
John	The fourth of . . . oh, Mrs. Baxter, the rent! I'm sorry it's late. I'll write you a check right now. Uh . . . do you have a pen I could use?
Mrs. Baxter	Yes, I do. Here you are.

Mrs. Baxter	Is that your girlfriend?
John	My girlfriend? Oh, you mean in the picture. No, that's my sister.
Mrs. Baxter	She's very pretty. Is she married?
John	Yes, married with two children—a boy and a girl.
Mrs. Baxter	Oh, how wonderful!
John	Do you have any children, Mrs. Baxter?
Mrs. Baxter	Mr. Pierce, I have six grandchildren!
John	Oh, really? (*Handing her the check*) Here you are, Mrs. Baxter.
Mrs. Baxter	Do you have a girlfriend?
John	No, not really.
Mrs. Baxter	What? A handsome man like you with a good job? Take my advice. Find yourself a girlfriend, get married, and have children. (*Rrring, rrring*)
John	Oh, there's the phone. Excuse me for just one moment, Mrs. Baxter . . .

37. Take my advice.

Write the following dialogue on the board:

Student: (*Knock, knock, knock!*)
Teacher: Who is it?
Student: It's (*student's name*).
Teacher: Come on in. How are you today/this
          morning/this evening?
Student: I'm fine/not bad/O.K.

Read the dialogue aloud with a student. Act it out with several other students. Then have the students work in pairs to take turns acting out the two roles in similar dialogues.

1. Conversation

BACKGROUND

John Pierce has forgotten to pay his rent. He is watching TV one evening when his landlady, Mrs. Baxter, comes to see him to ask for the rent. John writes a check for the rent, and he and Mrs. Baxter chat for a while.

LANGUAGE

Knock, knock... indicates the sound used to call someone to the door.

...please don't bother. is a polite way to refuse something.

...married with two children. is short for (She's) *married and has two children.*

...not really. is another way of saying "Actually not" and is used to express a slight degree of uncertainty.

...there's the phone. is another way of saying "The phone is ringing."

PROCEDURE

- Have students examine the illustrations. Point out Mrs. Baxter and John Pierce and the different situations. Ask questions and make statements like these:

  Where are Mrs. Baxter and John Pierce?
  John pays rent each month.
  Are there books in the picture?

- Have the students silently read over the conversation. Answer any questions they have about vocabulary or structures.

- As the students follow along in their books, play the cassette or read the conversation aloud.

2. Figure it out

1. *True* or *False*?

- Have the students read over the five statements. Tell them to listen to the conversation and answer *True* or *False* on separate paper.

- Have the students discuss their answers with a partner. Ask a student to write the answers on the board.

  ANSWERS
  1. True
  2. False
  3. False
  4. True
  5. False

  OPTION

  Have the students correct the false statements on separate paper. They can compare their corrections with a partner. Have a student write the corrections on the board for you to check and go over with the class.

2. What do you think? Does Mrs. Baxter have good advice?

- Read the instruction questions aloud. Discuss the difference between good and bad advice.

- Have the students locate the lines in the conversation where Mrs. Baxter gives John advice. Call on a student to read the lines aloud.

- Have the students work in small groups to discuss Mrs. Baxter's advice. Call on different groups to share their opinions with the class.

3. Listen in

- Read the instructions aloud as the students follow along in their books. Remind the students that their task is to complete the statements. Tell them they can write down either words or figures for the numbers in their answers.

- Tell the students to just listen the first time you play the cassette or read the tapescript aloud. Then have the students listen again and complete the statements.

- Call on a student to read the statements aloud as you write the answers on the board.

  TAPESCRIPT
  John Hello?
  Gloria Hello, John. This is Gloria. Where are you?
  John I'm at home. What do you mean?

Gloria John, it's Friday night, December fourth...
John Oh, no! Your birthday! Is everyone at the restaurant?
Gloria Yes. We're at the House of China at 352 Eleventh Avenue, near 23rd Street.
John Hey, slow down!
Gloria 352 Eleventh Avenue, near 23rd Street.
John I'll be right there. And uh...happy birthday, Gloria.

ANSWERS
1. Eleventh/11th
2. December fourth/4th

4. Your turn

- Read aloud the instructions and the four statements. Answer any questions students have about vocabulary or structures. If necessary, provide an example of an interviewer's question: "Where are you from, Mr. Schwarzenegger?"

- Have students work in pairs to take turns playing the roles of Arnold Schwarzenegger and the interviewer. Go around the classroom and select the best conversations for presentation to the class.

5. How to say it

- Read the conversations aloud or play them on cassette. Then present them again and have the students repeat each line. Slightly exaggerate the reduced pronunciation of the underlined words and have the students repeat after you.

- Practice the conversations with another student in front of the class. Then have the students practice in pairs. Move around the room and check their work, giving help where needed.

PRONUNCIATION NOTE

This exercise presents examples of vowel and consonant reduction and blending that often occur in normal conversational speech. The phonetic symbols at the right represent the reduced and blended sounds of the underlined words. These symbols are meant to be a guide to the pronunciation of the underlined words.

FOLLOW-UP

Students can write out their conversations from exercise 4.

WORKBOOK Lesson 37, p. 49

2. Figure it out

1. *True* or *False*?

1. John's rent check is late.
2. John has a girlfriend.
3. Mrs. Baxter has no children.
4. Mrs. Baxter's advice is, "Get married and have children."
5. John is happy to listen to Mrs. Baxter's advice.

2. What do you think? Does Mrs. Baxter have good advice?

📼 3. Listen in

John forgets to meet his friend Gloria. Read the statements below. Then listen to the conversation and complete them.

1. The House of China is at 352 _____ Avenue.
2. Gloria's birthday is _____ .

4. Your turn

Arnold Schwarzenegger is interviewed on television. Act out a conversation between him and the interviewer. Use this information:

Arnold Schwarzenegger is from Austria.
He lives in California now.
He speaks German and English.
He's an actor and a businessman.

📼 5. How to say it

Listen to the conversations.

1. **A** My brother is 22.
   B Does he live at home?   ['dəzi]
   A No, he lives with friends.
   B What does he do?   ['wədəzi]
   A He's an actor.

2. **A** My sister is 24.
   B Does she live with you?   ['dəʃi]
   A No, she's married.
   B What does she do?   ['wədəʃi]
   A She's a doctor.

38.

SO YOU WANT TO LEARN ENGLISH ... *FAST!*

You need to improve your English for work or travel. You want to practice your language skills, but you don't have the opportunity. What do you do?

Learn the IST way! Take a "study vacation" and travel to English-speaking countries.

With IST, International Student Travel, you can spend one to three months abroad improving your speaking, listening, reading and writing skills. Live with an English-speaking family. During the day, study full time in a high school or language institute. The choice is yours!

Where can you go? The United States and England are very popular for study holidays. Canada is another choice. And don't forget Australia and New Zealand, two more countries where people speak English. Each can provide you with the experience of a lifetime.

Enjoy the sights and learn English in Sydney.

London is an interesting place to study English.

Take a "Study Vacation" to Washington, D.C.

- -

INTERNATIONAL STUDENT TRAVEL
500 Fifth Avenue, 4th Floor
New York, NY   10020
U.S.A.

Yes! Please send me more information about opportunities to study in English-speaking countries.

Name _____

Address _____

Street and Number

_____

City   State   Zip Code

_____

Country

IST offers tours, short courses, and full-time study opportunities. For more information call us now at 1-800-555-2700 or send in the coupon.

INTERNATIONAL STUDENT TRAVEL can help you achieve your goals!

---

1. **Read the advertisement. Then scan it again and find . . .**

1. . . . five countries where you can learn English.
2. . . . three cities where you can study English with International Student Travel.
3. . . . another way to say "language school."
4. . . . the abbreviation for International Student Travel.
5. . . . the telephone number and address for International Student Travel.

2. **What are two ways that you can get more information about International Student Travel?**

38. SO YOU WANT TO LEARN ENGLISH...FAST!

BACKGROUND

This advertisement is a brochure from an international student travel service. It offers English language "study vacations" in English-speaking countries.

PROCEDURE

1. Read the advertisement.

- Read over the instructions with the students. Explain what an advertisement is. Then tell the students to read over the advertisement. After the students finish reading the ad, you may want to play the cassette or read the text aloud as the students follow along in their books.

- Go over the five items and tell the students to scan the article to find the information. (See the Methodology Note which follows.) Have the students work in pairs to compare answers.

- Ask different students to write the answers on the board. Then call on pairs of students. Have one student read an exercise item and the other the answer. Check their work.

ANSWERS
1. The United States, England, Canada, Australia, and New Zealand
2. Sydney, London, and Washington, D.C.
3. language institute
4. IST
5. 1-800-555-2700
   500 Fifth Avenue, 4th Floor
   New York, NY 10020
   U.S.A.

METHODOLOGY NOTE

Scanning is a reading technique in which the reader samples the text rather than reads word for word. Scanning involves first knowing which specific information to look for. To teach students to scan, tell them to read over the text quickly and look only for the information they have been asked to find. For example, in the first exercise item above, students should be told to look specifically for names of countries.

2. What are two ways that you can get more information about International Student Travel?

- Read the instruction question aloud. Tell the students to scan the advertisement for the answers.

- Call on different students to say the answers aloud. Ask a student to write them on the board.

SAMPLE ANSWERS
1. Call them at 1-800-555-2700.
2. Send in the coupon.

OPTION 1

Have the students read over the advertisement again. Point to relevant parts of it and use appropriate gestures or realia to help them understand the meanings of new words such as *abroad, achieve, choice, coupon, course, English-speaking, forget, goal, holiday, improve, lifetime, send,* and *tour.*

OPTION 2

Have the students work in small groups. Tell one student to play the role of someone who works for IST and gives information to students about IST's programs. Tell the other students to pretend they want to travel abroad to learn English. Have them ask questions about IST and its programs. Tell students to use the information from the advertisement to ask and answer questions. Also encourage them to make up additional questions and answers.

FOLLOW-UP

Students can write complete-sentence answers for exercise 1. For example, for item 1 they would write *The five countries where you can learn English are the United States, England, Canada, Australia, and New Zealand.*

WORKBOOK Lesson 38, p. 50. Point out to the students that most of their sentences will probably begin with *I.* Remind them to end each sentence with a period.

PREVIEW

Before you begin teaching, go over the functions/themes, language, and forms in the chart. This will give you a preview of what you will encounter as you guide the students through the unit.

Preview the conversations.

- Have the students examine the first illustration. Point out the two women, the names on the doors, and the desk. Ask the students where the women are. See if they can tell you the relationship between Melissa and Laura. Read the dialogue lines aloud and check for understanding. Discuss with the students the sentences under the illustration.

- Have the students examine the second illustration as you read aloud the dialogue lines. Check for understanding. Discuss the sentences under the illustration.

CULTURE CLOSE-UP

In the U.S., the language spoken in offices may be both formal and informal. Receptionists generally answer the telephone in a formal manner—for example, with a greeting followed by the name of the company, and the question "May I help you?" Employees in large companies usually address their employers with the appropriate title and last name—Mr. Rosansky, Dr. Baxter, Ms. Pierce, etc. Employers sometimes address their employees informally, on a first-name basis. Employees often address one another on a first-name basis as well.

FUNCTIONS/THEMES

Make a business telephone
  call
Leave a message

Say hello and good-bye

Talk about leisure plans

LANGUAGE

May I help you?
May I speak to Richard Lightner, please?
May I take a message?
Could you ask him to call me?
I'll give him the message.

Good morning/afternoon/evening.
  Good-bye./Good night./Have a nice
  weekend./See you tomorrow.

What are you going to do this weekend?
I'm going to visit a friend.
What is Rob going to do tonight/
  tomorrow evening/next weekend/on
  Sunday?

FORMS

Formulas *May I . . . ?* and *I'll . . .*
Object pronouns

Formulaic use of future with
  going to
Expressions of future time

Preview the conversations.

Notice how this receptionist answers the
phone. How do receptionists answer the
phone in your country?

The receptionist calls Bob Rosansky "Mr. Rosansky."
She calls her boss "Laura." Does Laura Martin call her
receptionist by her first name? When do you use first
names in your country?

39. Friday

It's a busy day for Melissa Harris, the receptionist at the law office of Laura Martin and Louis Brown.

A

Melissa Good morning, Martin and Brown. May I help you?

Bob Rosansky Yes. This is Bob Rosansky. May I speak to Laura Martin, please?

Melissa One moment, please. (*to Laura*) Do you want to speak to Bob Rosansky?

Laura No, Melissa. Not until Monday.

Melissa I'm sorry, Mr. Rosansky. She's busy right now. May I take a message?

Bob Rosansky Yes, could you ask her to call my office? My number there is 555-3492.

Melissa I'm sorry, could you repeat that?

Bob Rosansky 555-3492.

Melissa I'll give her the message.

B

Melissa Good afternoon, Martin and Brown. May I help you?

Bob Rosansky May I speak to Laura Martin or Louis Brown, please?

Melissa Who's calling, please?

Bob Rosansky Bob Rosansky.

Melissa I'm sorry. They're in a meeting right now. Can I give them a message, Mr. Rosansky?

Bob Rosansky No, I'll call back later.

C

Melissa Good afternoon, Martin and Brown. May I help you?

Bob Rosansky May I speak to Laura, please?

Melissa Who's calling, please?

Bob Rosansky Uh . . . it's her friend Bob.

Melissa Laura, your friend Bob is on the phone.

Laura Oh, thanks. Hi, Bob. How are you?

Bob Rosansky Ms. Martin? This is Bob Rosansky . . .

39. Friday

WARM-UP

Ask the students questions with *do/does* about things relevant to them. Prompt them to respond with short answers. For example:

T: Do we have class on Sundays?
S: No, we don't.
T: Does (*student's name*) speak Arabic?
S: Yes, she does.

You may also want to make up two questions about the illustrations on p. 67. Refer the class to the illustrations as you ask the questions. For example:

T: Does Melissa speak to Bob Rosansky?
S: Yes, she does.

T: Do Melissa and Laura work in the same office?
S: Yes, they do.

Encourage students to ask and answer additional questions about the illustrations and about the class.

BACKGROUND

Bob Rosansky makes three calls to the law office of Martin and Brown. Melissa Harris, the receptionist, answers the calls. Laura Martin succeeds in avoiding speaking to Bob Rosansky when he calls the first two times, but Bob finally tricks her into answering by using their first names so that she thinks he's a friend.

LANGUAGE

One moment, please. is a polite way to ask someone to wait.

…right now indicates at the present moment.

Can I…? is a less formal way of saying "May I…?"

Get some rest. is a friendly way of suggesting that someone seems tired and needs to relax.

…take it easy. is another way of saying "relax."

I guess… is another way of saying "I think."

PROCEDURE

- Point out and say the names of the different characters in the pictures as the students repeat after you. Make statements and ask simple questions about the pictures. For example:

  In the first picture, Laura is next to Melissa. Melissa speaks to Bob Rosansky on the phone.

- Play the cassette or read the conversations aloud as the students listen with their books closed. Have them listen again as they follow along in their books. Answer any questions they have about vocabulary or structures. Make sure students understand how Bob Rosansky gets Laura to finally talk to him: by pretending he's a friend of hers.

OPTION

If possible, have different students read the conversations with you. As they read the telephone conversations, have them pretend to talk into telephones.

Review the rising intonation pattern in "May I help you?" and the rising-falling pattern in "This is Bob Rosansky." Then have the students act out the conversations in small groups. Ask different groups to present the conversations to the class.

LANGUAGE NOTE

Note the frequent use of certain words in the formal register of office telephone calls—*May I…?, …please?, I'm sorry., …could you…?*

Figure it out

1. Listen to the conversations and answer the questions.

- Tell the students to silently read over the questions. Then read the questions aloud and have the students repeat.

- Have the students listen to the conversations and answer the questions. Tell them to write short answers on separate paper. Then have them work with a partner to compare answers and to take turns asking and answering the questions.

- Call on pairs to ask and answer the questions aloud. Have different students write the answers on the board.

  ANSWERS
  2. No, they're not./No, they aren't.
  3. Yes, he does.
  4. No, she doesn't.
  5. No, he doesn't.
  6. Yes, she does.

OPTION

You can ask students additional questions such as:

1. Does Bob Rosansky want to talk to Melissa?
2. Is Bob really Laura's friend?

See if the students can come up with any additional questions of their own. Write them on the board and call on other students to answer them.

2. Listen again. Complete the sentences with *a*, *b*, or *c*.

- Read the instructions to the students. Point out the *a*, *b*, and *c* on the right. You may want to review the different titles: *Mr.*, *Mrs.*, *Miss*, and *Ms.* Tell the students to read the statements to themselves before they listen.

- Read the conversations aloud or play them on cassette. Have the students try to do the exercise without referring to the conversations in their books. Then have them compare their answers with a partner.

- Tell the students to check their answers by looking at the conversations in their books. Then call on different students to read aloud their completed sentences.

ANSWERS
1. b
2. c
3. a, a, c
4. a, a, a

3. Match.

- Have the students read over the sentences. Tell them to match each sentence in the left column with the correct response in the right column. Have them draw lines in their books or write the answers on separate paper.

- Have the students work in pairs to compare their answers and to practice the exchanges. Call on different pairs to read the matched sentences aloud. Ask a student to write the answers on the board.

  ANSWERS
  1. c
  2. e
  3. b
  4. f
  5. a
  6. d

FOLLOW-UP

Students can write out the six two-line exchanges they matched in exercise 3.

WORKBOOK Lesson 39, p. 51

Melissa Good night, Louis. Good night,
Laura. See you tomorrow.
Laura Tomorrow?
Melissa Wait a minute—what day is today?
Louis Friday.
Melissa Oh, yes—you're right.
Laura Have a nice weekend, Melissa.
Louis Yeah. Get some rest.
Melissa Thanks.

E

Laura What are you going to do this
weekend, Louis?
Louis Oh, I don't have any plans. I'm just
going to take it easy. What about you?
Laura I'd like to go to the beach, but I
guess I'm going to work on that contract
for Bob Rosansky. He wants it on
Monday morning.
Louis Well, have fun.
Laura You too. See you Monday.

Figure it out

1. Listen to the conversations and answer the questions.

1. Does Laura Martin want to speak with Bob Rosansky? *No, she doesn't.*
2. Are Laura and Louis really in a meeting?
3. Does Bob Rosansky finally talk to Laura?
4. Does Melissa work on Saturday?
5. Does Louis have plans for the weekend?
6. Does Laura have plans for the weekend?

2. Listen again. Complete the sentences with *a*, *b*, or *c*.

1. In conversations A and B, Bob Rosansky identifies himself by his __*b*__ .
   When he asks to speak to Laura Martin, he uses her _____ .
2. When Melissa, the receptionist, speaks to Bob Rosansky, she uses his _____ .
3. In conversation C, Bob Rosansky identifies himself by his _____ . When he
   asks to speak to Laura Martin, he uses her _____ . When he finally speaks to
   Laura Martin, he uses her _____ .
4. When Melissa speaks to Laura Martin, she uses her _____ . When she speaks
   to Louis Brown, she uses his _____ . When the two lawyers speak to the
   receptionist, they use her _____ .

a. first name
b. first and last names
c. title and last name

3. Match.

1. Could you repeat your number, please?
2. Have a nice weekend.
3. Good night.
4. Good morning.
5. May I speak to Laura Martin, please?
6. May I take a message?

a. She's in a meeting right now.
b. See you tomorrow.
c. It's 555-3492.
d. No, I'll call back later.
e. You too. See you Monday.
f. Hello. How are you today?

40. May I take a message?

 1 ▶ Listen to the two possible business calls below.
▶ Act out the calls with a partner. Call Global Travel in the afternoon and ask to speak to a classmate. Then call back in the evening.

A *(Dials number) Rrring, rrring*

B Good morning, Global Travel. May I help you?

A May I speak to Richard Lightner, please?

B I'm sorry, he isn't here right now. **B** Just a moment, please.

A Thank you. I'll call back later. **A** Thank you.

morning

afternoon

evening

MAKE A BUSINESS CALL • LEAVE A MESSAGE

 2 ▶ Listen and complete the message with the caller's last name and telephone number.

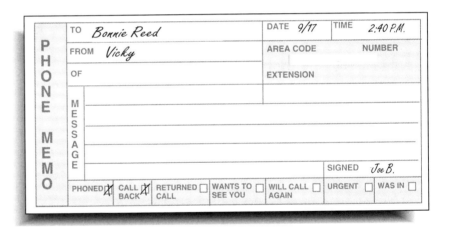

PHONE MEMO	TO	*Bonnie Reed*		DATE *9/17*	TIME *2:40 P.M.*
	FROM	*Vicky*		AREA CODE	NUMBER
	OF			EXTENSION	
	MESSAGE				
				SIGNED	*Joe B.*
	PHONED ☒	CALL BACK ☒	RETURNED CALL ☐	WANTS TO SEE YOU ☐ WILL CALL AGAIN ☐	URGENT ☐ WAS IN ☐

---

 3 ▶ Complete the conversation below with the sentences in the box.
▶ Listen to confirm your answers.
▶ Act out the conversation. Ask to speak to a classmate and substitute your own name for Rob Vale.

Receptionist _____
Rob Vale May I speak to Mrs. Reed, please?
Receptionist _____
Rob Vale Yes. This is Rob Vale. Could you ask her to call me?
Receptionist _____
Rob Vale "V" as in "Victor"—A-L-E.
Receptionist _____
Rob Vale No, she doesn't. It's 555-2811.
Receptionist _____
Rob Vale Thank you.

> Mrs. Reed = her
> Rob Vale = him

Certainly. Could you spell your last name, please?
I'll give her the message.
Does she have your number?
Global Travel. May I help you?
She isn't here right now. May I take a message?

Some difficult sounds

"V" as in "Victor" "R" as in "Robert"
"B" as in "boy" "S" as in "Sally"
"L" as in "Linda" "F" as in "Frank"

40. May I take a message?

WARM-UP

Pretend you are a receptionist. Tell the students to call and ask for someone. Hold an imaginary telephone receiver as you answer their calls. Write a sample conversation on the board for them to follow:

(*Rrring, rring*)

T: Good morning, (*name of school*). May I help you?

S: (*Person's name*), please.

T: I'm sorry, (*person's name*)'s busy. Who's calling, please?

S: (*Student's name*).

T: Could you spell that, please?

S: (Spells name.)

Have the students work in pairs to call each other.

MAKE A BUSINESS CALL

- Tell the students to follow along in their books and listen as you play the cassette or read aloud the two possible business calls. Have them listen a second time as you read the conversations aloud with two students. Have each of the two students say a different B response.

- Read the second set of instructions aloud. Tell the students to work in pairs to take turns playing the two different roles. Have them model their exchanges on the sample conversation. Make sure they understand they are to act out two separate calls, one in the afternoon and the other in the evening.

- Call on different pairs of students to act out the calls for the class.

MAKE A BUSINESS CALL • LEAVE A MESSAGE

- Have the students look at the phone memo in their books as you point out the two yellow areas. Tell them to listen to the message and complete the phone memo with the caller's last name and telephone number.

- Play the cassette or read the tapescript aloud while the students write the answers.

- Call on different students to say the answers. Ask a student to write the answers on the board.

TAPESCRIPT AND ANSWERS

A Good afternoon, Worldwide Airways. May I help you?

B May I speak to Bonnie Reed, please?

A I'm sorry, she isn't here right now. May I take a message?

B Yes. Could you ask her to call Vicky Gonzalez?

A Could you spell your last name, please?

B G-O-N-Z-A-L-E-Z.

A Does she have your number, Ms. Gonzalez?

B No, she doesn't. It's area code 215 555-6263.

A 215 555-6263. I'll give her the message.

B Thank you.

- Have the students repeat the sentences in the first box after you. Point to the small blue box and explain that *her* refers to Mrs. Reed and *him* refers to Rob Vale.

- Tell the students to use the sentences in the first box to complete the conversation. They can write their answers on separate paper.

- Play the cassette or read the conversation aloud with a student as the rest of the students confirm their answers. Have a student write the answers on the board.

ANSWERS

Global Travel. May I help you?
She isn't here right now. May I take a message?
Certainly. Could you spell your last name, please?
Does she have your number?
I'll give her the message.

- Point to the box entitled *Some difficult sounds*. Model the letters and the example words for the students. Then have them repeat after you.

- Tell the students to work in pairs to act out the conversation. Have them take turns playing the two roles. Tell the students to ask to speak to a classmate instead of to Mrs. Reed and to use their own names instead of Rob Vale's.

- Call on different pairs to act out their conversations for the class.

FORMAL AND INFORMAL LANGUAGE

- Point out the blue box. Use the language in it to form complete sentences. For example, on the board, write:

  May I speak to Mrs. Baxter?
  Can I speak to Loretta?
  Is Jeff there?

  Use appropriate body language to indicate the formality and informality of the situation as you say each of the questions aloud. For example, sit up straight and slightly exaggerate the enunciation of the first question. Have the students repeat after you.

- Point to the two messages. Read them aloud and ask the students where the messages are from—home or work? (Pink message: work/Yellow message: home)

- Read aloud the two greetings. Explain that *Good morning. May I help you?* is formal and is used for answering a business phone.

- Have the students read over the exercise choices. Have them look for formal and informal language.

- Read aloud the first set of instructions. Explain that there are two telephone conversations in this exercise—one takes place at home and the other at work. Answer any questions students have about the procedure. Tell them to read the pairs of sentences and to choose *home* or *work* for each line.

- Have the students work in pairs to compare answers. Then have them confirm their answers as you play the cassette or read the conversations aloud with a student.

- Call on students to read their answers aloud. Ask two students to write the answers on the board.

  ANSWERS

work **B**	*work* **A**	*work* **B**
home **B**	*home* **A**	*home* **B**

home **A**	*home* **B**
work **A**	*work* **B**

home **B**	*work* **A**
work **B**	*home* **A**

- Have students work in pairs to take turns acting out the different parts in the conversations. Then tell the pairs to take turns acting out the different parts again, this time asking to speak to someone of their choice.

- Tell the pairs to write down the messages from their conversations and to confirm them with their partners. Then call on different pairs to act out their conversations for the class. They can write their messages on the board.

MAKE A TELEPHONE CALL • OBJECT PRONOUNS

- Tell students to study the frame. Read aloud the possible sentences from the frame and have the students repeat after you.

OPTION

Make up some sentences with object pronouns. Make them relevant to the students and say them aloud as you point to different students. For example:

I know you.
I know him/her.
You know me.
He knows her.

- Read the instructions aloud. Tell the students to read over the incomplete conversations.

- Have the students complete the conversations, using the object pronouns listed in exercise 5.

- Play the cassette or read the conversations aloud with a student as the rest of the students check their answers. Ask a student to write the answers on the board.

  ANSWERS
  1. **A** me
  2. **A** them, me
     B them
     A it

- Have the students act out the conversations in pairs. Call on different pairs to present their conversations to the class.

FOLLOW-UP

Students can write out the possible sentences from the frame in exercise 5.

WORKBOOK Lesson 40, pp. 52-54

4

▶ **Brian calls his friend Liz at work. Then he calls her at home. To find the two conversations, choose *home* or *work* for each line below.**

▶ **Listen to confirm your answers.**

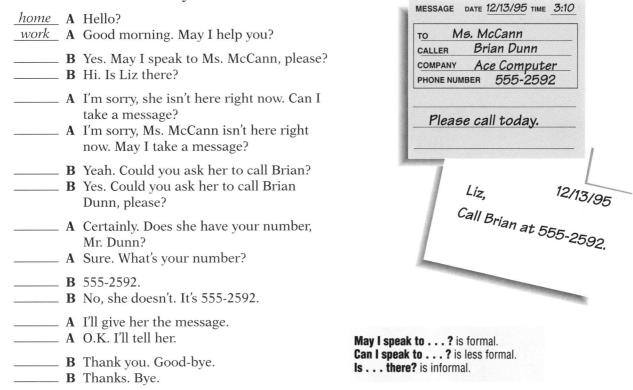

home	**A**	Hello?
work	**A**	Good morning. May I help you?
_____	**B**	Yes. May I speak to Ms. McCann, please?
_____	**B**	Hi. Is Liz there?
_____	**A**	I'm sorry, she isn't here right now. Can I take a message?
_____	**A**	I'm sorry, Ms. McCann isn't here right now. May I take a message?
_____	**B**	Yeah. Could you ask her to call Brian?
_____	**B**	Yes. Could you ask her to call Brian Dunn, please?
_____	**A**	Certainly. Does she have your number, Mr. Dunn?
_____	**A**	Sure. What's your number?
_____	**B**	555-2592.
_____	**B**	No, she doesn't. It's 555-2592.
_____	**A**	I'll give her the message.
_____	**A**	O.K. I'll tell her.
_____	**B**	Thank you. Good-bye.
_____	**B**	Thanks. Bye.

MESSAGE DATE 12/13/95 TIME 3:10

TO *Ms. McCann*
CALLER *Brian Dunn*
COMPANY *Ace Computer*
PHONE NUMBER *555-2592*

Please call today.

Liz,   *12/13/95*
Call Brian at 555-2592.

May I speak to . . . ? is formal.
Can I speak to . . . ? is less formal.
Is . . . there? is informal.

▶ **Act out the conversations with a partner. Ask to speak to someone of your choice.**

▶ **Take messages like the ones above.**

5 ▶ **Study the frame: Object Pronouns**

Laura Martin doesn't know	me. you. him. her. us. them.
I don't have	**it** (the number).

  6

▶ **Complete the conversations below with object pronouns.**

▶ **Listen to the conversations to check your answers.**

1. **A** Can I speak to Nina Janik, please?
   B Nina isn't here right now. Can I give ___*her*___ a message?
   A Well, Nina doesn't know _____ . My name is Marcella. I have a message from her sister in Prague.

2. **A** Hi, Suzy. Are your parents home?
   B No, they aren't.
   A Well, could you ask _____ to call _____ tonight? This is Mrs. Fox.
   B Sure. I'll tell _____ . Oh, what's your number?
   A I think they have _____ , but it's 555-6679.

41. Have a nice weekend!

1 ▶ **Match the activities below with the pictures.**
▶ **Working in groups, make a list of your classmates' leisure-time activities.**

1. go to the movies *c*
2. visit my parents
3. read a good book
4. watch TV

5. do my homework
6. go to the beach
7. go to the country
8. take it easy

9. play tennis
10. have dinner with friends

41. Have a nice weekend!

Tell the class about a leisure-time activity that you enjoy. If possible, show them pictures or photos of the activity or demonstrate it to the class. Call on students and ask them if they participate in the same activity.

LEISURE-TIME ACTIVITIES

- Have the students look at the list of activities. Answer any questions they have about the vocabulary.

- Have the students look at the pictures. Tell them to match the pictures with the activities. Have them write their answers on separate paper.

- Call on different students to read their answers aloud as you write them on the board.

  ANSWERS

2. j	5. a	8. e
3. g	6. d	9. b
4. i	7. f	10. h

- Divide the class into groups. Have each group make a list of the leisure-time activities of the group's members. Students in each group can write down the names of their group's members and the leisure-time activities next to the names.

- Call on members from different groups and have them tell the class about their group's leisure-time activities.

OPTION 1

Have the students close their books. Divide the class into small groups. Tell the groups to write down as many of the leisure-time activities as they can remember from the list on p. 72. The group with the most correct answers wins.

Then have the groups write down as many additional leisure-time activities as they can think of. Call on a member from each group to read aloud the group's list of activities and to write them on the board. The group with the most responses wins.

OPTION 2

Tell the students to demonstrate leisure-time activities for the class. Have them work in small groups to decide which activities they will demonstrate. Tell them to practice miming or acting out the activities. For example, two students can go through the motions of playing tennis. Other students might pretend they're watching television. Finally, have the group members act out their activities for the class. The class guesses the name of each leisure activity after it's acted out.

Note that the *-ing* form has not been taught yet. Since this form should be used when the students guess the names of the activities, you should write a sample "guess" on the board and have the class repeat it after you. For example:

They're playing tennis. OR Playing tennis.

TALK ABOUT PLANS • EXPRESSIONS OF FUTURE TIME

- Have the students look at Rob Vale's calendar and read the entries. Answer any questions they have about the language. Have them look at the calendar again as you play the cassette or read the conversation aloud.

- As you say the expressions in the first box, have the students repeat them. Read aloud the information in the second box.

- Read the second set of instructions aloud. Tell the students to work in pairs to act out the conversation, using personal information.

- Have the students move around the classroom to find out what two classmates are going to do this weekend. Tell them to use the conversation as a model.

- Call on different pairs to act out their conversations for the class. You or a student can write the leisure-time activities mentioned on the board.

- Go over the expressions of future time in the box with the students. Have them repeat the expressions after you. Use actual dates to give them examples of words such as *today*, *tomorrow*, *on Saturday*, etc.

- Have the students work in pairs. Tell them to look at Rob Vale's calendar and to imagine today is Wednesday, January 20, 1993. Tell them to take turns asking and answering questions 1-3. Then have them take turns asking and answering similar questions for items 4-6.

- Call on different pairs to say their exchanges for the class. The different partners who answer can write the answers on the board.

POSSIBLE ANSWERS

2. He's going to have dinner with Mrs. Reed.
3. He's going to take it easy.
4. What is he going to do this weekend?
   On Saturday, he's going to visit Fred.
   On Sunday, he's going to go to the beach.
5. What is he going to do next Wednesday?
   He's going to have dinner with his mom and dad.
6. What is he going to do next weekend?
   He's going to go to the country.

- Tell students to use separate paper to make a calendar for this week and next week. Have them use Rob Vale's calendar as a guide. Tell them to use personal information or to make up appointments.

- Have the students move around the classroom and use their calendars to interview three classmates. Tell them to find out their classmates' plans for this week and next week.

- Call on different students to report their findings to the class. You can also ask different students to copy their calendars on the board. Then ask other students to interview them.

FOLLOW-UP

Students can write out the exchanges in exercise 3.

WORKBOOK Lesson 41, pp. 55-56

JANUARY 1993

Monday 18

Tuesday 19

Wednesday 20
   see Citizen Kane at 8 P.M.

Thursday 21
   have dinner with Mrs. Reed

Friday 22
   evening—take it easy

Saturday 23   Sunday 24
   visit Fred   *go to the beach*

JANUARY 1993

Monday 25

Tuesday 26

Wednesday 27
   have dinner with Mom and Dad

Thursday 28

Friday 29
   evening—play tennis with Eva

Saturday 30   Sunday 31
   go to the country

2 ▶ **Look at Rob Vale's calendar as you listen to his conversation below.**
▶ **Act out the conversation using personal information. Find out what two classmates are going to do this weekend.**

Rob What are you going to do this weekend?
Amy I don't have any plans. What about you?
Rob On Saturday, I'm going to visit a friend.
And on Sunday, I'm going to go to the beach.
Amy Well, have a good time.
Rob Thanks. See you Monday.
Amy Bye.

Some ways to say good-bye

Good-bye. (Bye.) Have a good time.
Good night.   See you Monday.

Good night means **good-bye** and is used any time after the end of the work day.

 ▶ **Imagine that today is Wednesday. Answer questions 1-3 about Rob Vale.**
Then ask similar questions using the expressions of future time in items 4-6.

1. What is Rob going to do tonight?
   He's going to see Citizen Kane.

2. What is he going to do tomorrow evening?
3. What is he going to do Friday evening?
4. . . . this weekend?
5. . . . next Wednesday?
6. . . . next weekend?

Some expressions of future time

today	tomorrow
tonight	tomorrow night
this morning	tomorrow morning
this afternoon	tomorrow afternoon
this evening	tomorrow evening
this weekend	next weekend
on Saturday/Sunday/Monday . . .	

▶ **Make your own calendar for this week and next week.**
▶ **Using the expressions of future time in the box, find out three classmates' plans for this week and next week.**

42. Win a trip for two.

On a cold day in New York, George enters a contest for a trip to Florida. Then he runs into his friend Nick.

1. How to say it

Listen to the conversation.

give them	ask him	give him	give her
['gɪvðəm]	['æskəm]	['gɪvəm]	['gɪvər]

A Can I speak to Eric or Cora, please?
B They're not here. Can I give them a message?
A No, that's O.K. Is John there?
B No, he's at work.
A Could you please ask him to call Harold?
B O.K. I'll give him the message.
A Oh, and what about Mary? Is she there?
B No, she's at work, too. Can I give her a message?
A No. I'll call back later.

2. Listen in

Ayako Ono calls Arno's Coffee Shop and talks to Jeff. Read the questions below. Then listen to the phone conversation and answer the questions.

1. What day is George going to call back?
2. What's Ayako's phone number?

42. Win a trip for two.

WARM-UP

Have the students practice object pronouns. Read aloud the following sentences and have the students write *him*, *her*, or *them* for the persons' names in the sentences. Be sure to read at natural speed.

I can give George a message. (him)
Say hello to Loretta. (her)
I know Laura Martin and Louis Brown. (them)
I'll give Melissa the message. (her)
Ask Rob Vale to call me. (him)
I'm going to visit Mr. and Mrs. Vale. (them)

Write the sentences on the board. After you say each sentence, call on a student to say the sentence with the appropriate pronoun in place of the name(s).

1. How to say it

- Have the students repeat the reduced forms of the verbs + pronouns after you. Then write the verbs + pronouns on the board. Point to each of the pairs and call on students to say them. If necessary, repeat them after the students with the correct reduced pronunciation.

- Read the conversation aloud or play it on cassette. Then present it again and have the students repeat each line.

- Have the students practice the conversation in pairs. Move around the room and check their pronunciation.

OPTION

Divide the class into small groups. Give each group four slips of paper. On the board, write *ask him*, *give them*, *give her*, and *give him*. Tell the groups to write one verb + pronoun on each slip. Tell them you will play the cassette or read the conversation aloud and they should hold up the appropriate verb + pronoun after they hear it. Stop the cassette or leave a pause after you say each reduced form so that the groups can decide which slip of paper to hold up. To confirm their responses, point to the appropriate verb + pronoun on the board.

PRONUNCIATION NOTE

In American English, vowels in unstressed syllables often are pronounced [ə].

2. Listen in

- Read the instructions aloud as the students follow along in their books. Tell the students to read over the questions.

- Play the cassette or read the tapescript aloud. Tell the students to answer the questions on separate paper. Have them listen as many times as necessary.

- Have the students compare their answers with a partner. Call on a pair of students to read the questions and answers aloud. Write the answers on the board.

TAPESCRIPT
Jeff   Arno's Coffee Shop.
Ayako Hello! This is Ayako Ono. Is George there?
Jeff   No, he's not here right now. He isn't working today. Would you like him to call you on Monday?
Ayako Yes, please.
Jeff   Does he have your number?
Ayako Hmm. I'm not sure. It's 555-3478.
Jeff   555-3478. I'll give him the message.

ANSWERS
1. Monday
2. 555-3478

3. Conversation

BACKGROUND

George Arno enters a contest for a trip to Florida. Then he runs into his friend Nick Pappas. They strike up a conversation and make plans to watch the football game together.

LANGUAGE

Some (weather)... is used to point out that something (the weather) is unusually good or bad (in this case, "terrible").

...huh? is a casual way to ask for confirmation.

Well... has no actual meaning and is used to introduce a remark or as a filler to indicate hesitation.

...good luck! is a way to express the hope that someone will be fortunate and/or successful.

By the way... is used to introduce a new subject.

Hey is an informal expression used to attract attention.

Any time! is an informal response to *Thanks* or *Thank you* and means about the same as *You're welcome.*

...me too means *So do I.*

So long! is an informal way of saying "Good-bye."

PROCEDURE

- Point out George in the two illustrations on p. 74 and again with Nick in the illustration on p. 75. Make comments and ask questions about what's going on.

- Have the students follow along in their books as you play the cassette or read the conversation aloud. Answer any questions students have about vocabulary or structures.

OPTION

Have the students work in pairs. Tell them to take turns reading the parts of Nick and George.

4. Figure it out

True, False, or *It doesn't say?*

- Have the students read over the statements before they listen.

- Play the cassette or read the conversation aloud. Tell the students to answer *True, False,* or *It doesn't say.*

- Call on different students to say their answers aloud. Have a student write the answers on the board.

ANSWERS

1. It doesn't say.
2. False
3. True
4. True
5. False
6. True
7. It doesn't say.

5. Your turn

- Have the students follow along in their books as you read the instructions aloud. Ask a student to say who Loretta is. (She's George's wife.)

- Have the students work in pairs to play the roles of Loretta and Max. Tell the student who plays Loretta to write down the message from Max Shear. The following is a sample dialogue that you can write on the board and present with another student:

Loretta Arno's Coffee Shop.
Max May I speak to George, please?
Loretta George isn't here right now. May I take a message?
Max Yes. Please tell him to call Max Shear this afternoon.
Loretta Of course. Could you spell your last name?
Max Shear—S-H-E-A-R.
Loretta S-H-E-A-R.
Max Yes, that's right. And my phone number is 555-2276.
Loretta 555-2276. I'll give him the message.
Max Thank you. Good-bye.
Loretta Good-bye.

FOLLOW-UP

Students can write out exercise 1 on p. 74, substituting their own friends' or relatives' names for those in the exercise.

WORKBOOK Lesson 42, p. 57

3

Nick	Hi, George! Some weather, huh?
George	Yeah, it's terrible . . . but maybe I'll win a trip to Florida.
Nick	Win a trip to Florida?
George	Yeah, I just entered a contest.
Nick	Well, good luck!
George	By the way, your daughter Christine was in the coffee shop today.
Nick	Oh, yeah?
George	She sometimes comes in to talk to Jeff.
Nick	Jeff? Who's Jeff?
George	Well, you know, Jeff Hunt—the boy who works for me in the coffee shop.
Nick	Oh, yeah . . . well, he's a nice guy. Hey, George, are you going to watch the football game tomorrow night?
George	What a question! Of course I am!
Nick	Well, our TV isn't working. Could I . . .
George	Sure! Come over and watch the game with me. Bring Stella too!
Nick	Hey, thanks a lot, George.
George	Any time! Well, listen, I've got to get back.
Nick	Yeah, me too. Say hello to Loretta for me. Tell her to call Stella.
George	O.K. So long! See you tomorrow.

4. Figure it out

***True, False,* or *It doesn't say*?**

1. George is going to win a trip to Florida.
2. The weather is terrible in Florida.
3. Jeff and Christine are friends.
4. Nick is Christine's father.
5. George doesn't know Christine.
6. Nick is going to watch the football game with George.
7. Stella wants to watch the football game.

5. Your turn

Loretta answers the phone at Arno's and takes a message for George. The caller's name is Max Shear. Act out a possible conversation between Loretta and Max.

43.

Tips for Success on the Telephone ☎

By Amelia Peretti

You arrive at the airport in another country, but your luggage does not arrive with you. When the airport staff cannot find it, you go unhappily to your hotel room. Now you have to use the telephone for help.

Will someone at the airline help you quickly? Yes, if you are friendly and polite. Good manners are the key to success on the telephone. Here are a few suggestions:

• Speak slowly and pronounce your words clearly. You want the other person to understand you.

• Speak with a smile. People like to hear a pleasant voice.

• Always identify yourself right away. For example, if you make a business call, start with, "Hello, this is Bob Blair. May I speak to Carmen Rivera, please?" For an informal or personal call, you say, "Hi, this is Koji. Is Grace there, please?"

• Be sure to leave a complete message. You can say, "Please ask Ms. Rivera to call me at 555-6821 about our meeting tomorrow" or "Please ask Grace to give me a call about the party on Saturday."

• Finally, always thank the person you speak with. After all, he or she took the time to talk to you. Be sure to use the person's name if you know it. Say, "Thank you very much for your help, Ms. Rivera" or "Thanks a lot, Grace."

These are just a few telephone tips. Try them in *your* next phone call and watch what happens.✆

1. **Read the article. Then scan it again and say which of these suggestions it gives.**

1. Always give your name when you ask to speak to someone.
2. Speak slowly and clearly.
3. Always leave your phone number.
4. When you thank someone, use the person's name.
5. Always say "hello" and not "hi" when you ask to speak to someone.

2. **Do you agree with the tips for success in the article? Which are the most important? Are these tips useful in your country?**

43. Tips for Success on the Telephone

BACKGROUND

This article offers advice on using the telephone. It gives five suggestions to follow.

PROCEDURE

1. Read the article.

- Read the instructions aloud as the students read along in their books. Then have them silently read the exercise items and the article. Finally, you may want to play the cassette or read the article aloud as the students follow along in their books.

- Have the students scan the article. Call on different students to say *Yes* if the article gives the suggestion and *No* if it doesn't. Have a student write the answers on the board.

  ANSWERS
  1. Yes
  2. Yes
  3. No
  4. Yes
  5. No

2. Do you agree with the tips for success in the article?

- Read aloud the questions for exercise 2. Make sure the students understand.

- Have the students work in small groups to answer and discuss the questions. Go around the classroom and give help where needed.

- Call on different groups to share their answers with the class.

OPTION 1

Have the students underline or write down on separate paper any words they don't understand. Use gestures, realia, pictures, or words the students already know to help them understand the meanings of these words.

OPTION 2

Conduct an opinion poll to see which suggestion in the article the students rate as most important. Have a student say each suggestion aloud and then ask for a show of hands. Have another student tally the results on the board.

CULTURE CLOSE-UP

In the U.S., many people have answering machines that take messages for them in their absence or when they don't want to answer the phone. Many large companies also have answering machines that give the caller pre-recorded instructions on how to obtain different kinds of information. Some persons find this type of service to be very impersonal and even annoying.

FOLLOW-UP

Students can write down telephone tips that are useful in their country.

WORKBOOK Lesson 43, p. 58. When assigning the workbook activity, encourage students to write as complete a message as they can. Point out that Danai Aswin is a man.

Review of units 5-7

- Read aloud the first set of instructions and the information on the registration card as the students follow along in their books. Tell the students to copy the form on separate paper and complete it with personal information.

- Read the other instructions aloud. Tell the students to work with a partner. Have them exchange registration cards. Tell them to refer to the card they now hold as they introduce their partners to the class. Write a sample introduction on the board:

This is Eloida Jaico.
She's an accountant.

- Review the use of *in*, *on*, and *at* with specific locations. Read the instructions aloud to the students. Tell them to read over the paragraphs. Answer any questions they have about vocabulary or structures.

- Have the students work individually on the exercise. Then tell them to work in pairs to compare their answers.

- Have different students take turns reading aloud the sentences from the paragraphs. Have a student write the answers on the board.

ANSWERS
in, at, on, in, at, on, in, on

3

- Review singular and plural forms of nouns and the indefinite articles *a* and *an* by writing the following words on the board:

a teacher   teachers
an actor   actors

- Read the instructions aloud. Then have the students work individually to complete the sentences.

- Tell the students to check their answers with a partner. Call on students to read the answers aloud. Ask a student to write the answers on the board.

ANSWERS
2. waitresses
3. a receptionist
4. a cook
5. secretaries
6. an accountant
7. a doctor

OPTION

Have each student go to the board and on a line write his or her name, occupation, and country. The students can pretend they're from different countries and have different occupations. Point to a line of information on the board and say, for example, "Keiko is from Brazil. She's a doctor." Call on different students to make similar statements about their classmates by referring to the information on the board.

Review of units 5-7

1 ▶ **You're a guest at the Blue Water Hotel in Miami. Look at the registration card below. Then copy the form and complete it with personal information.**

The Blue Water Hotel
Miami, Florida

Date_____

Last Name _____ First Name _____

Address (Number and Street) _____

City _____ State _____ Zip Code _____ Country _____

Home Telephone _____ Business Telephone _____

Occupation _____ Place of Employment _____

▶ **Exchange registration cards with a partner.**

▶ **Introduce your partner to the class. Give his or her name and occupation.**

2 ▶ **Anna Stasiak is in Miami this week. Complete the paragraphs about her. Fill in the blanks with *in*, *on*, and *at*.**

Anna Stasiak is originally from Krakow, Poland, but she now lives and works ____ London, England. Anna works ____ the Polish Embassy ____ Weymouth Street. She is a translator and interpreter.

Right now, Anna is on vacation ____ Miami. She loves Miami and visits every year. This year she is a guest ____ the Blue Water Hotel ____ Collins Avenue. Anna likes tall buildings and the Blue Water Hotel is very tall. Anna is ____ Room 2234 ____ the twenty-second floor of the hotel.

3 ▶ **Complete the sentences about the staff at the Blue Water Hotel, using the correct singular or plural forms of the nouns in parentheses. Use *a* or *an* if necessary.**

1. Paulo Silva is _*a waiter*_ from Brazil. (waiter)
2. Judy Reinbeck is from Canada, and Maria Lopez is from Mexico. They're both _____ . (waitress)
3. Danielle Michaud is _____. She's from France. (receptionist)
4. Henri Dubois also speaks French. He's _____ from Haiti. (cook)
5. Mike Ito and Laura Conti are _____ . Mike is from California, and Laura is from New York. (secretary)
6. Bob Schubert is _____ from Miami. (accountant)
7. Lin Wang is _____ . She's from Taiwan. (doctor)

4 ► Imagine you're going to Miami on vacation and you meet another tourist on the flight. Introduce yourself and find out where he or she is from.

A Hi. My name's ———— .
B ————————— .
A Are you from Miami?
B ———— . ————————— ?
A I'm from ———— .

5 ► Write ten interview questions using the words below to help you. Be sure to use the correct forms of the present tense.

what	brother(s)	wife	parents	Chinese (Spanish, etc.)	speak	go	live	married
where	sister(s)	husband	you	school	have	do	work	

1. _____What do you do ?_____
2. _____
3. _____
4. _____
5. _____
6. _____
7. _____
8. _____
9. _____
10. _____

► Find a student you don't know very well. Interview your partner using the questions above. Write down his or her answers.
► Tell another classmate about your partner.

6 ► Talk about your plans for the weekend with a partner.

A ————————— ?
B On Saturday, ———————— .
   And on Sunday, ———————— . What about you?
A ———————— .
B Well, have a nice weekend.
A ———————— .

7 ► Complete the notes. Fill in the blanks with *me, you, him, her, it, us,* and *them.*

1.
Jim,
I'm at the movies.
Mrs. King is going
to call later.
Could you ask
_____ to call
_____ at the
office tomorrow
morning? Thanks,
Alan

2.
Emilio:
Mr. Garvey
called. Please
call _____ at
home tonight.

Bill

3.
Maria,
How about a
movie? I'll call
_____ tonight.

Alex

4.
Taro:
What is Noriko Kitano's
phone number? I don't
have _____ .
Steve

5.
Mike,
Aunt Norma and Uncle Frank are in town
this weekend. Please call _____ at 555-
4693.

Mother

6.
Bob and Ann,
Please call _____ . It's
very important.
Thanks,
Susan and Martin

- Read the instructions aloud. Act out the conversation with a student in front of the class. For example:

  A Hi. My name's Carlos.
  B Hi. My name's Bob.
  A Are you from Miami?
  B Yes, I am. Where are you from?
  A I'm from Chile.

- Tell the students to work in pairs to take turns acting out the two roles in the exchange. If the level of the students is high enough, they can expand on the conversation.

- Call on different pairs to act out their conversations for the class. Check their work.

- Read the instructions and the first question to the students. Review the present tense. Help the students make up some additional questions using the words in the box.

- Have the students write the ten interview questions on separate paper. Tell them to leave spaces for answers.

- Have them find a classmate they don't know very well to interview with the questions. Tell them to write down the answers.

- Have the students choose another classmate to report their findings to. Provide an example of what they should say:

  1. Carlos is a mechanic.
  2. He works at Bob's Garage.

  Go around the classroom and check their work.

- Tell the students to read over the instructions and the incomplete conversation. Help them come up with the opening question and write it on the board—for example, *What are you going to do this weekend?*

- Have the students work in pairs to take turns practicing the two roles in the conversation. Tell them to write their exchanges down on separate paper.

- Call on different pairs to present their exchanges to the class. Have a pair of students write their exchanges on the board. Check their work.

- Review object pronouns with the students by going over the frame on p. 71. Then read the instructions aloud.

- Tell the students to complete the notes by filling in the missing pronouns. Then have them check their answers with a partner.

- Call on different students to read the notes aloud for the class. Have a student write the missing words on the board.

  ANSWERS
  1. her, me
  2. him
  3. you
  4. it
  5. them
  6. us

OPTION

Have the students work in pairs to write each other notes. Tell them to use at least one object pronoun. Then tell them to exchange notes and read them aloud to each other. Go around the classroom and check their work. Call on pairs with "interesting" notes to write them on the board and to read them aloud.

- Tell the students to read the instructions and the incomplete messages. Play the cassette or read the tapescript aloud while the students complete the two messages. Have them listen again to check their work.

- Call on different students to read the completed messages aloud. Write the answers on the board.

TAPESCRIPT

A Hello?

B Hello. Can I speak to Marta, please?

A She isn't here right now. Can I take a message?

B Yes, this is her friend Mary Boostani. I'm in town for the week.

A Does she have your number, Mary?

B No, she doesn't. I'm at the Blue Water Hotel, room 402. The number there is 555-7498.

A Room 402, 555-7498. I'll give her the message.

B Thanks a lot.

A Blue Water Hotel. May I help you?

B Yes. May I speak to Mary Boostani in room 402, please?

A One moment, please.

A I'm sorry, there's no answer. May I take a message?

B Yes. This is Marta Lorenzo. My number is 555-0931.

A 555-0931. And could you spell your last name, please?

B Yes. It's L-O-R-E-N-Z-O.

A I'll leave a message.

B Thank you.

ANSWERS

Mary	402	555-7498
Lorenzo	Lorenzo	555-0931

- Read the instructions aloud to the students. Write the name *Roberto Mendez* on the board and explain that he's the person A is trying to reach.

- Tell the students to read over the incomplete conversation. Answer any questions they have about vocabulary or structures. If necessary, translate the Spanish in B's first line: "Good morning, Aztec (Export Company). May I help you?" Tell the students to work individually to complete the conversation.

- Tell the students to work in pairs. Have them act out the conversation. You can tell them to sit back to back and simulate a telephone conversation.

- Call on a pair of students to act out the conversation for the class. Have another pair write the exchanges on the board.

POSSIBLE ANSWERS

A Do you speak English?

A Yes. May I speak to Roberto Mendez?

A Yes, this is (*student's name*).

A *A says and then spells last name.*

A Yes, he does. OR No, he doesn't. It's (*student's telephone number*).

- Read aloud the instructions for exercise 10A on p. 79 and 10B on p. 80. If any students need help understanding how to do the exercise, ask the first question about Melinda Chan and have the students answer by looking at the article on p. 80.

- Have the students work in pairs. They can take turns playing the roles of Student A and Student B.

- Call on different pairs of students to ask and answer the questions about the newspaper articles. Check their work and have a student help you write the pairs' sentences on the board.

POSSIBLE 10A ANSWERS

A Where is Melinda Chan from?

B She's from Taipei.

A How old is she?

B She's 19 (years old).

A What languages does she sing in?

B She sings in Taiwanese, Chinese, French, and English.

A Where does she live?

B She lives in a small apartment.

A Does she live with her family?

B Yes. She lives with her parents.

8 ► Listen to the telephone calls and complete the two messages.

Marta— _____ Boostani is at the Blue Water Hotel, Room _____. The phone number is _____.

Mom

WHILE YOU WERE OUT

FOR Ms. Boostani   **DATE** 6/25/93
FROM Marta _____ **TIME** 2:30 P.M.

Please call Marta _____
at _____ .

 9 ► You work in Miami and you're trying to reach Roberto Mendez at the Aztec Export Company in Mexico City. Complete the conversation below.
► Act out the conversation in pairs.

A (*Dials number*) *Rrring, rrring*
B *Buenos días, Aztec. ¿Dígame?*
A _____ ?
B Yes, I do. May I help you?
A _____ ?
B I'm sorry, but he's busy right now. May I give him a message?
A _____ ?
B Could you spell your last name, please?
A _____ .
B And does he have your telephone number?
A _____ .
B Thank you. I'll give him the message.

 10A ► Student A follows the instructions below.
Student B follows the instructions on p. 80.

Student A Read the newspaper articles below. Ask your partner questions about Melinda Chan to fill in the blanks. Then answer your partner's questions about Eduardo Sanchez.

The Miami Independent

July 19, 1993

In Miami This Week . . .

MELINDA CHAN TO SING AT ALLIGATOR CLUB

The popular singer Melinda Chan, from _____ , is going to be at the Alligator Club in the Blue Water Hotel on Friday and Saturday, July 23 and 24. She will sing songs from her new hit record *Love Is the Answer*.

Melinda, who is only _____ years old, is popular in many countries around the world. She sings in four languages—Taiwanese, Chinese, _____ , and _____ . "I like languages," she says. "For me, a new language is a new world."

Melinda is rich and famous, but she still lives in a small _____ with her _____ . "My family is very important to me," she says, "and I like my neighbors. I don't want to move."

Melinda likes to travel. This is her first visit to Miami. Next weekend Melinda is going to California to sing in Hollywood. "I'm very excited about that!" she says.

COLOMBIAN COFFEE BUSINESS GOOD IN JAPAN

Eduardo Sanchez, from Colombia, is a very busy international businessman. He visits countries in North and South America, Europe, and Asia and sells coffee. Eduardo is very successful. He is only 38 years old, but he is already a millionaire. "I like my job," he says.

Eduardo speaks Spanish, English, and Japanese. "Japanese is very difficult," he says, "but I try."

Japan is an important country for Eduardo. "The Japanese like coffee and they have many popular coffee houses and cafes in Tokyo, Osaka, Kyoto, and other big cities."

Eduardo lives in Cali, Colombia, the city where he was born, with his wife, Gloria, his son, Carlos, and his daughter, Silvia.

Eduardo is here in Miami this week on vacation. Next week he is going to travel to Italy and Spain.

10B ▶ Student B follows the instructions below.
Student A follows the instructions on p. 79.

Student B Read the newspaper articles below. Answer your partner's questions about Melinda Chan. Then ask your partner questions about Eduardo Sanchez to fill in the blanks.

The Miami Independent

July 19, 1993

In Miami This Week . . .

MELINDA CHAN TO SING AT ALLIGATOR CLUB

The popular singer Melinda Chan, from _____ , is going to be at the Alligator Club in the Blue Water Hotel on Friday and Saturday, July 23 and 24. She will sing songs from her new hit record *Love Is the Answer*.

Melinda, who is only _____ years old, is popular in many countries around the world. She sings in four languages—Taiwanese, Chinese, _____ , and _____ . "I like languages," she says. "For me, a new language is a new world."

Melinda is rich and famous, but she still lives in a small apartment with her parents. "My family is very important to me," she says, "and I like my neighbors. I don't want to move."

Melinda likes to travel. This is her first visit to Miami. Next weekend Melinda is going to California to sing in Hollywood. "I'm very excited about that!" she says.

COLOMBIAN COFFEE BUSINESS GOOD IN JAPAN

Eduardo Sanchez, from _____ , is a very busy international _____ . He visits countries in North and South America, Europe, and Asia and sells coffee. Eduardo is very successful. He is only _____ years old, but he is already a millionaire. "I like my job," he says.

Eduardo speaks _____ , _____ , and Japanese. "Japanese is very difficult," he says, "but I try."

Japan is an important country for Eduardo. "The Japanese like coffee and they have many popular coffee houses and cafes in Tokyo, Osaka, Kyoto, and other big cities."

Eduardo lives in _____ , Colombia, the city where he was born, with his _____ , Gloria, his son, Carlos, and his _____ , Silvia.

Eduardo is here in Miami this week on vacation. Next week he is going to travel to _____ and _____ .

---

 11 ▶ Write conversations for these people at Arno's Coffee Shop, using the words in parentheses. Be sure to use the correct forms of the present of *be* and the simple present.
▶ Act out the conversations with a partner.

1. Maggie Sloane and Nick Pappas meet for the first time.

    Nick (where?)
Maggie (Brooklyn Hospital.)
    Nick (nurse?)
Maggie (lab technician.)

    Nick *Where do you work?*
Maggie *I work at Brooklyn Hospital. . . .*

2. Nick then talks to Maggie's friend Ruth Aguirre.

Nick (what?)
Ruth (biologist.)
Nick (Brooklyn Hospital?)
Ruth (Brooklyn College.)

3. Jeff Hunt wants to call Christine Pappas about some homework. He calls a friend, Gail Gooden, for her phone number.

Jeff (*Dials number*) *Rrring, rrring*
Gail (Hello?)
Jeff (there?)
Gail (Gail.)
Jeff (Jeff.)
Gail (how?)
Jeff (fine.) (Christine's phone number?)
Gail (555-3217.)

POSSIBLE 10B ANSWERS

A Where is Eduardo Sanchez from?
B He's from Colombia.

A What's his occupation?/What does he do?
B He's a businessman.

A How old is he?
B He's 38 (years old).

A What languages does he speak?
B He speaks Spanish, English, and Japanese.

A Where does he live?
B He lives in Cali, Colombia.

A Does he live with his parents?
B No. He lives with wife, his son, and his daughter.

A Where is he going to travel to next week?
B He's going to travel to Italy and Spain.

11

- Read the instructions aloud. Then have the students read over the conversation introductions and clues. Read the first exchange aloud with a student.

- Have the students work in pairs. Tell them to first write down the conversations and then to act them out.

- Call on different pairs to act out their conversations for the class. Have other pairs write them on the board. Check their work.

POSSIBLE ANSWERS

1.   **Nick** Are you a nurse?
   Maggie No, I'm a lab technician.

2.   **Nick** What do you do?
   Ruth I'm a biologist.
   Nick Do you work at Brooklyn Hospital?
   Ruth No, I don't. I work at Brooklyn College.

3.   **Gail** Hello?
   Jeff Hello. Is Gail there?
   Gail This is Gail.
   Jeff Oh, hi. This is Jeff.
   Gail How are you, Jeff?
   Jeff I'm fine, thanks. Do you have Christine's telephone number?
   Gail Yes. It's 555-3217.

WORKBOOK Review of units 5-7, pp. 59-60

PREVIEW

Before you begin teaching, go over the functions/themes, language, and forms in the chart. This will give you a preview of what you will encounter as you guide the students through the unit.

Preview the conversations.

- Have the students look at the first illustration. Point out Amanda and read aloud her statement. Discuss the questions with the students. Ask them if they have ever lost anything.

- Have the students look at the second illustration as you read the exchange aloud. Discuss the sentences with the students. Compliment different students on something they're wearing.

CULTURE CLOSE-UP

In the U.S. it is common for someone who has been complimented to express thanks. The person complimented will sometimes add a remark related to the compliment such as "It was a gift" or "I bought it in Mexico."

PREVIEW

FUNCTIONS/THEMES	LANGUAGE	FORMS
Clothing and personal belongings	What color are her gloves?	Colors
Compliment someone	That's a nice blouse.	Demonstrative pronouns (*that, those*)
Look for a lost item	They're on the table. I don't have my keys!	*In, on, under,* and *behind* Possessive adjectives
Ask where something is Give directions	Is there a telephone near here? There's one upstairs.	*There is*
Talk about the past	Where were you?	The past of *be*

Preview the conversations.

What's Amanda's problem? What do you think she does?

The man above is giving a friend a compliment. Do you compliment your friends? When?

44. Lost and Found

 Amanda Kelly goes to the hospital to see her doctor.

A

Nurse Here you are, Mrs. Kelly. Your next appointment with Dr. Wood is on Tuesday, April 6th, at ten o'clock.
Mrs. Kelly Thank you.
Nurse By the way, that's a nice dress. You look good in green.
Mrs. Kelly Oh, thank you. It's my favorite color. Uh . . . is there a pay phone on this floor?
Nurse Yes, there's one next to the elevators.
Mrs. Kelly Which way are the elevators?
Nurse Down the hall on the right. Just follow the blue line.
Mrs. Kelly Thank you.
Nurse Good-bye, Mrs. Kelly. See you next month.
Mrs. Kelly Bye.

B

Woman Excuse me, I found this wallet on the floor over there.
Nurse Oh, thank you. I'll take it to the Lost and Found.

44. Lost and Found

Practice different formulaic expressions with the students. Move around the classroom and greet different students, compliment them, prompt them to reply, etc. For example:

T: Hello, (*student's name*). How are you?
S: Fine.
T: That's a nice necklace!
S: Thank you.

BACKGROUND

Amanda Kelly has just had an appointment with her doctor. She loses her wallet, but fortunately someone finds it.

LANGUAGE

By the way... is another way of saying "incidentally." It's used to change the subject of the conversation.

...look good in (green) means a certain color (green) suits or is flattering to the person.

Uh is used to express uncertainty or hesitation.

Down (the hall) means somewhere along (the hall).

...over there indicates a location a slight distance away, as in *on the other side of the street, room, etc.*

There you are. is another way of saying "You're finally here."

...after six is short for *after six o'clock.*

...remember? is short for *Do you remember?*

What's wrong? is another way of saying "What's the problem?"

...by any chance means *maybe* or *possibly.*

PROCEDURE

- Point out and say the names of the different characters in the pictures. Make statements and ask simple questions about what's going on. For example:

  In the first picture, Mrs. Kelly is in the doctor's office.
  Where's Mrs. Kelly in the next picture?

- Play the cassette or read the conversations aloud as the students listen with their books closed. Have them listen again as they follow along in their books. (If you are reading the conversations aloud, speak at a normal speed and perform each role as realistically as possible. Show the change in speakers by shifting your position or by pointing to the appropriate character in the illustrations.)

- Students can listen to the conversations as many times as they need to in order to understand the language introduced. Before they listen for the second time, have them go over the questions in exercise 1 of **Figure it out**. This will focus their attention on specific details of the conversations. They can go over exercise 2 before listening a third time.

- Make sure the students understand what happens from one picture to the next. For example, see if they understand what happens between D and E (Mrs. Kelly decides to call Lost and Found at the hospital).

CULTURE CLOSE-UP

Many public places such as airports, hospitals, office complexes, and shopping malls in the U.S. have Lost and Found departments where possessions left on the premises can be claimed by their owners. The owner of a lost item can call or go to the Lost and Found and identify the item and then recover it.

Figure it out

1. Listen to the conversations. Say *true* or *false*.

- Have the students read the statements to themselves before they listen.

- Read the conversations aloud or play them on cassette. Tell the students to cover the dialogue boxes and to look only at the pictures as they listen. Have them answer *True* or *False* on separate paper.

- Tell the students to compare and discuss their answers with a partner. Then call on different students to read the statements and their answers aloud. Have a student write the answers on the board.

  ANSWERS
  2. True
  3. False
  4. True

2. Listen again. Match.

- Tell the students to read over the sentences. Then have them listen to the conversations again. Tell them to match each sentence in the left column with the correct response in the right column. Have them draw lines in their books or write the answers on separate paper.

- Have the students work in pairs to compare their answers and to practice the exchanges. Call on different pairs to read the matched sentences aloud. Ask a student to write the answers on the board.

  ANSWERS
  2. b
  3. d
  4. e
  5. a

FOLLOW-UP

Students can write out the exchanges in exercise 2.

WORKBOOK Lesson 44, p. 61

C

Mr. Kelly Amanda! There you are. It's after six. Where were you? I was worried.
Mrs. Kelly I was at the doctor's office, remember?
Mr. Kelly Oh, that's right. Is everything O.K.?
Mrs. Kelly Yes, everything's fine. How was your day?
Mr. Kelly Not bad.

D

Mrs. Kelly Oh, no!
Mr. Kelly What's wrong?
Mrs. Kelly I don't have my wallet!

E

Clerk Lost and Found. May I help you?
Mrs. Kelly Yes, this is Amanda Kelly. I lost my wallet this afternoon. Do you have it by any chance?
Clerk Let's see. . . . What color is it?
Mrs. Kelly Red.
Clerk Just one moment, please. . . . Yes, it's here, Mrs. Kelly.
Mrs. Kelly Oh, what a relief! (*to husband*) He has it there.

LOST AND FOUND

Figure it out

1. Listen to the conversations. Say *true* or *false*.

1. Mrs. Kelly's wallet is blue. *False*
2. Mrs. Kelly's favorite color is green.
3. Mrs. Kelly lost her wallet in the elevator.
4. Mrs. Kelly's husband was worried.

2. Listen again. Match.

1. You look good in green.   a. Red.
2. Is there a pay phone on   b. There's one next
   this floor?   to the elevators.
3. Which way are the   c. Oh, thank you.
   elevators?   d. Down the hall on
4. How was your day?   the right.
5. What color is it?   e. Not bad.

45. That's a nice dress!

 1 ▶ **Look at the picture. Match the questions and answers.**
▶ **Listen to check your work.**

1. What color is Angela's dress?
2. What color are her gloves?
3. What color is Michael's suit?
4. What color are his shoes?

a. They're black.
b. It's blue.
c. They're brown.
d. It's gray.

| Angela**'s** dress | ➡ | **her** dress |
| Michael**'s** suit | ➡ | **his** suit |

2 ▶ **Ask and answer questions about the people in the picture.**

3 ▶ **Describe someone in your class. The other students will guess the person.**

A His pants are blue. His shirt is yellow and white. And his shoes are brown.
B Is it Nick?
A Yes, it is. (No, it isn't. It's John.)

4 ▶ **Listen to the descriptions of the people in the picture. Who is it?**

1. _____
2. _____
3. _____
4. _____

 5 ▶ **The four people above are talking. Listen and complete their conversations.**

1. **Kevin** That's a nice _____ . You look good in _____ .
   Angela Thank you.

Singular	Plural
That's a nice hat.	**Those are** nice gloves.
It was a gift.	**They were** a gift.

2. **Michael** Those are beautiful _____ .
   Carla Thanks. They were a gift.

▶ **Compliment each of your classmates on a personal belonging or item of clothing.**

84 Unit 8

45. That's a nice dress!

WARM-UP

Have the students follow along in their books as you point to the twelve circles and name the colors. Point again and have the students repeat the names of the colors.

CLOTHING AND PERSONAL BELONGINGS • COLORS

- Point out the blue box to the students. Read aloud the phrases in the box as you hold up your book and point to the picture of Angela's dress and Michael's suit. Point again and say "This is Angela's dress. It's her dress. This is Michael's suit. It's his suit." Substitute students' names and articles of clothing and say the sentences again as you point to the students' clothes.

- Have the students read over the exercise items. Then read the instructions aloud. Tell the students to write their answers on separate paper.

- Have the students compare their answers with a partner. Then read the exchanges aloud or play the cassette as students check their work. Write the answers on the board.

ANSWERS

1. b   2. c   3. d   4. a

 (item 2 marker)

- Have the students repeat the names of the four people in the picture after you. Then point to the different items in the picture as you say the names of the items aloud. Point again and have the students repeat after you. If possible, point out the same items in the classroom and have the class repeat the names after you.

- Read the instructions aloud. Have the students work in pairs to take turns asking and answering the questions about the people in the picture. Tell them to model their exchanges on those in exercise 1.

- Go around the class and check students' work. Call on different pairs to present their exchanges to the class.

3

- Read aloud the sample conversation with another student. Then read aloud the instructions. Give the students time to move around the classroom to take note of what their classmates are wearing. You can have them write their descriptions on separate paper.

- Ask a student to describe another student to the class. Have the other students guess who the person is. Call on other students and continue the practice.

4

- Tell the students to carefully examine the picture as you play the cassette or read the tapescript. Tell them to identify the people and write their names in their books or on separate paper. Have them listen again if necessary.

- Call on different students to say the answers aloud. Have another student write the answers on the board.

TAPESCRIPT AND ANSWERS

1. Her skirt is purple and her blouse is white. She has a red scarf and red socks. Let's see, what else? Oh, yes, her earrings are silver. (Carla)
2. His suit is gray and his shirt is white. His tie is green, and he has a brown briefcase. (Michael)
3. His jacket is green and his sweater is yellow. His pants are blue. Oh, yes, and he has red glasses. (Kevin)
4. Her shoes are black. Her hat and her dress are blue. Her coat is red and she has a red umbrella, too. (Angela)

COMPLIMENT SOMEONE

 (item 5 marker)

- Have the students study the frame. Read aloud the sentences in the frame and have the students repeat them after you. Point to singular and plural items in the picture and say similar sentences. Answer any questions students have about the sentence structures.

- Tell the students to read over the incomplete conversations. Then have them listen to the conversations and write down the missing words on separate paper.

- Have the students compare their answers with a partner. Then call on a pair to read the conversations aloud. Ask a student to write the missing words on the board.

ANSWERS

1. dress, blue   2. earrings

- Read aloud the second set of instructions. Have the students work in groups. Tell them to take turns complimenting each member of their group.

WORKBOOK Lesson 45, pp. 62-63

46. I lost my keys!

WARM-UP

Go around the classroom and pretend you've lost something. After looking for it, pretend to find it. For example:

Oh, no! I lost my book. …
(*Finding book*) Here it is. What a relief!

LOOK FOR A LOST ITEM • *IN*, *ON*, *UNDER*, AND *BEHIND*

- Point to the different locations in the picture as you say the expressions aloud. Have the students repeat the expressions after you.

- Tell the students to read over the incomplete conversation. Then have them complete it with the appropriate expressions. Have them write their answers on separate paper.

- So the students can check their answers, have them listen to the conversation as many times as necessary. Ask two students to write the answers on the board.

- Have the students work in pairs to act out the conversation. Go around the classroom and check their work. Call on a pair to present the conversation to the class.

  ### ANSWERS
  A on the coffee table
  A under the desk
  A behind the sofa
  B in the closet

OPTION

Practice the prepositional phrases from the lesson by placing different objects in different locations in the classroom. Point to the objects and have the students repeat the locations after you. For example, point to a pencil placed under a desk as you say "The pencil is under the desk."

- Tell the students to look at the pictures as you read the phrases under the pictures. Then have them repeat the phrases after you. Next have them listen to the sample conversation.

- Tell the students to work in pairs. Have them practice the sample conversation aloud. Then tell them to use the information in the pictures to make up similar conversations. Go around the classroom and check their work.

- Call on different pairs to present the conversations to the class so you can check their

work. Have different pairs write the different conversations on the board.

POSSIBLE PARTIAL ANSWERS
A I lost my shoes.
B They're over there behind the door.

A I lost my keys.
B They're in your pocket.

A I lost my glasses.
B They're over there on the desk.

A I lost my credit card.
B It's over there under the sofa.

LOOK FOR A LOST ITEM • POSSESSIVE ADJECTIVES

- Have the students study the frame as you read aloud the heading and possible sentences. Answer any questions they have.

OPTION

As you read aloud the possible sentences, act them out. For example, gesture frustration and point to yourself as you say "I lost my gloves." Then point to a student as you say "You lost your gloves." Point to a male student as you say "He lost his gloves," etc. Say the sentences again and have the students repeat.

- Have the students look at the illustration and read over the incomplete sentences. Read the instructions aloud.

- Tell the students to complete the sentences with the appropriate possessive adjectives from exercise 3. Have them fill in the blanks or write their answers on separate paper.

- Have the students compare their answers with a partner. Then call on different students to read the sentences aloud. Ask a student to write the answers on the board.

  ### ANSWERS
  my, our, her, their, your

OPTION

Have the students work in groups to act out a situation like the one in the illustration. Tell each group to appoint a student to play the role of the Lost and Found employee. Have the other group members pretend they're trying to recover lost items. Call on a group to act out their conversations for the class.

WORKBOOK Lesson 46, p. 64

46. I lost my keys!

LOOK FOR A LOST ITEM • *IN, ON, UNDER,* AND *BEHIND*

1 ▶ Complete the conversation with the expressions in the picture.
▶ Listen to check your answers.
▶ Act out the conversation with a partner.

A Hurry! We're late!
B Wait. I don't have my keys.
A They're right there _____ .
B You're right. But where's my wallet?

A Is that it _____ ?
B Yes. Thanks. Now I just need my coat and hat.
A Look. Your hat is _____ .
B Great! And here's my coat . . . _____ .

in the closet

on the coffee table

under the desk

behind the sofa

2 ▶ Listen to the conversation below.
▶ Practice similar conversations using the information in the pictures.

A Oh, no!
B What's wrong?
A I lost my gloves.
B They're over there on the table.
A Oh, what a relief!

gloves on the table

shoes behind the door

keys in my pocket

glasses on the desk

credit card under the sofa

LOOK FOR A LOST ITEM • POSSESSIVE ADJECTIVES

3 ▶ Study the frame.

4 ▶ Fill in the blanks with the correct possessive adjectives.

Possessive adjectives

I		my	
You		your	
He		his	
She	lost	her	gloves.
We		our	
They		their	

I lost _____ glasses.

My wife and I lost _____ traveler's checks.

My daughter lost _____ umbrella.

These people lost _____ passports.

Here's _____ wallet, sir.

47. Locations in a building

ASK WHERE SOMETHING IS • GIVE DIRECTIONS

 1 ▶ **Answer the questions using the pictures below.**
▶ **Listen to check your answers.**

1. Is there a telephone near here? *Yes. There's one upstairs.*
2. Excuse me. Where's the drinking fountain? *It's down the hall on the left.*
3. Excuse me. Which way are the restrooms?
4. Is there a cafeteria here?
5. Which way is the exit?
6. Excuse me. Which way are the elevators?

Is there a cafeteria here?
Yes, **there's one** downstairs.
No, **there isn't**.

upstairs

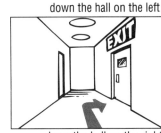

down the hall on the left

over there

downstairs

down the hall on the right

that way

2 ▶ **Ask and answer questions about the places in the floor plan below.**

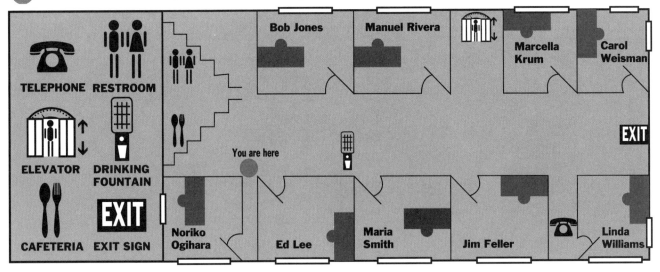

3 ▶ **Talk with your classmates.**

Ask where places are in your school building. Use
the questions in the box or your own questions.

Where are the restrooms?
Is there a drinking fountain on this floor?
Which way is the exit?
Is there a cafeteria near here?

47. Locations in a building

WARM-UP

Ask the students the locations of different personal items in the classroom. Use *Where's...?* and *Where are...?* For example:

T: Where's your dictionary?
S: It's on my desk.
T: Where are our coats?
S: They're in the closet.

ASK WHERE SOMETHING IS • GIVE DIRECTIONS

- Introduce *there is*. Have the students look at the blue box as you read the sentences aloud. Answer any questions students have. Explain that the word *there* in the sentences doesn't have any meaning in itself.

- Tell the students to examine the pictures as you read aloud the words under them. Then have the students read over the exercise items. Read aloud the first two items with a student. You may want to make sure students can distinguish the yes-no from the information (wh-) questions.

- Tell the students to use the pictures to answer the questions. Have them write their answers on separate paper.

- Have the students work in pairs to compare answers. Then have them listen to check their answers. Ask different students to write the answers on the board.

ANSWERS
3. They're over there.
4. Yes. There's one downstairs.
5. It's down the hall on the right.
6. They're that way.

LANGUAGE NOTE

The word *there* in sentences such as *There's one downstairs* has no meaning in itself. It's called a nonreferential or "dummy" subject. Many languages like Spanish and Italian do not have "dummy" subjects, with the result that speakers of these languages often forget to include them in English.

- Have the students examine the floor plan as you read aloud the questions in the box at the bottom of the page. Call on a student to answer the first question for the class.

- Read the instructions aloud. Then have the students work in pairs to take turns asking and answering questions about the places on the floor plan. Point out the red dot on the floor plan and explain that *You are here* means this is the location they should pretend they're at. Tell them to begin with the questions in the box. Remind them to ask additional questions such as *Where's Bob Jones's office?*

- Go around the classroom and check students' work, giving help when needed. Call on different pairs to present their exchanges to the class. Ask different pairs to write the exchanges on the board for you to check.

SAMPLE ANSWERS
A Where are the restrooms?
B They're upstairs.

A Is there a drinking fountain on this floor?
B Yes. It's over there.

A Where is Bob Jones's office?
B It's across the hall.

- Read aloud the instructions and the two sentences of additional information. Tell the students to move around the classroom to ask their classmates the location of different places in the school.

- Move around the classroom and check the students' work, giving help when needed. Have different students present their exchanges to the class.

FOLLOW-UP

Students can write out the exchanges in exercise 2 and/or exercise 3.

WORKBOOK Lesson 47, p. 65

48. Where were you?

WARM-UP

Have the students practice questions and answers with *where*. Ask them where classmates, relatives, and friends are. For example:

T: Where's (*student's name*)?
S: He/She's over there.

T: Where's your father?
S: He's at work.

TALK ABOUT THE PAST • THE PAST OF *BE*

- Introduce the past tense. Use a word signaling the past tense with one of the sentences from the frames—for example, write on the board and say "We weren't (were) at school yesterday." Translate *yesterday* if necessary.

- Have the students study the frames as you read aloud the headings and possible sentences. Answer any questions they have.

- Tell the students to read over the incomplete conversations. Answer any questions they have about vocabulary or structures.

- Have the students complete the conversations. Tell them to write their answers in the book or on separate paper.

- So the students can check their answers, have them listen to the conversations as many times as necessary. Ask two students to write the answers on the board.

- Have the students work in pairs to act out the conversations. Go around the classroom and check their work. Call on different pairs to present the conversations to the class.

ANSWERS
1. **B** was, was
   A was
   B wasn't
2. **B** were
   A were
3. **A** weren't, were
   B were
   A was
   B was

- Tell the students to look over the illustration. Point out the teacher's facial expression, the time written on the board, and the time on the clock on the wall. See if the students can identify the four places pictured at the top of the illustration (hall, water fountain, restroom, cafeteria).

- Have the students listen to the sample conversation and then repeat it after you. Say the names of the students in the illustration and have the class repeat after you.

- Have the students work in pairs to act out the conversations that the teacher has with the students in the picture. Tell the students to take turns playing the role of the teacher and the students. Tell them to use the sample conversation as a guide. Go around the class and check the students' work.

ANSWERS
Teacher Todd and Gina, you're late. Where were you?
Todd and
Gina We were in the hall.

Teacher Burt, you're late. Where were you?
Burt I was at the drinking fountain.

Teacher Ralph, you're late. Where were you?
Ralph I was in the cafeteria.

CULTURE CLOSE-UP

Punctuality is very important in American society. In the U.S., people are expected to be on time for scheduled events. Arriving late for classes, meetings, or appointments is usually frowned upon, and the person who arrives late may be reprimanded. Being on time is expected even at social gatherings such as dinner parties.

FOLLOW-UP

Students can write out the conversations from exercise 3.

WORKBOOK Lesson 48, p. 66

48. Where were you?

1 ► **Study the frames: The Past of *Be***

Information questions		
	was	he? she? your wallet?
Where		
	were	you? they?

Affirmative statements		
He She It I	**was**	at work.
We They	**were**	

Negative statements		
He She It I	**wasn't** **(was not)**	at school.
We They	**weren't** **(were not)**	

2 ► **Complete the conversations with the past tense of *be*.**
► **Listen to check your answers.**
► **Act out the conversations with a partner.**

1. **A** Where __*were*__ you
   yesterday?
   B I _____ sick. How
   _____ class?
   A It _____ interesting.
   B I'm sorry I _____ (not)
   here.

2. **A** I found my glasses.
   B Where _____ they?
   A They _____ in my car.
   B I'm glad you found them.

3. **A** You _____ (not) at work
   on Monday. Where
   _____ you?
   B We _____ at home.
   A Oh? What _____ wrong?
   B Our son _____ sick.

3 ► **Listen to the conversation below.**
► **Act out the conversations the teacher has with each student in the picture.**

Teacher Susan, you're late. Where were you?
Susan I was in the restroom.

49. Tryout

Carolyn Duval is trying out for a part in a television commercial.

(1)

Carolyn Good morning, my name's Carolyn Duval. I have a ten o'clock appointment with Mr. Anderson.

Mr. Anderson Yes, hello, Ms. Duval. I'm Jack Anderson. It's nice to meet you. This is my assistant Vicky Wu.

Vicky Wu Here's the script. Take a minute or two to read it over. That's Bob Velez over there. He's also trying out for this commercial.

(2)

Husband (*Holds up shirt*) Honey, this isn't my shirt.

Wife Yes, it is.

Husband But my shirts aren't this white.

Wife They weren't before, but they are now — now that we use *All-Bright*. (*Holds up box*)

Husband *All-Bright*? What's that?

Wife A new detergent — it gets all our laundry clean and bright. I was lost until I found *All-Bright*. What a wonderful detergent!

Husband (*Kisses wife*) What a wonderful wife!

3. Figure it out

True or *false*?

1. Carolyn Duval has a ten o'clock appointment at the doctor's office. *False.*
2. Carolyn Duval and Bob Velez are married.
3. Carolyn wants a part in a television commercial.
4. *All-Bright* is a detergent for washing clothes.

49. Tryout

WARM-UP

Practice three different uses of *what*. Go around the classroom and make exclamations about different matters. For example:

What a nice day (evening)!
What a difficult lesson!
(*Pointing out a student*) What a beautiful sweater!

Then practice *what* in questions. Ask different students questions such as "What are you going to do tomorrow evening?" and "What about you?"

1. & 2. Conversation

BACKGROUND

Carolyn is trying out for a part in a television commercial. She is playing the part of a wife recommending a new laundry detergent. Bob Velez is playing the part of the husband.

LANGUAGE

...*to read it over* means *to read through something.*

...*trying out for* refers to the process of competing for a place on a sports team or a role in a movie or play—or in this case, a part in a television commercial.

...*this* (white) is used to emphasize the adjective *white*. It's another way of saying "so."

...*now that* is another way of saying "because now."

...*(it) gets* is another way of saying "(it) makes."

PROCEDURE

- Have students examine the illustrations. Point out the different characters and the two scenes. Ask questions and make statements like these:

  What's Carolyn Duval's occupation?
  Carolyn is in a television studio.
  Is she sitting down?
  What are the two people doing in the second picture?

- Have the students silently read over the conversation. Answer any questions they have about vocabulary or structures.

- Have the students listen to the conversations twice, first with their books closed and then with their books open.

3. Figure it out

True or *false*?

- Have the students read over the statements. Then have them cover the dialogue boxes and look only at the pictures as they listen to the conversations and answer *True* or *False*. They can write their responses on separate paper.

- Have the students discuss their answers with a partner before listening to the conversations again. Tell them to uncover the conversations and check their answers. Ask a student to write the answers on the board.

ANSWERS
2. False
3. True
4. True

4. Listen in

- Read the instructions to the students as they follow along in their books. Tell them to read over the statements before they listen to the conversation.

- Have the students listen as many times as necessary to complete the exercise. Call on two students to say the answers.

TAPESCRIPT

Mr. Anderson Thank you very much, Ms. Duval. We'll call you in a few days.

Carolyn O.K. Thanks for your time, Mr. Anderson. Oh, by the way, is there a pay phone in the building?

Mr. Anderson Yes, there's one in the lobby, next to the coffee shop.

Carolyn Let's see. Is that near the Fifth Avenue entrance?

Mr. Anderson Yes, that's right. Just take the elevator to the first floor. The telephones will be on your left.

Carolyn Thanks a lot.

ANSWERS
1. True
2. False

5. Your turn

- Read the instructions to the students. Tell them to read over the incomplete conversation. Refer the students to the top picture on p. 88 for the question about color.

- Have the students work in pairs to complete the conversation. Tell them that answers may vary slightly.

- Have the pairs act out the conversation. The partners can take turns playing the two roles. Finally, call on different pairs to present their versions to the class.

SAMPLE ANSWERS
Oh, no!
I lost my umbrella.
Purple.
Oh, what a relief!

6. How to say it

- Have the students listen to the conversation. Then present it again and have them repeat each line.

- Refer the students to their books and point out the lines used to show rising and falling intonation and the inverted triangles to indicate syllables with the strongest stress. You can write the exchanges and the intonation lines on the board and trace them with your finger as you read the sentences aloud for the students to repeat.

- Practice the conversation with a student in front of the class. Then have the students practice in pairs. Move around the room and check their work, giving help where needed.

- Call on pairs of students to read the conversation aloud. If necessary, repeat each line with the correct syllable stress and the appropriate intonation.

7. Listen in

- Read the instructions to the students as they follow along in their books. Tell them to read over the incomplete conversation before they listen to it.

- Have the students listen as many times as necessary to complete the conversation. Then have them work in pairs to compare answers. Ask a pair to write the answers on the board.

TAPESCRIPT AND ANSWERS
George Hey, look! It's <u>Carolyn Duval</u>.
Loretta You're <u>right</u>! What a surprise!
Stella Carolyn Duval…who's that?
Loretta She <u>lives</u> next door. She's an <u>actress</u>.
Nick She's really <u>good</u>!
Loretta Shh!

OPTION

Model the conversation with another student. Be sure to use appropriate stress, intonation, and gestures. Then have the pairs act out the conversation. Go around the classroom and check their work. Finally, call on a pair to act out the conversation for the class.

FOLLOW-UP

Students can write out the conversation they practiced in **Your turn**.

WORKBOOK Lesson 49, p. 67

Thank you very much, Ms. Duval. We'll call you in a few days.

O.K. Thanks for your time, Mr. Anderson.

▭ 4. Listen in

Carolyn needs to make a phone call. Read the statements below. Then listen to the conversation and say *true* or *false*.

1. The phone is in the lobby next to the coffee shop.
2. The lobby is on the second floor.

5. Your turn

Carolyn lost her umbrella at the tryout. Complete the conversation below. Then act it out with a partner.

Carolyn _____
  Vicky What's wrong?
Carolyn _____
  Vicky What color is it?
Carolyn _____
  Vicky I think it's over there in the corner.
Carolyn _____

▭ 6. How to say it

Practice this conversation.

A Oh, no!

B What's wrong?

A I lost my wallet!

B Is this it?

A Yes! What a relief!

▭ 7. Listen in

Carolyn got the part. Two months later, George and Loretta are watching TV with Nick and Stella, and they see Carolyn's commercial. Read the conversation below. Then listen to the conversation and fill in the missing words.

George Hey, look! It's _____ .
Loretta You're _____ ! What a surprise!
  Stella Carolyn Duval . . . who's that?
Loretta She _____ next door. She's an _____ .
    Nick She's really _____ .
Loretta Shh!

Unit 8 **89**

50. Do People Watch Too Much TV?

Koji Kawabe

I know a lot of parents are worried because their children watch TV all the time. In fact, I read somewhere that the average child in the United States watches 19,000 hours of TV by the time he or she finishes high school. And that truly is a lot. But personally, I don't think TV is so bad. There are a lot of interesting programs on TV and you can learn a lot about the world. It's a great invention.

Rosa Hernandez

The real problem is the commercials. They stop every ten minutes to show a commercial. When I get home at night, I want to relax and enjoy myself. I'm not interested in watching ads for perfume and laundry detergent and breakfast cereal. I certainly don't think I'll be a better person or more beautiful or healthy if I buy those things.

William Owen

I like to watch TV, but I think people spend too much time in front of their TV sets. There are a lot of dumb programs on TV. Also, the television is not a very social machine. People should do things together—spend time with friends, play sports, go to plays and concerts, things like that.

Cheryl Brady

Definitely. We all watch too much. TV influences and changes our lives — not always for the better. For example, many experts feel that violent TV programs make children more aggressive—they fight or interrupt other children who are playing calmly—and that they will grow up to be aggressive adults.

1. **Read the survey. Who doesn't answer the question?**

2. **What's your opinion? Do people watch too much television?**

50. Do People Watch Too Much TV?

BACKGROUND

This survey asks if people watch too much television. It's a good example of an opinion survey one might find in a newspaper or on radio or television.

PROCEDURE

- Have the students read over the questions at the bottom of the page. After making sure they understand the questions, have them read the survey. Then play the cassette or read the text aloud as the students follow along in their books.

- Tell the students to answer the questions and then to work with a partner to compare and discuss their answers. Call on pairs to share their answers with the class.

   ANSWERS
   1. Rosa Hernandez
   2. Answers will vary.

OPTION 1

Have the students underline or write down on separate paper any words or structures from the survey which they don't understand. Use gestures, realia, pictures, or words they already know to help them with unfamiliar language. Give only basic and simple explanations of new words and structures at this time.

OPTION 2

Have two students conduct a survey of the class to find out how many class members think people watch too much television, how many think people watch just enough, and how many think people don't watch enough. One student can ask for a show of hands. The other can tally the results under three columns on the board entitled *Too Much TV*, *Just Enough TV*, and *Not Enough TV*.

FOLLOW-UP

Students can write down their opinions from exercise 2 on p. 90. Tell them to write down the reason for their answer to the question *Do people watch too much television?*

WORKBOOK Lesson 50, p. 68. Before assigning the writing task, you may want to point out the periods at the end of sentences and remind students to capitalize the first word of each sentence.

Before you begin teaching, go over the functions/themes, language, and forms in the chart. This will give you a preview of what you will encounter as you guide the students through the unit.

Preview the conversations.

- Have the students look at the first photograph. Read aloud the sentences in the box and point out the restaurant in the photograph. Discuss the sentences.

- Have the students look at the second photograph as you read aloud the information in the box. Point out the architecture in the first and second photographs. Discuss the sentence in the box.

- Point out the third photograph. Read aloud the sentences in the box. Refer to the photograph as you discuss the sentences with the students. Ask the students about jazz in their country.

- Read aloud and discuss the questions at the bottom of the page. You may want to refer to the text on p. 102 for more information about the city of New Orleans and its history.

POSSIBLE ANSWERS
1. New Orleans is located in the state of Louisiana in the southern part of the United States.
2. New Orleans is famous for its French Quarter, jazz, Mardi Gras, restaurants, and a tradition of good living.
3. You can eat out, shop, listen to jazz, and walk through the French Quarter.

CULTURE CLOSE-UP

Jazz is the only kind of modern music which originated in the U.S., and many Americans are proud of this fact. The African-Americans who first developed and played jazz rhythms lived in the southern part of the U.S., where jazz is still very popular. Over the past several decades, its popularity has spread to most major cities in the U.S., and it has had a great influence on other types of music such as rock.

FUNCTIONS/THEMES	LANGUAGE	FORMS
Talk about what people are doing	He's reading a book.	The present continuous
Talk about the weather	It's hot and sunny.	Weather
Make a suggestion Object or agree Ask what time it is Find out hours	Let's go to a museum. That's a good idea./That's too boring. What time is it? What time do you open?	*Let's* . . . Articles: *a*, *an*, and *the* Time
Talk about movies Talk about likes and dislikes Talk about feelings	What's playing this week? I don't really like old movies. I'm having a wonderful time.	Subject questions Placement of adjectives

Preview the conversations.

French influence is very strong in New Orleans, especially in the French Quarter. There are many good French restaurants there.

There is also a Spanish influence in the city, particularly in the architecture.

African-Americans in New Orleans developed jazz in the late 1800s. It is now popular all over the world.

Discuss these questions with the class.

1. Where's New Orleans?
2. Think of things that New Orleans is famous for.
3. What kind of things can you do in New Orleans?

UNIT 9 • LESSONS 51–57

51. Any suggestions?

Patty and Paul Sasa are spending their honeymoon in New Orleans.

 A

Patty What a beautiful
day! Are you having a
good time?
Paul Yeah, I'm having a
wonderful time.
Patty I am too. I just love
New Orleans!
Paul I do too!

B

Patty Paul . . . What are you doing?
Paul I'm calling my mother. *(Dialing phone)*
Mrs. Sasa Hello?
Paul Hi, Mom. It's Paul.
Mrs. Sasa Paul! How's New Orleans?
Paul Great! We're sightseeing and going to
museums.
Mrs. Sasa How's the weather?
Paul Oh, it's sunny and beautiful.
Mrs. Sasa Lucky you. It's cold here, and
it's snowing.

 C

Patty Uh-oh. . .
Paul What's wrong?
Patty Uh . . . I think it's . . .
raining!
Paul Come on! Let's run.

D

Paul What do you want to do? Any
suggestions?
Patty Let's go to a movie. *Love on a Rainy
Afternoon* is playing near the hotel.
Paul But we go to the movies all the time at
home.
Patty O.K., then, let's go to a museum.
Paul Good idea. Oh, wait—what time is it?
Patty It's a quarter after five.
Paul Too late. The museums close at five.
Patty Oh, right. They're open from ten to five.

51. Any suggestions?

WARM-UP

Tell the students what you are going to do on the weekend and ask volunteers to tell you their plans. Write other activities they mention on the board.

T: I'm going to see a movie this weekend. What about you?
S: I'm going to play tennis.

BACKGROUND

Patty and Paul Sasa are on their honeymoon in New Orleans. Paul calls his mother. Then he and his wife discuss what to do in New Orleans that evening.

LANGUAGE

*It's (*Paul*).* is another way of saying "This is (Paul)."

Uh-oh... is an informal and very casual way of saying "Something is wrong."

Come on! is used to encourage someone to hurry up.

Any suggestions? is short for *Do you have any suggestions?*

Good idea. is short for *That's a good idea.*

Too late. is short for *It's too late.*

Oh, right. is short for *Oh, you're right.*

...after six is short for *after six o'clock.*

Me too. is another way of saying "I am too."

*How about (*oysters*)?* is a way of suggesting something. It's another way of saying "Would you like (oysters)?"

*It's only (*twenty to ten*)!* is a way of saying "It's not very (late)."

PROCEDURE

- Follow a procedure similar to that indicated for the opening conversations in previous units.

- Have students listen to the conversations as they follow along in their books. If you read the conversations aloud, be sure to use appropriate stress, intonation, and gestures.

Figure it out

1. Listen to the conversations. Say *true*, *false*, or *it doesn't say.*

■ Tell the students to read over the instructions and the statements. Explain that *It doesn't say* means the information isn't in the conversations. Then have the students listen to the conversations again and answer *True, False,* or *It doesn't say.*

■ Call on different students to read the statements aloud. Call on others to say their answers. Ask a student to write the correct answers on the board.

ANSWERS
2. False
3. True
4. It doesn't say.
5. False
6. False

OPTION

Have the students correct the false statements. Help them get started by writing on the board the correction of a false statement from **Figure it out 1** on p. 83. For example:

Mrs. Kelly's wallet is red.

Have the students work in pairs to compare answers. Call on different students to read their answers aloud. Ask two students to write the answers on the board.

POSSIBLE ANSWERS
1. Patty and Paul just love New Orleans.
2. Paul calls his mother from New Orleans.
3. Patty and Paul don't go to a French restaurant.
4. At twenty to ten, Paul wants to go to a jazz club.

2. Listen again and choose the best response to each sentence.

■ Have the students listen to the conversations again. Then tell them to read the sentences and choose the correct responses. Students can work in pairs to compare their answers and practice the exchanges.

■ Call on different pairs to read the exchanges aloud. Ask a student to write the answers on the board.

ANSWERS
2. b
3. a
4. b
5. a
6. a
7. b

FOLLOW-UP

Students can write out the exchanges in exercise 2 on p. 93.

WORKBOOK Lesson 51, p. 69

E

Paul I'm hungry.
Patty Me too. Let's go out to dinner.
Paul O.K. What do you want to eat?
Patty How about oysters? New Orleans is famous for its oysters.
Paul You know I don't like oysters.
Patty Well, how about a French restaurant?
Paul No. That's too expensive.
Patty Well, where *do* you want to go?

F

Patty I'm exhausted. Let's go back to the hotel.
Paul It's too early. It's only twenty to ten! Let's go to a jazz club. Now let's see . . . who's playing?
Patty Oh, honey . . . I'm too tired.
Paul Oh, look! Toots Bixler is playing at the Savoy. The show starts at ten o'clock. Come on! Let's go!

Figure it out

1. Listen to the conversations. Say *true, false,* or *it doesn't say.*

1. Patty and Paul don't like New Orleans. *False.*
2. Patty calls her mother from New Orleans.
3. Patty likes oysters.
4. Paul likes French food.
5. Patty and Paul go to a French restaurant.
6. At twenty to ten, Paul wants to go back to the hotel.

2. Listen again and choose the best response to each sentence.

1. I just love New Orleans!
   a. I do too.
   b. I am too.

2. How's the weather?
   a. That's good.
   b. It's beautiful.

3. Any suggestions?
   a. Let's go to a movie.
   b. We're sightseeing.

4. Let's go to a museum.
   a. Me too.
   b. That's a good idea.

5. What time is it?
   a. It's a quarter after five.
   b. It's sunny.

6. What are you doing?
   a. I'm calling my mother.
   b. Let's go back to the hotel.

7. Who's playing?
   a. *Love on a Rainy Afternoon.*
   b. Toots Bixler.

52. What are you doing?

  1 ▶ Study the picture and complete the sentences.
▶ Listen to check your answers.

1. *Boris* is dancing.
2. _____ is drinking wine.
3. _____ is going to a movie.

4. _____ are talking in the street.
5. _____ is playing jazz.
6. _____ are eating oysters.

2 ▶ Study the frames: The Present Continuous

Information questions		Statements				Yes-no questions			Short answers			
	you	I	**'m**				you		Yes,	I	**am.**	
are						**Are**			No,		**'m not.**	
	they	We	**'re**				they		Yes,	we	**are.**	
		They		(not)	eating.			**listening?**	No,	they	**aren't.**	
What							he		Yes,	he	**is.**	
is	he	He	**'s**			**Is**			No,	she	**isn't.**	
		She					she		Yes,	it	**is.**	
	she								No,		**isn't.**	
		It	**'s**		raining.	**Is**	it	**raining?**				

do + **ing** ➜ doing	
have + **ing** ➜ having	
run + **ing** ➜ running	

  3 ▶ Listen to the conversation below.
▶ Have a similar conversation about the people in the picture.

A What's Boris doing?
B He's dancing.
A Is he having a good time?
B Yes, he is.

 4 ▶ Talk with your classmates.

What are you doing? What about your family and friends? Where are they right now? What are they doing?

My father is at work right now. He's probably talking on the telephone.

52. What are you doing?

WARM-UP

As you perform or mimic different actions, describe what you are doing. Use the present continuous. For example, as you pretend to dial a telephone, say "I'm calling a friend."

TALK ABOUT WHAT PEOPLE ARE DOING • THE PRESENT CONTINUOUS

- Point out the different characters in the illustration and have the students repeat their names after you. Then tell the students to read over the instructions and the exercise items. Have the students complete the exercise.

- Have the students listen to the sentences as many times as necessary. Then have them compare their answers with a partner. Ask a student to write the answers on the board.

ANSWERS
2. Jane
3. Hiroko
4. Antonia and Arthur
5. Korhan
6. Mae Ling and Ashok

- Have the students study the frames as you read aloud the headings and possible sentences. Answer any questions the students have.

- Point out the blue box to the right. Read aloud the contents and have the students repeat.

LANGUAGE NOTE

If a verb ends in *e*, the *e* is dropped before adding *ing* (have + **ing** = having). If a verb consists of or ends in a consonant + vowel + consonant, the final consonant is doubled before adding *ing* (run + **ing** = running). With most other verbs such as *do*, *listen*, and *rain*, the *ing* is simply added (do + **ing** = doing).

- Have the students listen to the sample conversation as they follow along in their books. Then read aloud the instructions.

- Have students work in pairs to take turns asking and answering questions about the people in the picture. Go around the classroom and check students' work.

- Call on different pairs to present their conversations to the class. Also have them write the conversations on the board.

POSSIBLE ANSWERS
A What's Hiroko doing?
B She's going to a movie.
A Is she having a good time?
B Yes, she is.

A What are Antonia and Arthur doing?
B They're talking in the street.
A Are they having a good time?
B Yes, they are.

A What are Jane and Paitoon doing?
B They're eating dinner in a restaurant.
A Are they having a good time?
B Yes, they are.

A What's Korhan doing?
B He's playing jazz.
A Is he having a good time?
B Yes, he is.

A What are Mae Ling and Ashok doing?
B They're eating oysters.
A Are they having a good time?
B No, they aren't.

4

- Read aloud the instruction and the questions. Then ask the question "What is your father doing?" and read the answer from the book.

- Have the students move around the classroom to talk with their classmates. Tell them to ask their classmates the questions from the book. You might suggest they write the answers on separate paper.

- Call on different pairs of students to act out their conversations. Have them write some of their questions and answers on the board.

WORKBOOK Lesson 52, p. 70

53. How's the weather?

Practice *How was...?* For example, go around the classroom and ask different students "How was the game yesterday?" and "How was the movie on TV last night?"

TALK ABOUT THE WEATHER

- Point out the weather map and talk about weather reports and the use of the symbols and color chart. Have the students repeat the place names and other words on the map after you. Then point out and talk about the four illustrations. Have the students repeat the sentences under each illustration after you.

- Read aloud the first instruction and have the students complete the exercise. Then have them compare and discuss their answers with a partner.

- So the students can check their answers, have them listen to the weather report as many times as necessary. Ask a student to write the answers on the board.

TAPESCRIPT
1. In Reykjavik, it's very cold and snowing.
2. In Dublin, it's cool and raining.
3. In Prague, it's cloudy and cool.
4. In Lisbon, it's warm and raining.

ANSWERS
1. a
2. b
3. b
4. a

2

- Read aloud the instructions as the students follow along in their books. Then point out Dublin on the map and read aloud the sample exchange with a student.

- Have the students work in pairs to take turns asking and answering questions about the map. Tell them to use the sample exchange as a model.

- Call on different pairs to present their exchanges to the class. You can ask other pairs to write the exchanges on the board.

- Read aloud the instructions. Tell the students to work with two or more classmates to discuss the weather in their own country or countries.

- Call on different students to describe to the class the current weather in their country.

OPTION

Have the students work in small groups. Tell them to draw a weather map of their own country on separate paper. Have them indicate different cities and possible weather patterns. Call on different groups to reproduce their weather maps on the board. Have group members describe the weather conditions on their maps for the class.

> ### CULTURE CLOSE-UP
>
> The weather is a common and frequent topic of discussion in the U.S. Americans are known to talk about the weather at the drop of a hat, sometimes as "small talk" or as a way to "break the ice" with a stranger. Weather reports on television and radio occur around the clock. In fact, there are television stations which broadcast nothing but weather reports and forecasts.

FOLLOW-UP

Students can write out their descriptions of the weather in their own country from exercise 3.

WORKBOOK Lesson 53, p. 71

53. How's the weather?

 1 ▶ Read the weather map and circle *a* or *b*.
　　 ▶ Listen to check your answers.

1. In Reykjavik, it's . . .
　 a. very cold and snowing.
　 b. very cold and raining.

2. In Dublin, it's . . .
　 a. cool and snowing.
　 b. cool and raining.

3. In Prague, it's . . .
　 a. sunny and warm.
　 b. cloudy and cool.

4. In Lisbon, it's . . .
　 a. warm and raining.
　 b. cloudy and cool.

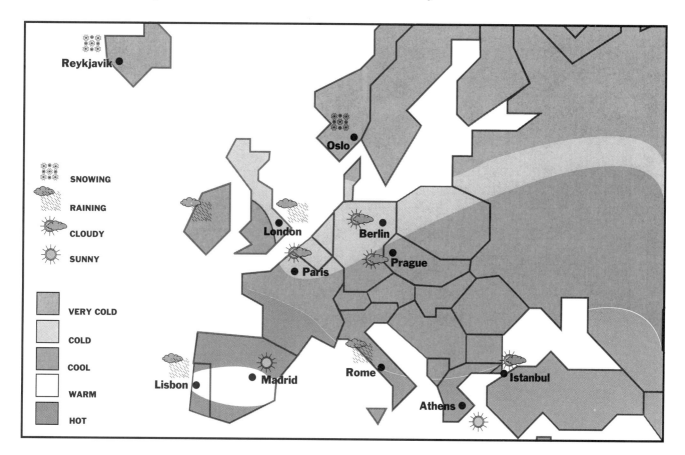

It's cold.

It's cool.

It's warm.

It's hot.

2 ▶ Ask and answer questions about the map.

 A How's the weather in Dublin?
B It's raining.

3 ▶ Talk with your classmates. How's the weather in your country right now?

54. Let's go to the beach.

 1
► Match the woman's suggestions below with her husband's objections.
► Listen to check your answers.

Let's go out to dinner.
Let's go dancing.
Let's go for a walk in the park.
Let's go to the beach.
Let's stay home and watch TV.

I'm too tired.   It's too cold.
That's too boring.   That's too dangerous.
That's too expensive.

 2
► Listen to the two possible conversations.
► Act out the conversations with a partner.

A What do you want to do? Any suggestions?

B Let's go to a movie.

A That's a good idea.   **A** That's too boring. Let's go dancing instead.

Let's + verb ➜ Let's go out to dinner.

3 ► Study the frame.

Articles: *a* (*an*) and *the*

Let's go to **a** museum.
O.K. How about **the** art museum on Rampart Street?

 4
► Complete the conversation with *a* (*an*) or *the*.
► Listen to check your answers.

A Let's go to _____ museum.

B O.K. How about _____ Voodoo Museum on Dumaine Street?

A No, I was there yesterday. Let's go to _____ art museum instead.

B No. I don't think that _____ art museum here is very interesting.

54. Let's go to the beach.

Ask students what kinds of leisure-time activities they like and dislike. Encourage them to provide reasons for why they like or dislike a particular activity.

MAKE A SUGGESTION • OBJECT OR AGREE

- Have the students examine the picture. Read the sentences aloud and have the students repeat. Use gestures, realia, pictures, or words the students already know to help them understand new words such as *dangerous*, *expensive*, *tired*, and *boring*.

- Tell the students to work in pairs to match the woman's suggestions with her husband's objections. Point out that the pictures will provide clues to help them answer. Go around the classroom and give help when needed.

- So they can check their answers, have the students listen to the exchanges. Call on different pairs of students to present their exchanges to the class.

TAPESCRIPT AND ANSWERS

Woman Let's go out to dinner.
   Man That's too expensive.
Woman Let's go dancing.
   Man I'm too tired.
Woman Let's go for a walk in the park.
   Man That's too dangerous.
Woman Let's go to the beach.
   Man It's too cold.
Woman Let's stay home and watch TV.
   Man That's too boring.

OPTION

Tell the students to work in small groups to discuss the reasons for their answers. Have them refer to the pictures and make comments about what they see. Call on different groups to share their reasons with the class.

LANGUAGE NOTE

The word *let's* is a contraction of *let* + *us* and is used to suggest a plan that includes the person spoken to.

- Point out the box and explain that *let's* is used to make a suggestion. Read aloud the words and the sentence in the box.

- Tell the students to follow along in their books as they listen to the two possible conversations. Have them listen a second time as you read the conversations aloud with a student.

- Tell the students to work in pairs to take turns playing the two different roles. Refer them to the picture in exercise 1 for the content of their exchanges. Have them model their exchanges on the sample conversation.

- Call on different pairs of students to act out the conversations for the class.

MAKE A SUGGESTION • ARTICLES *A* (*AN*) AND *THE*

- Have the students study the frame as you read aloud the heading and sentences. Provide additional examples such as "Let's go to a restaurant. O.K. How about the restaurant across the street?"

- See if the students can come up with the rule for when to use *a/an* and when to use *the*. (We use *a/an* when referring to something in general. We use *the* when referring to something specific.)

PRONUNCIATION NOTE

The word *the* is pronounced [ðə] before consonant sounds and [ði] before vowel sounds.

- Read aloud the instructions to the students. Tell them to read over the incomplete conversation. Then have them complete it with the appropriate articles.

- So they can check their answers, have the students listen to the conversation. Have two students write the answers on the board.

ANSWERS

A a
B the
A an
B the

OPTION

Have the students work in pairs to act out the conversation. Go around the classroom and check their work. Call on a pair to present the conversation to the class.

- Tell the students to examine the illustrations at the top of the page as you read aloud the information below each picture. Read the information again and have the students repeat. Answer any questions students have about telling time.

- Have the students look at the illustration on the right as you read aloud the exchange. Then have them listen to each conversation and circle the time they hear.

- Have the students compare their answers with a partner. Call on a student to write the answers on the board.

TAPESCRIPT

1. **A** What time is it, please?
   B It's a quarter after five.
   A Thanks a lot.

2. **A** Excuse me. Do you have the time?
   B Yes, it's half past nine.
   A Thank you very much.

3. **A** Excuse me. What time is it?
   B It's ten to ten.
   A Thanks.

4. **A** What time is it, please?
   B I'm sorry, I don't have a watch… . Oh, wait, there's a clock over there. It's noon.
   A Thanks.

ANSWERS

1. a   2. b   3. b   4. a

- Point out the first digital clock. Then read aloud the sample exchange with a student. Read aloud the instructions as the students follow along in their books.

- Have students work in pairs to take turns asking and answering questions about the digital clocks. Call on different pairs to share their exchanges with the class.

ANSWERS

2. It's twenty-five after ten.
3. It's a quarter to two.
4. It's half past three.

- Have the pairs ask each other what time it is now. Call on a pair to ask and answer the question for the class and to write the current time on the board.

- Tell the students to read over the conversation. Then play the cassette or read the conversation aloud with a student. If you read the conversation aloud, pretend you are using a telephone.

- Point out the boxes on the right. Read the contents aloud. Answer any questions about the information in the boxes.

- Read aloud the second set of instructions. Tell the students to work in pairs. Have different pairs call different places in the guidebook. Tell them to use the conversation in their books as a guide, but explain that conversations may vary. Go around the classroom and check their work, giving help when needed.

- Call on different pairs to act out possible conversations for the class.

SAMPLE ANSWERS

A *(Dials number) Rrring, rrring*
B The Voodoo Museum, may I help you?
A Yes. What time do you open?
B We're open from 10 a.m. to 5 p.m., but we're closed on Mondays.
A So you open at ten o'clock?
B Yes.
A O.K. Thank you.

A *(Dials number) Rrring, rrring*
B The Savoy, may I help you?
A Yes. What time do you open?
B We're open from 9 p.m. to 2 a.m., but we're closed on Sundays.
A So you open at ten o'clock?
B No. We open at nine o'clock.
A O.K. Thanks.

FOLLOW-UP

Students can write the words for the times from exercises 5 and 6.

WORKBOOK Lesson 54, pp. 72-73

ASK WHAT TIME IT IS • TIME

a quarter after five
five fifteen
5:15

half past five
five thirty
5:30

a quarter to five
four forty-five
4:45

ten to five
four fifty
4:50

ten after five
five ten
5:10

twelve noon
(midnight)
twelve o'clock
12:00

  5 ▶ **Listen to each conversation and circle the time you hear.**

1. a. 5:15 2. a. 9:00 3. a. 10:10 4. a. 12:00
   b. 5:45   b. 9:30   b. 9:50   b. 12:30

What time is it, please? I'm sorry. I don't have a watch.

6 ▶ **Ask and answer questions about the clocks in the picture.**

A What time is it?
B It's a quarter after eight.

1. **8:15** 2. **10:25** 3. **1:45** 4. **3:30**

5. **?**

▶ **What time is it now?**

FIND OUT HOURS

  7 ▶ **Listen to the telephone conversation.**
▶ **Act out the conversation. Call one of the places in the guidebook below.**

A (Dials number) Rrring, rrring
B Belle Monde Restaurant, may I help you?
A Yes. What time do you open?
B We're open from 6 p.m. to midnight.
A So you open at six o'clock?
B Yes.
A O.K. Thank you.

> on Mondays = every Monday

> a.m. = in the morning
> p.m. = in the afternoon
>   in the evening
>   at night

N E W O R L E A N S

MUSEUMS

The Voodoo Museum
724 Dumaine Street
10:00 a.m. – 5:00 p.m.
Closed Mondays

The Art Museum
110 Rampart Street
10:00 – 5:30 every day

**The Louisiana
State Museum**
701 Chartres Street
9:00 – 4:00, Tuesday
          to Saturday
11:00 – 3:00, Sunday
9:00 – 12:00, Monday

N E W O R L E A N S

MUSIC CLUBS

The Savoy
122 Bourbon Street
Toots Bixler and his
jazz band.
9:00 p.m. to 2:00 a.m.
Closed Sunday

The Music Hall
Good old Rock and Roll
7:30 to Midnight
every night
344 Royal Street

RESTAURANTS

The Belle Monde
400 Esplanade Avenue
6:00 p.m. to Midnight
Closed Mondays
Great French food
Expensive

Italian Villa
560 Bourbon Street
Noon – Midnight every day
Good and inexpensive

55. Do you want to go to a movie?

TALK ABOUT MOVIES • SUBJECT QUESTIONS

1 ► **Answer the questions using the information in the movie ads.**

1. What's playing this week?
2. Who's in *The Doctor's Office*?
3. Who's in *Love on a Rainy Afternoon*?
4. Who's David Contreras?
5. What's playing at the Baker Street Theater?
6. What's playing at midnight?
7. Who's in *Rock and Roll Cowboy*?
8. What's "the best science fiction movie in years"?

> Subject questions with **who** and **what**
>
> **What**'s playing? *The Lost Galaxy* (is playing).
> **Who**'s in *Rock and Roll Cowboy*? **Charlie Mills and Donna Sue Parker.**

 2 ► **Listen and say *true* or *false*.**

1. *The Doctor's Office* is playing at the Baker Street Theater. *False.*
2. *The Lost Galaxy* is a great adventure movie.
3. *Casablanca* starts at midnight.
4. Tessa Lake is in *Texas Charlie and the Last Frontier*.
5. The State Theater is on Monument Avenue.
6. The Circle Cinema is downtown.
7. *Rock and Roll Cowboy* is a comedy.

3 ► **Talk with your classmates.**

Name a film for each category. Use the movie ads above or talk about movies you know.

Some kinds of movies	
classic movies	comedies
horror movies	dramas
adventure movies	westerns
love stories	science fiction movies
documentaries	

55. Do you want to go to a movie?

WARM-UP

On the board, write *Let's go to a movie*. Have the students work in pairs to make suggestions for each other with *Let's...* . They can use the suggestions on p. 96.

TALK ABOUT MOVIES • SUBJECT QUESTIONS

- Point out the blue box. Read aloud the heading and the sentences. Make sure the students understand that *who* refers to persons and *what* refers to things. Explain the meaning of *is playing* and the use of *in*.

- Tell the students to read over the questions and the movie ads. Answer any questions they have about vocabulary. Then have the students work in pairs to answer the questions. Tell them to use the information in the movie ads. Go around the classroom, giving help when needed.

- Call on different pairs to ask and answer the questions. Check their work.

  ANSWERS
  1. *Rock and Roll Cowboy, Casablanca, The Story of Civilization, Love on a Rainy Afternoon, Claws II, The Lost Galaxy, The Doctor's Office,* and *Texas Charlie and the Last Frontier* (are playing).
  2. Drew Young and Julia Williams
  3. Duane Beam and Tessa Lake
  4. He's in *Texas Charlie and the Last Frontier*.
  5. *Love on a Rainy Afternoon*
  6. *Casablanca*
  7. Charlie Mills and Donna Sue Parker
  8. *The Lost Galaxy*

OPTION

Have the students practice the pronunciation of *who's* and *what's*. Note that the final sound in *who's* is the voiced [z] and the final sound in *what's* is the voiceless [s]. Have the students repeat the words after you. Then have them repeat the questions from the exercise.

- Have the students read over the statements. Then have them listen to the statements and answer *True* or *False*.

- After the class listens to each statement, call on a student to say "True" or "False." Write the answers on the board.

  ANSWERS
  2. True
  3. True
  4. False
  5. True
  6. False
  7. True

- Read the instructions aloud. Make sure the students understand the terms used to categorize movies.

- Have the students work in small groups. Tell them to name a movie for each category.

- Call on groups to name their choices for each category. Ask different students to name a movie from the ads on p. 98 for each category.

  ANSWERS
  classic movie - *Casablanca*
  horror movie - *Claws II*
  adventure movie - *The Lost Galaxy*
  love story - *Love on a Rainy Afternoon*
  documentary - *The Story of Civilization*
  comedy - *Rock and Roll Cowboy*
  drama - *The Doctor's Office*
  western - *Texas Charlie and the Last Frontier*
  science fiction movie - *The Lost Galaxy*

TALK ABOUT LIKES AND DISLIKES

- Tell the students to silently read over the instructions, the objections in the box, and the incomplete conversation. Answer any questions they have.

- Have the students work in pairs to complete the conversation. Tell them to use the information in the ads to help them choose the appropriate polite objection.

- So the students can check their answers, have them listen to the conversation as many times as necessary. Call on a pair to read the completed conversation aloud for the class.

ANSWERS
I don't really like horror movies.
I don't really like documentaries.
I don't really like love stories.
I don't really like movies.

- Have the students listen to the conversation. Then have them repeat each line after you.

- Have the students work in pairs to practice a similar conversation, giving information about themselves. Tell them to refer to the box at the bottom of p. 98 and to take turns playing each role.

- Call on different pairs to present their conversations to the class. Check their pronunciation and intonation.

TALK ABOUT FEELINGS • PLACEMENT OF ADJECTIVES

- Point out the frame and the box and read aloud the information in them. Substitute different adjectives from the box for *fantastic* in the frame and read aloud the new sentences. Help students understand the meanings of the adjectives by using gestures, pictures, or other words they already know. Point out that the adjectives in the left-hand column are "positive" and the ones to the right are "negative." Elicit from the students the rule for when to use *a* and when to use *an*. (We use *a* before consonant sounds and *an* before vowel sounds.)

- Read aloud the instructions. Then have the students follow along in their books as they listen to the two possible conversations. Have them listen a second time as you read the conversations aloud with two students. Have each of the two students say a different B response.

OPTION

Have the students work in pairs to practice the conversations. Call on different pairs to act out the conversations for the class.

- Have the students listen to the conversation. If you read it aloud, be sure to simulate a telephone conversation and to use appropriate intonation.

- Have the students work in pairs to act out the conversation. Go around the classroom and check their work. Call on a pair to present the conversation to the class.

- Have the students silently read the role-play instructions. Then read the instructions aloud as the students follow along in their books. Answer any questions they have about the procedure.

- Have the students work in pairs to play the roles. Go around the classroom to listen in and give help when needed.

- Call on different pairs of students to present their role-plays to the class. You can give a prize for the best role-play.

FOLLOW-UP

Students can write down their likes and dislikes in music, food, and movies. On the board, write some examples such as *I like jazz. I don't like rock and roll.*

WORKBOOK Lesson 55, p. 74

TALK ABOUT LIKES AND DISLIKES

4 ▶ **Complete the conversation with the objections in the box. Use the information in the ads.**
 ▶ **Listen to check your answers.**

A Let's go to a movie. *Casablanca* starts at midnight.
B *I don't really like old movies* . Besides, that's too late.
A O.K. *Claws II* is at the Circle Cinema.
B The Circle is too far away and _____ .
A How about *The Story of Civilization*?
B That's too long and _____ .
A Oh, look! *Love on a Rainy Afternoon* is at the Baker Street Theater.
B _____ .
A Well, what kind of movies *do* you like?
B _____ .

> **Some polite objections**
>
> I don't really like documentaries.
> I don't really like love stories.
> I don't really like movies.
> I don't really like horror movies.
> I don't really like old movies.

5 ▶ **Listen to the conversation.**
 ▶ **Have a similar conversation with a partner.**

A What kind of movies do you like?
B I like horror movies. How about you?
A I like love stories.

TALK ABOUT FEELINGS • PLACEMENT OF ADJECTIVES

6 ▶ **Imagine you are at a movie theater with a friend. Listen to the possible conversations.**

A Are you having a good time?

B Yeah, I'm having a wonderful time.
A *I'm* not. This movie is horrible.

B No, I'm having a terrible time.
A I am too. This is an awful movie.

> **Placement of adjectives**
>
> This movie is **fantastic**.
> This is a **fantastic** movie.

> **Some adjectives**
>
> | | |
> |---|---|
> | fantastic | horrible |
> | wonderful | awful |
> | excellent | terrible |
> | good | lousy |

7 ▶ **Listen to this conversation. Then act it out with a partner.**

A (*Dials number*) Rrring, rrring
B Hello.
A Hi, Jeff. It's Nabila. Do you want to go to a movie?
B O.K., but I don't have a newspaper. What's playing?
A Let's see. . . . *Rock and Roll Cowboy* is playing at the Palace.
B Oh, I don't really like westerns.
A How about *The Doctor's Office*?
B Who's in it?
A Drew Young and Julia Williams.
B What time does it start?
A There are shows at 7:15 and 9:30.
B Hmm. The 9:30 show is too late. Let's go to the 7:15 show.
A O.K.

8 ▶ **Play these roles.**

Student A Telephone Student B and suggest going to a movie. Use the information in the movie ads or your own newspaper to answer his or her questions.

Student B Student A calls to invite you to a movie. You don't have a newspaper. Ask for more information about the movies. Agree with or object to Student A's suggestions.

56. Two tickets, please.

 The Arnos go to a movie to get out of their cold apartment.

1

George	It's freezing in here! What's wrong with the heat anyway?
Loretta	I've got an idea. Why don't we go out?
George	Out? In this weather? It's snowing!
Loretta	I mean let's go somewhere warm . . . a movie, for instance. I think *Casablanca* is playing at the theater down the street.
George	*Casablanca*! You know I don't like old movies!
Loretta	Oh, George!
George	Really, Loretta, I . . .
Loretta	Come on, George. It'll be nice and warm in the theater . . . Let's see . . . It's a quarter after seven now. I'll call the theater and find out.

2. Listen in

It's a quarter after seven when Loretta calls the theater. Listen to the telephone recording. What time does the next show start?

3

ADULTS $7.00
CHILDREN $4.00
SENIOR CITIZENS $5.00

Two, please. Are we late?

The movie's just starting now, ma'am.

4. How to say it

Practice these conversations.

1. **A** I like old movies.

   B I do too.

2. **A** I like old movies.

   B Well, I don't.

3. **A** I don't like old movies.

   B Well, I do.

56. Two tickets, please.

Go around the classroom and ask different students questions about the weather and the time. Use structures from Lessons 53 and 54. For example:

How's the weather today? Is it cloudy and cool? What time is it now?

1., 3., 5., & 7. Conversation

BACKGROUND

To escape their cold apartment, the Arnos go to see the old movie classic *Casablanca*. After the movie, they find out they've won a free trip to Florida.

LANGUAGE

What's wrong with (the heat)? is another way of saying "What's the problem with (the heating system)?"

...for instance is another way of saying "for example."

Really... is used here to mean *honestly* or *truly*.

...is this seat taken? is another way of saying "Is anyone sitting here?"

...move down a seat means *move over one seat* (to the left or right).

Shh! is a rather impolite way to tell someone to be quiet.

At least... means *if nothing else*.

Yahoo is a very informal expression used to express great surprise and delight.

PROCEDURE

- Follow a procedure similar to that on p. 88.

2. Listen in

- Read the instructions to the students as they follow along in their books. Remind them to listen carefully for the show times.

- Have the students listen as many times as necessary. Call on a student to say the answer.

TAPESCRIPT AND ANSWER

Recording Thank you for calling the Brooklyn Heights Cinema. We're located at 70 Henry Street in Brooklyn. Playing now is that well-loved American classic *Casablanca*, starring Humphrey Bogart and Ingrid Bergman. Show times: 12:00, 3:50, and <u>7:40</u>.

OPTION

If you are teaching in an English-speaking country, have the students call a local theater to find out what is playing and at what times. Students can work in small groups to choose a theater and to assign a person to make the call. Have a student from each group report the information in the following class session.

4. How to say it

- Follow the basic procedure for **How to say it** in Unit 8 on p. 89.

6. Your turn

- Read the instructions to the students. Tell them to read over the incomplete conversation.

- Have the students work in pairs to complete the conversation. Tell them that answers will vary.

- Have the pairs act out the conversation. The partners can take turns playing the two roles. Finally, call on different pairs to present their versions to the class.

SAMPLE ANSWERS
Let's go to a movie.
How about *Claws II*?
Then how about *The Lost Galaxy*?
12:00, 3:50, and 7:40.
O.K.

8. Figure it out

True or *false*?

- Have the students read over the statements. Then have them cover the dialogue boxes and look only at the pictures as they listen to the conversations and answer *True* or *False*. They can write their responses on separate paper.

- Have the students discuss their answers with a partner before listening to the conversations again. Tell them to uncover the conversations and check their answers. Ask a student to write the answers on the board.

ANSWERS
2. False
3. True
4. False
5. True

FOLLOW-UP

Students can write out the conversation they practiced in **Your turn**.

WORKBOOK Lesson 56, p. 75

5

Loretta	Uh-oh . . .
George	What's wrong?
Loretta	I can't see! (*Turning to man*) Excuse me, sir—is this seat taken?
Man	Uh . . . no, it's not.
Loretta	Let's move down a seat, George.
Woman	Shh!

6. Your turn

A man and a woman are planning their evening. Act out the conversation. Refer to the movie section of a newspaper if possible.

Woman	What do you want to do tonight?
Man	_____ .
Woman	O.K. What do you want to see? Any suggestions?
Man	_____ .
Woman	No, I don't like that kind of movie.
Man	_____ .
Woman	That's fine. Do you know what time it starts?
Man	_____ .
Woman	Let's go to the last show.
Man	_____ .

7

Loretta	Oh, I just love Humphrey Bogart!
George	Yeah. Well, at least it was warm in there . . . What's that?
Loretta	Oh, I almost forgot. Remember that contest you entered last month?
George	Oh, yeah. For the free trip to Miami Beach.
Loretta	Well, this letter came today.

YAHOO! Pack your bikini, Loretta! We're going to Florida!

8. Figure it out

True or *false*?

1. It's very cold in the Arnos' apartment. *True.*
2. George wants to see *Casablanca*.
3. *Casablanca* is an old movie.
4. George likes the movie.
5. George and Loretta win a trip to Florida.

57. New Orleans:
A tradition of good living

New Orleans with its famous French Quarter (Vieux Carré) is a never-ending delight for visitors as well as natives. For shopping, dining, entertainment or just the pleasures of walking and watching, there's no place like it in the world.
— *The Greater New Orleans Tourist and Convention Commission*

New Orleans, at the mouth of the Mississippi River, is a city over 270 years old. The French built the first town in 1718 and named it in honor of the French Duc d'Orleans. Today, New Orleans has over 600,000 people and it is an important U.S. port and center for tourism.

New Orleans is a city with a European flavor and an interesting history. In 1762, France gave New Orleans and part of its Louisiana colony to Spain. It belonged to Spain for over 30 years. Then in 1800 Napoleon Bonaparte asked Spain to return the territory to France again. In 1803 President Thomas Jefferson bought the Louisiana Territory, including New Orleans, from France. The cost: $15 million.

The city of New Orleans has a tradition of good living. Perhaps that's why many American writers, such as Tennessee Williams and William Faulkner, lived there at some time during their lives. Its restaurants are famous for French and Creole food. It has many old houses and government buildings. Jazz, a famous musical tradition in New Orleans, dates from the African–American community of the late nineteenth century. And every spring New Orleans celebrates its legendary holiday, Mardi Gras. From colorful celebrations in the streets to formal masquerade balls, it is a magical time of costumes, parades, and parties.

For more information see your travel agent or call or write:
The Greater New Orleans Tourist and Convention Commission
1520 Sugar Bowl Drive
New Orleans, LA 70112
504-566-5011

---

1. Read the article. Then circle the things you can find in New Orleans.

a. good shopping
b. interesting old buildings
c. good weather
d. great beaches
e. excellent restaurants
f. jazz

2. Answer these questions.

1. What two European countries were important in the history of New Orleans?
2. What famous holiday does New Orleans celebrate?

57. *New Orleans: A tradition of good living*

BACKGROUND

This article is like an article one might find in the travel section of a newspaper. It traces the history of New Orleans, Louisiana, and highlights some of that city's outstanding features.

PROCEDURE

1. Read the article. Then circle the things you can find in New Orleans.

- Have the students read over the exercise items at the bottom of the page. After making sure they understand the vocabulary, have them read the article. Then you may want to have them listen to the article as they follow along in their books. Finally, tell them to choose the appropriate answers.

  ANSWERS
  a, b, e, f

2. Answer these questions.

- Have the students read the questions and answer them. Then call on different students to share their answers with the class. Ask a student to write the answers on the board.

  ANSWERS
  1. France and Spain
  2. Mardi Gras

OPTION

Have the students underline or write down on separate paper any words or structures from the article which they don't understand. Use gestures, realia, pictures, or words they already know to help them with unfamiliar language. Give only basic and simple explanations of new words and structures at this time.

FOLLOW-UP

Students can write down things which can be found in New Orleans that are not mentioned in exercise 1.

WORKBOOK Lesson 57, p. 76. Before assigning the writing task, have the students answer the questions in exercise 2, first with short answers and then with complete sentences. Point out the use of italics in the title of the movie in the movie review. Remind the students that titles of movies are italicized in print and that the equivalent in handwritten work is underlining.

PREVIEW

Before you begin teaching, go over the functions/themes, language, and forms in the chart. This will give you a preview of what you will encounter as you guide the students through the unit.

Preview the conversations.

- Have the students look at the illustration. Read aloud the names and prices of the fruits and vegetables and have the students repeat. Point out that *lb.* is the abbreviation for *pound*. Discuss the sentences in the first box.

- Read aloud the information in the bottom box and have the students repeat. Answer any questions students have about pounds, grams, and kilograms. You may want to refer students to the Weights and Measures chart on p. 166.

- Point out the prices in the picture. Then read aloud the sentences in the box to the right and discuss them with the students.

CULTURE CLOSE-UP

The system of measurement commonly used in the U.S. is different from the metric system, which is used in most countries in the world. In the U.S. system, terms such as *inch*, *foot*, and *yard* are used when measuring length; and *ounce* and *pound* are used when measuring weight.

PREVIEW

FUNCTIONS/THEMES

Talk about favorite foods
Shop for food

Ask about prices
Ask for something you want

Make a shopping list

LANGUAGE

Steak is my favorite food.
I'll take these bananas.

How much are oranges?
I'd like some pears, please.
Do you need any onions?

We need two pounds of chicken.

FORMS

Foods
Demonstrative adjectives: *this*, *that*,
   these, *those*

How much
Some and *any*

Preview the conversations.

In the United States, fruits and
vegetables are weighed in pounds.
How are they weighed in your country?

Do you think these prices are
expensive? How do they compare to
prices in your country?

1 pound (lb.) = 453.5 grams (g)
2.2 pounds (lbs.) = 1 kilogram (kg)

58. Anything else?

 Before they leave for work, Russ and Jill Perkins talk about what they want for dinner.

A

Jill What do you want for dinner tonight?

Russ How about chicken?

Jill Anything but chicken. We always have chicken.

Russ Then let's go to a restaurant. There's a new Japanese restaurant on the corner.

Jill You know, I'd really like to stay home tonight.

Russ Well . . . how about steak?

Jill Mmm . . . that's my favorite food. And let's have a salad and some potatoes too. . . . And then some melon for dessert.

Russ Great. You buy the fruit and vegetables and I'll get the meat.

Jill O.K. I'll see you at six.

B

Jill I'd like this head of lettuce and a pound of those potatoes, please.

Clerk Anything else?

Jill Oh, let me think. . . . Do you have any melons?

Clerk What kind? I have these nice, fresh cantaloupes and those watermelons over there.

Jill The cantaloupes look good. How much are they?

Clerk They're $1.99 each.

Jill I'll take two, please.

Clerk All right. Would you like anything else?

Jill No, that's all. How much is it?

Clerk Let's see. . . . That'll be $5.47.

58. Anything else?

Tell the students what you like to eat. Then go around the classroom and ask different students what they like to eat. Write their responses on the board.

BACKGROUND

Before they leave for work, Russ and Jill Perkins talk about what they want for dinner and plan the menu. Jill wants steak, not chicken. Each of them buys certain ingredients.

LANGUAGE

You know... is used to confirm or establish something as fact.

Mmm... is used to indicate that something tastes good.

Anything else? is short for *Would you like anything else?* The word *else* means something additional or more.

No, that's all. is another way of saying "No, nothing more."

*...all out of (*steak*)* means there is no more (steak).

...instead here means "in place of that."

PROCEDURE

- Follow a procedure similar to that indicated for the opening conversations in the previous units.

- Have students listen to the conversations as they follow along in their books. If you read the conversations aloud, be sure to use appropriate stress, intonation, and gestures.

CULTURE CLOSE-UP

The most common place to shop in the U.S. is in large supermarkets, many of which sell not only food but many other items as well, ranging from toiletries to hardware. Specialty shops are found in some neighborhoods. These include produce markets, bakeries, butcher shops, etc.

Figure it out

1. Listen to the conversation and answer the questions.

■ Have the students follow along in their books as you read aloud the instructions and the questions.

■ Have the students listen to the conversation and answer the questions. They can compare their answers with a partner.

■ Call on different students to say their answers aloud. See if they can provide reasons for their answers. Ask a student to write the answers on the board.

ANSWERS
1. No, he doesn't.
2. No, she doesn't.

2. Listen again. Say *true*, *false*, or *it doesn't say*.

■ Tell the students to read over the instructions and the statements. Then have them listen to the conversation again and answer *True*, *False*, or *It doesn't say*.

■ Call on different students to read the statements aloud. Call on others to say the answers. Ask a student to write the correct answers on the board.

ANSWERS
2. It doesn't say.
3. False
4. False
5. True

3. Match.

■ Tell the students to read over the sentences. Have them match each sentence in the left column with the correct response in the right column.

■ Have the students work in pairs to compare their answers and to practice the exchanges. Call on different pairs to read the matched sentences aloud. Ask a student to write the answers on the board.

ANSWERS
2. c
3. a
4. d

FOLLOW-UP

Students can write out the exchanges they matched in exercise 3.

WORKBOOK Lesson 58, p. 77

Clerk May I help you?
Russ Yes. I'd like some steak, please.
Clerk I'm sorry. I'm all out of steak.
Russ Well . . . do you have any chicken?
Clerk Sure. I always have chicken.

Jill I'm really hungry. Where's the steak?
Russ Well . . . they were all out of steak.
So here's some chicken instead.
Jill Chicken?
Russ Yeah. Chicken.
Jill Russ, let's go to a restaurant.
Russ Well, how about Japanese food?
There's a new Japanese restaurant on
the corner, you know. . . .

Figure it out

1. Listen to the conversation and answer the questions.

1. Does Russ want to eat dinner at home?
2. Does Jill really want to eat in a restaurant?

2. Listen again. Say *true, false,* or *it doesn't say*.

1. Russ wants to eat in a restaurant. *True.*
2. The watermelons look bad.
3. Jill's favorite food is salad.
4. The store is out of chicken.
5. Russ and Jill are going to eat in a restaurant.

3. Match.

1. How about potatoes?
2. Anything else?
3. Where are the potatoes?
4. How much is it?

  a. They were out of potatoes.
  b. Anything but potatoes.
  c. No, that's all.
  d. $5.47.

59. Steak is my favorite food.

 1 ▶ **Listen to this magazine article and find each item in the picture.**

The four basic food groups are the *Fruit and Vegetable Group*; the *Meat, Fish, and Egg Group*; the *Milk Group*; and the *Grain Group*.

The Fruit and Vegetable Group includes bananas, grapes, apples, oranges, melons, spinach, potatoes, tomatoes, carrots, lettuce, and many more. The Meat, Fish, and Egg Group contains fish, eggs, and meats such as beef, pork, lamb, chicken, and turkey. The Milk Group includes foods like milk, cheese, and yogurt. Finally, the foods in the Grain Group are breads, pastas (like spaghetti), and cereals.

59. Steak is my favorite food.

WARM-UP

Tell the students to find as many food items as possible on pp. 103-105. Then have them close their books and name the food items they remember. Have other students write the names on the board. Finally, have them open their books to check and, if necessary, complete the list on the board.

FOODS

- Have the students examine the illustration and read the magazine article. Answer any questions they have. You may have to allow for translation to help students with the meanings of words for certain food items. Make sure they understand the concept of food groups.

- Have the students listen to the magazine article. As they listen a second time, pause after each food item so they can locate the items in the picture.

OPTION

Practice the pronunciation of the voiced plural ending of nouns—[z]. Say words from the picture and have the students repeat.

oranges
bananas
apples
eggs
melons
tomatoes
peppers
onions
potatoes

Now practice the voiceless plural ending [s] by having the students repeat the following words from the picture:

grapes
carrots

Say the words in sentences and have the students repeat. For example:

Do you have any oranges?
No, but I have bananas.
Are you out of grapes?
Yes, but I have apples.

TALK ABOUT FAVORITE FOODS

- Have the students follow along in their books as you read aloud the instructions and the exercise items. Make sure they understand the phrases *good for you* and *bad for you*.

- Have students work in pairs to take turns asking and answering the questions. Then call on different pairs to share their exchanges with the class. Discuss exercise item 4 with the class.

  ### SAMPLE ANSWERS
  1. Oranges, grapes, and apples.
  2. Carrots, onions, and potatoes.
  3. I eat (*student names items*).
     I don't eat (*student names items*).
  4. I think fish and chicken are good for you.
     I think pork and eggs are bad for you.

- Read aloud the sample exchanges with a student. Then tell the students to move around the classroom to find out their classmates' favorite foods.

- Call on different students to report their findings to the class.

SHOP FOR FOOD • DEMONSTRATIVE ADJECTIVES

- Have the students study the frame as you read aloud the heading and possible sentences. Answer any questions.

OPTION 1

Have the students practice the pronunciation contrast between *this* [ðɪs] and *these* [ðiz]. Have them repeat the words and the sentences in the frame after you. Then have them close their books. Say sentences which contain the words and have the students say "one" if they hear *this* and "two" if they hear *these*. For example:

T: I'll take this cheese.
S: One.
T: I don't want these apples.
S: Two.

OPTION 2

Use a book and some pencils to demonstrate the use of demonstrative adjectives. Place the objects on a desk. Stand next to the desk. Touch the book and say "I'll take this book." Then touch the pencils

and say "I'll take these pencils." Next move some distance from the desk, point to the book, and say "I'll take that book." Then point to the pencils and say "I'll take those pencils." Use different objects and have the students practice.

- Read the instructions aloud. Then tell the students to read over the incomplete conversation. Explain that *ugh* and *yuk* are both ways of expressing disgust or distaste.

- Have the students work individually to complete the conversation. Then have them work in pairs to practice the conversation.

- So they can check their answers, have the students listen to the conversation as many times as necessary. Call on a pair to act out the conversation for the class. Ask two students to write the answers on the board.

  ### ANSWERS
  A those
  B these, this
  B These
  A those

- Read aloud the information in the boxes and have the students repeat. Use the adjectives in complete sentences, say the sentences, and have the students repeat.

- Read aloud the instructions and the example sentences. Have the students repeat the sentences after you.

- Have students work in pairs to take turns comparing the fruit at the two stands in the picture. Tell them to use the example sentences as a model and to point as they make their comparisons. Go around the classroom and check their work.

- Call on different pairs to hold up their books, point, and say the sentences for the class. Ask two students to write the sentences on the board.

  ### SAMPLE ANSWERS
  These apples are 69¢ a pound. Those apples are 73¢ a pound.
  This watermelon is fresh. That watermelon is old.

FOLLOW-UP

Students can write out their answers to the questions in exercise 2.

WORKBOOK Lesson 59, pp. 78-79

TALK ABOUT FAVORITE FOODS

2 ▶ **Answer these questions.**

1. Name three kinds of fruit.
2. Name three vegetables.
3. Which of the foods in the article do you eat? Which of these foods don't you eat?
4. Which foods do you think are good for you and which ones do you think are bad for you?

3 ▶ **Interview your classmates. Ask about each student's favorite foods.**

A What's your favorite fruit?
B Apples.

A What's your favorite vegetable?
B Carrots.

SHOP FOR FOOD • DEMONSTRATIVE ADJECTIVES

4 ▶ **Study the frame.**

Demonstrative adjectives

| I'll take | **this** banana. |
| | **these** bananas. |

| I don't want | **that** banana. |
| | **those** bananas. |

 5 ▶ **Fill in the blanks with *this*, *that*, *these*, or *those*.**
▶ **Listen to check your answers.**

A O.K. What do we need?
B Bananas, apples, and watermelon.
A Well, _____ bananas look terrible.
B Yeah, but _____ bananas are ripe. And _____ watermelon is fresh, too.
A What about the apples?
B Ugh . . . look! _____ apples are rotten!
A Yuk! Let's take _____ apples instead.

 6 ▶ **Compare the fruit at the two stands.**

This watermelon is 49¢ a pound. That watermelon is 45¢ a pound.
These apples are rotten. Those apples are fresh.
These bananas are ripe. Those bananas are too ripe.

49¢ lb. = forty-nine cents a pound.

Some adjectives

| fresh | old |
| rotten | ripe |

60. How much are oranges?

  1 ▶ Listen to the radio ad. Find the items in the picture.

▶ Listen again. There are two mistakes in the radio ad. What are they?

▶ Ask and answer questions like the ones below.

1. How much is a bag of potatoes?
2. How much are tomatoes?
3. How much are oranges?
4. How much are bananas?
5. How much is salmon?
6. How much is chicken?
7. How much are these things at your local market?

55¢ ea. = fifty-five cents each
3/$1 = three for a dollar

potato + es ➡ potato**es**
tomato + es ➡ tomato**es**

Nick's Grocery
S P E C I A L   S A L E

VEGETABLES

Potatoes $2.49
5 lb. bag
Tomatoes 89¢ lb.
Head of Lettuce 99¢
Head of Garlic $1.29 lb.
Onions 59¢ lb.

FRUITS

Oranges 3/$1
Bananas 89¢ lb.
Pears 79¢ lb.
Watermelon 49¢ lb.
Grapes 99¢ lb.
Apples 55¢ lb.

MEATS

Pork Chops $2.29 lb.
Lamb Chops $3.19 lb.
Chicken $2.49 lb.
Ground Beef $2.29 lb.

FISH

Salmon $7.99 lb.
Flounder $5.99 lb.

chicken   pork   beef   lamb   turkey   fish

Sale Starts March 3 and Ends March 8

2 ▶ Study the frame.

Some and **any**

I have	**some**	
I don't have	**any**	onions.
Do you have	**any**	onions?

Some is used in polite requests:
*Would you like **some** onions?*

  3 ▶ Complete the conversation with *some* or *any*.
▶ Listen to check your work.

A I'd like *some* pears, please.
B I'm sorry. I don't have _____ pears.
A Do you have _____ apples?
B Yes. I have _____ nice apples.
A Great. I'll take three, please.
B O.K. Anything else?
A Yes. I'd like _____ bananas too.
B Sure. They're 89¢ a pound.
A O.K. Give me six, please.

60. How much are oranges?

WARM-UP

Have the students work in pairs to act out a conversation similar to Conversation C on p. 105. Tell them to use the picture on p. 107 as the setting for their role-plays.

ASK ABOUT PRICES • *HOW MUCH*

- Have the students examine the picture. Read the contents aloud and have the students repeat. Answer any questions about vocabulary. If possible, use pictures to help explain pork chops, lamb chops, ground beef, salmon, and flounder.

- Point out the blue boxes, read aloud the information in them, and have the students repeat. Make sure they understand that *ea.* is the abbreviation for *each* and that / means *for*. Give an example of when to use *each*—for example, say "Melons are a dollar ninety-nine each."

- Have the students listen to the radio ad. Provide a pause after each food item so they can locate the item in the picture.

- Read aloud the second set of instructions. Explain to the students that they will have to listen and read very carefully in order to find the two mistakes. When they've finished listening, call on different students to identify the two mistakes.

TAPESCRIPT AND ANSWERS

Come to Nick's Grocery! This week there's a special sale at Nick's Grocery. In our vegetable department, potatoes are two forty-nine a bag, and tomatoes are eighty-nine cents a pound. Lettuce is only ninety-nine cents a head. You can buy garlic for a dollar twenty-nine and onions for fifty-nine cents a pound.

In our fruit department, oranges are two for a dollar, and bananas are eighty-nine cents a pound. Pears are on sale for seventy-nine cents a pound, watermelon for forty-nine cents, and grapes are ninety-nine cents a pound. Buy apples for only fifty-five cents a pound.

Shop in our meat and fish departments and purchase pork chops for two twenty-nine a pound, lamb chops at three nineteen, and chicken for two forty-nine a pound. And ground beef is only a dollar nine a pound! Have salmon for dinner tonight for seven ninety-nine a pound or flounder for only five ninety-nine.

Remember, shop at Nick's Grocery, where there's always a bargain.

- Have the students work in pairs to take turns asking and answering the questions. Encourage them to ask and answer additional questions.

ASK FOR SOMETHING YOU WANT • *SOME* AND *ANY*

- Have the students study the frame and the box as you read aloud the heading and the sentences. Provide additional sentence examples with *some* and *any*.

- Try to elicit the rule for when to use *some* and when to use *any*. (Use *some* in affirmative statements and polite requests. Use *any* in negative statements and questions.)

OPTION

Go around the classroom and ask different students questions with *some* and *any* such as "Do you have any books in your desk?" and "Would you like some fruit?" Prompt them to answer truthfully.

- Read the instructions aloud. Then tell the students to read over the incomplete conversation.

- Have the students work individually to complete the conversation. Then have them work in pairs to practice the conversation.

- So they can check their answers, have the students listen to the conversation as many times as necessary. Call on a pair to act out the conversation for the class. Ask a student to write the answers on the board.

ANSWERS
B any
A any
B some
A some

OPTION

You and your students can bring pictures of different food items (or the actual food items) to class. Create a grocery store environment in the classroom. Use desk tops as counters to display the different types of food items. Have some students stand behind the counters and act as grocery store clerks. Have other students pretend they're customers.

ASK FOR SOMETHING YOU WANT

- Point out the first box and read aloud the heading and the possible sentences. Read aloud the information in the second box. Answer any questions.

- Read aloud the instructions. Then have the students follow along in their books as they listen to the two possible conversations. Have them listen a second time as you read the conversations aloud with two students. Have each of the two students say a different B response.

- Have the students work in pairs to take turns acting out the two possible conversations. Call on different pairs of students to act out the conversations for the class.

MAKE A SHOPPING LIST

- Have the students read over the conversation before they listen to it.

- Have the students read over the pink shopping list. Then have them listen a second time as you read the conversation aloud with a student.

- Read aloud the second set of instructions. Then have the students work in pairs to take turns playing the two roles in the conversations. Tell them to use the three shopping lists and the information in the gray box to help construct their conversations.

- Call on different pairs to present the conversations to the class.

POSSIBLE ANSWERS

2. **A** May I help you?
   B Yes. I'd like four bananas, please.
   A Anything else?
   B Yes. I'd also like a pound of grapes.
   A I'm sorry. I'm all out of grapes.
   B Oh...do you have any cantaloupes?
   A Yes, they're right over here.
   B O.K. I'll take two cantaloupes.
   A Would you like anything else?
   B Yes. I'd like two pounds of apples, please.
   A Sure. That'll be _____.

3. **A** May I help you?
   B Yes. I'd like three pounds of ground beef, please.
   A Anything else?
   B Yes. I'd also like a pound of chicken.
   A Would you like anything else?
   B Yes. I'd like a pound of bananas.
   A Anything else?
   B Yes. I'd like two pounds of pork chops.

A Sorry. We're all out of pork chops.
B Oh.
A That'll be _____.

- Read aloud the instructions. Then read aloud the items on the shopping list and have the students repeat.

- As they listen to the conversation, have the students identify the items the woman buys. Have them listen as many times as necessary.

- Call on a student to read aloud the list of items which the woman buys.

TAPESCRIPT
Clerk May I help you?
Woman Yes. I'd like a pound of tomatoes and a head of lettuce, please.
Clerk Anything else?
Woman Yes. I'd also like a bag of potatoes.
Clerk I'm sorry. I'm all out of potatoes. They were on sale, and I don't have any more.
Woman Do you have any onions?
Clerk No. I'm all out of onions too.
Woman How about apples?
Clerk Yes. How many would you like?
Woman Eight.
Clerk Anything else?
Woman Six oranges, and I think that's all.
Clerk All right.
Woman Oh, I almost forgot. I need some pears too. Let's see. Give me two pounds.
Clerk O.K. That'll be five ninety-eight.

ANSWERS
1 lb. tomatoes   2 lbs. pears
1 head of lettuce   6 oranges
8 apples

- Tell the students to read over the conversation. Then have them listen to it. You can also read aloud each line from the conversation and have the students repeat.

- Have the students work in groups of four. Tell them to take the different parts and read aloud the conversation they've just listened to.

- Read aloud the second set of instructions. Tell the groups to role-play the activity. Go around the classroom and give help where needed. Choose the best role-play and have the group present it to the class.

FOLLOW-UP

Students can write out their original conversations from exercise 7.

WORKBOOK Lesson 60, pp. 80-82

4
▶ **Listen to the possible conversations.**
▶ **Imagine you are at Nick's Grocery. Act out the conversation with a partner.**

A May I help you?
B Yes. I'd like two pounds of tomatoes, please.
A Anything else?
B Yes, do you have any onions?

A No. I'm all out of onions.
B O.K. That's all then.
A Let's see. . . . That'll be $1.78.

A Yes, they're right over here.
B Great. Give me a pound, please.
A Let's see. . . . That'll be $2.37.

You can say:

I'll take
I'd like   two pounds, please.
Give me

I'd like . . . is more polite than *I want* . . .

MAKE A SHOPPING LIST

  5
▶ **Listen to the conversation.**

A May I help you?
B Yes. I'd like two pounds of tomatoes, please.
A Anything else?
B Yes. I'd also like a pound of onions.
A I'm sorry. I'm all out of onions.
B Oh . . . do you have any garlic?
A Yes, it's right over here.
B O.K. I'll take a head of garlic.
A Would you like anything else?
B Yes. I'd like a watermelon, please.
A Sure. That'll be $6.20.

▶ **Have similar conversations using the shopping lists.**

1.

Shopping List
2 lbs. tomatoes
1 lb. onions
1 head garlic
1 watermelon

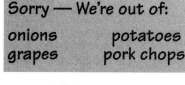

Sorry — We're out of:
onions   potatoes
grapes   pork chops

3.

Shopping List
3 lbs. ground beef
1 lb. chicken
1 lb. bananas
2 lbs. pork chops

2.

Shopping List
4 bananas
1 lb. grapes
2 cantaloupes
2 lbs. apples

  6
▶ **A woman is shopping at Nick's Grocery. Listen to the conversation and check the items she buys.**

Shopping List

____ 1 lb. tomatoes
____ 1 bag of potatoes
____ 1 head of lettuce
____ 1 lb. onions
____ 8 apples
____ 2 lbs. pears
____ 6 oranges

  7
▶ **Listen to the conversation.**

A What do you want for dinner?
B Let's have chicken.
C How much is it?
D It's $2.49 a pound at Nick's Grocery.
B O.K. We need two pounds. That'll be about $5.00.
A What kind of vegetable do you want? . . .

▶ **Solve this problem.**

Work in groups of four. Imagine you are preparing dinner tonight and you have only $10.00 for food. Agree on what food to buy from Nick's Grocery and make a shopping list.

61. Department store

 Loretta is shopping for a bathing suit with Stella.

1

Clerk May I help you?

Loretta Yes. I'm going to Florida and I need a new bathing suit.

Clerk Well, we have some very nice bathing suits right over here. I'm sure we have one just for you. What size do you wear — a twelve?

Loretta *(Laughs)* No. I need a fourteen.

Clerk The fourteens are over here. . . . This is beautiful, don't you think?

Stella Oh, that *is* pretty, Loretta.

Loretta No. I don't like all those flowers.

Clerk But that's the style this year. Everyone's wearing flowers.

Loretta Well, not me!

2

Stella How about those over there?

Clerk Those are bikinis.

Loretta *(Laughing)* Me in a bikini? I don't think so.

Clerk Well, do you like this?

Loretta Hmm . . . that's not bad. What do you think, Stella?

Stella Oh, it's very nice. I like it.

Loretta How much is it?

Clerk $59.98.

Loretta Oh, no. That's too expensive for . . .

Stella Oh, come on, Loretta. Try it on!

3

Loretta Well? What do you think?

Stella You look terrific! George is going to love it!

Loretta O.K. I'll take it.

4. Figure it out

***True, false,* or *it doesn't say*?**

1. Loretta wants a new bathing suit for Florida.
2. Loretta wants a bikini.
3. George likes bathing suits with lots of flowers.
4. Loretta tries on a bathing suit with flowers.
5. Loretta buys a bathing suit for $59.98.

61. Department store

WARM-UP

On the board, write the following exchanges:

May I help you?
Yes, I need a watermelon.

May I help you?
Yes, I need some apples.

Practice the exchanges with a student in front of the class. Then have the students work in pairs to take turns asking and answering the question. Tell them they can use food items from pp. 106-107 in their answers.

1., 2., & 3. Conversation

BACKGROUND

Loretta and Stella are shopping in a large department store. Loretta is looking for a bathing suit to wear in Florida.

LANGUAGE

...*right* (over here) means *immediately* or *directly* (over here).

...*just* (for you) means *especially* (for you).

...*a twelve* is short for *a size twelve*.

Try it on. means to put something on to see if it fits and/or looks good.

PROCEDURE

- Follow a procedure similar to that on p. 88.

4. Figure it out

***True, false,* or *it doesn't say*?**

- Tell the students to read over the instructions and the statements. Then have them listen to the conversation again and answer *True, False,* or *It doesn't say*.

- Call on different students to read the statements aloud. Call on others to say their answers. Ask a student to write the correct answers on the board.

ANSWERS
1. True
2. False
3. It doesn't say.
4. False
5. True

5. Listen in

- Read aloud the instructions as the students follow along in their books. Talk about each picture. For example, for picture **b**, you might say "A woman is at the Video Center. They rent and sell movies at the Video Center."

- Have the students listen to the four conversations as many times as necessary. Then have them compare their answers with a partner.

- Call on different students to say the answers. Write the answers on the board.

  TAPESCRIPT

  1. **Clerk**   How are they?
     Customer   They're too big.

  2. **Clerk**   How many would you like?
     Customer   I'll take six.

  3. **Clerk**   How much is this?
     Customer   Forty-five ninety-nine.

  4. **Clerk**   What kind of movies does your friend like?
     Customer   Comedies.

  ANSWERS
  1. d
  2. a
  3. c
  4. b

OPTION

Have the students work in pairs. Tell them to make up possible conversations for the people in the different pictures. Go around the classroom and check their work, giving help where needed. When they finish practicing their conversations, call on different pairs to present them to the class.

6. How to say it

- Follow the basic procedure for **How to say it** on p. 89.

PRONUNCIATION NOTE

Compound nouns, consisting of two words—such as *sunglasses*—receive primary stress on the first word.

7. Your turn

- Point out the sunglass department at the bottom of the page. Then read the instructions to the students. Tell them to read over the incomplete conversation.

- Have the students work in pairs to complete the conversation. Tell them that answers will vary.

- Have the pairs act out the conversation. The partners can take turns playing the two roles. Finally, call on different pairs to present their versions to the class.

SAMPLE ANSWERS
Yes. I like those sunglasses.
No, the brown sunglasses.
How much are they?
I'll take them.
No. That's all.

CULTURE CLOSE-UP

Large department stores in the U.S. often have many different sections or departments. Each department specializes in the sale of certain items. Typical departments are men's clothing, women's clothing, children's clothing, shoes, jewelry, and cosmetics. There may also be departments for hardware, household appliances, garden supplies, pet supplies, etc.

Shopping malls are similar to large department stores in that they contain separate shops which specialize in the sale of certain items. The difference is that these shops have different owners, whereas a large department store has only one owner. Incidentally, shopping malls often also house large department stores.

FOLLOW-UP

Students can write out the conversation they practiced in **Your turn**.

WORKBOOK Lesson 61, p. 83

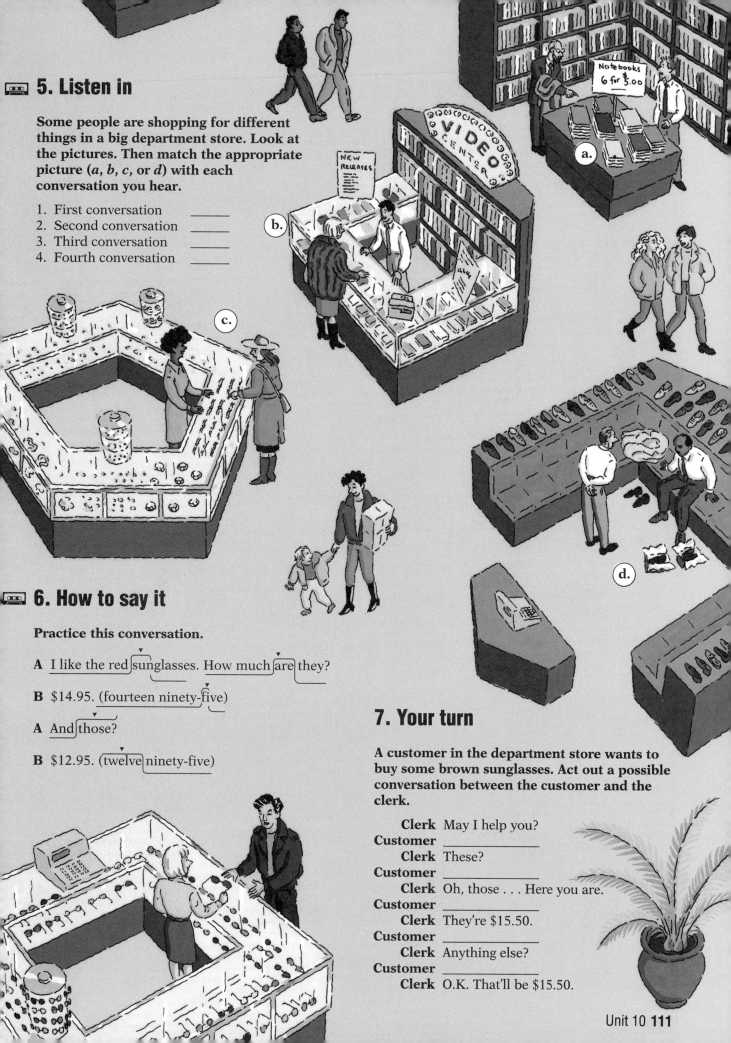

5. Listen in

Some people are shopping for different things in a big department store. Look at the pictures. Then match the appropriate picture (*a*, *b*, *c*, or *d*) with each conversation you hear.

1. First conversation _____
2. Second conversation _____
3. Third conversation _____
4. Fourth conversation _____

Notebooks 6 for $5.00

VIDEO CENTER

NEW RELEASES

6. How to say it

Practice this conversation.

A I like the red sunglasses. How much are they?

B $14.95. (fourteen ninety-five)

A And those?

B $12.95. (twelve ninety-five)

7. Your turn

A customer in the department store wants to buy some brown sunglasses. Act out a possible conversation between the customer and the clerk.

Clerk May I help you?
Customer _____
Clerk These?
Customer _____
Clerk Oh, those . . . Here you are.
Customer _____
Clerk They're $15.50.
Customer _____
Clerk Anything else?
Customer _____
Clerk O.K. That'll be $15.50.

World Travelers

1 It grows best in hot, wet weather and young plants usually grow in fields under water. It originally comes from India and China where it grew 3,000 to 5,000 years ago. Today it also grows in North and South America, but more than 95% of the world's supply comes from Southeast Asia. We only eat the seeds of this plant, but you have to cook them.

peanut

2 In the sixteenth century, Spanish explorers found them in Peru and took them back to Spain. At about the same time, Sir Walter Raleigh introduced them to England and Ireland. People have to wash them very well because they grow under the ground. Today, the French style of cooking them is very popular and North America, Northern Europe, and the former Soviet Union are the biggest producers.

rice

3 Peru was their native home, but they first became an important food in Mexico. Spanish explorers took them from South America to Europe, but most Europeans would not eat them. They thought they were poisonous. Today people eat them raw or cooked, and they are very popular in Italian cooking. The United States, Italy, Spain, Brazil, and Japan are the major producers of this food.

banana

4 Originally, they grew wild in the tropical jungles of Asia. They traveled across the islands of the Pacific and also across the Indian Ocean to Africa. Later they traveled across the Atlantic to the West Indies and America. You cut them when they are green, then they ripen and turn yellow and sweet. They are delicious raw, but you can also cook them. Central and South America and the West Indies grow them for export.

potato

5 One interesting story is that Spanish explorers found them in South America in the sixteenth century and took them back to Spain. At about the same time, explorers probably carried them from South America across the Pacific to China. The Spanish and Portuguese traded them in Africa for spices and elephant tusks. When slave ships went from Africa to North America, this food went back to America. Today, China, parts of Africa, and the United States grow most of them.

tomato

1. Read the article and match the descriptions with the names under the pictures.

2. Answer the questions.

1. Which three foods are originally from South America?
2. Which two are from Asia?

62. World Travelers

BACKGROUND

This article is like a guessing game. It talks about five different foods without telling the reader the names of the foods.

PROCEDURE

1. Read the article and match the descriptions with the names under the pictures.

- Read aloud the instructions. Make sure the students understand the procedure. Then have them read the article and do the exercise. They can also listen to the article as they follow along in their books.

- Call on different students to say the paragraph numbers and the corresponding food names. Ask two students to write the answers on the board.

  ANSWERS
  1. rice
  2. potato
  3. tomato
  4. banana
  5. peanut

2. Answer the questions.

- Tell the students to read the questions and write the answers on separate paper.

- Call on different students to read aloud the questions and their answers. Ask a student to write the answers on the board.

  ANSWERS
  1. Potatoes, tomatoes, and peanuts
  2. Rice and bananas

OPTION 1

Have the students underline or write down on separate paper any words or structures from the article which they don't understand. Use gestures, pictures, or words they already know to help them with unfamiliar language. Give only basic and simple explanations of new words and structures at this time.

OPTION 2

Have the students substitute the name of the food for the appropriate pronoun in each sentence. Write the first two sentences on the board:

Rice grows best in hot, wet weather and young plants usually grow in fields under water.

Rice originally comes from India and China where it grew 3,000 to 5,000 years ago.

Continue by having different students come to the board and write the other sentences.

FOLLOW-UP

Students can write complete-sentence answers for exercise 2.

WORKBOOK Lesson 62, p. 84. Before assigning the writing task, point out the use of commas in the list in Mike's note. Explain that we put a comma after each thing on a list when the list is written as part of a sentence. Point out that the comma before the word *and* is optional; this comma is called the serial comma, and although used throughout the *Spectrum* series, can be left out.

PREVIEW

Before you begin teaching, go over the functions/themes, language, and forms in the chart. This will give you a preview of what you will encounter as you guide the students through the unit.

Preview the conversations.

- Have the students look at the illustrations. Read aloud the name of the movie and the word *ice cream* and have the students repeat.

- Discuss the sentences in the box. Ask the students about classic old movies in their country. Find out what kind of movies they like.

CULTURE CLOSE-UP

The classic American movie *Gone with the Wind* has been around since 1939. It is probably the most famous American film ever made. It stars Clark Gable and Vivien Leigh and is the story of romance and adventure in the Old South during the Civil War. *Gone with the Wind* is sometimes called a "cult classic." This means that it has a following of people who have seen it many times and who usually know many of the film's details.

FUNCTIONS/THEMES	LANGUAGE	FORMS
Talk about past activities	They visited their friends. They went to the ballet	The past tense
Ask about the weekend	How was your weekend?	
Ask about the past	What did you do?	Information questions in the past tense
Talk about the past	She went to the office. She was at the office. She was in the office.	*To*, *at*, *in* with the definite article

Preview the conversations.

On Saturday night, Jenny and Sherry went to a movie. What movie did they see? What did they do after the movie?

63. Saturday night . . .

Jenny and her friend Sherry see *Gone with the Wind* for the third time.

A

Jenny Well, what did you think of the movie?

Sherry Oh, it was wonderful! I loved it!

Jenny Me too. I'd like to see it again.

Sherry Yeah, it's a classic. So, do you want to get some ice cream?

Jenny Sure.

B

Sherry So, are you still working at the Stop and Shop?

Jenny Just on Mondays and Wednesdays. Do you know who works there now? Gary Selby.

Sherry No kidding! I saw him last week at a party. He's a pretty nice guy.

Jenny Yeah, he is.

63. Saturday night...

WARM-UP

Tell the students the name of your favorite movie. Then go around the classroom and ask different students what their favorite movies are.

T: What's your favorite movie?
S: *Gone with the Wind*.

Now see if students can remember what their classmates said. For example:

T: What's his (her) favorite movie?
S: It's *Gone with the Wind*.

BACKGROUND

After seeing the movie *Gone with the Wind*, Jenny and her friend Sherry have some ice cream and talk about a mutual friend, Gary Selby.

LANGUAGE

...a classic is a traditional favorite or a masterpiece.

Just (on Mondays...) means *only* (on Mondays...).

No kidding! is like *You're kidding!* and is used to express mild doubt or surprise.

...pretty (nice guy) means *rather* or *somewhat*.

...actually is another way of saying "in fact."

...went out refers to going somewhere for entertainment or fun.

PROCEDURE

- Follow a procedure similar to that indicated for the opening conversations in the previous units.

- Have students listen to the conversations as they follow along in their books. If you read the conversations aloud, be sure to use appropriate stress, intonation, and gestures.

Figure it out

1. Listen to the conversation. Then complete the sentences with *good* or *boring*.

- Have the students follow along in their books as you read aloud the instructions. Then have them listen to the conversations and complete the sentences.

- Call on different students to say their answers aloud. Ask a student to write the answers on the board.

ANSWERS
1. good
2. boring

2. Listen again and answer *true, false,* or *it doesn't say.*

- Tell the students to read over the instructions and the statements. Then have them listen to the conversations again and answer *True, False,* or *It doesn't say.*

- Call on different students to read the statements aloud. Call on others to say the answers. Ask a student to write the correct answers on the board.

ANSWERS
1. True
2. It doesn't say.
3. True
4. True
5. It doesn't say.
6. True
7. True
8. False

3. Match each verb with its past form.

- Read aloud the verbs in each column as the students follow along in their books. Then have them match each verb in the left column with the correct past tense form in the right column.

- Call on different students to read the answers aloud. Ask a student to write the answers on the board.

ANSWERS
2. f
3. d
4. g
5. c
6. e
7. h
8. a

OPTION

Have the students make up sentences about the class, using the verbs in the present and past tense. Help them get started by writing some examples on the board:

I always ask questions in class.
I asked questions in class yesterday.

We have class on Mondays.
We had class yesterday.

FOLLOW-UP

Students can write down all the activities in Conversation C that are written in the past tense.

WORKBOOK Lesson 63, p. 85

C

Jenny How was your weekend?

Gary It was pretty boring, actually. I visited my parents on Saturday and I studied all day yesterday. Last night I was tired so I went to bed early. How about you? What did you do?

Jenny Sherry and I went out Saturday night.

Gary So, what did you do?

Jenny Oh, we went to the movies.

Gary What did you see?

Jenny We saw *Gone with the Wind*.

Gary Oh, I saw that last year. I didn't like it much, though.

Jenny Really? Why not?

Gary I guess I just don't like romantic movies.

Figure it out

1. **Listen to the conversation. Then complete the sentences with *good* or *boring*.**

Jenny's weekend was pretty _____ .
Gary's weekend was pretty _____ .

2. **Listen again and answer *true*, *false*, or *it doesn't say*.**

1. Jenny and Sherry went out Saturday night.
2. They had a pizza before the movie.
3. They thought the movie was great.
4. They got ice cream after the movie.
5. Jenny worked on Sunday.
6. Sherry knows Gary.
7. Gary studied on Sunday.
8. Both Jenny and Gary liked *Gone with the Wind*.

3. **Match each verb with its past form.**

1. ask   a. got
2. have   b. asked
3. study   c. did
4. go   d. studied
5. do   e. saw
6. see   f. had
7. love   g. went
8. get   h. loved

64. How was your weekend?

 1 ▶ **Listen to what the people in the pictures did yesterday.**
▶ **Match the descriptions with the pictures.**

1. He had dinner with a friend.
2. She got ice cream.
3. They went to the ballet.
4. She did her homework.
5. He lost his wallet.

6. She visited her parents.
7. They studied at the library.
8. She worked all day.
9. He relaxed at home.
10. They watched TV.

64. How was your weekend?

Write the following exchange on the board:

T: How was your weekend?
S: Wonderful!

Go around the classroom and ask different students how their weekend was. List their answers on the board.

TALK ABOUT PAST ACTIVITIES

- Read the instructions aloud and have the students repeat the sentences after you. Check for understanding of the vocabulary.

- Tell the students to examine the pictures. Then have them listen to the descriptions.

- Have the students match the descriptions with the pictures. Then have them compare their answers with a partner. Call on different students to say the answers. Ask two students to write the answers on the board.

ANSWERS

1. h	6. j
2. d	7. f
3. a	8. i
4. g	9. b
5. c	10. e

OPTION 1

Tell the students to cover the descriptions. Hold up your book and point to a picture. See if the class can say the appropriate description. Have the students work in pairs to take turns pointing to different pictures and saying the descriptions.

OPTION 2

Make copies of p. 116 and cut out the individual pictures. Give each student a picture. Call on different students to describe their pictures in the past tense. Then have the students trade pictures with a partner. Have them describe one another's pictures. Go around the classroom and check their work, giving help when needed.

ASK ABOUT THE WEEKEND • PAST TENSE

- Have the students study the frames as you read aloud the contents. Explain what is meant by *regular verbs* and *irregular verbs*. Point out the consistent occurrence of *-ed* and contrast it with the varying forms of the irregular verbs. Answer any questions the students have.

- Pronounce the three regular verbs in the past tense, slightly exaggerating the final sounds. Then have the students repeat them after you. Read aloud the language from the frames again and have the students repeat.

PRONUNCIATION NOTE

The regular past tense ending *-ed* is pronounced [əd] after the sounds [t] and [d], [d] after all other voiced sounds, and [t] after all other voiceless sounds.

- Have the students follow along in their books as you read aloud the instructions. Make sure they understand the language and the procedure mentioned in the instructions.

- Tell the students to read over the incomplete conversation and to look at the illustrations. Then have them work in pairs to complete the conversation.

- Have the students listen to the conversation to check their answers. Have two students write the answers on the board.

    ### ANSWERS
    I went to a party
    I played tennis, I studied
    I went to the ballet

OPTION 1

Have the students practice the conversation in pairs. Call on different pairs to present the conversation to the class. Then have the students use personal information and practice the conversation again. Call on different pairs to present their original conversations to the class.

OPTION 2

Call on various students to describe the pictures in the past tense. You can also have the students work in pairs to take turns describing the pictures to one another.

- Have the students move around the classroom and ask their classmates about their weekend. Tell them to use the conversation in exercise 3 as a model. You might have them take notes on their findings.

- Call on different students to report their findings to the class. Check their pronunciation and structures.

FOLLOW-UP

Students can use the past tense to write descriptions of the pictures in exercise 3.

WORKBOOK Lesson 64, pp. 86-87

2 ▶ **Study the frames: Past Tense**

Affirmative statements

I	**liked** [t]	the movie a lot.
We		
She	**studied** [d]	French last night.
He		
They	**visited** [əd]	their friends yesterday.

Past tense of regular verbs

like + **ed** ➔ **liked**

visit + **ed** ➔ **visited**

study + **ed** ➔ **studied**

Some irregular verbs

do	**did**	have	**had**
get	**got**	lose	**lost**
go	**went**		

They **went** to the beach.

  3 ▶ **Gary's weekend was boring, but the weekend before last, he had more fun. Complete the conversation using the information in the pictures.**
▶ **Listen to check your answers.**

Jim How was your weekend, Gary?
Gary Oh, it was pretty good. On Friday night _____ .
Jim How about Saturday?
Gary Well, in the morning _____ . On Saturday night _____ .
Jim Sunday night too?
Gary No, _____ .

Friday 11:30 PM

Saturday 11:00 AM

Saturday 10:00 PM

Sunday 8:00 PM

 4 ▶ **Talk with your classmates. Ask about their weekend.**

65. What did you do?

  1 ▶ **Complete the paragraphs about Jenny's mother, Mrs. Wilcox. Use the past tense of the verbs in parentheses.**
▶ **Listen to check your work.**

Mrs. Wilcox _____ (have) a terrible day on Monday. You see, her entire life is in her appointment book and she _____ (lose) it.

She _____ (go) to Chicago for a business meeting. At the meeting, she looked in her briefcase for her appointment book, but it wasn't there. She _____ (think) maybe she _____ (put) it in her handbag, but it wasn't there either.

After her meeting she _____ (have) dinner and _____ (see) a movie. Then she returned to the hotel. At the hotel she _____ (get) a surprise. There was a message from the airline. They _____ (say) they _____ (find) her appointment book. She _____ (leave) it on the plane.

Some more irregular verbs			
find	**found**	see	**saw**
leave	**left**	take	**took**
put	**put**	think	**thought**
say	**said**		

2 ▶ **Look at Mrs. Wilcox's appointment book. Answer the questions.**

1. Where did she go on Sunday afternoon?
2. What time did she have a meeting at City Bank?
3. What did she do Monday evening?
4. Where did she go on Tuesday?
5. Who did she see?
6. What did she do on Friday?

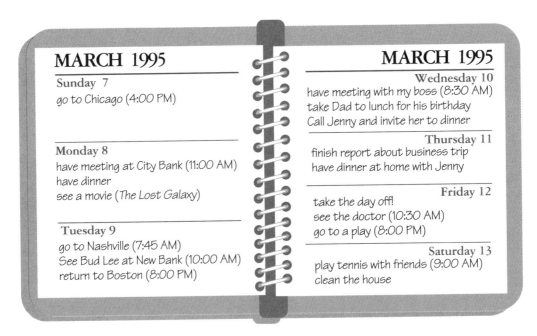

MARCH 1995

Sunday 7
go to Chicago (4:00 PM)

Monday 8
have meeting at City Bank (11:00 AM)
have dinner
see a movie (*The Lost Galaxy*)

Tuesday 9
go to Nashville (7:45 AM)
See Bud Lee at New Bank (10:00 AM)
return to Boston (8:00 PM)

MARCH 1995

Wednesday 10
have meeting with my boss (8:30 AM)
take Dad to lunch for his birthday
Call Jenny and invite her to dinner

Thursday 11
finish report about business trip
have dinner at home with Jenny

Friday 12
take the day off!
see the doctor (10:30 AM)
go to a play (8:00 PM)

Saturday 13
play tennis with friends (9:00 AM)
clean the house

3 ▶ **Study the frame: Information Questions in the Past Tense**

Information questions

Where			**go**?		**went** to Nashville.
What	**did**	you	**do**?	I	**had** a meeting.
Who			**see**?		**saw** Bud Lee.

 4 ▶ **Imagine it's Saturday. Ask and answer questions about Mrs. Wilcox's week.**

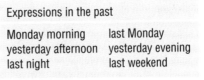

Expressions in the past

Monday morning	last Monday
yesterday afternoon	yesterday evening
last night	last weekend

65. What did you do?

WARM-UP

As you write them on the board, say verbs from the previous lesson in the present tense. Then point to each verb and have the class say the past tense. Next say some sentences from the lesson in the present tense, using the verbs on the board. See if different students can say the sentences in the past tense. For example:

T: They go to the ballet every Friday night.
S: They went to the ballet last Friday night.

ASK ABOUT THE PAST • INFORMATION QUESTIONS IN THE PAST TENSE

- Have the students look at the box and repeat as you read the contents aloud. Check for understanding of the meanings of the verbs.

- Tell the students to read over the incomplete paragraphs. Answer any questions they have about vocabulary or structures. Then have them complete the paragraphs.

- So they can check their answers, have the students listen to the paragraphs as many times as necessary. Ask two students to write the answers on the board.

ANSWERS

had	had, saw
lost	got
went	said, found
thought, put	left

- Have the students read over the instructions, exercise items, and the pages from Mrs. Wilcox's appointment book. Answer any questions about vocabulary or structures.

- Have the students work in pairs to take turns asking and answering the questions. Remind them to answer the questions in the past tense. Tell them to write their answers on separate paper.

- Call on different pairs to read their exchanges aloud. Ask other students to write the answers on the board.

ANSWERS
1. She went to Chicago.
2. She had a meeting at City Bank at 11 a.m.
3. She had dinner and saw a movie.
4. She went to Nashville.

5. She saw Bud Lee.
6. She took the day off, saw her doctor, and went to a play.

OPTION

Have the students write down additional questions about Mrs. Wilcox's appointments. Then have them work in pairs to take turns asking and answering one another's questions. Go around the classroom and check their work.

- Have the students study the frame and repeat as you read aloud the heading and possible sentences. Answer any questions.

OPTION

Ask different students the questions from the frame. Add the word *yesterday* to the first question.

- Have the students examine the box as you read aloud the contents. On the board, write some information questions with the expressions from the box. Use the information-question patterns from the blue box in exercise 3. Ask the questions about Mrs. Wilcox. For example:

  What did Mrs. Wilcox do on Monday morning?
  Where did she go yesterday evening?

- Read aloud the instructions. Ask the students the questions you wrote on the board. Then have them work in pairs to take turns asking and answering additional questions about Mrs. Wilcox's week.

- Call on different pairs to say their exchanges aloud and to write them on the board.

SAMPLE ANSWERS
A: Where did Mrs. Wilcox go on Monday morning?
B: She went to City Bank.
A: What did Mrs. Wilcox do last Monday?
B: She had a meeting at City Bank, had dinner, and saw a movie.
A: What did Mrs. Wilcox do yesterday afternoon?
B: I don't know what she did yesterday afternoon.
A: Where did Mrs. Wilcox go yesterday evening?
B: She went to a play.

WORKBOOK Lesson 65, pp. 88-89

66. Yesterday

WARM-UP

On the board, write and then read aloud the following exchange:

S1: Where did you go last night?
S2: I went to the movies.

Have the students make up an information question to ask a partner. Call on pairs to say their exchanges to the class. Write some of the exchanges on the board.

TALK ABOUT THE PAST • *TO*, *AT*, AND *IN* WITH THE DEFINITE ARTICLE

- Have the students read over the instructions and the exercise items. Answer any questions.

- Have the students listen to the conversation and check the things Jenny did yesterday. Have them listen as many times as necessary.

- Call on different students to read aloud the sentences they checked. Have other students write the sentences on the board.

TAPESCRIPT

Sherry Hey, Jenny!
Jenny Oh, hi, Sherry.
Sherry So, what did you do yesterday?
Jenny Yesterday? Wednesday?
Sherry Yeah. I called you, but you weren't at home.
Jenny Oh, I was pretty busy all day. I went to the hospital, and then I went to work.
Sherry To the hospital? Were you sick?
Jenny No. My friend Mark is in the hospital. I took some books to him.
Sherry What did you do after work?
Jenny I went shopping. I needed a new watch. And then it was six o'clock, and I went to class.
Sherry Did you get a watch?
Jenny Yeah. Look!
Sherry Oh, nice!

ANSWERS
1, 2, 5, 7, 8

- Have the students study the frame as you read aloud the heading and the possible sentences. Have the students look at the pictures as you read the sentences below them.

- Read the sentences from the frame again and have the students repeat. Answer any questions.

- Read the instructions aloud and explain that the words in parentheses may or may not be needed in the blanks. Also make sure the students understand that not all blanks necessarily have to be filled.

- Have the students read over the incomplete paragraph and then complete it. Tell them to compare their answers with a partner.

- Call on different students to read aloud the sentences from the paragraph as you write the answers on the board.

ANSWERS
in the
to the
at the
to
at
to
No answer needed.

4

- Read aloud the instructions as the students follow along in their books. Then read aloud the questions in the box and have the students repeat.

- Have the students work in pairs. Tell them to interview their partners. You might suggest that they write down what their partners say.

- Have the students tell another classmate what they found out about their partners. Call on different students to report their findings to the class.

FOLLOW-UP

Students can write down answers about themselves to the questions in the box in exercise 4.

WORKBOOK Lesson 66, p. 90

66. Yesterday

TALK ABOUT THE PAST • *TO, AT,* AND *IN* WITH THE DEFINITE ARTICLE

1 ▶ **Jenny is talking to her friend Sherry. Listen and check the things she did yesterday.**

1. _____ She went to the hospital.
2. _____ She took some books to a friend.
3. _____ She did her homework in the hospital.
4. _____ She had lunch with her mother at home.
5. _____ She went shopping.
6. _____ She looked for a new wallet.
7. _____ She got a new watch.
8. _____ She went to class.

2 ▶ **Study the frame and look at the pictures.**

To, at, and *in* with the definite article

		the office.			**the** office.
		the hospital.			**the** hospital.
				at	work.
She went	to	work.	She was		school.
		school.			home.
		class.			**the** office.
					the hospital.
				in	
	home.				class.

She went to the hospital.

She was at the hospital.

She was in the hospital.

3 ▶ **Complete the paragraph with *to (the)*, *at (the)*, or *in (the)* if necessary.**

Jenny's friend Mark was _____ hospital. On Tuesday Jenny went _____ hospital to visit him. She was _____ hospital for an hour. Then she went _____ work. She was _____ work all day. After work she went shopping and then at six o'clock she went _____ class. Finally, at eight thirty she went _____ home.

4 ▶ **Interview a classmate.**

Find out what a classmate did yesterday. Use the questions in the box or your own questions. Tell another classmate about your partner.

Where were you yesterday?
What did you do there?
Where were you last night?
What did you do/see/have? Anything exciting?

67. Now think back . . .

George and Loretta arrive at the airport.

1

George	What did you put in these suitcases, lead?
Loretta	I'm sorry, George. We had a lot of things.
Employee	May I help you?
Loretta	Yes. We're going to Miami.
Employee	May I see your tickets, please?
Loretta	George . . .
George	Huh?
Loretta	Give her the tickets.
George	Oh, the tickets . . . uh–oh . . .
Loretta	What's the matter?
George	I don't have the tickets.

2

Loretta	You don't have the tickets! George, it's two thirty. The flight leaves in half an hour!
George	Now calm down, Loretta.
Loretta	O.K. . . . I gave them to you this morning, remember?
George	Right.
Loretta	At breakfast.
George	Right.
Loretta	Now think back. What did you do after that?
George	Let's see . . . I got up from the table . . .
Loretta	Yes . . .
George	. . . and I went into the bedroom . . .
Loretta	Yes . . .
George	. . . and I put them in the pocket of my jacket . . . and now they're not there. (*George looks in his pocket.*)
Loretta	That's not possible, George. Look again.
George	Wait! Now I remember! I put them in the pocket of my *blue* jacket! It's in my suitcase.

3. Figure it out

Now think back and put the events in the correct order.

_____ George went to the bedroom and put the tickets in the pocket of his blue jacket.

_____ Loretta gave George the tickets.

_____ George remembered that the tickets were in the pocket of his blue jacket.

_____ George and Loretta found the tickets.

_____ Loretta asked George for the tickets.

_____ George and Loretta went to the airport.

_____ George put his blue jacket in his suitcase.

_____ The tickets weren't in George's pocket.

67. Now think back...

Ask the students if they ever lost something very important. Then ask if they found it. Encourage them to say where they found it.

1. & 2. Conversation

BACKGROUND

George and Loretta are at the airport and are about to check their suitcases. They are frantic because George can't find the tickets.

LANGUAGE

What's the matter? is another way of saying "What's wrong?"

...calm down is used to tell someone nervous or upset to relax.

...think back is another way of saying "Try to remember."

...got up means *stood up*.

PROCEDURE

- Follow a procedure similar to that on p. 88.

3. Figure it out

- Read aloud the instructions. Have the students cover the dialogue boxes. Then tell them to read the sentences and put the events in order by numbering the sentences.

- Have the students compare their answers with a partner. Have them uncover the dialogue boxes and check their answers.

- Call on different students to read aloud the sentences in the correct order. Write the answers on the board.

ANSWERS
2
1
7
8
5
4
3
6

4. Listen in

- Tell the students to look at the picture. Read aloud the instructions and the questions as the students follow along in their books.

- Have the students listen to the conversation as many times as necessary. Then have them answer the questions.

- Call on different students to say the answers. Have a student write the answers on the board.

TAPESCRIPT

Man Listen, have a good time in Chicago, relax, and call me when you get there.

Woman O.K., I will. Oh, please say good-bye to your sister for me. I called her yesterday, but she wasn't at home.

Man Yeah, she went to Boston for a week.

Woman Oh, I didn't know that.

ANSWERS
1. She's going to Chicago.
2. She went to Boston.

5. Your turn

- Have the students look at the picture and the sentences as you read them aloud.

- Have the students work in pairs. Tell them to pretend they're in a situation identical to George and Loretta's. Have them act out a conversation. You might help them get started by writing a possible first line on the board:

  George: Look, Loretta! I found the tickets!

- Call on different pairs to act out their conversations for the class. Have the pairs write their conversations on the board for you to check.

SAMPLE ANSWERS
George Look, Loretta! I found the tickets!
Loretta Great! What a relief!

6. How to say it

- Have the students read over the conversation. Then read aloud the instructions and have the students listen to the conversation. Play the cassette or read it again and have the students repeat each line.

- Tell the students to work in pairs to practice the conversation. Have them take turns playing each role.

- Call on different pairs to present their conversations to the class. Check their work.

PRONUNCIATION NOTE

The phonetic transcriptions in brackets [ ] demonstrate how the sounds of the underlined words are reduced and blended into what sounds like one word in normal speech.

7. Your turn

- Point out the pilot and flight attendant at the bottom of the page. Then read the instructions to the students. Tell them to read over the incomplete conversation.

- Have the students work in pairs to complete the conversation. Tell them that answers will vary.

- Have the pairs act out the conversation. The partners can take turns playing the two roles. Finally, call on different pairs to present their versions to the class.

SAMPLE ANSWERS
Fine, thanks.
In Tokyo. How about you?
How was your trip?
How is she?

FOLLOW-UP

Students can write out the conversation they practiced in **7. Your turn**.

WORKBOOK Lesson 67, p. 91

4. Listen in

A man is saying good-bye to a woman at the airport. Read the questions below. Then listen to the conversation and answer the questions.

1. Where is the woman going?
2. Where did the man's sister go?

5. Your turn

George finds the tickets and shows them to Loretta. She is very relieved and happy. Act out the conversation.

6. How to say it

Listen to the conversation below. Then practice it.

A Where <u>did</u> <u>you</u> go?   [diʤuw]
B To Chicago.
A What <u>did</u> <u>you</u> do there?   [diʤuw]
B I visited some friends.
A When <u>did</u> <u>you</u> get back?   [diʤuw]
B Last night.

7. Your turn

Amy runs into her friend Lou in the airport. They were both away on trips. Act out the conversation.

Amy Lou! How are you doing?
Lou _____
Amy So, where were you this time?
Lou _____
Amy London.
Lou _____
Amy Oh, my trip was O.K. By the way, Ellen Mason was on the flight.
Lou _____
Amy She's fine. She says hello.

Tomorrow Is Another Day

On December 15, 1939, Rhett Butler and Scarlett O'Hara came alive on the movie screen. From the very first moment, people fell in love with a movie about life in the Old South. Based on Margaret Mitchell's 1936 novel, it is the story of a self-centered young woman who struggles to live through the American Civil War, but then loses the only man she loves.

Clark Gable was everyone's choice to play Rhett Butler. Thousands of people sent letters to the movie studio saying that Clark Gable was perfect for the part. Gable was not interested, but he had to take the part because he had a contract at the studio.

It was more difficult for Selznick to find a

When Margaret Mitchell was 35, she found herself at home in Atlanta with a broken ankle and nothing to do. She had read all of the books in the local library so her husband suggested that she write her own book. Its original title was Tomorrow Is Another Day. *When it was published, more than 100,000 copies sold immediately. It became a best-seller and David O. Selznick at the MGM movie studio bought the movie rights. Mitchell never wanted to write a sequel to her novel. For her, she said, the story had ended. She died in 1949 before anyone could change her mind. In 1991,* Scarlett, *a novel by Alexandra Ripley, was published with the approval of Margaret Mitchell's estate.*

female lead. Everyone tested for the part, from Lucille Ball to Joan Crawford. A young British actress named Vivien Leigh was in Hollywood visiting her boyfriend, the famous actor Lawrence Olivier. Selznick's brother Myron was Olivier's agent. When Myron Selznick met Vivien Leigh, he knew immediately that she would be the ideal Scarlett O'Hara. So he developed a plan. He arranged for her to meet David O. Selznick. For the meeting she wore a large hat and green eye shadow. Myron introduced her to David as Scarlett O'Hara. She got the part.

The movie won eight Academy Awards, including best picture, best performance by an actress (Vivien Leigh), and best performance by a supporting actress (Hattie McDaniel, the first African-American actor to receive an Oscar). The movie's spectacular sets, romantic costumes, and dramatic music make it as popular today as it was more than fifty years ago.

1. **What is the real name of this famous novel and movie?**

2. **Answer these questions.**

1. Who wrote the original novel?
2. Why did Clark Gable take the part?
3. Who played Scarlett O'Hara? Where was the actress from?
4. Is there a sequel to the novel? Who wrote it?

68. Tomorrow Is Another Day

BACKGROUND

This article is about how a famous movie came to be. It also talks about the book on which the movie was based and the book's author. It's the kind of article one might find in the arts or entertainment section of a newspaper.

PROCEDURE

1. What is the real name of this famous novel and movie?

- Have the students read through the article. Tell them to look for the real name of the movie in the first pages of this unit.

- Call on a student to write the real name of the novel and movie on the board.

ANSWER
Gone with the Wind

2. Answer these questions.

- Tell the students to read through the questions. Then have them listen to the article as they read it a second time. Make sure they understand the meanings of new words such as *sequel*. Have them answer the questions with complete sentences.

- Have the students work with a partner to compare answers. Ask different students to write the answers on the board. Check their work.

POSSIBLE ANSWERS
1. Margaret Mitchell wrote the original novel.
2. Clark Gable took the part because he had a contract at the MGM movie studio.
3. Vivien Leigh played Scarlett O'Hara. She was from England.
4. Yes. There's a sequel to the novel called *Scarlett*. Alexandra Ripley wrote it.

OPTION

Have the students underline or write down on separate paper any words or structures from the article which they don't understand. Use gestures, pictures, or words they already know to help them with unfamiliar language. Give only basic and simple explanations of new words and structures at this time.

FOLLOW-UP

Students can write additional questions and answers for exercise 2—for example, *What is the movie about?* (*The movie is about life in the Old South*).

WORKBOOK Lesson 68, p. 92. Before assigning the writing task, point out the different features of the letter such as the date, opening greeting, and closing remark. You might also point out the paragraph indentation and remind students to indent their own paragraphs.

Review of units 8-11

1

- Read aloud the first set of instructions to the students. Then have the students read over the incomplete conversation.

- Have the students work in pairs to complete the conversation and to act it out. Go around the classroom and check their work.

- Call on different pairs to act out their conversations for the class. Have two students write sample answers on the board.

  SAMPLE ANSWERS
  Hello. How are you?
  Fine. What are you doing?
  How nice! Do you like Los Angeles?
  How's the weather in Los Angeles?
  I'm listening to the radio.

- Have the students look over the weather report. Call on different students to read the contents aloud.

- Go over the remaining instructions with the students. Tell the pairs to take turns playing the two roles. Remind them to choose a city from the weather report.

- Call on different pairs to act out their conversations for the class. Check their pronunciation and intonation.

2

- Read aloud the instructions for exercise 2A on p. 123 and 2B on p. 124. Divide the class into pairs. Have them decide who will be Student A and who will be Student B. So the pairs have a model, call on a student and practice asking about and locating the department store. For example:

  A Is there a department store in the neighborhood?
  B Yes, there is.
  A Where is it?
  B It's on Main Street.

- Have the pairs follow the instructions and take turns playing the roles of Student A and Student B. Go around the classroom and listen in, giving help when needed.

- Call on different pairs of students to share their exchanges with the class. You can have other pairs write the exchanges on the board.

POSSIBLE 2A ANSWERS
A Is there a bookstore in the neighborhood?
B Yes, there is.
A Where is it?
B It's on Elm Street, across from the park.

A Is there a shoe store in the neighborhood?
B No, there isn't.

A Is there a grocery store in the neighborhood?
B Yes, there is.
A Where is it?
B It's on the corner of Maple and Elm.

A Is there a drugstore in the neighborhood?
B Yes, there is.
A Where is it?
B It's on the corner of Maple and Elm.

POSSIBLE 2B ANSWERS
A Is there a video store in the neighborhood?
B No, there isn't.

A Is there a drugstore in the neighborhood?
B Yes, there is.
A Where is it?
B It's on the corner of Maple and Elm.

A Is there a bank in the neighborhood?
B Yes, there is.
A Where is it?
B It's on the corner of Main and Maple.

A Is there a movie theater in the neighborhood?
B Yes, there is.
A Where is it?
B It's on the corner of Main and Pine.

3

- As the students follow along in their books, read aloud the instructions for exercise 3A on p. 123 and 3B on p. 124. If necessary, call on a student and practice asking about and locating the cafeteria.

- Have the pairs follow the instructions. Go around the classroom and listen in, giving help when needed.

- Call on a pair of students to share their exchanges with the class. You can have another pair write the exchanges on the board.

Review of units 8-11

 ▶ You are calling a friend who has moved to Los Angeles. Complete the phone conversation.

▶ Imagine your partner moved to one of the cities in the weather report. Act out a similar conversation.

A _____
B Oh, pretty good. How are you?
A _____
B Nothing much. I'm just sitting here and reading a book, and I decided to call you.
A _____
B Yes. I like Los Angeles a lot.
A _____
B It's very hot today. So, what are you doing now?
A _____

WEATHER REPORT

Athens	65°		cloudy
Cairo	95°		sunny
Helsinki	20°		snowing
London	72°		raining
Los Angeles	86°		sunny
Madrid	50°		windy
Moscow	40°		cloudy
Seoul	55°		raining

 ▶ Student A follows the instructions below. Student B follows the instructions on page 124.

Student A Ask your partner if there's a *department store*, a *bookstore*, a *shoe store,* and a *grocery store* in the neighborhood shown on the map. Locate the places if they exist. Then answer your partner's questions.

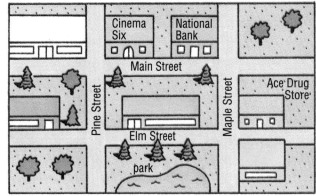

3A ▶ Student A follows the instructions below. Student B follows the instructions on page 124.

Student A You and your partner are coming out of the elevators in Brennan's Department Store. Ask your partner for directions to the *cafeteria,* the *restrooms,* the *drinking fountain,* and the *stairs.* Locate each place on the floor plan. Then answer your partner's questions.

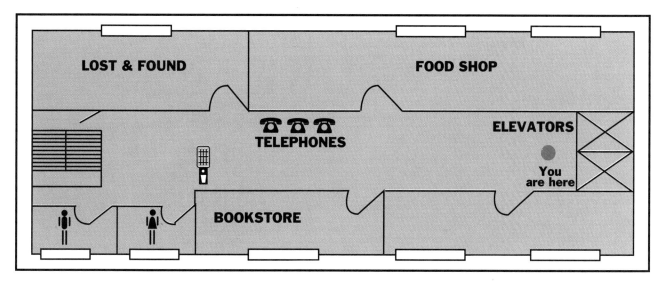

2B ▶ **Student B follows the instructions below. Student A follows the instructions on page 123.**

Student B Use the map to answer your partner's questions. Then ask your partner if there's a *video store*, a *drugstore*, a *bank*, and a *movie theater* in the neighborhood. Locate the places on the map.

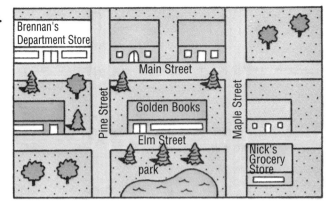

3B ▶ **Student B follows the instructions below. Student A follows the instructions on page 123.**

Student B You and your partner are coming out of the elevators in Brennan's Department Store. Answer your partner's questions. Then ask your partner for directions to the *food shop*, the *telephones*, the *bookstore*, and the *Lost and Found*. Locate each place on the floor plan.

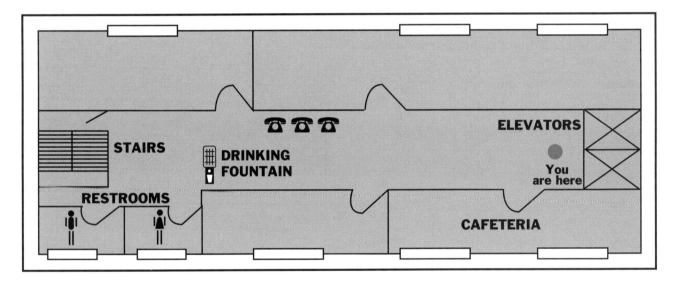

  ▶ Listen to the radio commercial for Brennan's Department Store. Then complete the newspaper ad with the correct address and store hours.

POSSIBLE 3A ANSWERS

A Excuse me. Where's the cafeteria?
B It's on your left.

A Excuse me. Where way are the restrooms?
B They're down the hall on the left.

A Excuse me. Where's the drinking fountain?
B It's down the hall on the left.

A Excuse me. Where are the stairs?
B They're down the hall.

POSSIBLE 3B ANSWERS

A Excuse me. Where's the food shop?
B It's on your right.

A Excuse me. Where are the telephones?
B They're down the hall on the right.

A Excuse me. Where's the bookstore?
B It's down the hall on the left.

A Excuse me. Where's the Lost and Found?
B It's down the hall on the right.

- Read aloud the contents of the newspaper ad as the students follow along in their books. Then read the exercise instructions aloud.

- Have the students listen to the radio commercial and complete the ad. Then have them compare their answers with a partner. Finally, call on a student to write the answers on the board.

TAPESCRIPT

Brennan's Department Store has everything you need for your family and the home. And this week, Brennan's is having its annual back-to-school sale with up to thirty percent off on all boys' and girls' clothes. Brennan's is open from ten to nine Monday through Friday, ten to six on Saturday, and twelve to six on Sunday. So come to Brennan's, located at 1742 Park Avenue. Brennan's—where all the smart shoppers go!

ANSWERS
1742 Park
10 to 9
10 to 6
12 to 6

- Read aloud the first set of instructions. Then have the students examine the picture and read over the incomplete conversation.

- Have the students work in pairs to complete the conversation. Then call on a pair to act out the conversation for the class. Ask a pair of students to write the answers on the board. Finally, you can have the pairs practice the conversation.

  SAMPLE ANSWERS
  They're $28.00.
  Do you like these cotton ties?
  $15.00.
  Anything else?
  $30.00.

- Read aloud the second set of instructions. Have the pairs act out similar conversations. Go around the classroom and listen in, giving help if needed.

- Call on different pairs to act out their conversations for the class.

OPTION

Call on different pairs of students to act out the conversation in their books. Check their pronunciation and intonation.

- Hold up your book and point to the sale table in the picture as you read the first sentence of the instructions. Point to the table and then to the counter as you read the second sentence.

- As you point to the items, read the sample sentences aloud. Have the class repeat after you.

- Tell the students to work in pairs to compare the items. Call on different pairs to write the comparisons on the board and to read them aloud.

  ANSWERS
  These ties are $15.00.
  Those ties are $28.00.

  These wallets are plastic.
  Those wallets are leather.

  These sweaters are cotton.
  Those sweaters are wool.

  These sweaters are $36.00.
  Those sweaters are $46.00.

OPTION

Have the students work in pairs. Tell them to make up a conversation between a customer and the salesperson in the picture. Then have them act out the conversation. Go around the classroom and listen in. Choose the best conversation for presentation to the class.

- Have the students read over the incomplete conversation and then complete it. Tell them to compare their answers with a partner.

  SAMPLE ANSWERS
  Uh-oh…
  I lost my sweater.
  Oh, what a relief!

OPTION

Call on different pairs of students to act out the conversation. Check their pronunciation and intonation.

- Read aloud the instructions as the students follow along in their books.

- Have the students work in pairs. Tell them to take turns closing their eyes as their partner hides one of their personal belongings. Then have them act out conversations like the one in exercise 7.

5 ▶ You are in the men's department of Brennan's. Look at the picture and complete the conversation.

▶ Act out a similar conversation with a partner, talking about other items in the picture.

Customer Excuse me, how much are these silk ties?
Salesperson _____
Customer Oh, they're too expensive.
Salesperson _____
Customer Yes. They are pretty nice. How much are they?
Salesperson _____
Customer Good. I'll take a blue tie and a green tie.
Salesperson _____
Customer No. That's all. How much is it?
Salesperson _____

6 ▶ You are standing at the sale table in the men's department. Compare the items on the table with those on the counter.

These ties are cotton.
Those ties are silk.

These wallets are $3.50.
Those wallets are $10.00.

7 ▶ Complete the conversation.

A _____
B What's wrong?
A _____
B Your sweater? It's over there on the teacher's desk.
A _____

8 ▶ Play a game.

Your partner will hide one of your personal belongings. Act out a conversation like the one on the left.

9 ▶ You are in the food shop at Brennan's. Complete the conversation.
  ▶ Look at the picture and act out a similar conversation with a partner.

You Excuse me. Do you have any pears?
Clerk _____
You Oh, no! Well, give me six oranges instead.
Clerk _____
You No. That's all.
Clerk _____

10 ▶ Imagine you are having coffee at Brennan's cafeteria and you see a friend. Greet your friend and ask about his or her weekend. Tell about your weekend. Use the sentences in the box.

How was your weekend?
What did you do?

11 ▶ Complete the conversation.

A Let's go to a movie.
B _____
A *Gone with the Wind* is playing at the Winthrop.
B _____
A How about *Sylvia's Adventures*? It's playing at the Cinema Center.
B _____
A There are shows at 8:20 and 10:30.
B _____
A O.K.

▶ Act out a similar conversation with a partner. Suggest going to see a movie shown in the ad or one advertised in your local newspaper.

- Read aloud the first set of instructions. Then have the students examine the picture and complete the conversation.

- Have the students work in pairs to compare answers and to practice the conversation. Then ask a pair of students to write the answers on the board.

  SAMPLE ANSWERS
  No. I'm sorry. We're all out of pears.
  Anything else?
  Let's see…That'll be $1.50.

- Read aloud the second set of instructions. Have the pairs act out similar conversations. Go around the classroom and listen in, giving help when needed.

- Call on different pairs to act out their conversations for the class.

- Read aloud the instructions as the students follow along in their books. Then point out the box, read the questions in it, and have the class repeat.

- Have the students work in pairs to take turns asking and answering the questions about one another's weekend. Go around the classroom and check their work.

- Call on different pairs to present their conversations to the class.

- Have the students read over the incomplete conversation and then complete it. They can compare their answers with a partner.

  SAMPLE ANSWERS
  What's playing tonight?
  You know I don't like old movies.
  What time does the next show start?
  Let's go to the 8:20 show.

- Read aloud the second set of instructions as the students follow along in their books. Then have the students read over the ad.

- Have the students work in pairs to act out a conversation similar to the one in their books. They can use the ad in their books or one from their local newspaper.

- Call on different pairs to act out their conversations for the class. You may want to give a prize for the best presentation.

WORKBOOK Review of units 8-11, pp. 93-94

PREVIEW

Before you begin teaching, go over the functions/themes, language, and forms in the chart. This will give you a preview of what you will encounter as you guide the students through the unit.

Preview the conversations.

- Have the students look at the illustration. Read aloud the question at the bottom of the picture and then discuss it with the class. Talk about your own experiences in starting a conversation with a stranger. Invite the students to share their own experiences as well.

CULTURE CLOSE-UP

The use of "small talk" is a common way to start up a conversation in the U.S. Small talk refers to conversation about very ordinary or mundane topics such as the weather. Small talk is often used to "break the ice" when a person wants to talk to a stranger. Small talk can be used to lead into more specific or personal conversation—for example, after talking about the weather, a person might say what he or she likes to do on a sunny or cloudy day.

UNIT 12 • LESSONS 69–73

PREVIEW

FUNCTIONS/THEMES	LANGUAGE	FORMS
Make small talk	Nice day.	*There is* and *there are*
Talk about places to live Give an opinion	I live in the city. There's always something to do. In my opinion, it's the only place to live.	
Talk about favorite cities	New York is my favorite city.	
Talk about likes and dislikes	Robert likes classical music, and I do too. Robert doesn't like mystery novels, and I don't either.	Rejoinders: *too* and *either*
Talk about what you have in common	How old are you? Twenty-five. Oh, I am too! I love nightclubs. But the nightclubs here are awful.	Nouns with and without *the*

Preview the conversations.

In your country, if you don't know someone and want to start a conversation, how do you begin?

69. In my opinion . . .

 Two strangers on their lunch hour are talking in the park in New York City.

A

Todd Nice day.
Kim Yeah, it is.
Todd Don't you work at the Plaza Hotel?
Kim Uh-huh.
Todd I thought so. Me too. I just started there last week.

B

Todd Do you live here in the city?
Kim No. I live in the country.
Todd Oh? Where?
Kim Cold Spring. It's a small town about an hour from here.
Todd That's pretty far.
Kim I know, but I like the country. It's very quiet — especially after a long day at work.
Todd How do you get to work?
Kim I take the train. It takes me about an hour.

C

Kim Where do *you* live?
Todd Here in the city.
Kim Do you like it?
Todd Yeah. In my opinion, it's the only place to live.
Kim Why do you say that?
Todd Because there's always something to do and it's never boring.
Kim But the country isn't boring either. You can swim, fish, hike, have a garden — all kinds of things.
Todd I guess.

69. In my opinion...

WARM-UP

Introduce small talk and review questions with *do* by going around the class and asking different students questions. For example:

Nice evening. Do you live near here?
Cool weather. Do you like it?

BACKGROUND

Two strangers meet in a park in New York City. They strike up a conversation about life in the city versus life in the country.

LANGUAGE

I thought so. is used to confirm or establish something as fact.

...about (an hour) means *approximately* (an hour).

It takes... is another way of saying "It requires... ."

In my opinion is another way of saying "I think" or "I believe."

So... has no actual meaning and is used to introduce a remark.

It puts me to sleep. is another way of saying "It tires (or bores) me."

PROCEDURE

- Follow a procedure similar to that indicated for the opening conversations in the previous units.

- Have students listen to the conversations as they follow along in their books. If you read the conversations aloud, be sure to use appropriate stress, intonation, and gestures.

Figure it out

1. Listen to the conversation and answer *true* **or** *false*.

■ Have the students follow along in their books as you read aloud the instructions and the statements.

■ Have the students listen to the conversation and then answer *True* or *False*.

■ Call on different students to say the answers aloud. See if they can provide reasons for their answers.

ANSWERS
1. True
2. False

OPTION

Have the students write down additional true/false statements. You can write some examples on the board:

Cold Spring is a small town. (True)
The man and the woman both live in the city. (False)

Tell the students to work in pairs and to take turns trying their statements out on each other. Finally, call on different students to try out their statements on the class.

LANGUAGE NOTE

Rap music became popular in the 1980s. Its lyrics are spoken rather than sung. Electronic rhythms provide background music to rap's street-wise chants and rhymes, which reflect the concerns of urban youth living in a tough world.

2. Match.

■ Tell the students to read over the sentences. Have them match each sentence in the left column with the correct response in the right column.

■ Have the students work in pairs to compare their answers and to practice the exchanges. Call on different pairs to read the matched sentences aloud. Ask a student to write the answers on the board.

ANSWERS
2. d
3. e
4. b
5. f
6. a

OPTION

Have students practice the rising intonation pattern of yes-no questions and the rising-falling pattern of wh- information questions and statements. Read the exchanges from the exercise aloud and have the students repeat. Then tell the students you will read aloud the exchanges again. Explain that this time, after you read each part of an exchange, they should say "one" if they hear a rising pattern and "two" if they hear a falling pattern.

FOLLOW-UP

Students can write out the exchanges they matched in exercise 2.

WORKBOOK Lesson 69, p. 95

D

Todd What are you reading?
Kim It's a new book by Robert Ludlum.
Todd Oh, he's great.
Kim I agree. I like most mystery writers, but Ludlum's my favorite.

E

Todd So, what kind of music do you like?
Kim Most kinds. Rock, rap, jazz…
Todd Me too, but I like classical music best.
Kim Oh, that's the only kind of music I don't like. It puts me to sleep.

Figure it out

1. Listen to the conversation and answer *true* or *false*.

1. The man and the woman both like mystery writers.
2. The man and the woman both like classical music.

2. Match.

1. Do you live here in the city?
2. Nice day.
3. Where do you live?
4. Why do you say that?
5. Oh, he's a good writer.
6. What kind of music do you like?

a. Most kinds.
b. Because it's never boring.
c. No.
d. Yes, it is.
e. Here in the city.
f. I agree.

70. Nice day

 1 ▶ Listen to the conversation.
▶ Start a conversation and find out about someone you don't know very well.

A Beautiful day.
B Yes, it is.
A Do you work near here?
B Uh-huh. On Fifth Avenue.
A And do you live here in the city?
B No. I live in the country.
A How do you get to work?
B I take the train. It takes about an hour.

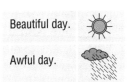

 I take the train.   I take the subway.   I ride my motorcycle.

 I take the bus.   I ride my bike.   I walk.  I drive.

TALK ABOUT PLACES TO LIVE • GIVE AN OPINION • *THERE IS* AND *THERE ARE*

 2 ▶ Listen to the conversation. Put an *M* in front of the things the man likes about the city.
▶ Listen again. Put a *W* in front of the woman's opinions about the city.

Some Opinions

There's always something to do.	There's nothing to do.
There are a lot of great restaurants.	There aren't many good restaurants.
There are discos.	There aren't any discos.
There are excellent museums.	There aren't any museums.
There are a lot of trees and flowers.	There aren't many trees and flowers.
It's exciting.	It's boring.
It's safe.	It's dangerous.
It's too quiet.	It's too noisy.
It's clean.	It's dirty.
It's cheap.	It's expensive.

  3 ▶ Listen to these possible conversations.
▶ Have a similar conversation with a partner.

A Do you live here in the city?
B Uh-huh.
A Do you like it?
B Yeah. In my opinion, it's the only place to live. There's always something to do.
A I agree. It's very exciting.

A Do you live here in the city?
B No. I live in the country about an hour from here.
A Do you like it?
B Not really. In my opinion, it's boring.
A Oh, I disagree. There are lots of things to do in the country.

the city

the suburbs

a small town

the country

70. Nice day

WARM-UP

Practice questions with *Is it...?* and *Is there...?* Ask different students questions about their immediate surroundings or environment. For example:

T: Is it raining?
S: Yes, it is. (No, it isn't.)
T: Is there a drinking fountain near here?
S: Yes, there is. (No, there isn't.)

MAKE SMALL TALK

- Have the students look at the illustrations and repeat the sentences under them as you read the sentences aloud. Point out the box and read the two phrases in it aloud, using appropriate intonation and facial expressions.

- Tell the students to read over the conversation. Then have them listen to it.

- Read aloud the second set of instructions. Tell the students to move around the classroom and to start a conversation with someone. Have them take notes on what they find out about their classmate.

- Call on different students to report their findings to the class.

OPTION

Have the students work in pairs. Tell them to look at the illustrations and talk about how they get around. They can discuss their preferences for different modes of transportation. Go around the classroom and join the discussions.

TALK ABOUT PLACES TO LIVE • GIVE AN OPINION • *THERE IS* AND *THERE ARE*

- Have the students follow along in their books and repeat after you as you read aloud the opinions in the box. Answer any questions.

- Read aloud the first set of instructions. Then have the students listen to the conversation and identify the things the man likes about the city.

- Read aloud the second set of instructions. Then have the students identify the woman's opinions.

- Call on different students to read aloud the answers and write them on the board.

TAPESCRIPT

Woman Do you live here in the city?
Man Uh-huh.
Woman Do you like it?
Man Yeah. In my opinion, it's the only place to live.
Woman Why do you say that?
Man Because there's always something to do, and it's exciting.
Woman But there are things to do in the country.
Man That's true, but there are a lot of great restaurants and discos in the city. And there are excellent museums too. You can't find things like that in the country.
Woman Maybe you're right, but cities are very expensive. And I think they're dirty too.

ANSWERS

M: There's always something to do.
M: There are a lot of great restaurants.
M: There are discos.
M: There are excellent museums.
M: It's exciting.
W: It's dirty.
W: It's expensive.

- Tell the students to look at the photos as you read aloud the words at the bottom of each photo. Answer any questions about the vocabulary.

- Have the students read over the instructions and the conversations. Then have them listen to the conversations.

- Have the students work in pairs. Tell them to have conversations similar to the ones in their books. Call on different pairs to present their conversations to the class.

TALK ABOUT FAVORITE CITIES • *THERE IS* AND *THERE ARE*

4

- Have the students study the frames as you read aloud the heading and possible sentences. Answer any questions.

5

- Point out the box, say the two words, and have the students repeat. Use the words in context to show cause and effect. For example, point to the box in exercise 1 on p. 130 and say "Why is it an awful day? Because it's raining."

- Have the students read over the conversation and listen to it. Then have them work in pairs to practice the conversation.

- Call on a pair of students to present the conversation to the class.

6

- Point out the box, read the phrases aloud, and have the students repeat. Check for understanding of the vocabulary. If necessary, use pictures to help get the meanings across.

- Read aloud the instructions. Then have the students work in small groups. Tell the group members to describe their favorite cities or other places of interest.

- Call on different students to share their descriptions with the class. On the board, write any descriptive phrases students use which are not in the box.

7

- Read aloud the instructions. Point out that *there*, *their*, and *they're* are all pronounced the same way—[ðer].

- Have the students read over the ad. Answer any questions. Then tell the students to complete the ad with the appropriate words.

- So students can check their work, read the completed ad aloud. Ask a student to write the answers on the board.

ANSWERS
There
They're
their
They're
their
there
There
They're

FOLLOW-UP

Students can write the descriptions of their favorite cities or other locations from exercise 6.

WORKBOOK Lesson 70, pp. 96-98

4 ▶ **Study the frames.**

There is and *there are*

There	is	always something to do.
	isn't	anything to do.
	are	excellent museums.
	aren't	any discos.

| Is | there | a zoo in New York City? | Yes, **there is**. No, **there isn't**. |
| Are | | any good restaurants? | Yes, **there are**. No, **there aren't**. |

5 ▶ **Listen to the conversation.**
▶ **Practice the conversation with a partner.**

A New York is my favorite city.
B Why do you say that?
A Because there are great restaurants and nightclubs.
B Is there a good museum there?
A Yes, there is. There's the Museum of Modern Art.

Why . . . ?
Because . . .

6 ▶ **Talk to your classmates.**

Tell about your favorite city. Use the words in the box or your own information.

beautiful old houses	fantastic nightclubs
beautiful streets	great beaches
delicious food	friendly people

7 ▶ **Complete this travel ad with *there, their,* and *they're*.**

New York is Art

_____ are several very well known museums in New York City, for example, the Metropolitan Museum of Art, the Museum of Modern Art and the Guggenheim Museum. _____ all excellent and _____ exhibits change regularly. _____ open from about 10 A.M. to 5 P.M. and closed one day a week. Call first for _____ hours.

Is _____ a museum children will enjoy? Definitely. _____ is the Museum of Natural History and the Museum of the American Indian. _____ very popular with children and school groups.

71. What kind of music do you like?

classical music
rock music
historical novels
mystery novels
romance novels
jazz
country music
science fiction novels

1 ▶ **Work with a partner. Look at the chart and check the things you like.**

What do you like? Check the appropriate categories.

	YOU	YOUR PARTNER
MUSIC		
classical music	_____	_____
jazz	_____	_____
rock music	_____	_____
country music	_____	_____
other	_____	_____
BOOKS		
mysteries	_____	_____
science fiction novels	_____	_____
romance novels	_____	_____
historical novels	_____	_____
other	_____	_____

2 ▶ **Listen to the sentences below. Then compare yourself to your partner.**

Robert likes classical music and I do too.
Robert doesn't like rock music, but I do.

Robert doesn't like mystery novels and I don't either.
Robert doesn't like romance novels, but I do.

3 ▶ **Study the frames.**

Rejoinders with *too*

I'm single.	I He She	am is	**too.**
I'm reading a book.	We They	are	
He likes classical music.	I We They She	do does	**too.**

Rejoinders with *either*

I'm not married.	I He She	'm not isn't	**either.**
We're not doing anything.	We They	aren't	
She doesn't like jazz.	I We They She	don't doesn't	**either.**

71. What kind of music do you like?

On the board, write *I (like/don't like) (cities/ classical music/science fiction movies) because...* . Have the students use the words on the board to write complete sentences, stating their own opinions. Then call on different students to say their completed sentences. Write some of their sentences on the board.

TALK ABOUT LIKES AND DISLIKES • REJOINDERS *TOO* AND *EITHER*

- Have the students look at the illustrations as you read aloud and have them repeat the surrounding words. Answer any questions about vocabulary.

- Tell the students to look over the chart. Then read aloud the instructions.

- Have the students work with a partner. Tell them to first identify the things they like on the chart and then to interview their partner about what he or she likes.

- Call on different students to report to the class on what they and their partners like.

- Have the students follow along in their books as you read aloud the instructions and exercise sentences or play the cassette. (You can model the exercise for the class by first doing exercise 1 with a student and then comparing yourself to that student.)

- Have the students work with their partners. Tell them to use their completed charts in exercise 1 to compare their likes and dislikes. Have them use the sentences in exercise 2 as a model.

- Call on different pairs to share their comparisons with the class.

OPTION

If possible, bring in recordings of different kinds of music—classical, country, rock, and jazz. Randomly play different selections and see if the students can identify the kind of music by name. Have the students talk about their likes and dislikes for the different kinds of music.

- Have the students study the frames as you read aloud the headings and possible sentences. Answer any questions. Make sure the students understand that *too* is used in affirmative sentences and *either* is used in negative sentences.

TALK ABOUT WHAT YOU HAVE IN COMMON • NOUNS WITH AND WITHOUT *THE*

- Read aloud the first set of instructions. Then tell the students to read over the incomplete conversation. Answer any questions they have.

- Have the students complete the conversation. Then have them compare their completed versions with a partner.

- So they can check their answers, have the students listen to the conversation as many times as necessary. Ask two students to write the answers on the board.

ANSWERS
Mary I am too.
Mary I'm not either.
John I do too.
Mary I do too.
John I don't either.
Mary I am too.

OPTION

Have the students work in pairs to act out the conversation. Go around the classroom and check their work. Call on a pair to present the conversation to the class.

- Read aloud the instructions. Then tell the students to read the sentences and to put the events in order by numbering the sentences.

- Have the students compare their answers with a partner. So they can check their answers, have the students listen to the conversation as many times as necessary.

- Call on different students to read aloud the sentences in the correct order. Write the answers on the board.

ANSWERS
1 — What kind of music do you like?
2 — I like rap best.
3 — Oh, me too. Who's your favorite singer or group?
4 — Hammer. He's great.
5 — I agree. Do you like classical music?
6 — No, not really.
7 — Me either. It puts me to sleep.

- Point out the box, read the contents aloud, and have the students repeat. Then read aloud the instructions.

- Have the students work in small groups. Tell the group members to find out what they have in common with their classmates. Go around the classroom and listen in, giving help when needed.

- Call on different groups to share what they found out with the class.

METHODOLOGY NOTE

Working in small groups of three to six students is beneficial for language practice. In such small groups, each student has more opportunity to use the language. This is especially beneficial for students who are uncomfortable speaking in front of the entire class. Monitor the small groups' activities by circulating throughout the classroom. You can note pronunciation and intonation errors.

- Have the students study the pictures as you read aloud the sentences at the bottom. Try to elicit the rule for when to use *the* and when not to. (Use *the* when the noun which follows is specific. Use no article if the noun is talked about in general.)

- Read aloud the instructions. Tell the students to read over the conversation. Then have them read it again and complete it.

- Have the students compare their answers with a partner. Ask two students to write the answers on the board.

ANSWERS
A the
B The
   No article, the
   No article
A *No article*
B the

OPTION

Have the students practice the conversation in pairs. Tell them to take turns playing each role. Call on a pair to present the conversation to the class.

FOLLOW-UP

Students can write out their findings from exercise 6.

WORKBOOK Lesson 71, pp. 99-100

4

▶ **John and Mary find out they have a lot in common. Complete the conversation.**

▶ **Listen to check your answers.**

Mary How old are you?
John Twenty-five.
Mary Oh, _____ . Are you married?
John No, I'm not.
Mary _____ . I have a roommate.
John _____ . We live in the suburbs.
Mary How do you get to work?
John I take the bus.
Mary _____ . I have a car, but I don't like to drive into the city.
John _____ .
Mary What kind of music do you like?
John Mostly rock. But I like rap too. In fact, I'm going to the Hammer concert tonight.
Mary _____ . Maybe I'll see you there.

 5

▶ **Put the lines of the conversation in order.**

▶ **Listen to check your answers.**

_____ I like rap best.
_____ I agree. Do you like classical music?
_____ Oh, me too. Who's your favorite singer or group?
_____ What kind of music do you like?
_____ No, not really.
_____ Me either. It puts me to sleep.
_____ Hammer. He's great.

6

▶ **Talk with your classmates.**

Find out what you have in common with your classmates. Ask what music and books they like.

Me too. = I do too.
Me either (Me neither). = I don't either.

7

▶ **Study the pictures. Then complete the conversation with *the* where necessary.**

I love nightclubs.

But the nightclubs here are awful.

A I'm going to New York. How is _____ night life there?
B _____ night life in New York in wonderful. I really like _____ discos and nightclubs, and _____ nightclubs in New York are terrific. Do you like _____ music?
A Yeah, I always listen to _____ music, especially jazz.
B Well, _____ jazz in New York is great. Only New Orleans has better jazz clubs. You'll have a good time.

72. What a life!

Loretta and George are enjoying the sun in Miami Beach.

1

Loretta Oh, it's so beautiful here, George!

George Yeah, I'd like to live here someday.

Loretta Oh, I don't know. I love the city — the neighborhood, all the excitement. . .

George Excitement?! Is working twelve hours a day, seven days a week exciting? And the cold weather and the dirty snow? . . . Give me this beautiful sunshine any day!

Loretta Well, *I* like New York.

George Think of it, Loretta. . . . We could move here and open another little coffee shop — "Arno's South" — open from ten o'clock to one o'clock, three or four days a week. Oh, what a life!

Loretta What time is it now?

George It's a little after ten. Hmm . . . Nick is probably at the coffee shop right now, drinking his morning cup of coffee and talking to Jeff. And . . .

Loretta George, don't think about work. We're on vacation! Here, put on some more suntan lotion.

George Nah, I don't need any more.

Loretta You're going to get a terrible sunburn. This Florida sun is hot!

George Hey, that guy looks terrific. I think I'll get up and run with him. I need a little exercise.

Loretta Now don't do too much, George. You're not twenty years old.

George Don't worry, Loretta. I know what I'm doing. I'm just a little out of shape. I'll take it easy.

2. Figure it out

True, false, or ***it doesn't say?***

1. The suntan lotion is going to give George a sunburn.
2. George is thinking about the coffee shop in New York.
3. Loretta likes to exercise.
4. George would like to move to Florida.
5. Loretta likes New York.
6. Loretta likes the snow.

72. What a life!

WARM-UP

Have the students look at the picture and describe it. Help them get started by writing a sentence on the board.

Loretta and George are on the beach.

1. Conversation

BACKGROUND

George and Loretta are relaxing on the beach in Florida. George mentions his friend Nick Pappas and Jeff Hunt, the high school student who works at Arno's Coffee Shop. George suggests they move to Florida. Loretta is worried that George will get a bad sunburn and will do too much exercise.

LANGUAGE

"Arno's South" is a name for Arno's Coffee Shop, referring to its location in Florida, which is in the southern part of the U.S.

What a (life)! is a way of making an exclamation about something. In this case it's short for *What a great life this is!*

It's a little after ten. is another way of saying "It's a few minutes after ten (o'clock)."

...on vacation means *having a vacation.*

I'm a little out of shape is another way of saying "I'm only slightly unfit."

PROCEDURE

- Follow a procedure similar to that on p. 88.

2. Figure it out

True, false, or *it doesn't say?*

- Tell the students to read over the statements. Then have them listen to the conversation again and answer *True, False,* or *It doesn't say.*

- Call on different students to read the statements aloud. Call on others to say their answers. Ask a student to write the correct answers on the board.

ANSWERS
1. False
2. True
3. It doesn't say.
4. True
5. True
6. It doesn't say.

OPTION

Have the students make up additional *True, False,* or *It doesn't say* statements about the conversation. Then call on different students to say their statements. Call on other students to respond. Some examples of additional statements are:

Loretta thinks it's beautiful on the beach. (True)
George asks Loretta the time. (False)
Loretta needs a little exercise. (It doesn't say.)

3. Listen in

- Read aloud the instructions as the students follow along in their books. Then have them silently read the questions.

- Have the students listen to the conversation as many times as necessary. Then have them answer the questions with short answers.

- Call on different students to say the answers. Write the answers on the board.

TAPESCRIPT

George Hi! Nice weather, huh?
Runner Yeah.
George Listen, can I ask you something? How old are you?
Runner I'm thirty-eight.
George No kidding! Hey, you're in great shape. Do you run a lot?
Runner Six miles a day, rain or shine.
George Really?
Runner I don't even drive to work. I run.
George Yeah, I don't drive to work either. I just walk downstairs to my coffee shop.

ANSWERS
1. Thirty-eight
2. He runs.

OPTION

Tell the students to continue the conversation between George and the runner. Have them work in pairs to make up additional lines for the conversation. Then call on different pairs to present their extended conversations to the class.

4. How to say it

- Follow the basic procedure for **How to say it** on pp. 9 and 89.

5. Your turn

- Point out the picture above exercise 5. Then read the instructions to the students. Tell them to read over the incomplete conversation.

- Have the students work in pairs to complete the conversation. Tell them that answers will vary.

- Have the pairs act out the conversation. The partners can take turns playing the two roles. Finally, call on different pairs to present their versions to the class.

SAMPLE ANSWERS
Hello.
Nice day.
What are you listening to?
Sometimes.
Sure.
I don't like them.
No, I don't.

FOLLOW-UP

Students can write out the conversation they practiced in **Your turn**.

WORKBOOK Lesson 72, p. 101

📼 3. Listen in

George talks to the runner.
Read the questions below.
Then listen to the conversation
and answer the questions.

1. How old is the runner?
2. How does he get to work?

📼 4. How to say it

Listen to the conversation.

A How do you get to work?

B I drive. How do you get to

   work?

A I take the train.

5. Your turn

Donna is listening to her cassette player when
Rob comes up and starts talking. What do you
think he's saying? Act out the conversation.

Rob _____
Donna Oh, hi.
Rob _____
Donna Yeah, it's a great day.
Rob _____
Donna Oh, I'm listening to a new rock group
   called Fishbone. Do you like rock music?
Rob _____
Donna Well, this group is fantastic. Would you
   like to listen to them?
Rob _____ (*Puts on headset.*)
Donna What's your opinion?
Rob _____
Donna What about rap music? Do you like that?
Rob _____
Donna Me either.

73.

Hotel Flamingo GARDENS

To help us give you the best service, the Flamingo Gardens Hotel would like the following information. Please take a minute to answer these questions.

1. What is the purpose of your trip to Miami?
   a. Vacation
   b. Business
   c. Other _____

2. How did you travel here?
   a. Plane
   b. Private Car
   c. Train
   d. Boat/ship

3. How did you learn about the Flamingo Gardens Hotel?
   a. Magazine Ad
   b. Newspaper Ad
   c. Travel Agent
   d. Other _____

4. How would you grade your room for:

APPEARANCE	COMFORT
a. Excellent	a. Excellent
b. Good	b. Good
c. Fair	c. Fair
d. Poor	d. Poor

5. How would you grade the restaurant for:

FOOD QUALITY	SERVICE
a. Excellent	a. Excellent
b. Good	b. Good
c. Fair	c. Fair
d. Poor	d. Poor

6. How would you grade the hotel staff for:

COURTESY	EFFICIENCY
a. Excellent	a. Excellent
b. Good	b. Good
c. Fair	c. Fair
d. Poor	d. Poor

Today's Date _____   Room _____
Name _____
Address _____
_____
Telephone _____

---

1. What's the purpose of the Flamingo Gardens Hotel Guest Survey? Scan the survey and choose the correct answer.

1. The hotel wants to improve its services.
2. The hotel wants to make a list of its guests' names and addresses.

2. Imagine you and your partner are guests at this hotel. Use the information below to complete the survey.

1. You came to Miami for a vacation on the beach.
2. You arrived on flight 21 from your country.
3. Your travel agent, IntraTours, chose the hotel.
4. The room is beautiful, but it is on the second floor and you can hear the traffic all night long.
5. You had lunch in the hotel restaurant. The food was pretty good and the service was fast.
6. The hotel staff was very courteous and efficient.

73. Hotel Flamingo Gardens

BACKGROUND

This guest survey is much like those which are often found in hotel rooms. Hotel managers hope guests will fill out the surveys to give the managers feedback about which services and accommodations at the hotel may need improvement.

PROCEDURE

1. What's the purpose of the Flamingo Gardens Hotel Guest Survey?

- Read aloud the instructions. Explain that to scan means *to read over for specific information*. Also make sure students understand what *survey* means.

- Have the students scan the survey and choose the best answer. They can also listen to the survey as they read along in their books.

- Call on a student to read the correct answer aloud.

ANSWER
1

2. Imagine you and your partner are guests at this hotel.

- Read aloud the instructions. Then have the students read over the information needed to complete the survey.

- Have the students work in pairs to complete the survey with the listed information.

- Call on different partners to report the information on their surveys to the class.

POSSIBLE ANSWERS
1. a
2. a
3. c
4. a, d
5. b, a
6. a, a

OPTION 1

Have the students underline or write down on separate paper any words or structures from the survey and the exercises which they don't understand. Use gestures, pictures, or words they already know to help them with unfamiliar language. Give only basic and simple explanations of new words and structures at this time.

OPTION 2

Have the students work in small groups to design their own surveys. You can suggest different places for them to create surveys for—for example, restaurants, hotels, nightclubs, etc. Call on different groups to write their surveys on the board.

FOLLOW-UP

Students can write complete-sentence answers for exercise 2. For example, for item 1, they would write *We came to Miami for vacation.*

WORKBOOK Lesson 73, p. 102. Before assigning the writing task, point out the first sentence in each paragraph of Marisa's letter. Explain that the first sentence of a paragraph is often the "topic sentence," a sentence which capsulizes or sets the stage for the other sentences in the paragraph.

Before you begin teaching, go over the functions/themes, language, and forms in the chart. This will give you a preview of what you will encounter as you guide the students through the unit.

Preview the conversations.

- Have the students examine the first photograph. Point out Paula, Jim, and Bob. Read aloud the dialogue lines and have the students repeat. Explain that Paula is inviting Jim to go to a baseball game with her and Bob.

- Have the students examine the second photograph. Point out Jack. Read aloud the dialogue lines and have the students repeat. Discuss the sentences in the boxes. You may need to explain that Jim's refusal is more polite than Jack's, because he gives a reason for not being able to accept the invitation. Ask the students how people refuse invitations in their country.

CULTURE CLOSE-UP

In the U.S., invitations to social events such as weddings, anniversaries, and christenings are usually formal. An invitation to a birthday party can be either formal or informal. Formal invitations consist of specially designed and worded invitation cards which are sent through the mail. The language of these cards is usually very formal and includes a request for a reply with the French initials *R.S.V.P.—Répondez, s'il vous plaît.*

PREVIEW

FUNCTIONS/THEMES	LANGUAGE	FORMS
Make a request	Could you open the window? Could you answer it for me?	*Could you . . . ?* Pronouns as objects of prepositions
Talk about the present	What do you do? What are you doing?	Simple present vs. present continuous
Say how you're doing Ask about an acquaintance Send greetings	I'm doing just great. How's Betsy doing? Say hi to her for me.	
Invite someone informally	I've got two tickets for the baseball game. Do you want to go?	*Have got*
Invite someone formally	Would you like to join us? I'd like to, but I can't. I have to work on Saturday.	*Have to* and *have got to*
Invite a friend to a party	When is it? In December. / On Sunday. / At five o'clock.	Prepositions *in, on,* and *at*

Preview the conversations.

"We're going to go to a baseball game on Saturday. Would you like to join us?"

"I'd like to, but I can't. I have to take my car to the garage on Saturday."

"We're going out after work. Do you want to come?"

"I'm sorry, I can't."

Here are two ways to invite someone. Both are appropriate for informal situations. Which one is also appropriate for formal situations?

Notice how these people refuse invitations. Which way is more polite? Why?

74. Would you like to join us?

 Some people are making plans to go to a baseball game.

A

Paula We're going to a baseball game on Saturday and we've got an extra ticket. Would you like to join us?

Jim Oh, I'd like to, but I can't. I have to take my car to the garage on Saturday. But thanks for inviting me.

Bob Are you sure? Rachel's going to go too.

Jim Oh, how's Rachel doing?

Paula She's doing fine. She loves her new job.

Jim Well, I really can't go, but say hi to her for me, O.K.?

Bob O.K. We will.

B

Bob Hey, Jack! Paula and I have an extra ticket to the baseball game. Do you want to go?

Jack That sounds great. When is it?

Bob Saturday at two.

Jack Oh, I'd really like to, but I have to work this Saturday.

Bob Oh, that's too bad. Well, maybe some other time.

C

Paula So, what are we going to do with that extra ticket?

Bob I don't know. Could you call Rachel after work? Maybe she knows someone who wants to go.

Paula O.K.

74. Would you like to join us?

WARM-UP

Ask the students to look through their books, point to different characters, and say what they're doing. Begin by pointing to Paula on p. 139 and saying "She's calling her friend." Other examples are on pp. 45, 51, 72, 133, and 135.

BACKGROUND

Paula and Bob are going to a baseball game and are inviting others to join them. Unfortunately, none of the others are able to join them.

LANGUAGE

That sounds great. is used to reply favorably and with enthusiasm to a suggestion.

…that's too bad. is an informal expression of regret.

…we've…got is another way of saying "we have."

PROCEDURE

- Follow a procedure similar to that indicated for the opening conversations in the previous units.

- Have students listen to the conversations as they follow along in their books. If you read the conversations aloud, be sure to use appropriate stress, intonation, and gestures.

Figure it out

1. Listen to the conversations. Then answer the questions.

- Tell the students to silently read over the questions. Then read the questions aloud and have the students repeat.

- Have the students listen to the conversations and answer the questions. Tell them to write short answers on separate paper. Then have them work with a partner to compare answers and to take turns asking and answering the questions.

- Call on pairs to ask and answer the questions aloud. Have a student write the answers on the board.

  ANSWERS
  1. Three
  2. Paula and Bob

2. Listen again and answer *true*, *false*, or *it doesn't say*.

- Tell the students to read over the instructions and the statements. Then have them listen to the conversation again and answer *True, False,* or *It doesn't say*.

- Call on different students to read the statements aloud. Call on others to say the answers. Ask a student to write the correct answers on the board.

  ANSWERS
  1. True
  2. False
  3. False
  4. It doesn't say.
  5. True
  6. False

3. Find another way to say it.

- Read aloud the instructions and the sentences and have the students repeat.

- Have the students work in pairs on the exercise. Tell them to look through the conversation for other ways to say the expressions. Have them write the other versions on separate paper.

- Call on different pairs. Have one partner read aloud the answer and the other write it on the board.

  ANSWERS
  1. Would you like to join us?
  2. We've got an extra ticket.
  3. She's doing fine.
  4. Saturday at two.
  5. Is Rachel there?
  6. How are you doing?

FOLLOW-UP

Students can write complete-sentence answers for the questions in exercise 1.

WORKBOOK Lesson 74, p. 103

Mrs. Walters Hello?
Paula Hello, Mrs. Walters. This is Paula. Is Rachel there?
Mrs. Walters She's eating dinner right now, Paula. Could you call her back in about half an hour?
Paula Sure.

Rachel Hello?
Paula Hi, Rachel. This is Paula.
Rachel Hi. How are you doing?
Paula Pretty good. I saw Jim today. He says hello.
Rachel Oh, really? How's he doing?
Paula Oh, he's fine. Listen, we've still got one ticket for the baseball game. That's why I'm calling. Do you know anyone who wants it?
Rachel Oh, Paula, I forgot to tell you. I can't go either. Mom's having a birthday party for my sister Saturday, and I have to help.

Figure it out

1. Listen to the conversations. Then answer the questions.

1. How many tickets do Paula and Bob have?
2. Who's going to go to the baseball game?

2. Listen again and say *true*, *false*, or *it doesn't say*.

1. Something is wrong with Jim's car.
2. Rachel is Jim's girlfriend.
3. Rachel hates her new job.
4. Jack has to work every Saturday.
5. Paula calls Rachel about the extra ticket.
6. Rachel's birthday is Saturday.

3. Find another way to say it.

1. Would you like to go with us?
2. We have an extra ticket.
3. She's fine.
4. On Saturday at two o'clock.
5. Is Rachel at home?
6. How are you?

75. Could you call him for me?

  1

▶ **What are they saying? Complete the requests with the sentences in the box.**

▶ **Listen to check your work.**

> Could you answer it for me?
> Could you close the door?
> Could you open the window?
> Could you help me with them?

▶ **Work with a partner. Make your own requests.**

PRONOUNS AS OBJECTS OF PREPOSITIONS

  2

▶ **Complete the conversation with object pronouns.**
▶ **Listen to check your work.**

Lawyer Mr. and Mrs. Walters and I are going to have lunch today. Do you want to come with _____ ?
Assistant Thanks, but I can't. I have to meet my son for lunch.
Lawyer Oh, that's nice. Say hi to _____ for _____ .
Assistant I will. What time are you going to meet the Walters?
Lawyer Good question! Could you call _____ for _____ and find out?
Assistant Sure.

Pronouns as objects of prepositions

		me?
		us?
Could you call him for		**him?**
		her?
		them?

CALL SOMEONE • MAKE A REQUEST

  3

▶ **Listen to the conversation.**
▶ **Look at each picture and act out similar conversations with a partner.**

A Hello. Is Kenji there?
B He's eating dinner right now. Could you call him back in an hour?
A Sure. Thanks.

> **Could you call back . . . ?**
>
> | | |
> |---|---|
> | in half an hour | at about nine |
> | in ten minutes | before eleven |
> | at ten thirty | after seven |

75. Could you call him for me?

WARM-UP

Invite different students to do something with you. Use the expression *Would you like to...?* Encourage students to try out some of the expressions in the conversations on pp. 138-139. For example:

T: Would you like to go to a concert tonight?
S: Oh, I'd like to, but I can't.

MAKE A REQUEST • *COULD YOU...?*

- Tell the students to read over the instructions, the dialogue lines, and the questions in the box. Answer any questions they have.

- Have the students work in pairs to complete the requests. Tell them to select the most appropriate question for each blank from the box.

- So they can check their answers, have the students listen to the requests as many times as necessary. Then tell the pairs to practice saying the requests. Call on different students to write the answers on the board.

  ### ANSWERS
  Could you answer it for me?
  Could you close the door?
  Could you help me with them?
  Could you open the window?

- Read aloud the third set of instructions. Tell the partners to take turns making requests. Have them model their requests on those in the exercise. Go around the classroom and check their work, giving help where needed.

- Call on different pairs of students to share their requests with the class.

OPTION

On the board, list possible ways for the students to respond to the requests. For example:

Sure.
O.K.
I'm sorry, I can't.

Have the pairs practice again, this time including responses to the requests.

- Point out the blue box. Read aloud the heading and the possible sentences and have the students repeat. Have them identify the preposition *for* and the object pronouns in the box.

- Tell the students to read over the incomplete conversation and then to write the missing pronouns on separate paper.

- So they can check their answers, have the students listen to the conversation as many times as necessary. Ask a student to write the answers on the board. Finally, have the students practice the conversation with a partner.

  ### ANSWERS
  us
  him, me
  them, me

- Point out the box, read aloud the possible questions, and have the students repeat. Next point out the picture of Kenji. Then have the students listen to the conversation.

- Tell the students to look at each picture and repeat the surrounding words after you. Then have them work in pairs to act out conversations similar to the one in their books. Tell them to use the pictures and the expressions in the box. Remind them to pretend they are talking on the phone.

- Call on different pairs to act out their conversations for the class. Have different pairs write the possible conversations on the board.

  ### POSSIBLE ANSWERS
  A Hello. Is Julia there?
  B She's sleeping right now. Could you call her back in half an hour?

  A Hello. Is Alan there?
  B He's taking a shower right now. Could you call him back in ten minutes?

OPTION

Bring to class pictures of people engaged in different activities which could prevent them from coming to the phone. Make sure to choose only activities the students already know the verbs for. Hand each pair a picture. Have them give the person in their picture a name. Then tell them to act out conversations based on their pictures. For example:

(For a picture of a man studying...)

S1: Hello. Is Jack there?
S2: He's studying right now. Could you call him back after seven?

FOLLOW-UP

Students can write out one of the conversations they practiced in exercise 3.

WORKBOOK Lesson 75, p. 104

76. How's she doing?

WARM-UP

Practice the simple present and the present continuous. Go around the classroom and ask different students what other students do or are doing. For example:

T: What does (*student's name*) do?
S: She works in an office.

T: What's (*student's name*) doing?
S: He's reading a newspaper.

TALK ABOUT THE PRESENT • SIMPLE PRESENT VS. PRESENT CONTINUOUS

- Have the students study the frame as you read aloud the heading and the sentences. Answer any questions the students have. Point out *right now* as an expression which is often used with the present continuous. If necessary, provide other sentence examples contrasting the simple present with the present continuous.

2

- Tell the students to read over the incomplete conversations. Then have the students complete them with the verbs in parentheses.

- So they can check their answers, have the students listen to the conversation as many times as necessary. Ask two students to write the answers on the board.

ANSWERS
1. **B** are you doing
   A I'm reading
      Are you cooking
   B I don't cook
      I go out

2. **A** Is he working
   B he doesn't work
   A is he visiting
   B He visits

SAY HOW YOU'RE DOING

- Have the students examine each picture. Then have them listen to the sentences under each picture as they follow along in their books. You can have the students repeat the sentences after you.

- Call on each student to tell the class how he or she's doing. If the class is very large, you may want to have the students do this activity in groups. Check their work.

- Read aloud the instructions as the students follow along in their books. Then read aloud the questions in the box and have the students repeat.

- Have the students work in pairs to complete the conversation. Then have them listen to the conversation so they can check their work. Call on a pair to present the conversation to the class and to write the answers on the board.

ANSWERS
Oh, how's she doing?
Does she work on weekends?
Well, say hi to her for me, O.K.?

- Call on a student to read the third set of instructions aloud. Then tell the students to work in pairs. Have them take turns asking and answering questions about Daniel and Maria. Tell them to use the information in items 2 and 3 in exercise 3 and the questions from exercise 4.

- Go around the class and check the pairs' work. Call on different pairs to share their conversations with the class.

SAMPLE ANSWERS
A I'm going to see Daniel tonight.
B Oh, how's he doing?
A He's doing fine. He's not studying English now.
B Does he have a job?
A Yes. He works for the telephone company.
B Well, say hi to him for me, O.K.?
A O.K. I will.

A I'm going to see Maria tonight.
B Oh, how's she doing?
A She's doing pretty well, but her mother isn't feeling well these days.
B Does she live alone?
A No. In fact, she lives with her mother, so she takes care of her.
B Well, say hi to her for me, O.K.?
A O.K. I will.

FOLLOW-UP

Students can write down answers about themselves to the questions in the frame in exercise 1.

WORKBOOK Lesson 76, pp. 105-106

76. How's she doing?

 1 ▶ **Study the frame.**

Simple present vs. present continuous

What **do** you **do**?	I **teach** English.
Do you **work** every day?	I **don't work** on Sundays.
What **are** you **doing**?	I**'m teaching** a class right now.
Are you **working** now?	I**'m not working** today.

 2 ▶ **Complete the conversations with the verbs in parentheses.**
▶ **Listen to check your work.**

1. **A** Hello?
    B Hi, Tom. What _____ (do)?
    A Right now? _____ (read) a book. How about you? _____ (cook) dinner?
    B No. _____ (not cook) on Saturdays and Sundays. _____ (go out) for dinner on the weekends.

2. **A** I called Jim, but he wasn't at home. _____ (work) at the store today?
    B No, _____ (work) on Sundays. He's in Los Angeles.
    A Oh, _____ (visit) his brother?
    B Yes. _____ (visit) him every Sunday.

 3 ▶ **Listen to what these people say about themselves.**
▶ **Tell your classmates how you're doing.**

1. I'm doing fine. I'm working a lot these days. But I'm lucky, I don't work on weekends. I play tennis every weekend.

2. I'm doing just great. I'm not studying English now. I have a job. In fact, I work for the telephone company.

3. I'm doing pretty well, but my mother isn't feeling well these days. I live with her now, so I take care of her.

 4 ▶ **Two people are talking about Betsy, above. Complete this conversation with the sentences in the box.**
▶ **Listen to check your work.**

A I'm going to have dinner with Betsy tonight.
B _____
A She's doing fine. She's working a lot these days.
B _____
A No. In fact, she plays tennis every weekend.
B _____
A O.K. I will.

> Does she work on weekends?
> Oh, how's she doing?
> Well, say hi to her for me, O.K.?

▶ **Imagine you are going to see Daniel or call Maria. Have similar conversations.**

77. I'd like to, but I can't.

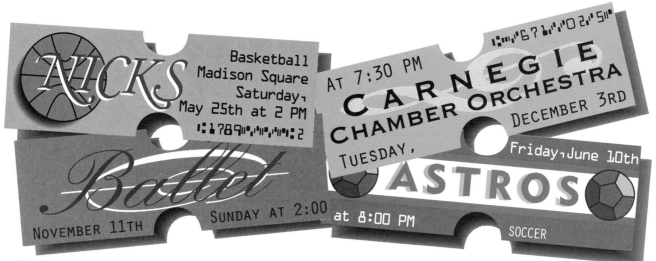

1

▶ **Listen to the two possible conversations.**

▶ **Imagine you have two of the tickets above. Invite a friend to go to one of the events.**

A I've got two tickets for the basketball game. Do you want to go?

B When is it?

A Saturday at two.

B That sounds great.   **B** Oh, I'd really like to, but I can't on Saturday.

                         A Oh, that's too bad.

Have got

| I **have** | two tickets |
| **I've got** | |

2

▶ **Listen to the two possible conversations.**

▶ **Work in groups of three. Invite someone you don't know very well to join you for coffee, lunch, or dinner.**

A We're going out for dinner tonight. Would you like to join us?

B I'd love to. What time   **B** I'd like to, but I can't. I already have plans. I have to make
    are you going?   dinner for my family tonight. But thanks for inviting me.

A At seven o'clock.   **A** Well, maybe some other time.

Have to and *have got to*

	work on Saturday.
	help my mother.
I **have to**	go home right after work.
I've got to	work late.
	go to the dentist.
	take my car to the garage.

77. I'd like to, but I can't.

WARM-UP

On the board, write *What are you doing right now? Would you like to...?* Have the students move around the classroom and invite different classmates to do different things. Tell them to use the questions on the board.

INVITE SOMEONE INFORMALLY • *HAVE GOT*

- As the students look over the illustrations, read aloud the information on the tickets. Then point out the box and have the students repeat as you read aloud the heading and possible sentences. Answer any questions.

- Tell the students to follow along in their books as they listen to the two possible conversations. Have them listen a second time as you read the conversations aloud with two students. Have each of the two students say a different B response.

- Tell the students to work in pairs to take turns playing the two different roles. Refer them to the tickets for the content of their exchanges. Have them model their exchanges on the sample conversation.

- Call on different pairs of students to act out the conversations for the class.

  SAMPLE ANSWERS
  A I've got two tickets for the ballet. Do you want to go?
  B When is it?
  A Sunday at two.
  B That sounds great.
    OR
  B Oh, I'd really like to, but I can't on Sunday.
  A Oh, that's too bad.

  A I've got two tickets for the soccer game. Do you want to go?
  B When is it?
  A Friday at eight.
  B That sounds great.
    OR
  B Oh, I'd really like to, but I can't on Friday.
  A Oh, that's too bad.

INVITE SOMEONE FORMALLY • *HAVE TO* AND *HAVE GOT TO*

- Point out the box and have the students repeat as you read aloud the heading and possible sentences. Answer any questions.

- Tell the students to follow along in their books as they listen to the two possible conversations. Have them listen a second time as you read the conversations aloud with two students. Have each of the two students say a different B response.

- Read aloud the second set of instructions as the students follow along in their books. Tell them to work in groups of three. Have them take turns playing the three different roles. Tell them to use the sentences in the box for the second B response. Have them model their exchanges on the sample conversation.

- Call on different groups to act out the conversations for the class.

  SAMPLE ANSWER
  A We're going out for lunch today. Would you like to join us?
  B I'd like to, but I can't. I already have plans. I have to go to the dentist. But thanks for inviting me.
  A Well, maybe some other time.

PRONUNCIATION NOTE

In casual speech, the expressions *have to* and *got to* are reduced and pronounced "haftah" [hæftə] and "gotta" [gadə].

- Tell the students to look at the illustration and to read over the incomplete conversation. Then have them complete it with the appropriate prepositions.

- So they can check their answers, have the students listen to the conversation as many times as necessary. Ask a student to write the answers on the board.

ANSWERS
Fred On
June on
June at, in
June on
Fred At

- Have the students study the frame and repeat after you as you read aloud the heading and possible sentences. Provide other examples of answers with prepositions + dates, days, or times.

- Read aloud the instructions and have the students look at the guest list. Then have them listen to the conversations and identify which people are coming to Alice's party. Have them listen as many times as necessary.

- Call on a student to read aloud the answers and to write them on the board.

TAPESCRIPT
June Fred, this is June.
Fred Oh, hi, June.
June I talked to Bill. We *can* come to Alice's party on Tuesday, but we'll be a little late.
Fred That's fine. See you then.

Fred Alex, this is Fred.
Alex Hi, Fred. What's going on?
Fred Alice's birthday is Tuesday. Can you come to her party?
Alex Sure. I'd love to.
Fred Good. Everybody's coming at about eight.
Alex Fine.

Ellen This is Ellen. I'm sorry, but I'm out of town right now. I'll be back next Thursday. Please leave your name and telephone number, and I'll call you then.

Fred Hello, Steve?
Steve Hi, Fred. I know why you're calling.
Fred You do?
Steve Yeah. I just talked to Bill and June. They told me about Alice's party.
Fred Well, can you and Kim come?
Steve We'd like to, but we can't. We already have plans on Tuesday.
Fred Oh, that's too bad.
Steve But thanks for inviting us.

ANSWERS
Yes June, Bill, Alex
No Ellen, Steve, Kim

- Have the students look at the illustration and repeat as you read the dialogue lines aloud. Have the second man in the illustration say "I would too."

- Have the students follow along in their books as you read aloud the instructions, the contents of the invitation, and the sample conversation. Answer any questions.

- Tell the students to work in pairs. Have them take turns inviting one another to Teresa's party. Tell them to use the sample conversation as a model and to complete it with the information in the invitation.

FOLLOW-UP

Students can make a list of five things they've got to do this week. For examples, you can refer them to the box in exercise 2 on p. 142.

WORKBOOK Lesson 77, pp. 107-108

3 ► Complete the telephone conversation with *in, on,* and *at*.
► Listen to check your work.

June Hello?
Fred June, it's Fred.
June Oh, hi, Fred.
Fred Listen, it's Alice's birthday next week. Would you like to come to her party?
June Sure. When is it?
Fred _____ Tuesday.
June Oh, we can't. Bill works late _____ Tuesdays.
Fred That's O.K. Come after work.
June Well, Bill isn't _____ home right now, but he'll be back _____ about an hour. Can I call you then?
Fred Sure.
June By the way, what time _____ Tuesday?
Fred _____ about eight o'clock.
June O.K. I'll check with Bill.

4 ► Study the frame.

In, on, and *at*

When is it?

In	December.
	two days.
On	Sunday.
At	five o'clock.

 5 ► Listen to these conversations. Which of these people are coming to Alice's party?

6 ► You just received this invitation to a party from your friend Teresa. Invite a friend to go with you.

A My friend Teresa is having a party. Do you want to go?
B Sure. When is it? . . .

78. Invite Jeff to come along.

🔊 Christine Pappas and her friends are talking after school.

①

Joe Hey, Chris . . . we're going out for pizza tonight. You want to come along?

Chris Gee, I'd really like to, but I have to ask my parents.

Joe Well, call me when you get home.

Katy Hey, look over there. Who's that with Ms. Rogers?

Chris I don't know, but I see them together a lot.

Joe He's probably her boyfriend.

Chris Shh! She'll hear you!

Joe Hey, Chris, there's Jeff.

Chris Hmm . . . maybe he'd like to come with us tonight.

Katy Yeah, Chris, invite Jeff to come along.

Chris *You* invite him, Katy. You know him better.

Katy O.K. Oh, wait — he can't come anyway. He has to work.

Chris Oh, that's right. He works on Wednesdays . . . Hey, does anyone know what time it is?

Katy Yeah, it's almost three thirty.

Chris Oh, it's late. I've got to get home. Well, maybe I'll see you later.

Joe Bye, Chris. Don't forget to call!

2. Figure it out

True, false,* or *it doesn't say?

1. Joe and Katy invite Chris for pizza. *True.*
2. Chris already has plans.
3. Joe thinks the man with Ms. Rogers is her boyfriend.
4. Jeff works after school on Wednesdays.
5. Ms. Rogers teaches English.
6. Katy invites Jeff to join them for pizza.
7. Chris is in a hurry to get home.

78. Invite Jeff to come along.

WARM-UP

Have the students comment on the picture on pp. 144-145. Encourage them to use the present continuous. Write an example on the board:

Two people are walking down the hall.

1. Conversation

BACKGROUND

Katy and her friend Joe invite Christine Pappas out for pizza. They talk about inviting Jeff Hunt but realize he has to work that night.

LANGUAGE

You want to come along? is another way of saying "Do you want to go with us?"

Gee is a very informal way to express mild surprise.

PROCEDURE

- Follow a procedure similar to that on pp. 8 and 88.

2. Figure it out

True, false, **or** *it doesn't say?*

- Tell the students to read over the instructions and the statements. Then have them listen to the conversation again and answer *True, False,* or *It doesn't say.*

- Call on different students to read the statements aloud and to say their answers. Ask a student to write the correct answers on the board.

ANSWERS
2. False
3. True
4. True
5. It doesn't say.
6. False
7. True

3. Listen in

- Read aloud the instructions. Tell the students to read over the incomplete sentences.

- Have the students listen to the conversation as many times as necessary. Then have them choose *a* or *b*.

- Call on different students to say the answers. Write the answers on the board.

TAPESCRIPT

Liz Hi, Paul! How was your day?
Paul Fine. How was yours?
Liz O.K.
Paul By the way, do you remember the Lees?
Liz Yeah, I do.
Paul Well, they called this morning and invited us to dinner Sunday night.
Liz Oh, how nice. What time?
Paul Seven o'clock.
Liz Oh, wait. This Sunday or next Sunday?
Paul Next Sunday, the twenty-sixth.
Liz Oh, no. I've got to go to my parents' house for dinner.

ANSWERS

1. b
2. b

4. How to say it

- Have the students read over the conversation and then listen to it.

- After the students repeat each line of the conversation, tell them to work in pairs to practice the conversation. Have them take turns playing each role.

- Call on different pairs to present the conversation to the class. Check their pronunciation.

PRONUNCIATION NOTE

The phonetic transcriptions in brackets [ ] demonstrate how the sounds of the underlined words are reduced and blended into what sounds like one word in normal speech.

5. Your turn

- Have the students look at the picture of Jeff and Bill. Read aloud the instructions. Then have the students read over the incomplete conversation.

- Tell the students to work in pairs. Have them complete the conversation and act it out.

- Call on different pairs to act out the conversation for the class.

SAMPLE ANSWERS

Do you want to play basketball?
Where do you work?
Do you work every day?
Do you want to play tomorrow?
See you tomorrow. Good-bye.

FOLLOW-UP

Students can write out the conversation they practiced in **Your turn**.

WORKBOOK Lesson 78, p. 109

Liz Rogers's friend Paul meets her at school. He tells her that their friends the Lees have invited them to dinner. Read the statements below. Then listen to the conversation and choose a or b.

1. The Lees invite Liz and Paul to dinner _____ .
   a. this Sunday
   b. next Sunday

2. Liz _____ have dinner with the Lees.
   a. can
   b. can't

🔊 **4. How to say it**

Listen to the conversation.

A Do you <u>want to</u> go to a movie after work? [wanə]

B Oh, I'd really <u>like to</u> go, but I can't. I <u>have to</u> make dinner for my family. [layktə] [hæftə]

5. Your turn

It's Wednesday. Jeff's friend Bill invites him to play basketball, but Jeff has to work. Act out the conversation.

Bill _____

Jeff I'd really like to, but I can't. I have to work.

Bill _____

Jeff Oh, I work at Arno's Coffee Shop.

Bill _____

Jeff No, I don't work every day. Just Wednesdays, Fridays, and Saturdays.

Bill _____

Jeff Tomorrow? Sure. That sounds good.

Bill _____

Jeff O.K. Bye.

79.

Did You Know?

Here are some things you may or may not know about people in the United States and the way they live. Some of them may surprise you.

- The U.S. population is approximately 250 million.
- Between 1980 and 1990, forty percent of the population increase in the U.S. was due to immigration.
- Most of today's immigrants are from Mexico, the Philippines and China.
- California has a larger population than either Canada or Australia.
- The average annual income is about $25,000 although 7% of the population is unemployed.
- About twenty percent of the population moves every year.
- On the average, a person in the U.S. changes jobs about every four years.
- There are an estimated 250,000 homeless people in the cities and towns of the U.S.
- The average cost of college tuition per year is $11,269 at a private university and $4,711 at a public university.
- Approximately twenty-three percent of American women and thirty percent of American men never marry.
- On the average, people spend only 20 minutes eating dinner.
- Americans eat an average of 16 lbs. of ice cream every year.

Answer the questions with *true, false,* or *it doesn't say*.

1. People in the U.S. move a lot.
2. Everyone has a job in the U.S.
3. People change their jobs every year.
4. Everyone has a home.
5. A college education is usually free.
6. The population of California is larger than the population of Australia.
7. Most immigrants to the U.S. come from Europe.
8. Everyone in the U.S. gets married.
9. People in the U.S. like long dinners.
10. People usually eat ice cream at dinner.

79. Did You Know?

BACKGROUND

This article is mostly a list of facts, the result of surveys and research. It's the kind of article one might find in a magazine or newspaper.

PROCEDURE

- Tell the students to read through the statements at the bottom of the page. Then have them read the article. You may also want the students to listen to the article as they follow along in their books.

- Tell the students to write the answers to the questions on separate paper. Then have them compare their answers with a partner.

- Call on different students to say the answers. Have different students write the answers on the board.

ANSWERS
1. True
2. False
3. False
4. False
5. False
6. True
7. False
8. False
9. False
10. It doesn't say.

OPTION 1

Have the students underline or write down on separate paper any words or structures from the article which they don't understand. Use gestures, pictures, or words they already know to help them with unfamiliar language. Give only basic and simple explanations of new words and structures at this time.

OPTION 2

Have the students work in pairs to correct the false statements. Tell the pairs to compare and discuss their corrections with other pairs. Call on different students to read aloud the corrections and to write them on the board. Check their work.

CULTURE CLOSE-UP

Americans are known for their rushed eating habits. "Eat and run" is an expression often heard in the U.S., especially at lunchtime when most workers have only an hour or less off and cannot enjoy a leisurely meal. Places where lunch is served promptly and eaten in a hurry are appropriately called "fast-food restaurants."

FOLLOW-UP

Students can write additional true/false statements based on the article. Then they can work in pairs and try out their items on one another.

WORKBOOK Lesson 79, p. 110. Before assigning the writing task, point out the different uses of commas, periods, and capital letters in the invitation cards and the letter.

PREVIEW

Before you begin teaching, go over the functions/themes, language, and forms in the chart. This will give you a preview of what you will encounter as you guide the students through the unit.

Preview the conversations.

- Have the students examine the first picture. Point out Pete and Al. Discuss the picture and the sentences in the first box.

- Have the students look at the second picture. Point out the waitress and the other people in the coffee shop. Discuss the questions in the bottom box. Ask the students about meals in their country.

CULTURE CLOSE-UP

In large U.S. cities, coffee shops are usually crowded places where breakfast and lunch are served at a counter and nearby small tables. Often orders are taken and the food is served in a hurry, with little personal attention given the customer. In many U.S. towns, however, the local coffee shop has traditionally been the place to meet friends and exchange news in a relaxed and friendly atmosphere. With the appearance of malls and shopping centers, particularly in larger towns, many traditional coffee shops are being replaced by fast-food establishments.

PREVIEW

FUNCTIONS/THEMES	LANGUAGE	FORMS
Ask about something you found	I found this pen. Is it yours?	Possessive adjectives and pronouns
Talk about possessions	This is my pen.	
Listen to opinions about jobs Give opinions about jobs	Elena is a teacher. She likes it a lot. A plumber's job is hard work, but the pay is good.	
Ask where to buy something Give directions Offer to do a favor	Where can you get some aspirin? There's a drugstore on Ridge Road. Can I get you anything?	Impersonal pronoun *you*
Compare yourself to someone Talk about eating habits	I'm like Manolo. I always have a big lunch around 2:00 P.M.	Frequency adverbs

Preview the conversations.

These two men live and work in the United States. Like most Americans, they eat three meals a day — breakfast, lunch, and dinner. Sometimes they have coffee or eat snacks between meals.

How many meals do you usually eat every day? Do you ever get hungry between meals? What do you eat or drink then?

80. First day on the job?

 Pete Hall is starting a new job.

A

Pete Uh . . . Is this your hammer or mine?
Al It's mine. I think yours is over there.
Pete Oh, yeah. Thanks.

B

Al First day on the job?
Pete Yeah. I'm Pete Hall.
Al Al Johnson.
Pete How do you like it here?
Al It's O.K. The pay is good.
Pete Yeah, it is. I think I'm going to like construction work.
Al Where did you work before?
Pete In a shoe factory.
Al Oh, how was that?
Pete I didn't like it. The hours were long, and the pay was terrible.

C

Pete I need to take a break. Where can I get some coffee around here?
Al I always bring coffee from home, but there's a coffee shop across the street.
Pete And where do you eat lunch?
Al Well, I usually bring my lunch too, but sometimes I eat across the street. The food's not great, but it's fast and cheap.
Pete When is lunchtime?
Al At noon. We get an hour. In fact, it's noon now.
Pete Great! I guess I'll try that coffee shop. Can I get you anything?
Al Uh . . yeah. Could you bring me a cola? I have a sandwich, but I don't have anything to drink.
Pete Sure.

80. First day on the job?

Ask different students what they did the night before. For example:

T: What did you do last night?
S: I went to a movie.
T: How was it?
S: Great!

BACKGROUND

Pete Hall is starting a new job at a construction site. He meets a co-worker, Al Johnson. After talking a while, they take a break for lunch.

LANGUAGE

First day on the job? is short for *Is this your first day on the job?*

The hours were long. means the work schedule included many hours each day.

...take a break. means to stop what one is doing for a while and rest.

To stay or to go? is short for *Do you want to stay and eat (the food) here or take it with you?*

(Two colas) then. means *(Two colas) in that case.*

PROCEDURE

- Follow a procedure similar to that indicated for the opening conversations in the previous units.

- Have students listen to the conversations as they follow along in their books. If you read the conversations aloud, be sure to use appropriate stress, intonation, and gestures.

Figure it out

1. Listen to the conversations and choose *a*, *b*, or *c*.

- Tell the students to silently read over the instructions and the statements. Then have them listen to the conversation and write their answers on separate paper.

- Call on two students to say the answers and write them on the board.

  ANSWERS
  1. a
  2. b

2. Listen again. Say *true*, *false*, or *it doesn't say*.

- Tell the students to read over the instructions and the statements. Then have them listen to the conversation again and write their answers on separate paper.

- Call on different students to read the statements aloud. Call on others to say the answers. Ask a student to write the correct answers on the board.

  ANSWERS
  2. True
  3. True
  4. It doesn't say.
  5. True
  6. False

3. Find another way to say it.

- Read aloud the instructions and the sentences and have the students repeat.

- Have the students work in pairs on the exercise. Tell them to look through the conversation for other ways to say the expressions. Have them write the other versions down on separate paper.

- Call on different pairs. Have one partner read aloud a sentence from the book. Then have the other partner read aloud the other version and write it on the board. Check their answers.

ANSWERS
2. Can I get you anything?
3. To stay or to go?
4. How's your coffee?
5. How do you like it here?
6. It's cheap.

In the U.S., many people who work outdoors such as construction workers bring lunch from home or purchase it from a mobile coffee truck or a nearby sandwich shop. In addition to a lunch period, workers usually get a brief rest period called a "coffee break."

Construction workers are sometimes referred to as "hard hats" because of the helmets they wear to protect themselves from falling debris.

FOLLOW-UP

Students can write down all the positive opinions from the conversation in one column and all the negative opinions in another. For example:

Positive	Negative
It's O.K.	The hours were long, and
The pay is good.	the pay was terrible.

WORKBOOK Lesson 80, p. 111

Waitress What would you like?
Pete A hamburger and french fries.
Waitress To stay or to go?
Pete To go, please.
Waitress Something to drink?
Pete Yeah. How's your coffee?
Waitress Uh . . . Well, I never drink it!
Pete Two colas then.
Waitress Anything else?
Pete No, that's all. Thanks.

Figure it out

1. Listen to the conversation and choose *a*, *b*, or *c*.

1. a. One of the men is going to have a hamburger for lunch.
   b. Both of the men are going to have hamburgers for lunch.
2. a. One of the men is going to have a cola with his lunch.
   b. Both of the men are going to have colas with their lunch.

2. Listen again. Say *true, false,* or *it doesn't say*.

1. Pete lost his hammer. *False.*
2. It's Pete's first day at work.
3. Pete would like a cup of coffee.
4. The waitress likes the food at the coffee shop.
5. Al always brings coffee from home.
6. Pete is going to eat his lunch in the coffee shop.

3. Find another way to say it.

1. It's my hammer. *It's mine.*
2. Do you want anything?
3. Do you want to eat here in the coffee shop or not?
4. Is your coffee good or bad?
5. What do you think of this job?
6. It's not expensive.

81. Is this yours?

 1 ▶ **Listen to the conversation.**
▶ **Have similar conversations with your classmates.**

A I found this pen. Is it yours?
B No. Mine is right here. Maybe it's his (hers).
A Excuse me, is this pen yours?
C Yes, it is. Thanks a lot.

 2 ▶ **Imagine you found one of the items in the box. Find the owner.**

Some personal possessions

pen	copy of *Spectrum*
keys	gloves
notebook	umbrella
wallet	coat

TALK ABOUT POSSESSIONS • POSSESSIVE ADJECTIVES AND PRONOUNS

 3 ▶ **Study the frames.**

Possessive adjectives		Possessive pronouns	
	my pen.		mine.
	your pen.		yours.
This is	his pen.	This pen is	his.
	her pen.		hers.
	our pen.		ours.
	their pen.		theirs.

Possessive adjectives and pronouns have one form. They do not change for plural nouns.

This is **my** pen.   This pen is **mine**.
These are **my** pens. These pens are **mine**.

  4 ▶ **Complete the conversations with possessive pronouns.**
▶ **Listen to check your answers.**

Is this your earring?

Yes. _____ .

Is this your English book?

No. _____ .
Your name is in it.

Is this your calculator?

No. I think _____ .

Is this your car?

Yes. _____ .
We're sorry.

Is this your address book?

No. I think _____ .

Are these your shoes?

No. I think _____ .

81. Is this yours?

WARM-UP

Touch different personal items in the classroom as you say sentences such as the following:

This is my book. It's mine.
This is (*student's name*)'s pencil. It's his (hers).

To practice production of *your*, point to different items and ask students questions such as the following:

T: (Point to your own book.) Is this (*student's name*)'s book?
S: No, it's your book.
T: (Point to your own pencil.) Is this my pencil?
S: Yes, it's your pencil.

ASK ABOUT SOMETHING YOU FOUND

- Tell the students to read over the instructions and the sample conversation. Then have them listen to the conversation. You can act out the conversation with two students. Use a real pen and appropriate gestures and intonation.

- Have the students work in groups of three. Tell them to use real items as they act out similar conversations to the one in their books. Go around the classroom and listen in, giving help when needed.

- Call on different groups to act out their conversations for the class.

- Point out the box, read aloud the contents, and have the students repeat. Say *this* or *these* before each of the words in the box and have the students repeat.

- Have the students read the instructions. Tell them to choose an item from the box and to move around the classroom to find the owner. Tell them to use the conversation from exercise 1 as a guide. You might want to model a sample conversation with two students in front of the class before the students begin the exercise. If necessary, write it on the board.

- Go around the classroom and check students' work. Choose three students to act out their conversation for the class.

TALK ABOUT POSSESSIONS • POSSESSIVE ADJECTIVES AND PRONOUNS

- Have the students study the frames as you read aloud the headings and the possible sentences. Answer any questions the students have.

- Point out the box to the right and read aloud the contents. Answer any questions.

OPTION

As you read aloud the sentences with possessives, use gestures and point to different items in the classroom. You can also have the students repeat the sentences. Then have the students point to different items and say sentences with possessives.

4

- Have the students look at the illustrations and read over the incomplete conversations. Read aloud the instructions.

- Tell the students to complete the conversations with the appropriate possessive pronouns. You might remind them to use *it* or *they* + *is/are* + the possessive pronoun in their answers. Write the first answer on the board before they begin.

- So the students can check their answers, have them listen to the conversations as many times as necessary. Ask two students to write the answers on the board.

ANSWERS
It's mine.
It's yours.
it's hers
It's ours.
it's theirs
they're his

OPTION

Have the students work in pairs to act out the conversations. Go around the classroom and check their work. Call on different pairs to present the conversations to the class.

FOLLOW-UP

Students can write out the conversation they practiced in exercise 2.

WORKBOOK Lesson 81, p. 112

82. What do you do?

WARM-UP

Go around the classroom and ask different students "What do you do?" and "Do you like your job?" If students do not have jobs, ask about a parent or other relative.

LISTEN TO OPINIONS ABOUT JOBS • GIVE OPINIONS ABOUT JOBS

- Read aloud the instructions and the questions as the students follow along in their books. Then have them listen to the radio interview and answer the questions.

- Tell the students to work in pairs to compare their answers. Call on different pairs to read aloud the questions and their answers. Ask a student to write the answers on the board.

TAPESCRIPT

Interviewer	We have two guests on our show today, Elena Cardenas, from Santiago, Chile, and Jim Wilson, from Chicago, Illinois. Tell me, Elena, what do you do?
Elena	I'm a teacher.
Interviewer	Oh, how do you like it?
Elena	Well, it's hard work, but I like it a lot.
Interviewer	How about you, Jim? What do you do?
Jim	I'm a reporter. I work at the *Times*.
Interviewer	And how do you like your job?
Jim	Not too much, actually. The hours are long, and the pay isn't very good either.

ANSWERS

1. She's a teacher. Yes, she does.
2. He's a reporter. No, he doesn't.

- Have the students examine the survey chart. Call on different students to read aloud the sentences in the chart. Have the students repeat the names of the professions after you. Answer any questions about vocabulary.

- Read aloud the instructions and explain that the students should give their opinions by checking the appropriate boxes for each profession.

- Call on different students to state their opinions based on their completed surveys. Write a sample answer on the board.

SAMPLE ANSWER

An actor's job is interesting, but it's hard work.

- Read aloud the second set of instructions. Call on two students to read aloud the sample exchange.

- Have the students work in pairs to share their opinions about the jobs in the chart. Tell them to take turns asking and answering questions like in the sample exchange.

- Call on different pairs to say their exchanges for the class. Check their work.

3

- Have the students listen to the conversation as they follow along in their books. Answer any questions.

- Have the students practice the conversation in pairs. Call on a pair to act out the conversation for the class. Check their pronunciation and intonation.

4

- Read aloud the instructions. Then read aloud the sentences in the box and have the students repeat after you. Point out the faces on the right.

- Have the students go around the classroom to ask several classmates about their jobs. Tell them to use the questions from the conversation in exercise 3. When they finish, have pairs of students take turns asking and answering the questions in front of the class.

OPTION

Have the students interview at least three people outside the class about their jobs. Tell them to use the questions they've just practiced and to write down the results of their surveys to report in class.

FOLLOW-UP

Students can write out the first conversation from exercise 3, substituting information about themselves.

WORKBOOK Lesson 82, p. 113

82. What do you do?

  1 ▶ **Listen to a radio interview with Elena Cardenas from Santiago, Chile, and Jim Wilson from Chicago, Illinois. Then answer the questions below.**

1. What does Elena do? Does she like her job?
2. What does Jim do? Does he like his job?

2 ▶ **What's your opinion of these professions? Complete the survey.**

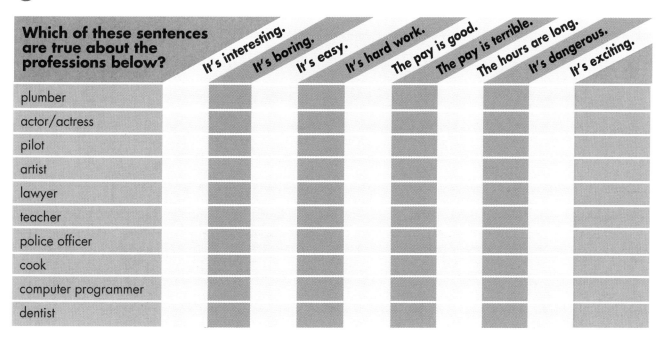

Which of these sentences are true about the professions below?	It's interesting.	It's boring.	It's easy.	It's hard work.	The pay is good.	The pay is terrible.	The hours are long.	It's dangerous.	It's exciting.
plumber								
actor/actress								
pilot								
artist								
lawyer								
teacher								
police officer								
cook								
computer programmer								
dentist								

▶ **Share your opinions about jobs.**

A What do you think about a plumber's job?
B Well, it's hard work, but the pay is good.

  3 ▶ **Listen to the conversation.**
▶ **Practice the conversation with a partner.**

A What do you do?
B I'm a pilot.
A Oh, how do you like it?
B Well, I like it a lot, but it's hard work. How about you? What do you do?
A I'm a computer programmer.
B How do you like your job?
A Not too much, actually. The pay is good, but it's boring.

4 ▶ **Talk with your classmates.**

Now talk about your own job or imagine you have one of the jobs in exercise 2. Tell your classmates how you like it.

How do you like your job?	
It's great. I like it a lot.	😊
It's O.K. It's not too bad.	😐
Not too much. I don't like it at all.	🙁

83. Where can I get some coffee?

ASK WHERE TO BUY SOMETHING • IMPERSONAL PRONOUN *YOU*

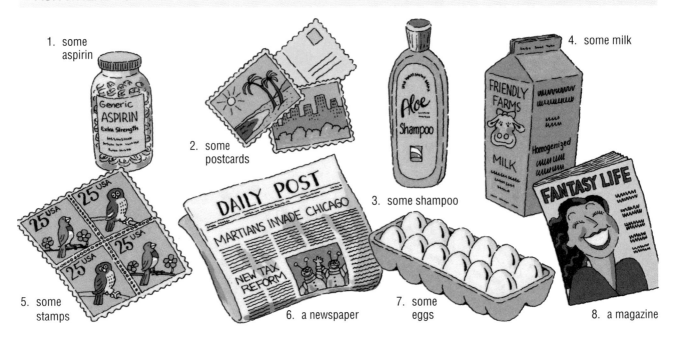

1. some aspirin
2. some postcards
3. some shampoo
4. some milk
5. some stamps
6. a newspaper
7. some eggs
8. a magazine

a. post office   b. drugstore (pharmacy)   c. newsstand   d. grocery store   e. other: _____

 1 ▶ **Listen to the conversation below.**

A Where can you get some coffee?
B You can get some coffee at a coffee shop.

▶ **Act out the conversation using the items in the pictures.**

GIVE DIRECTIONS • OFFER TO DO A FAVOR

 2 ▶ **Listen to the conversation.**
    ▶ **Fill in the blanks.**

Minoru Where can I get some _____ around here?
  Paul Well, there's a _____ on _____ Street.
Minoru Where's _____ Street?
  Paul Just walk to the _____ and turn _____ . Go
      _____ ahead for _____ blocks. The _____
      is on the _____ .
Minoru Thanks. Can I get you anything?
  Paul Yes. Could you get me some _____ ?
Minoru Sure.

3 ▶ **Talk with your classmates.**

Ask where you can get the items
above in your own neighborhood.
Ask for directions to each place.

83. Where can I get some coffee?

WARM-UP

Point out the items pictured at the top of the page and have the students repeat the names after you. Then ask different students if they have any of the items. For example:

T: Do you have any aspirin?
S: No, I don't have any.

ASK WHERE TO BUY SOMETHING • IMPERSONAL PRONOUN *YOU*

- Have the students look over the illustrations and repeat the names of the locations after you. Then have them listen to the sample conversation. Explain the use of the impersonal pronoun *you*. (See Language Note below.)

- Have a student read the second set of instructions. Then have the students work in pairs to take turns acting out the conversation, using the items and the places in the pictures.

- Call on various pairs to act out their conversations for the class. Ask different pairs to write the answers on the board.

POSSIBLE ANSWERS
1. **A** Where can you get some aspirin?
   B You can get some aspirin at a drugstore (pharmacy).
2. **A** Where can you get some postcards?
   B You can get some postcards at a drugstore.
3. **A** Where can you get some shampoo?
   B You can get some shampoo at a drugstore.
4. **A** Where can you get some milk?
   B You can get some milk at a grocery store.
5. **A** Where can you get some stamps?
   B You can get some stamps at a post office.
6. **A** Where can you get a newspaper?
   B You can get a newspaper at a newsstand.
7. **A** Where can you get some eggs?
   B You can get some eggs at a grocery store.
8. **A** Where can you get a magazine?
   B You can get a magazine at a newsstand.

LANGUAGE NOTE

The pronoun *you* can be used impersonally or generically to indicate "anyone." The word *one* can be used in the same way.

GIVE DIRECTIONS • OFFER TO DO A FAVOR

- Have the students read over the incomplete conversation. Tell them to guess what kinds of words might go in the blanks.

- Tell the students to listen to the conversation and to fill in the blanks. Call on a pair of students to read the conversation aloud. Have another pair write the answers on the board.

ANSWERS
Minoru aspirin
  Paul drugstore, Ridge
Minoru Ridge
  Paul corner, left, straight, two, drugstore, right
  Paul shampoo

- Read aloud the instructions. To help the students get started, you might have a student present a sample conversation with you in front of the class. Use the conversation in exercise 2 as a model.

- Have the students move around the classroom to ask their classmates where to get the items in the pictures and how to get to each place in the local neighborhood.

- Call different students to the front of the class and have them ask different class members the questions. Check their work.

FOLLOW-UP

Students can write out some of the conversations they practiced in exercise 3.

WORKBOOK Lesson 83, p. 114

84. I always go out to lunch.

Go around the classroom and talk about food. Have students say what they are hungry for right now—for example, ask "What would you like to eat right now?" If necessary, refer them to the pictures of food on pp. 106-107 in their books. Write their answers on the board.

COMPARE YOURSELF TO SOMEONE

- If possible, use a map or globe to point out where the people in the pictures are from. Then have the students read what the people say.

- Have the students listen to what the people say as they read along in their books. Then call on three different students to read aloud the comments.

- Read aloud the sample conversation with a student. Then have a student read aloud the instructions.

- Tell the students to talk to at least two classmates to compare their lunchtime routines to those of the people in exercise 1. Call on different students to make their comparisons for the class.

TALK ABOUT EATING HABITS • FREQUENCY ADVERBS

- Have the students study the frame as you read aloud the heading and possible sentences. Check to see if the students understand the purpose of the percentages to the right of the frames. If necessary, use graphics, gestures, and words the students already know to help them understand the meaning of the frequency adverbs.

OPTION

Ask different students the possible questions from the frame. Then have the students close their books. Ask students the questions again, this time substituting different times.

- Have the students read over the conversation. Check for understanding. Then have them listen to it.

- Tell the students to practice the conversation with a partner. Then call on a pair of students to present the conversation to the class.

OPTION

Change the first A question to "Do you ever go out for dinner?" and have the pairs practice the conversation, using personal information. Call on different pairs to present their conversations to the class.

- Read aloud the instructions. On the board, write *What do you usually do for lunch?* Tell the students to use this question to interview three classmates.

- Call on different students to report their findings to the class.

- Have the students examine the picture and read over the conversation. Then have them listen to the conversation.

- Have the students repeat the words surrounding the pictures. Then read aloud the second set of instructions. Have the students work in pairs to take turns playing the two parts in the conversation. Remind them to use personal information in the B part.

- Call on different pairs to act out the conversation for the class. Check their pronunciation and intonation.

OPTION

Have the students pretend the classroom is a restaurant. Arrange some desks as tables and have small groups of students sit around them. Have different students serve the restaurant customers. (Before the students begin their role-plays, you might want to provide a model by going to a table and taking the students' orders.)

WORKBOOK Lesson 84, pp. 115-116

84. I always go out to lunch.

  1 ▶ Read along as you listen to what these people say about eating lunch.

What do you usually do for lunch?

Margarida Silva
Translator
Porto Alegre,
Brazil

I always go out for lunch — usually around 3:00. I never go home.

Manolo Gonzalez
Store manager
Guadalajara,
Mexico

I always go home for lunch. I usually have a very big lunch around 2:00.

Suzanne Jackson
Accountant
Baltimore,
Maryland, U.S.A.

I usually eat around 12:30. I often take my lunch to work. Restaurants are so expensive.

2 ▶ Talk to your classmates. Compare yourself to the people above.

A I'm like Manolo. I always have a big lunch around 2:00.
B I'm like Suzanne. I usually eat early, at about 12:00 or 12:30 — but I don't take my lunch to work.

 3 ▶ Study the frame.

Frequency adverbs

Do you	**always** **usually** **often**	eat at two o'clock?	I	**always** **usually** **often**	eat at two o'clock.	100%
Are you	**sometimes** **ever**	hungry at noon?	I'm	**sometimes** **never**	hungry at noon.	0%

  4 ▶ Listen to the conversation below.
▶ Practice the conversation with a partner.

A Do you ever go home for lunch?
B No. I always eat at a restaurant near work. I only have a half hour for lunch.
A What do you eat?
B I usually have a sandwich.

 5 ▶ Interview your classmates.

Find out what three classmates usually do for lunch.

  6 ▶ Listen to the conversation.
▶ Order your own lunch. Work in pairs and act out the conversation.

A What would you like?
B A hamburger and french fries.
A Is that to stay or to go?
B To go, please.
A Something to drink?
B A cup of coffee.
A Anything else?
B No, that's all, thanks.

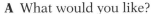

orange juice   cola   tea   coffee

chicken sandwich

hamburger   french fries   cheeseburger

85. Is your postcard from the Arnos?

George and Loretta are in their hotel room.

View of Miami Beach, Miami, Florida

Dear Nick and Stella,
Greetings from Miami Beach!

See you soon!   Love,
                 Loretta and George

P.S. We miss you!

Mr. and Mrs. N. Pappas
27 Willow Street
Brooklyn, NY 11201

1. Listen in

Back in their hotel room, George and Loretta are talking while Loretta writes some postcards. Read the statements below. Then listen to the conversation and say *true* or *false*.

1. Loretta doesn't want to go to a restaurant.
2. George has a sunburn.

2. Your turn

Complete the postcard for Loretta. Include this information.

1. Loretta tells Nick and Stella they're having a wonderful time.
2. She tells them the weather in Miami is beautiful.
3. She asks about the weather in New York.
4. She sends greetings to Christine.

85. Is your postcard from the Arnos?

WARM-UP

Talk about writing postcards and letters. Ask the students questions such as the following:

Do you ever send postcards or letters?
When do you send them?
Who do you write to?

BACKGROUND

Back in their hotel room, George is recovering from a sunburn and Loretta is writing some postcards. Meanwhile, on Willow Street back in Brooklyn, Carolyn Duval and John Pierce finally meet.

LANGUAGE

...*just* (like it) means *exactly* (like it).

Why, (yes!) is used for emphasis and is similar to *as a matter of fact*.

(The "J") is for (John). means that the letter "J" stands for or represents the word *John*.

1. Listen in

- Read the instructions aloud as the students follow along in their books. Check for understanding.

- Tell the students to read the two statements. Then have them listen to the conversation.

- Call on different students to say the statements and their answers. Write the answers on the board.

TAPESCRIPT

George Ohh.

Loretta Now, let me see. Do the Pappases live at 25 or 27?

George Oh, Loretta.

Loretta I'll put 27.

George Loretta.

Loretta Yes, dear.

George I'm hungry, Loretta. Could you call room service and get us something to eat?

Loretta I hear there's a nice little restaurant just down the street.

George Oh, Loretta, I can't move.

Loretta O.K., dear, I'll call in a few minutes. I just have two or three postcards to write.

ANSWERS

1. False
2. True

2. Your turn

- Have the students look at the postcard and follow along as you read the phrases on it. Answer any questions about vocabulary.

- Read the instructions aloud. Then tell the students to read over the four sentences. You might want to help the class write the first sentence as it would appear in the postcard. On the board, write *We're having a wonderful time*.

- Have the students complete the postcard and then compare their work with a partner. Call on different students to write their postcard messages on the board. Check their work.

3., 4., & 5. Conversation

PROCEDURE

- Follow a procedure similar to that on pp. 8 and 88.

6. Figure it out

True, false, or *it doesn't say*?

- Tell the students to read over the instructions and the statements. Then have them listen to the conversation again and answer *True, False,* or *It doesn't say*.

- Call on different students to read the statements aloud and to say their answers. Ask a student to write the correct answers on the board.

ANSWERS
2. True
3. True
4. False
5. It doesn't say.

7. Your turn

- Have the students follow along in their books as you read aloud the instructions. Then have them read over the incomplete conversation.

- Tell the students to work in pairs. Have them complete the conversation and act it out.

- Call on different pairs to act out the conversation for the class.

SAMPLE ANSWERS
No, I'm not.
How do you like it?
Sure.

8. How to say it

- Tell the students to read over the conversation. Then have them listen to it and repeat each line.

- Tell the students to work in pairs to practice the conversation. Have them take turns playing each role.

- Call on different pairs to present the conversation to the class. Check their pronunciation.

OPTION

Have the pairs make up their own conversations along the lines of the one in **How to say it**. Encourage them to add additional lines such as *How do you like your work now?* When the students finish practicing their conversations, call on different pairs to act them out for the class.

FOLLOW-UP

Students can write out the conversation they practiced in **7. Your turn**.

WORKBOOK Lesson 85, p. 117

Meanwhile, back on Willow Street . . .

3

John Excuse me, miss — is this yours?
Carolyn Oh . . . yes, it is. Thanks.
John Wait a minute. . . . I got a postcard just like it. Is yours from the Arnos?
Carolyn (*Surprised*) Why, yes! Do you know them?
John Well, they're my neighbors.
Carolyn Really? They're mine too.

4

John Oh, yeah? Where do you live?
Carolyn In that building over there — number 3.
John Me too. I live in 1B.
Carolyn No kidding! I live right above you — in 2B.
John Oh, then you must be Carolyn Laval.
Carolyn *Du*val. And you're . . . don't tell me . . . J. Pierce.
John Right! The "J" is for John.

5

Carolyn What do you play?
John Huh? Oh, you mean this. . . . I play the saxophone.
Carolyn Really? Do you play any jazz?
John Sure. I love jazz.
Carolyn I do too. I play the string bass.

6. Figure it out

***True*, *false*, or *it doesn't say*?**

1. Carolyn got a card from the Arnos and John did too. *True.*
2. Carolyn lives at 3 Willow Street and John does too.
3. Carolyn likes jazz and John does too.
4. Carolyn plays the string bass and John does too.
5. Carolyn plays well and John does too.

7. Your turn

How do you think Carolyn and John's conversation ends? Act out the conversation, finishing John's part.

Carolyn Are you a professional musician?
John _____
Carolyn I'm not either. I'm an actress.
John _____
Carolyn I like it a lot — when I'm working! Say, would you like to go out for coffee?
John _____

8. How to say it

Listen to the conversation.

A <u>Where do you</u> work? [werdəyuw]
B At the *Press*.
A <u>Where did you</u> work before? [werdɪdʒuw]
B At the *Record*.

To begin their day, many people around the world wake up and have a cup of coffee or tea. But as for what people eat in the morning the variety is almost as great as the number of countries. We were not able to include all of the responses we received, but we think you'll find these examples interesting.

Olivier Barre
Nancy, France

My favorite thing for breakfast is croissants. Croissants are a kind of bread and in my family we always have them on Sundays. We get them fresh from the bakery down the street. I have mine with a cup of hot chocolate. My parents have coffee.

Kamala Natarajan
Madras, India

Besides coffee, we have several things for breakfast. For example, there is *idli*, a kind of warm rice cake, and *dosa*, a thin pancake made with rice and lentils. Also, there is something called *upma* which is ground wheat cooked with spices. We eat all this with *chutney*, a kind of jam made from coconut or mangoes.

Costa Vassos
Salonika, Greece

A simple breakfast of butter and honey on fresh bread is what my family eats. We also have coffee — good strong Greek coffee. Sometimes we eat yogurt and we put honey in that too.

Shirley Luck
Leeds, England

I like a big breakfast in the morning — fried eggs and bacon, or maybe porridge, kippers, and toast. Porridge is boiled cereal and kippers are a type of smoked fish. And, of course, I always have a pot of good breakfast tea.

Cesar Mendoza
Monterrey, Mexico

My favorite breakfast is *huevos rancheros. Huevos rancheros* are fried eggs served with hot sauce on top of fried beans and a tortilla. When I have them for breakfast, I don't need any lunch.

Yoko Higuchi
Tokyo, Japan

When I have time, I have a bowl of hot rice with a raw egg and some dried fish. Sometimes, just coffee and toast is good too. In any case, I usually don't eat much for breakfast.

Read the article. Then answer *true, false,* or *it doesn't say.*

1. *Huevos rancheros* is a big breakfast for Cesar Mendoza.
2. Olivier Barre lives near a bakery.
3. Yoko Higuchi doesn't always have time for a breakfast of rice, egg, and fish.
4. Costa Vassos has two cups of Greek coffee with his breakfast.
5. Shirley Luck has coffee with her breakfast.
6. Kamala Natarajan eats *chutney* with every meal.

86. World Note

This article is like a survey. It asks different people from around the world to comment on what they have for breakfast.

PROCEDURE

- Have the students read through the statements at the bottom of the page. Then have them read the article. You may also want the students to listen to the article as they follow along in their books.

- Tell the students to answer the questions with *True, False,* or *It doesn't say*. Then have them compare their answers with a partner.

- Call on various students to say the answers. Have different students write the answers on the board.

  ANSWERS
  1. True
  2. True
  3. True
  4. It doesn't say.
  5. False
  6. It doesn't say.

OPTION 1

Have the students underline or write down on separate paper any words or structures from the article which they don't understand. Use gestures, pictures, or words they already know to help them with unfamiliar language. Give only basic and simple explanations of new words and structures at this time.

OPTION 2

Have the students work in pairs to make up additional *true, false,* or *It doesn't say* statements about the article. Then have each pair try their statements out on another pair. You can also have the pairs try their statements out on the class.

CULTURE CLOSE-UP

A light breakfast in the U.S. usually consists of juice, coffee or tea, toast, and sometimes cereal. A heavy breakfast includes one or more of the following— bacon, ham, or sausages; eggs (fried, scrambled, boiled, or poached); waffles, pancakes, or french toast; and fruit. In the South, a heavy breakfast usually includes grits, a hot cereal made from ground corn.

FOLLOW-UP

Students can use the comments from the article as a guide and write down what they like for breakfast.

WORKBOOK Lesson 86, p. 118. Before assigning the writing task, point out different features of the postcard such as the opening greeting, closing remark, and the placement of Trahn's name and address.

Review of units 12-14

- Have the students read over the instructions and the incomplete conversation. Answer any questions they have about vocabulary or structures.

- Tell the students to fill in the blanks with prepositions. Then have them compare their answers with a partner. Tell the pairs to act out the conversation.

- Call on a pair to act out the conversation for the class. Have two students write the answers on the board.

  ANSWERS
  to, at, at, at, in, in, for, with, on

- Point out the items in the picture and have the students repeat the name of each item after you. Read aloud the instructions and the sample exchanges with a student. Check for understanding of the procedure the students are to follow.

- Have the students work in pairs to take turns playing the two roles. Remind them that they can use personal items. Go around the classroom and check their work, giving help when needed.

- Have different pairs present their exchanges to the class. You can also have them write their exchanges on the board.

- After reading the instructions aloud, point out that Jim and Ann are talking on the telephone. Refer the students to the chart on the right, say the types of foods, and have the students repeat.

- Have the students listen to the conversation the first time for general comprehension. Then tell them to check the foods as they listen again.

- Tell the students to check their answers with a partner. Call on two students to read the answers aloud. Ask a student to write the answers on the board.

  TAPESCRIPT
  Ann Hello?
  Jim Hi, Ann. I have your book. Ellen found it at the library.
  Ann Oh, great. I thought I lost it.
  Jim I'll give it to you on Sunday.
  Ann O.K.
  Jim So, where do you want to have lunch on Sunday?

Ann Oh, I don't know. What kind of food do you like?
Jim Well, I like Chinese and Japanese food. And I like all kinds of seafood. What about you?
Ann I don't really like seafood, but Chinese or Japanese sounds good.
Jim Or what about an Italian restaurant? I love Italian food.
Ann I do too. I just don't want to go to an Indian restaurant. I don't like Indian food.
Jim That's fine. I don't either.
Ann And I don't like French food.
Jim Me either.
Ann How about a Mexican restaurant?
Jim No, I don't really like Mexican food.
Ann So, where do you want to go?
Jim I can't decide.
Ann Well, we can always have a hamburger!
Jim Oh, good idea. And french fries! Let's go to that new fast-food place near the university.
Ann Oh, you mean Lulu's. Fine. Let's meet there at noon.
Jim O.K.

ANSWERS
Jim Seafood, Italian food, Chinese food, Japanese food, Fast food
Ann Italian food, Chinese food, Japanese food, Mexican food, Fast food

- Have the students read the instructions. Then have them follow along in their books as you read the sample dialogue with a student.

- Have the students work with a partner to compare Jim's and Ann's likes and dislikes. Tell them to refer to the sample dialogue and the chart. Go around the classroom and check their exchanges.

- Read aloud the instructions. Tell the students to make charts on separate paper. Remind them to include the foods from the chart in their books and three blank columns.

- Tell the students to use their charts to interview three classmates.

- Call on different students to report their findings to the class.

OPTION

As they did in exercise 4, the students can make comparisons about the information in their charts.

Review of units 12-14

1 ► Jim Eldred and Tom Kio go to college in San Francisco. Fill in the blanks with prepositions.
► Act out the conversation with a partner.

Tom How was your day?

Jim Not too good. I went _____ the library, but I was bored and I left _____ noon.

Tom Oh, I was _____ the library, too. In fact, I found this book there. Is it yours?

Jim No, I think it's Ann Lorca's book.

Tom Do you think she's _____ home now?

Jim No, she's _____ class, but she'll be back _____ an hour.

Tom Well, could you give her the book _____ me?

Jim Sure. I'm going to have lunch _____ her _____ Sunday.

Tom Great.

2 ► Imagine you found something. Try to find the owner. Use the items in the pictures or other items.

A I found this book in the library. Is it yours?
B Yes, it's mine. Thanks.

A I found these glasses on the table. Are they yours?
B No, they're not mine. I think they're Ann's.

 3 ► It's Friday night and Jim Eldred and Ann Lorca are talking. Listen and check the kinds of food they like.

	Jim	Ann
Seafood		
French food		
Italian food		
Indian food		
Chinese food		
Japanese food		
Mexican food		
Fast food		

4 ► Make comments about Jim and Ann.

A Jim likes seafood, but Ann doesn't.
B Jim doesn't like French food and Ann doesn't either.

5 ► Interview your classmates.

Make a chart like the one above. Ask three classmates about the foods they like.

6 ▶ **Tom wants to go out to dinner with his friend Gina. Fill in the blanks with** *the* **where necessary.**

Tom Do you like _____ hamburgers?
Gina Sure. Why?
Tom Well, there's a restaurant called Lulu's and _____ hamburgers there are excellent. Would you like to go tonight?
Gina I'd like to, but I can't. I have to babysit for _____ neighbors.
Tom Well, maybe some other time.
Gina O.K. Oh, by the way, I know you like _____ rock music. _____ music at the Underground Club is great. You really have to go!
Tom Yeah, I know. Maybe this weekend.

▶ **Act out the conversation with a partner. Use the ads on the right or your own information.**

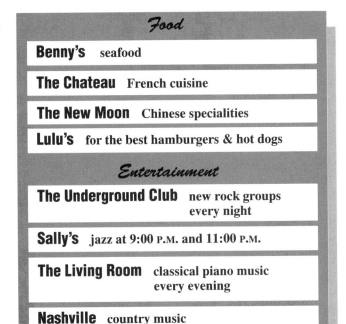

Food

Benny's   seafood

The Chateau   French cuisine

The New Moon   Chinese specialities

Lulu's   for the best hamburgers & hot dogs

Entertainment

The Underground Club   new rock groups every night

Sally's   jazz at 9:00 P.M. and 11:00 P.M.

The Living Room   classical piano music every evening

Nashville   country music

7 ▶ **It's Saturday. Ann meets her friend Helene Garcia at the library. Complete Helene's part of the conversation.**

Ann I'm going to have lunch with Jim tomorrow. Would you like to join us?
Helene _____
Ann At about noon.
Helene _____
Ann Oh, that's too bad. Well, maybe some other time.
Helene _____
Ann By the way, I've got two tickets for the ballet next Saturday night. Do you want to go?
Helene _____
Ann Great! I'll meet you at the theater at ten to eight.

▶ **Invite your partner to join you for a meal and for the ballet or a concert.**

8 ▶ **Complete the conversation.**
▶ **Act out a similar conversation with a partner.**

Helene _____
Ann Oh, Jim's doing fine.
Helene _____
Ann No, he doesn't live here in San Francisco now. He moved to a small town in the country.
Helene _____
Ann He loves it. In his opinion, it's quiet and cheap.
Helene _____
Ann He takes the train. It takes him about forty-five minutes.
Helene _____
Ann O.K.

- Review the rule for when to use *the*. Then read aloud the instructions. Remind the students that some blanks in the exercise may not require *the*.

- Have the students fill in the blanks and then compare their answers with a partner. Call on two students to read aloud the conversation and to write the answers on the board.

ANSWERS
no article, the, the, *no article*, The

- Tell the students to examine the ads on the right as you read them aloud. Then read aloud the second set of instructions. Remind students to use either the information in the ads or their own information in their conversations.

- Have the students work in pairs to act out the conversation. Go around the classroom and check their work, giving help when needed.

- Call on different pairs to act out their conversations for the class.

OPTION

Have the students work in pairs. Have each partner choose a different food and entertainment establishment from the ads. Tell the students to invite their partners to the places they chose. They can pretend to invite one another by telephone.

- Have a student read aloud the instructions. Then have the students read over the incomplete conversation.

- Have the students work in pairs to complete the conversation. Then call on a pair to write Helene's lines on the board. Check their work.

POSSIBLE ANSWERS
What time?
I'm sorry. I can't. I have to take my car to the garage.
Yeah.
Sure.

- Have the students act out their completed conversations. Go around the classroom and listen in, giving help if needed. Then call on a pair to act out their conversation for the class.

- Read aloud the second set of instructions. Have the students choose places to invite their partners to. Tell them they can use the places mentioned on p. 158 or their own ideas.

- Have the pairs act out their invitations. Go around the classroom and check their work. Then call on different pairs to present their conversations to the class.

- Tell the students to read the instructions and the incomplete conversation. Then have them work with a partner to complete the conversation.

- Call on a pair to act out the conversation and to write Helene's lines on the board. Check their work.

POSSIBLE ANSWERS
How's Jim?
Does he still live here?
How does he like it?
How does he get to work?
Say hello to him for me.

- Have the pairs act out a similar conversation, using their own information. Go around the classroom and check their work.

- Call on different pairs to present their original conversations to the class.

9

- Read the instructions aloud to the students. Then have them read over the incomplete conversation and the sentences in the box.

- Tell the students to work in pairs to complete the conversation. Then have a pair read the conversation aloud as they write the answers on the board.

  ANSWERS
  Yes, it is.
  Yes, I do.
  I like it very much.
  Because the city is beautiful. There are interesting old houses and wonderful parks.
  I'm a doctor.
  The hours are long, but I like it very much.

- Read aloud the second set of instructions as the students follow along in their books. On the board, write the following sample conversations:

  A: I like this city because there's always something to do.
  B: I agree. It's never boring.
  OR
  B: I disagree. It's boring and dirty.

- Have the students work with a partner to make up their own conversations. Tell them to use the sample on the board as a guide.

- Go around the classroom and listen in, giving help if necessary. Then call on different pairs to share their conversations with the class.

10

- Read aloud the instructions. Then have the students read over the menu. You can also read the menu aloud and have the students repeat. Answer any questions about the vocabulary.

- Have the students work in pairs to take turns playing the two roles of customer and waiter/waitress. Go around the classroom and check their work.

- Call on different pairs to act out their conversations for the class.

11

- Divide the class into pairs. Have them decide who will be Student A and who will be Student B. Have the A's read their instructions on p. 159 while the B's read theirs on p. 160. So the pairs have a model, call on a student and take turns asking and answering at least one question about each party.

- Have the pairs follow the instructions. Go around the classroom and listen in, giving help when needed.

- Call on a pair of students to present their conversation to the class. You can have another pair write the lines from the conversation on the board.

  SAMPLE 11A ANSWERS
  A My friend Ann is having a party. Would you like to go?
  B When is it?
  A On Friday, November 10th at 8 p.m.
  B I can't. I have class from 8 to 10.
  A Oh, that's too bad.

9 ▶ **It's Sunday and Ann is waiting for Jim at Lulu's. A stranger begins talking to her. Complete Ann's part of the conversation with the sentences in the box**

Man Beautiful day.
Ann _____
Man Do you live here in San Francisco?
Ann _____
Man Do you like it here?
Ann _____
Man Why?
Ann _____
Man What do you do for a living?
Ann _____
Man How do you like it?
Ann _____

I like it very much.
I'm a doctor.
Yes, I do.
The hours are long, but I like it very much.
Yes, it is.
Because the city is beautiful. There are interesting old houses and wonderful parks.

▶ **Work with a partner. Say why you like the place where you live. Your partner will agree or disagree.**

10 ▶ **You are at Lulu's restaurant. Look at the menu and order lunch. Your partner will write down your order.**

LULU'S Restaurant

SANDWICHES
hamburger
cheeseburger $3.95
with lettuce and tomato $4.95
hot dog $1.00 extra
$2.75
chicken sandwich
steak sandwich $3.50
fish sandwich $5.95
$4.75

SIDE ORDERS
french fries
potato salad $1.10
$1.10

DRINKS
soda
cola, diet cola, orange   small large
coffee, tea   .65   .95
milk   .65
    .45

11A ▶ **Student A follows the instructions below.**
Student B follows the instructions on page 160.

Student A Imagine you received this invitation to a party. Invite your partner and answer his or her questions. Then ask appropriate questions and accept or decline your partner's invitation.

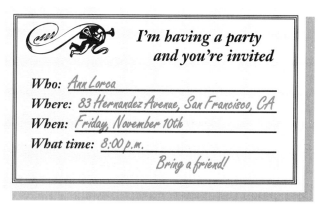

I'm having a party and you're invited

Who: *Ann Lorca*
Where: *83 Hernandez Avenue, San Francisco, CA*
When: *Friday, November 10th*
What time: *8:00 p.m.*
Bring a friend!

11B ▸ **Student B follows the instructions below.**

Student A follows the instruction on p. 159.

Student B Ask appropriate questions and accept or decline your partner's invitation. Then imagine you received this invitation to a picnic. Invite your partner and answer his or her questions.

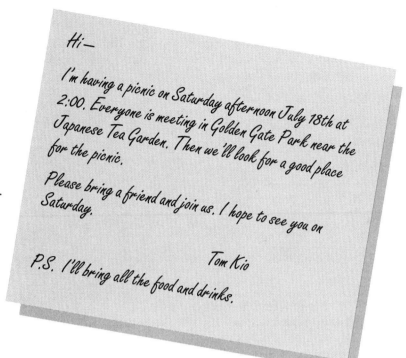

Hi—

I'm having a picnic on Saturday afternoon July 18th at 2:00. Everyone is meeting in Golden Gate Park near the Japanese Tea Garden. Then we'll look for a good place for the picnic.

Please bring a friend and join us. I hope to see you on Saturday.

Tom Kio

P.S. I'll bring all the food and drinks.

12 ▸ **You are preparing for a birthday party on Friday and you still need several things from the store. Ask your classmates where you can get these things in your neighborhood.**

some balloons

some paper napkins

some soda

some plastic forks

some paper plates

a cake

some paper cups

13 ▸ **Read the article about Tom and answer the questions.**
▸ **Ask your partner similar questions.**

1. Does Tom work hard?
2. Does he enjoy it?
3. Where does he usually eat lunch?
4. Does Tom play any sports? What sport(s)?
5. When does he play?
6. What does he do in the evenings?
7. What does he often do on weekends?

PROFILE: *Tom Kio*

Tom Kio is a very busy man. He's a student in the architecture department at San Francisco State University and he has a part-time job at Benning Design Associates. Tom works hard, but he enjoys what he does. He usually arrives at his office at eight o'clock in the morning and works until one. He always eats lunch at his desk at work. Then he leaves for the university.

Tom is busy in the evening, too. He usually studies for several hours every night. On Mondays and Wednesdays, however, he always plays tennis — he really loves sports. When he has time, he sometimes goes out for dinner or to a movie with friends.

On the weekends, Tom often invites 15 or 20 friends to join him for a picnic in the park. His favorite activity at a picnic — playing baseball.

SAMPLE 11B ANSWERS

B My friend Tom Kio is having a picnic in
Golden Gate Park. Would you like to go?
A When is it?
B On Saturday afternoon, July 18th.
A Sure. I'd love to go. What time is the picnic?
B At 2 p.m.

- As the students follow along in their books, read
aloud the instructions. Have the students look at
the illustrations as you read aloud the words
surrounding them and have the students repeat.

- Have the students work in small groups. Tell
them to take turns asking group members the
questions about the items. If necessary, write a
sample exchange on the board:

A: Where can you get a cake?
B: You can get a cake at Lorca's Bakery.

- Call on different groups to share their exchanges
with the class. Check students' intonation and
pronunciation.

OPTION

Have the students plan a class party. Have them
work as a group to decide who will bring the items
pictured on p. 160. Encourage them to add other
items. Appoint a student to ask for volunteers to
bring the different items. Have two students record
the items and the names of the volunteers on the
board. Then have another student ask for
volunteers to set things up and decorate the
classroom before the party and other volunteers to
clean up after the party. Have two students record
the names of the volunteers and their duties on the
board. If possible, actually have the party!

- Have the students read over the questions. Then
tell them to read the article and underline any
words or structures they don't understand.
Answer any questions they have.

- Have the students answer the exercise questions.
You can have them answer on separate paper
and then compare their answers with a partner.

- Call on different pairs of students to ask and
answer the questions and to write the answers
on the board. Check their work.

POSSIBLE ANSWERS

1. Yes, he does.
2. Yes, he does.
3. He always eats lunch at his desk at work.
4. Yes, he does. He plays tennis and baseball.
5. He plays tennis on Mondays and Wednesdays,
and on weekends he sometimes plays
baseball.
6. He usually studies for several hours; however,
sometimes he plays tennis or goes out for
dinner or to a movie with friends.
7. He often invites 15 or 20 friends to join him
for a picnic in the park.

- Read aloud the second set of instructions. Have
the students work in pairs to take turns asking
and answering similar questions about one
another. Go around the classroom and check
their work.

- Call on different pairs to share their exchanges
with the class.

OPTION

Have each student write his or her partner's name
and answers on separate paper. Collect the papers
and distribute them randomly throughout the class.
On the board, write *This person... . Who is he/she?*
Tell the students they are going to read aloud the
answers to the class. Tell them to start each
statement with the words *This person* and when
they finish to have the class guess who the person
is. Write an example on the board:

This person doesn't work very hard.
He doesn't enjoy his work at all.
He usually eats lunch at Arno's Coffee Shop.
etc. ...
Who is he?

WORKBOOK Review of units 12-14, pp. 119-120

VOCABULARY LIST

The list includes both productive and receptive words introduced in Student Book 1. Productive words are those which students use actively in interaction exercises. Receptive words are those which appear only in opening conversations, comprehension dialogues, readings, and instructions, and which students need only understand. Countries, languages, and nationalities are given in a separate list. The following abbreviations are used to identify words: V = verb, N = noun, ADJ = adjective, ADV = adverb, PR = pronoun, INTERJ = interjection, SUPER = superlative, COMP = comparative, 3RD PERS SING = third person singular, PL = plural, R = receptive. Page numbers indicate the first appearance of a word.

A
a 12 R
a few 76 R
a little 63
a lot of 61
a quarter 97
abbreviation 30 R
able 156 R
about ADV 140
abroad 66 R
academy 122 R
accept 159 R
according to 54 R
accountant 48
achieve 66 R
acquaintance 45 R
across 112 R
across from 34
activity 72 R
actor 65 R
actress 52 R
actually 151
ad (= advertisement) 29 R
address 27
address book 27 R
adult 90 R
adventure 98
advertisement 29 R
after 92 R
afternoon 70
again 3 R
aggressive 90 R
ago 112 R
Ah... 12 R
ahead (go ahead) 152 R
airline 76 R
airport 76 R
alive 122 R
all 30 R
all about it 10 R
all day 60
all over 91 R
all right 104 R
all the time 90 R
almost 101 R
alone 51
along 144 R
alphabet 7 R
already 142 R
also 40 R
always 20 R
am 4
an 48
and 7
ankle 122 R
answer N 14 R
answer V 25 R
any 61
Any time! 75 R
anyone 122 R
anything 104 R
anyway ADV 100 R
Anyway... INTERJ 52 R
apartment 35
apologize (for) 17 R
appearance 136 R
apple 106
appointment 82 R
approval 122 R
architect 20 R

architecture 91 R
are 5
area 40 R
aren't (= are not) 25
around ADV 153
around here 51
arrange 122 R
arrive 76 R
art 96
article 20 R
artist 57 R
as (work as a waiter) 57 R
as . . . as 122 R
as for 156 R
as well as 122 R
ask 7 R
aspirin 152
assistant 88 R
association 41 R
at 38 R
at (+ time) 82 R
at least 101 R
at night 57 R
attraction 40 R
aunt 59
avenue 32 R
average 90 R
award 122 R
awful 99

B
babysit 158 R
back ADV 93 R
back there 30 R
bacon 156 R
bad 20 R
bag (of) 108
bakery 156 R
ball (= dance) 102 R
ballet 116
balloon 160
banana 108
bank 34
banker 48
baseball 127 R
based (on) 122 R
basic 126 R
basketball 145
bathing suit 110 R
be asleep 20 R
be away 38 R
be buried 40 R
be excited about 79
be in a hurry 38 R
be located 34 R
be ready to 40 R
be related to 59 R
be...blocks/miles away 38 R
be...years old 40 R
beach 72
bean (fried beans) 156 R
beautiful 10 R
became (PAST of become) 112 R
because 90 R
bed (go to bed) 115 R
bedroom 120 R
beef (ground beef) 109
before 140
behind 85

believe 20 R
belong (to) 102 R
belt 84
besides 99
best (the best = SUPER of good) 40 R
best-seller 122 R
better (COMP of good) 144 R
between 34
big 156 R
biggest (SUPER of big) 112 R
bike (= bicycle) 130
bikini 101 R
bill 11 R
biology 60
birth date 58
birthday 58
black 84
block 50
blouse 84
blue 84
board N 33 R
board V 56 R
boat 136 R
boiled ADJ 156 R
book 72
bookstore 43
boring 96
borrow 63 R
boss 44
both 77
bother 64 R
bought (PAST of buy) 102 R
boulevard 30 R
bow V 45 R
bowl (of) 156 R
box 7 R
boy 64 R
bread 29
breakfast 30 R
briefcase 84
bright 88 R
broken ADJ 122 R
brother 59
brother-in-law 28 R
brown 84
building 37
built (PAST of build) 102 R
bus 130
bus stop 45 R
business 41 R
businessmen (PL of businessman) 44
businesswomen (PL of businesswoman) 44
busy 67 R
but 30 R
but (= except) 104 R
butter 156 R
buy 29 R
by any chance 83 R
by the time 90 R
by the way 75 R
by train 30 R
bye (= good-bye) 26

C
cafe 79
cafeteria 86
cake 160

calculator 150
calendar 58 R
call (by a name) 8 R
call (on the telephone) 12 R
call back 70
calm (down) V 120 R
calmly 90 R
came (PAST of come) 101 R
Can I...? 71
can V 91 R
can't (= cannot) 101 R
candy 43
cannot 76 R
cantaloupe 109
car 87
card (= postcard) 155 R
carrot 107
carry V 112 R
cassette player 135 R
celebrate 102 R
celebration 102 R
cemetery 40 R
cent 107
center 102 R
century 102 R
cereal 90 R
certain 160 R
Certainly. 70
change V 90 R
cheap 130 R
check N 64 R
check V 14 R
cheese 29
cheeseburger 153
chicken 108
child 90 R
children (PL of child) 61
chocolate 156 R
choice 66 R
chose (PAST of choose) 136 R
citizenship 57 R
city 24 R
classic 98
classical 129 R
classmate 4 R
clean ADJ 88 R
clean V 118
clearly 76 R
close V 33 R
closed ADJ 131 R
closet 85
clothing 84 R
cloudy 95
club 93 R
coat 84
coconut 156 R
coffee 26
coffee house 79 R
coffee shop 8 R
coffee table 85
coin 11 R
cola 153
cold 74 R
colleague 42
college 157 R
colony 102 R
color 84
colorful 102 R
come along 144 R

smoked ADJ 156 R
snack 147 R
snack bar 43 R
snow V 95
so ADV 52 R
so INTERJ 18 R
So long. 75 R
soccer 139 R
social 90 R
sock 84
soda 26
sofa 85
sold (PAST of sell) 122 R
sold out 126
solve 37
someday 28 R
someone 5 R
something 21 R
sometime 8 R
sometimes 38 R
somewhere 90 R
son 59
song 79
soon 10 R
sound V 52 R
South 30 R
spaghetti 106 R
speak 62
speaker 59 R
speaking of... 52 R
spectacular 122 R
spell 7
spelling N 7 R
spend 66 R
spice 112 R
spinach 106 R
sport 90 R
spring (season) 102 R
staff 76 R
stair 123
stamp 152
stand for 30 R
stand up 33 R
start V 99
statement 28 R
stay V 96 R
steak 104 R
stop V 90 R
stop in 18 R
store 36
story 112 R
straight 33 R
straight ahead 35
stranger 55 R
street 37
string bass 155 R
strong 81 R
struggle V 122 R
student 20 R
studio 122 R
study V 4 R
style 110 R
suburb 130 R
subway 130
success 76 R
successful 79
such as 102 R
sugar 23 R
suggest 99 R
suggestion 76 R
suit 84
suitcase 120 R
sun 130 R
sunburn 134 R
sunglasses 111
sunny 95
sunshine 134 R
suntan 134 R
supply N 112 R
supporting ADJ 122 R
sure ADJ 32 R
Sure. INTERJ 63

surprise N 89
sweater 84
sweet 112 R
swim V 128 R

T table (coffee table) 85
take 38 R
take a break 148 R
take a message 71
take a minute or two 88 R
take an order 16 R
take care of 141 R
take it easy 72
take someone's advice 64 R
take the time to... 76 R
taken ADJ 101 R
talk V 20
tall 77
taxi 39 R
tea 26
teach 60
teacher 48
telephone 63
television 88 R
tell 10 R
terrible 38 R
terrific 110 R
test N 40 R
test V 122 R
than 122 R
Thank you. 17
thank V 76 R
Thanks. 6
Thanks anyway. 36
Thanks for... 50
Thanks a lot. 36
that PR 8 R
that ADJ 107
that way 86
that'll (= that will) 104 R
That's right. 7
the 3
The number has been
   changed. 19 R
theater 34
their 61
theirs 150
them 4 R
then (= at that time) 119
then (= in that case) 109
There are... 10 R
There you are 83 R
there's (there is) 86
these 5 R
they 25
they're (= they are) 25
thin 156 R
thing 90 R
think 30 R
this ADJ 14 R
this PR 12 R
those ADJ 107
those PR 84
though 115 R
thought (PAST of think) 118
through 122 R
ticket 100 R
tie (necktie) N 84
time 90 R
tip 76 R
tired 28 R
title 6 R
toast 156 R
today 73
together 25 R
tomato 108
tomorrow 73
tonight 73
too (= in excess) 99
too (= also) 4
too much 90 R
took (PAST of take) 118

top (on top of) 156 R
tortilla 156 R
tour 66 R
tourism 102 R
tourist 78 R
town 102 R
town hall 40 R
trade V 112 R
tradition 102 R
traffic 38 R
train N 130
translator 77
travel 40 R
travel agent 102 R
traveler 112 R
traveler's check 85 R
tree 30 R
trip 22 R
tropical 112 R
true 3
truly 90 R
try on 110 R
try out (for) 88 R
try to 12 R
tryout N 88 R
turkey 106 R
turn 35
tusk 112 R
TV (= television) 72
type (of) 156 R

U Ugh! INTERJ 107 R
Uh... INTERJ 12 R
Uh-huh. (= yes) 130 R
uh-oh INTERJ 92 R
umbrella 84
uncle 59
under 85
understand 76 R
unhappily 76 R
university 160 R
until 68 R
up 134 R
upstairs 3 R
us 71
use V 63
usually 153

V variety 156 R
vegetable 103 R
very 20 R
very much 33
video store 124
violent 90 R
visit N 79
visit V 72
visitor 55 R
voice 76 R

W wait V 85
Wait a minute. 69 R
waiter 48
waitress 48
wake (up) V 156 R
walk N 96 R
walk V 35
wallet 85
want 8 R
warm 95
was 84
was/were born 58
wash V 112 R
watch (wristwatch) N 84
watch V 64 R
water 26
watermelon 103 R
we 25
we'll (= we will) 89 R
we're (= we are) 25
we've (= we have) 136 R
wear V 110 R
weather 75 R
week 98 R

weekend 153
weigh 103 R
Welcome to... 8 R
well ADV 54 R
Well, then... INTERJ 8 R
Well... INTERJ 28 R
went (PAST of go) 118
were 84
west 30 R
western 98
wet 112 R
What a...! 75 R
What about...? 11 R
What are you going to...? 73
What do you do? 49
What does...mean? 63
What else...? 54 R
What kind of...? 52 R
What time is it? 97
What's the matter? 120 R
What...? 7
when 64 R
Where...? 24
Which way? 86
Which...? 27
white 84
Who's...? 60
Who's calling, please? 68 R
whole 36 R
why 10 R
Why! INTERJ 155 R
widest (SUPER of wide)
   40 R
wife 59
wild 112 R
will V 8 R
win 75 R
window 140
windy 123
women (PL of woman) 43
won (PAST of win) 122 R
wonderful 64 R
wool 125
wore (PAST of wear) 122 R
work V 48
world 40 R
worried ADJ 83 R
worry V 134 R
would 112 R
write 7 R
write a check 64 R
write down 16 R
writer 102 R
wrong 17
wrote (PAST of write) 122 R

Y Yahoo! INTERJ 101 R
yeah (= yes) 38 R
yellow 84
yes 5
Yes, please. 26
yesterday 87
yogurt 106 R
you 5
You're kidding! 46 R
You're welcome. 17
young 29 R
your 7
yours 66 R
yourself 4 R
Yuk! INTERJ 107 R

Z Zip Code 30 R
zoo 131 R

S U P P L E M E N T A R Y   V O C A B U L A R Y

SOME COUNTRIES AND NATIONALITIES

SOME LANGUAGES

Country	Nationality	Country	Nationality	
Algeria	Algerian	Kuwait	Kuwaiti	Arabic
Argentina	Argentine	Korea	Korean	Bengali
Afghanistan	Afghan	Laos	Laotian	Cantonese
Australia	Australian	Lebanon	Lebanese	Czech
Austria	Austrian	Lithuania	Lithuanian	Danish
Bolivia	Bolivian	Malaysia	Malaysian	Dutch
Brazil	Brazilian	Mexico	Mexican	English
Bulgaria	Bulgarian	Mongolia	Mongolian	Farsi
Canada	Canadian	Morocco	Moroccan	Finnish
Chad	Chadian	Nepal	Nepalese	French
Chile	Chilean	Nicaragua	Nicaraguan	German
China	Chinese	Nigeria	Nigerian	Greek
Colombia	Colombian	Norway	Norwegian	Hausa
Costa Rica	Costa Rican	Pakistan	Pakistani	Hebrew
Cuba	Cuban	Paraguay	Paraguayan	Hindi
Czechoslovakia	Czech	Peru	Peruvian	Hungarian
Ecuador	Ecuadorian	Panama	Panamanian	Italian
Egypt	Egyptian	Poland	Polish	Japanese
Ethiopia	Ethiopian	Portugal	Portuguese	Korean
Finland	Finnish	Saudi Arabia	Saudi	Mandarin
France	French	Spain	Spanish	Mongolian
Gambia	Gambian	Somalia	Somalian	Nahuatl
Germany	German	Sweden	Swedish	Norwegian
Guyana	Guyanese	Switzerland	Swiss	Polish
Ghana	Ghanan	Syria	Syrian	Portuguese
Greece	Greek	Thailand	Thai	Quechua
Guatemala	Guatemalan	The Dominican Republic	Dominican	Romanian
Haiti	Haitian	The Netherlands	Dutch	Russian
Honduras	Honduran	The Philippines	Filipino	Spanish
Hungary	Hungarian	The United Kingdom	British	Swahili
India	Indian	The United States of America	American	Swedish
Indonesia	Indonesian			Tagalog
Iran	Iranian	Tunisia	Tunisian	Tamil
Iraq	Iraqi	Turkey	Turkish	Thai
Ireland	Irish	Venezuela	Venezuelan	Turkish
Israel	Israeli	Vietnam	Vietnamese	Urdu
Italy	Italian	Yugoslavia	Yugoslavian	Vietnamese
Japan	Japanese	Zaire	Zairian	Zulu
Jordan	Jordanian	Zambia	Zambian	
Kenya	Kenyan			

WEIGHTS AND MEASURES

English System

Linear Measure

12 inches (in.)	=	1 foot (ft.)
3 feet	=	1 yard (yd.)
1760 yards (5280 feet)	=	1 mile (mi.)

Liquid Measure

16 fluid ounces (oz.)	=	1 pint (pt.)
2 pints	=	1 quart (qt.)
4 quarts	=	1 gallon (gal.)

Weight

16 ounces	=	1 pound (lb.)
1 ton	=	2000 pounds (U.S.)
	=	2240 pounds (Great Britain)

Metric and English Equivalents

Linear Measure

1 inch (in.)	=	2.54 centimeters (cm)
1 foot	=	30.48 centimeters
1 yard	=	0.9144 meters (m)
1 mile	=	1609.3 meters

Liquid Measure

1 quart	=	0.946 liters
1 gallon	=	13.78 liters

Weight

1 ounce	=	28.3 grams (g)
1 pound	=	0.45 kilograms (kg)
1 ton (U.S.)	=	907.18 kilograms
1 ton (Great Britain)	=	1,016 kilograms

PRONUNCIATION

STRESS AND INTONATION

Affirmative statement: Nice to meet you.

Yes-no question: Hello, is Susan there?

Information question: Where are you from?

> The numbers above and below the intonation lines indicate the pitch: 1 is for the lowest level and 3 is for the highest.

PHONETIC SYMBOLS*

Consonants

[p]	pen, apple
[b]	bank, cabbage
[f]	far, after
[v]	very, have
[k]	coffee, like
[g]	good, again
[l]	letter, mile
[m]	many, name
[n]	never, money
[w]	water, away
[θ]	think, with
[ð]	the, mother
[s]	some, dress
[z]	zero, busy
[ʃ]	shoe, information
[ʒ]	pleasure, measure
[tʃ]	children, teach
[dʒ]	job, age
[r]	right, hurry
[y]	year, million
[h]	he, hat, who
[t]	ten, can't
[d]	dinner, idea

Vowels

[I]	in, visit
[i]	meet, tea
[ɛ]	end, let, any
[æ]	ask, family
[a]	father, hot
[ɔ]	water, long
[ʊ]	could, put
[u]	you, room
[ə]	across, but
[ər]	her, work
[e]	wait, great
[o]	home, go
[aI]	dime, night
[ɔI]	toy, boy
[aʊ]	found, house

*[ə] and [ər] are used in this book, for both stressed and unstressed syllables. [y] is used instead of the International Phonetic Alphabet (IPA) [j].

ANSWERS

Exercise 3, page 5

1. Tom Cruise is an American actor.
2. Janet Jackson is an American singer.
3. Yumi Matsutoya is a Japanese singer/songwriter.
4. Emmanuel is a Mexican singer.

Exercise 4, page 63

Mucho gusto means "Nice to meet you" in Spanish.
Shukran means "Thank you" in Arabic.
Parakalo means "Please" in Greek.
Obrigado means "Thank you" in Portuguese.
Do svidanye means "Good-bye" in Russian.
Habari gani means "How are you?" in Swahili.
Arigato means "Thank you" in Japanese.
Pen yangai means "How are you?" in Thai.

WORKBOOK TAPESCRIPT

UNIT 1

Lesson 3 (p. 3)

2 1. **Charles** Excuse me—are you Marie Thomas?
   Woman No, I'm not.

2. **Marie** Excuse me—are you Charles Lowe?
   Man No, I'm not.
   Marie Sorry.

3. **Jeff** Hi. Are you a neighbor?
   Charles Yes, I am. I'm Charles Lowe.
   Jeff Nice to meet you. I'm Jeff Bowen.

4. **Charles** Hello. I'm Charles Lowe. Uh…are you Marie Thomas?
   Jennifer No, I'm not. My name's Jennifer Hayes.
   Charles Nice to meet you, Jennifer.

5. **Marie** Excuse me—are you Charles Lowe?
   Charles Yes, I am.
   Marie Well, I'm Marie Thomas.
   Charles Oh, hello, Marie! It's nice to meet you!

Lesson 6 (p. 7)

1 1. **Registrar** Could you spell your last name, please?
   Student 1 L-E-A-R. Lear.

2. **Registrar** Spell your last name, please.
   Student 2 A-N-D-E-R-S-O-N. Anderson.

3. **Registrar** Your last name, please?
   Student 3 It's Lopez. L-O-P-E-Z.

4. **Registrar** Your name, please?
   Student 4 Gary Hough. H-O-U-G-H.

5. **Registrar** What's your last name?
   Student 5 Klein. K-L-E-I-N.

6. **Registrar** Your last name, please?
   Student 6 Stewart.
   Registrar How do you spell that?
   Student 6 S-T-E-W-A-R-T.

7. **Registrar** Could you spell your last name, please?
   Student 7 It's Cook. C-O-O-K.

8. **Registrar** Your name, please?
   Student 8 Young. Y-O-U-N-G.

9. **Registrar** Spell your last name, please.
   Student 9 S-M-Y-T-H.
   Registrar Oh, Smyth with a "Y."
   Student 9 That's right.

10. **Registrar** What's your last name?
   Student 10 Brown. B-R-O-W-N.

UNIT 2

Lesson 10 (p. 12)

2 1. **Operator** Directory Assistance. May I help you?
   Man Yes, I'd like the number of Barbara Gomez, please.
   Operator The number is 555-1310.
   Man 1301?
   Operator No, 555-1310.

2. **Man** Hello?
   Woman Hello, is Bob there?
   Man Bob? No, I'm sorry, you have the wrong number.
   Woman Is this 555-2518?
   Man No, it's 555-2918.

3. **Woman** Hello?
   Man Is this 555-6431?
   Woman No, you have the wrong number. This is 555-6421.

4. **Man** Hello?
   Woman Hello, is Mrs. Chang there?
   Man I think you have the wrong number.
   Woman Is this 555-6704?
   Man No, it's 555-6705.
   Woman Oh. Sorry.
   Man That's O.K.

Lesson 11 (p. 14)

5 1. Hello?
   2. Let's see.
   3. May I help you?
   4. Could you spell that, please?
   5. You're welcome.
   6. Hello, is Jill there?
   7. The number is 555-4883.
   8. Is this 555-5071?
   9. I'm sorry, she's at work.
   10. Do you have change for a dollar?

Lesson 12 (p. 15)

1 1. **Operator** Directory Assistance. May I help you?
   Woman I'd like the number of Mary Quinn. Q-U-I-N-N.
   Operator The first name?
   Woman Mary.

2. **Man** Hello, is Bill there?
   Woman No, I'm sorry, he's at work right now.

2 1. **Man** Hello?
   Woman Hello, is Joe Hecht there?
   Man You have the wrong number.
   Woman Is this 555-2094?
   Man No, it's 555-3094.

2. **Operator** Directory Assistance.
   Woman I'd like the number of Al Franco, please.
   Operator The number is 555-8695.

❸ 1. **Man** Are you Mrs. Andrews?
   Woman No, I'm not.

2. **Woman** Your last name?
   Mr. Corelli Corelli.
   Woman Could you spell that, please?
   Mr. Corelli C-O-R-E-L-L-I.

3. **Woman** Do you have change for a quarter?
   Man Yes, I do.
   Woman Thank you.

4. **Woman** Hello?
   Man Hello, is Sally there?
   Woman No, she's at work right now.

UNIT 3

Lesson 15 (p. 18)

❶
1. The United States.
2. Canada.
3. Germany.
4. The Soviet Union.
5. Japan.
6. Taiwan.
7. Australia.
8. Indonesia.
9. Thailand.
10. Kenya.
11. Morocco.
12. Brazil.
13. Chile.
14. Colombia.

❸ 1. **James** Lynn, this is Ana Alvarez, and this is Luis Alvarez. The Alvarezes are from Argentina.
   Lynn Hello. It's nice to meet you.

2. **James** Hi. My name's James Black.
   Lynn And I'm James's wife, Lynn.
   Jean I'm Jean Silver. Are you from the United States?
   Lynn No, we're not. We're from Canada.

3. **Jean** Excuse me—are you Rosa Nunes?
   Rosa Yes, I am.
   Jean I'm Jean Silver, and this is my husband, Mike. We're from England.
   Rosa Nice to meet you.

4. **Jean** Mike, are Rosa and Paulo Nunes from Mexico?
   Mike No, they aren't. The Nuneses are from Brazil.

5. **Rosa** Where are Yoko and Akira Ozawa from?
   Paulo The Ozawas are from Japan. From Tokyo, I think.

6. **Rosa** What about the Lees? Are they from Korea?
   Paulo Yes, that's right. They're from Seoul.

Lesson 17 (p. 22)

❸ 1. **Woman** Hi there. 11 Valley Road, please.
   Cab driver O.K. 11 Valley Road.

2. **Cab driver** Hello. Where are you going?
   Man 14 Pine Street.
   Cab driver 14?
   Man That's right.

3. **Woman** 19 River Street, please.
   Cab driver 90 or 19?
   Woman 19.

4. **Man** North Avenue, please.
   Cab driver O.K., but what number?
   Man Sorry. 230.
   Cab driver O.K. 230 North Avenue.

5. **Cab driver** Where to, ma'am?
   Woman 50 Park Road.
   Cab driver Where?
   Woman 50 Park Road.

6. **Cab driver** Yes, sir?
   Man 80 Western Avenue.
   Cab driver 18?
   Man No, 80.

Lesson 18 (p. 23)

❶ 1. **Woman** Hi, Fred. How are you?
   Fred Fine, thanks.
   Woman How about your wife?

2. **Woman** This is my first trip to Miami.
   Man Oh? Where are you from?

3. **Woman** Do you want some coffee, Joe?

4. **Woman** 16 Front Street, please.
   Cab driver 16 or 60?

5. **Woman** Your sister's very nice. Where's she from?

6. **Man** Where are your neighbors from?

7. **Woman** Joe, this is Fred Wilson. Fred, this is Joe Hecht. He's an old friend from school.

8. **Joe** Good-bye, Fred.
   Fred Bye, Joe.

❷ 1. **Man** How are you and Bob?
   Woman We're fine.

2. **Man** Do you want some coffee?
   Woman Yes, please.

3. **Man** Cream and sugar?
   Woman No, thank you.

4. **Man** Do you have change for a five?
   Woman No, I don't. Sorry.

5. **Man** Uh…Do you have change for a dollar?
   Woman Yes. Here you are.

6. **Man** So, how are your friends, the Nuneses?
   Woman They're fine.

7. **Man** Are they from Mexico?
   Woman No, they aren't.

8. **Man** Where are they from?
   Woman They're from Brazil.

9. **Man** Are you and Carlos from Argentina?
Woman No, we're from Chile.

10. **Man** Good-bye, Laura.
Woman Bye. Nice meeting you.

❸ 1. **Paul** Hello. 90 Olive Street, please.
Cab driver 90?
Paul Yes, that's right.

2. **Cab driver** Olive Street...Is that near the Civic Center?
Paul I don't know. This is my first trip to San Francisco.
Cab driver Let me check my city directory. Olive Street. There it is.

3. **Cab driver** So this is your first trip to San Francisco. Where are you from?
Paul I'm from Canada.
Cab driver Oh? Where in Canada? Montreal? I have friends in Montreal.
Paul No, I'm not from Montreal. I'm from Toronto.

4. **Cab driver** Here you are. 90 Olive Street. That's fifteen dollars.
Paul Fifteen? Do you have change for a twenty?
Cab driver Sure.
Paul O.K. Thanks.
Cab driver Thank you. Enjoy your visit!

5. **Woman** Paul! Welcome! How are you?
Paul Fine, thanks. How are you and Roberto?
Woman We're fine. Roberto's not home yet. He's still at work.

6. **Woman** Do you want some coffee, Paul?
Paul No, thanks.
Woman How about some tea?
Paul Yes, please. That sounds good.

UNIT 4

Lesson 23 (p. 30)

1. **Man** Excuse me—where's Elena's Coffee Shop?
Woman It's on the corner of Taft and Columbus, across from Spiffo's Clothing Store. It's next to the Taft Street Theater.

2. **Woman** Excuse me—is Drucker's Grocery Store near here?
Man Drucker's...Drucker's...Oh, yes. It's on Toledo Avenue between the Hip Hop Discotheque and Northwood High School.

3. **Woman** Where's Sharp's Clothing? Is it near here?
Man Sharp's is on Taft between Toledo and Cleveland. It's next to the fire department, right across from Dollop's Restaurant.

4. **Man** Excuse me—where's Lou's Restaurant?
Woman It's on Hayes Street, across from the park. It's next to Whipple's Grocery Store.

5. **Woman** Excuse me—is the Museum of Modern Art near here?
Man Yes, it is. It's on the corner of Hayes and Cleveland, across from General Hospital.

6. **Man** Excuse me—where's Scribbler's Bookstore?
Woman It's on Garfield Street, next to Dupree's Restaurant.

Lesson 24 (p. 31)

❷ 1. Is the bank near Second Street?
2. The hotel is on Fourth Street.
3. Is Fifth Street near the park?
4. Is First Street that way?
5. Where's State Street?
6. Walk two blocks to Eighth Street. Then turn right.
7. The discotheque is on the corner of Third and Main.
8. Go straight ahead to Third Street.

❸ 1. **Man 1** Excuse me—is the City Library near here?
Man 2 Yes, it is. Walk to the corner of Harrison and Toledo and turn right. Go straight ahead for two blocks. The City Library is on the corner.
Woman 1 No, that's not right. Listen...go to the corner of Harrison and Cleveland and turn left. Walk straight ahead for two blocks. It's on the left.

2. **Woman 2** Excuse me—is the Hamm Theater near here?
Man 2 The Hamm Theater? Yes, it is. Go to Cleveland Avenue and turn left. Then walk about two blocks. It's on the right, next to the Old Mill Museum.
Woman 1 No...the Hamm Theater is on Taft Street. Walk to Columbus Avenue and turn right. Go one block and turn left. The Hamm Theater is on the left, across from Spiffo's.

3. **Man 3** Excuse me—where's Dante's Bookstore?
Man 2 Dante's Bookstore...Go to Toledo Avenue and turn right. Walk straight ahead for three blocks and turn left on Garfield. Walk one block. Dante's is on the corner.
Woman 1 No, dear. Dante's is not on Garfield Street. Walk to Columbus and turn right. Then walk two blocks. Dante's is on your left.

4. **Woman 3** Excuse me—is the Babel Language School near here?
   Man 2 Yes, it is. Walk to the corner and turn right on Toledo. Then go straight ahead for three blocks and turn right on Garfield. The Babel Language School is on the left.
   Woman 1 No, that's not right. Walk straight ahead on Toledo for only two blocks and turn right on Hayes Street. The school is on Hayes, across from the park.

UNIT 5

Lesson 29 (p. 40)

3 1. **Man 1** Hello, Susan. How are you?
   Woman 1 Hi, Mark.
   Man 1 Do you work in this neighborhood?

2. **Man 1** So, where do you work?
   Woman 1 In an office on Main Street.
   Man 1 Oh, what do you do?

3. **Woman 1** How about you? What do you do?
   Man 1 I'm a lawyer.
   Woman 1 Do you work around here?

4. **Man 2** Here's my bus.
   Woman 2 That's my bus, too.
   Man 2 Oh? Where do you live?

5. **Man 2** Where do you live on Washington Avenue?
   Woman 2 In an apartment building between First and Second. It's at 18 Washington Avenue.
   Man 2 Really? I live in the same building. What floor are you on?

6. **Man 2** I have an apartment on the second floor.
   Woman 2 Do you live alone?
   Man 2 Yes, I do. I'm single. What about you?

Lesson 30 (p. 41)

1 1. **Ann** Hello, Bob. How are you?
   Bob Ann! It's nice to see you.
   Ann Do you work in this neighborhood, Bob?
   Bob No, but I live near here. I live in a house down the street.

2. **Bob** What about you? Do you work around here?
   Ann Yes. I work across the street.
   Bob At First National Bank?
   Ann No, at Sam's Restaurant.

3. **Bob** Are you a waitress?
   Ann No, I'm a cook.
   Bob That sounds interesting.
   Ann You're right. It really is.

4. **Ann** What kind of work do you do, Bob?
   Bob Well, I'm a mechanic, but I'm out of work right now. I'm looking for a job in a garage.
   Ann I hope you find something soon.
   Bob I do, too.

2 **Part 1**
   Barber Next!...And how are you today, sir?
   Jonathan Pretty good, thanks. And you?
   Barber Not bad. New in town?
   Jonathan Yes, we just moved here from Washington.
   Barber We? Are you married?
   Jonathan Yes, I am. My wife and I have two children, a son and a daughter.

Part 2
   Barber Live around here?
   Jonathan Yes, right across the street.
   Barber In one of those new apartments?
   Jonathan Uh-huh. That's right.
   Barber What do you do for a living?
   Jonathan I'm a banker.
   Barber First National Bank?
   Jonathan No, the Second National, over on First Street.
   Barber What's your name, by the way?
   Jonathan Riley. Jonathan Riley.

UNIT 6

Lesson 33 (p. 44)

3 1. **Girl 1** Are you sixteen yet?
   Boy 1 Not yet, but my birthday is in March.
   Girl 1 When in March?
   Boy 1 It's March 20th.

2. **Man 1** There's a party for my daughter tonight. It's her twelfth birthday.
   Woman 1 I hope you have a good time.

3. **Marie** Sylvia! What are you doing here?
   Sylvia Oh, hi, Marie. I'm getting a birthday present for my son. It's his thirtieth birthday this year.
   Marie You're kidding! My son is the very same age.

4. **Man 2** I hear today's your birthday. Congratulations!
   Man 3 Thanks. Yeah, it's my twenty-first birthday...I'm finally twenty-one.

5. **Grandma** What's the date today?
   Grandpa The twenty-seventh.
   Grandma ...Oh, no! It's our grandson's birthday and we forgot.

6. **Girl 2** What are you getting Vicki for her birthday?
   Boy 2 When is her birthday?
   Girl 2 It's the fifteenth of June. Today. Vicki's your girlfriend, and you don't know her birthday?

Lesson 37 (p. 49)

1 1. **Man 1** What's your date of birth?
Woman 1 Excuse me?
Man 1 When were you born?

2. **Woman 2** Are you married or single?
Man 2 I'm single. What about you?

3. **Man 1** Could you fill out these forms? They're in Spanish.
Woman 1 My mother and I don't speak Spanish. Could you help us?

4. **Woman 2** Do you speak French?
Man 2 Yes, I do.
Woman 2 Are you from France?

5. **Woman 3** I think our rent is late.
Man 3 Well, what's today's date?

6. **Woman 1** Where are you from?
Man 2 Brazil.
Woman 1 Oh, do you speak Spanish?

7. **Man 2** When is your birthday?
Woman 2 It's in May.
Man 2 When in May?

8. **Man 1** Could you write down your name for me?
Woman 1 Sure...could I borrow your pencil?

9. **Woman 1** Do you speak Portuguese?
Man 2 Well, a little.
Woman 1 How do you say, "How are you?" in Portuguese?

10. **Woman 1** Where's your friend from?
Woman 2 Algeria.
Woman 1 Does he speak both French and Arabic?

2 **Clerk** What's your name?
Michiko Could you speak a little slower, please?
Clerk Sure. What's your name?
Michiko Michiko Nishida. M-I-C-H-I-K-O, N-I-S-H-I-D-A.
Clerk Your address?
Michiko 213 Sixth Street...Dallas, Texas.
Clerk 213 or 230?
Michiko 213.
Clerk O.K. 213 Sixth Street, Dallas, Texas.
Michiko That's right.
Clerk And the ZIP code?
Michiko The ZIP code is 87501.
Clerk Your telephone number?
Michiko (505) 555-9037.
Clerk Date of birth?
Michiko June 23, 1972.
Clerk Where are you from?
Michiko Japan.

UNIT 7

Lesson 40 (p. 53)

4 1. **Woman 1** May I speak with Suzanne Gould?
Man 1 Just a moment, please. May I ask who's calling?

2. **Man 2** Say, can you ask John to call me tonight?
Janet O.K. I'll tell him.
Man 2 Thanks a lot.
Janet Sure. See you later.

3. **Man 1** Good afternoon, Western Industries. May I help you?
Alice Yes, I'd like to speak to Janet Davis, please.

4. **Man 1** I'm sorry, Ms. Davis is in a meeting right now. May I take a message?
Alice Yes, please. Could you ask her to call Alice Young?

5. **Alice** Hi. Is Janet there?
Man 2 No, she's still at work.
Alice O.K. I'll call her later.

6. **Man 2** Hello?
Alice Hello. Is Janet there?
Man 3 Yes. Just a minute...Uh...she's busy right now. Can she call you later?
Alice Sure.

7. **Man 2** Could you take a message, please?
Woman 2 Certainly. Could you spell your last name?

8. **Janet** Hi, Mrs. Young. This is Janet. Can I speak to Alice?
Woman 2 Just a minute, Janet. I'll get her.

6 1. **Man 1** Who's that?
Woman 1 That's my lawyer, Mrs. Rose. Would you like to meet her?

2. **Man 2** Are your parents here?
Woman 2 Yes, but I don't see them.

3. **Man 1** Do you speak Spanish?
Man 2 I don't speak it, but I understand it.

4. **Woman 1** My friend doesn't speak much English.
Man 1 Maybe I could help her.

5. **Man 2** Hello? Is your father there?
Woman 2 No, he isn't. Would you like to leave a message for him?

6. **Man 1** May I have a form?
Man 2 Here you are. Fill it out and bring it back to me.

7. **Woman 1** When was he born?
Woman 2 I don't know, but I can ask him.

8. **Woman 1** Does your wife speak Chinese at home?
Man 2 Yes, with her parents, but I don't understand her!

Lesson 42 (p. 57)

 1. **Assistant** Good afternoon, Lee Import-Export. May I help you?

George Ah, yes. May I speak to Mrs. Lee, please?

Assistant Who's calling, please?

George This is George Greene.

Assistant I'm sorry, Mr. Greene, but Mrs. Lee isn't here right now. May I take a message?

George Could you ask her to call me at my office?

Assistant Does she have your number?

George Maybe not. It's 555-4371.

Assistant 555-4371?

George That's right. That's my number at work.

Assistant And your name is George Greene.

George Yes, Greene with an "E."

Assistant You mean G-R-E-E-N-E?

George Right.

Assistant O.K., Mr. Greene. I'll give her the message.

George Thank you. Good-bye.

Assistant Good-bye.

2. **Assistant** Good afternoon, Lee Import-Export. May I help you?

Catherine Could I speak to Amy Lee, please?

Assistant Who's calling, please?

Catherine This is her friend Catherine Barr.

Assistant I'm sorry, Ms. Barr, but Mrs. Lee isn't here right now. May I take a message?

Catherine Could you ask her to call me at home this evening?

Assistant Does she have your number?

Catherine No, she doesn't. I have a new number. It's 555-9283.

Assistant 555-9283?

Catherine That's right.

Assistant And could you spell your name?

Catherine My first name is Catherine— C-A-T-H-E-R-I-N-E, and my last name is Barr—"B" as in "boy"- A-R-R.

Assistant Thank you, Ms. Barr. I'll give her the message.

Catherine Thank you. Good-bye.

 Tony Hi, Dang. How are things going?

Dang Not bad.

Tony Any plans for the weekend?

Dang Well, on Saturday I'm going to visit my parents.

Tony Hmm…Where do they live?

Dang In the country.

Tony Nice…So you're going to the country…Are you going to work or just relax?

Dang I hope I can take it easy. I'm tired this week. What about you? What are you going to do?

Tony Well, I'm going to go to the beach on Saturday. And then Saturday evening I'm going to have dinner with some friends.

Dang That sounds like fun. Any plans for Sunday?

Tony I'm going to stay home and watch the baseball game on TV.

Dang Great…Listen, I've got to go now, but have a wonderful weekend.

Tony You, too. Enjoy the country.

U N I T 8

Lesson 45 (p. 63)

④ 1. That's a nice jacket.
2. It's red.
3. His glasses are silver.
4. They're new.
5. Those are interesting earrings.
6. They were a gift.

⑤ 1. **Man** That's a beautiful scarf.
Woman Thanks.
Man Gold is a nice color.

2. **Woman** That's a nice shirt. You look good in blue.
Man Thanks.

3. **Woman 1** What color is your new skirt?
Woman 2 It's green.

4. **Man 1** Oh, no!
Man 2 What's wrong?
Man 1 I don't have my gloves.
Man 2 What color are they?
Man 1 They're gray.
Man 2 Are those yours? Over there?
Man 1 Yes. Thanks!

5. **Woman** What color are those shoes?

6. **Man** Black. Are they O.K.?
Woman With brown socks?

⑥ 1. **Man** That's a beautiful scarf.
Woman Thanks.
Man Gold is a nice color.

2. **Woman** That's a nice shirt. You look good in blue.
Man Thanks.

3. **Woman 1** What color is your new skirt?
   Woman 2 It's green.

4. **Man 1** Oh, no!
   Man 2 What's wrong?
   Man 1 I don't have my gloves.
   Man 2 What color are they?
   Man 1 They're gray.
   Man 2 Are those yours? Over there?
   Man 1 Yes. Thanks!

5. **Woman** What color are those shoes?

6. **Man** Black. Are they O.K.?
   Woman With brown socks?

Lesson 47 (p. 65)

2 1. **Receptionist** It's down the hall on the right, near the stairs.

2. **Receptionist** There's one upstairs.

3. **Receptionist** They're over there, near the exit.

4. **Receptionist** It's down the hall on the left, near the stairs.

5. **Receptionist** It's downstairs.

Lesson 48 (p. 66)

2 1. **Woman** Where were your credit cards?
   Man They were on the table.

2. **Man** Where were your keys? Were they in your pocket?
   Woman No, they were in my handbag.

3. **Man 1** Well, I have my glasses.
   Man 2 Where were they?
   Man 1 They were right here in my pocket.

4. **Woman 1** Is this your wallet?
   Woman 2 Yes, it is! What a relief! Where was it?
   Woman 1 Under the sofa.

Lesson 49 (p. 67)

2 1. **Woman** That's a terrific briefcase. Is it new?
   Man Thank you. Yes, it was a gift.

2. **Woman** Oh, no!
   Man What's wrong?
   Woman I don't have my credit card.

3. **Woman** Where was your wallet?
   Man On my desk.
   Woman Where? In your desk?
   Man No, *on* my desk.

4. **Man** Excuse me, is there a pay phone in the building?
   Woman Yes, there's one down the hall on the right, next to the employment office.

5. **Woman** Excuse me, which way is the employment office?
   Man It's downstairs, on the second floor.

6. **Man 1** Where are the restrooms?
   Man 2 Down the hall on the left, near the exit.
   Man 1 This way?
   Man 2 No, that way.

7. **Woman** Where are my car keys?
   Man I don't have them.
   Woman What? You lost my car keys?
   Man I'm afraid so. But you can use mine. Here!

8. **Man 1** Were you at work yesterday?
   Man 2 No, I wasn't. Were you?
   Man 1 No. I was sick.
   Man 2 Uh-huh. Beautiful day, wasn't it?
   Man 1 Yeah. It was.

UNIT 9

Lesson 53 (p. 71)

2 1. **Jean Claude** Allo?
   Frank Jean Claude? Hi, it's Frank Larson. How ya' doing?
   Jean Claude Frank! It's good to hear from you. What's new?
   Frank Not much. How are things in Montreal? Is it snowing there?
   Jean Claude No, but it's cold and raining.

2. **Frank** Hi, Terry. It's your Uncle Frank.
   Terry Well, hi, Uncle Frank. How are you?
   Frank Not bad. You?
   Terry O.K.
   Frank How's the weather there in Washington?
   Terry Well, it's cloudy today. And cool. It isn't very nice. In fact, I think I'm catching cold.

3. **Frank** Well, how's my favorite person in Vancouver?
   Woman 1 I'm fine, Frank. How are you?
   Frank Oh, everything's O.K. I called earlier, but you weren't there.
   Woman 1 No, I was out. Then it started raining, so I came home.
   Frank Oh, it's raining there now?
   Woman 1 Yes, but at least it isn't cold. It's warm, in fact.

4. **Alfredo** ¿Bueno?
   Frank Hello, Alfredo. This is Frank Larson, in San Francisco.
   Alfredo Well, Frank! It's good to hear from you. When are you coming back to Mexico?
   Frank Maybe next month. I'm ready for some Mexican sunshine. Is it sunny now?
   Alfredo Yes, it's sunny, but cool. You know Mexico City in January.

5.   **Woman 2** Yes, it's snowing here in Denver, Frank. We have about a foot of snow already, and it isn't stopping. And it's cold. We should be with Dad in Miami. Have you called him lately?
     Frank I'm going to call him next, sis...

6.   **Dad** Hot and sunny, Frank, hot and sunny. Just like always. That's Miami. How's your sister?
     Frank Fine, Dad. She sends her love...

Lesson 54 (p. 73)

3 1.   **Man 1** Let's eat out tonight.
          Woman 1 OK. Where?
          Man 1 Paul Havens?
          Woman 1 It's closed on Tuesdays.
          Man 1 That's right. How about the new Mexican restaurant?
          Woman 1 Is it open Tuesdays?
          Man 1 Yes, it's open seven days a week.
          Woman 1 Good. I like Mexican food. What time do they open?
          Man 1 I'm not sure. Where's the newspaper? Here. They open at seven.
          Woman 1 Let's go at seven thirty.
          Man 1 O.K.

2.   **Woman 2** Do you want to go to a museum tomorrow? There are three very good ones in town.
     Man 2 Well, maybe. What are they?
     Woman 2 There's an art museum. Oh, too bad. It isn't open on Fridays.
     Man 2 Good. Art museums are boring.
     Woman 2 There's a clothing museum. They have clothes from all over the world. Some of them are hundreds of years old.
     Man 2 You've got to be kidding. A museum of old clothes? Forget it!
     Woman 2 O.K., here you go. A transportation museum: old cars and trains.
     Man 2 Now, that's a good idea! When is it open?
     Woman 2 From nine to six thirty.
     Man 2 Let's do that. Is it O.K. with you?
     Woman 2 I guess so, but Saturday we're going to the art museum or the clothing museum.
     Man 2 All right.

Lesson 56 (p. 75)

1 1. **Woman** Are you hungry?

2.   **Woman** Are you hungry?
     Man Yes!
     Woman Me too. Where do you want to eat?

3.   **Man** Do you like Washington, D.C.?

4.   **Man** Do you like Washington, D.C.?
     Woman Yes, I like it a lot. How about you?

5.   **Man** Are you having a good time?

6.   **Man** Are you having a good time?
     Woman Yeah, I'm having a wonderful time.

7.   **Woman** What's playing at the Ridge Theater tonight?

8.   **Woman** What's playing at the Ridge Theater tonight?
     Man *I Am the Vice-President*.
     Woman What kind of movie is it?

2 1.   **Man** This movie is bad.
          Woman Bad? It's a horrible movie.
          Both Let's go home!

2.   **Woman** How do you like San Francisco?
     Man I love it! How about you? Are you having a good time?
     Woman Well, no, I'm not.

3.   **Man** Let's go out for dinner.
     Woman OK. What do you want to eat?
     Man I like Japanese food.
     Woman Well, I don't. How about Italian? Do you like that? I do.
     Man I do too.

4.   **Woman** Do you want to go to the bank?
     Man Yes, I do. When does it close?
     Woman At three o' clock, I think. What time is it now?
     Man Quarter after three.
     Woman It's too late, then.

3 1. Are you having a good time?
2. Is it raining?
3. Does he like jazz?
4. Are you hungry?
5. Does it start at 7:30?
6. Are we late?
7. Do you like westerns?
8. Is she having dinner?
9. Do they open at nine?
10. Do they want to see it?
11. Is it expensive?
12. Are you listening?

U N I T   1 0

Lesson 59 (p. 78)

2 1.   **Man** What do you want for dinner tonight?
          Woman How about fish?

2.   **Woman** May I help you?
     Man Yes, I'd like some chicken, please.

3.   **Woman 1** What's your favorite fruit?
     Woman 2 I don't know. Apples, I guess.

4.   **Woman** Anything else?
     Man Yes, I'd like some beef, please.

5.   **Woman** Do we need any cheese?
     Man No, we have some cheese.

6.   **Man** What's your favorite vegetable?
     Woman Onions, believe it or not.

③
1. I'll take those bananas.
2. How much are these apples?
3. This lettuce is rotten.
4. Is this fish fresh?
5. How much are those grapes?
6. That cheese is two fifty-nine a pound.

Lesson 60 (p. 81)

④
1. **Grocery Clerk** They're eight for a dollar.
   Woman 1 Give me four, please.

2. **Woman 2** How much are the potatoes?
   Grocery Clerk They're thirty-nine a pound.
   Woman 2 I'll take three pounds, then.

3. **Woman 1** How are your apples today?
   Grocery Clerk Nice and fresh.
   Woman 1 How much are they?
   Grocery Clerk Three for a dollar.
   Woman 1 I'll take six.

4. **Woman 2** How much are your peppers?
   Grocery Clerk Thirty cents a pound, or two pounds for fifty-nine.
   Woman 2 Give me two pounds, please.

5. **Woman 1** That ground beef looks good.
   Grocery Clerk It is. I just made it.
   Woman 1 But a dollar ninety-eight a pound? That's kind of expensive.
   Grocery Clerk Well, it is good—and fresh.
   Woman 1 O.K., I'd like three pounds, please.

Lesson 61 (p. 83)

①
Clerk Do you need any peaches today?
Customer No, I have peaches at home. But I'll take some of those pears. How much are they?
Clerk A dollar for six. How many would you like?
Customer Give me six, please. Are those potatoes twenty-nine or thirty-nine cents a pound?
Clerk Twenty-nine a pound.
Customer I'll take five pounds, please.
Clerk Is there anything else? Some onions? Carrots? Tomatoes? Peppers? They're all fresh today.
Customer No, thanks. I don't need anything else.

UNIT 11

Lesson 65 (p. 89)

②
1. What did you do last night?
2. Where did you go for dinner?
3. What time did she return to Chicago?
4. How was your weekend?
5. What did they see there?
6. Who did he visit in the hospital?

③
1. **Woman** How do you like my coat?
   Man That depends. How much was it?

2. **Woman** How did you like the movie?

3. **Man** How's your family?
   Woman They're fine. Jason's a college student now, you know.

4. **Woman** Where did you have your meeting?

5. **Woman** I saw Mrs. Knight at that new Japanese restaurant.

6. **Man** Marge! Are you home?...Marge?... Marge!
   Woman Here I am.

Lesson 66 (p. 90)

①
1. **Man 1** Mr. Kelly wasn't at work last week.
   Man 2 No, he was in the hospital.

2. **Woman 1** I called you at eight this morning.
   Woman 2 I wasn't home. I went to work at seven. We have to finish that building.

3. **Man** Where were you last night?
   Woman I went to the office.

4. **Woman** Was Amanda at school today?
   Man Yes, she was.

5. **Man** I thought Mark was sick.
   Woman No, he was in class. He's O.K.

6. **Man 1** What did you do yesterday?
   Man 2 I went to the hospital. I saw Mr. Kelly.

Lesson 67 (p. 91)

① **Conversation 1**
Bill Hi, Tom. How was your weekend?
Tom Pretty good. Friday night I went to a movie with Ann.
Bill What did you see?
Tom *Cold Pizza*.
Bill How did you like it?
Tom It was terrific. I really like comedies.... Then Saturday I took Lisa to a party at Donna's house. By the way, how was your weekend?
Bill Don't ask. I worked the whole time.

Conversation 2
Lindsay What did you do last weekend, Maria?
Maria Not much. It was pretty boring. Friday I stayed home and watched television. I worked all day Saturday. Sunday I—
Lindsay What did you do Saturday night?
Maria Well, uh, actually, I stayed home and watched TV again.
Lindsay Oh. Sorry. What about yesterday?
Maria I visited my parents.
Lindsay Did you go out last night?
Maria Yeah, I saw a movie.
Lindsay Alone?
Maria No, I went with my sister.

UNIT 12

Lesson 70 (p. 98)

4

1. **Reporter** Excuse me, sir. Can I ask you a question?
   Man Well, I'm in a hurry, but O.K.
   Reporter Do you live here in the city?
   Man No, I don't. I live in a small town about half an hour from here.
   Reporter What do you think of the city? Do you like it?
   Man No, I just work here. I don't like it at all. It's too dangerous, and it's noisy and dirty.
   Reporter I see. Well, thank you.

2. **Reporter** Ma'am? Excuse me, may I ask you a question?
   Woman Yes, I suppose so. What would you like to know?
   Reporter Do you live in the city?
   Woman Yes, I do. I've lived here all my life—eighty-two years.
   Reporter Do you like the city?
   Woman That's two questions, young man. You said, "May I ask you a question?" But the answer is yes. I love the city, and I love living here, even after eighty-two years. There are a lot of excellent restaurants… theaters…museums…There's always something to do.
   Reporter Thank you, ma'am.
   Woman You're welcome, young man.

3. **Reporter** Do you work here in the city?
   Man Yes, I work in that building over there.
   Reporter Do you live here too?
   Man No, I live in the country, more than an hour from here. I take the bus to work.
   Reporter Do you like the city?
   Man Yes. I really want to live here, but I can't right now. I spend a lot of time here, though.
   Reporter What do you like about the city?
   Man The music. I like all kinds of music, and there are all kinds here: classical, rap, jazz—You name it, the city's got it. It's great.

4. **Woman** I wouldn't live in the city for anything. You couldn't pay me to live here. No, I live in the suburbs.
   Reporter You don't like the city, then?
   Woman No, I don't. I just come here to do some shopping. But everything's so expensive! And ugly. There aren't any trees or flowers, and it's dirty and dangerous. No, thank you. I would not want to live here. The suburbs are fine, just fine.

5 (Repeat conversations from exercise 4.)

Lesson 71 (p. 100)

4

1. I like classical music.
2. I'm single.
3. I don't like romance novels.
4. I'm reading a really good book right now.
5. I'm not doing anything tonight.
6. I like Mexican food.

Lesson 72 (p. 101)

1

1. **Woman 1** I think the movie was really great.
   Woman 2 I think so too.

2. **Man 1** I don't like the suburbs.
   Man 2 I don't either.

3. **Man** I had a good time. Did you?
   Woman Uh-huh.

4. **Man 1** I think the city is dirty and dangerous.
   Man 2 Well, I don't.

5. **Woman 1** I don't think small towns are boring.
   Woman 2 Oh, I do.

6. **Man** I'm pretty tired. How about you?
   Woman Oh, I'm fine.

7. **Man 1** I like the birds and trees and flowers in the country…
   Man 2 Me too.

8. **Woman** Hey, he's pretty good.
   Man What? I think he's awful.

9. **Man** In the suburbs there's nothing to do.
   Woman I don't really agree.

10. **Woman** Let's eat at this German restaurant.
    Man Hmm…it's too expensive for me.

2

1. **Woman** Don't you work in my building?

2. **Man** Do you live here in the city?

3. **Woman** Do you like it?

4. **Man** How do you get to work?

5. **Woman** Are there any good restaurants here?

6. **Man** Where?

7. **Woman** What are you reading?

8. **Man** Why do you say that?

UNIT 13

Lesson 76 (p. 105)

2

1. Could you call me later?
2. Do you want to come with us?
3. Thanks for inviting me.
4. Do you know them?
5. Where did you see her?
6. Could you call him back in about an hour?

Lesson 78 (p. 109)

1 1. **Man** Hurry! Our flight leaves in fifteen minutes!

2. **Woman** When were you born?
    Man 1962.
    Woman I was born in 1968.

3. **Woman** What time do you open?
    Man We open at eight thirty, Monday through Friday.

4. **Woman** Are you open on Sundays?
    Man No, we aren't.

5. **Woman** When's your birthday?
    Man It's in May. The 28th.

6. **Woman 1** When does school start?
    Woman 2 September 10th, in just two weeks.

7. **Man 1** Is Marie there?
    Man 2 No, she isn't. Could you call back in about half an hour?

8. **Man** When's the concert?
    Woman It's on January 17th.

9. **Man** Is your next appointment in the morning or the afternoon?
    Woman The morning. At eleven o' clock.

2 1. **Man** Would you like to go to a movie Friday?
    Woman Sorry, I can't. I work Fridays.

2. **Woman** Do you want to go with us?
    Man I'd like to, but I can't. I'm working.

3. **Woman 1** Can you come with us?
    Woman 2 Thank you, I'd love to.

4. **Woman** I've got tickets for the baseball game. Want to go with me?
    Man Sure. That sounds great.

5. **Man** There's a concert this Saturday. Would you like to go?
    Woman Sorry, I can't. Wait—did you say this Saturday?
    Man Yeah. This Saturday.
    Woman Then I can go.

3 **Don** Hello?
Greg Hi, Don. It's Greg.
Don Hey, Greg. How are you doing?
Greg Great. You?
Don O.K. What's up?
Greg I've got two tickets for the football game this Saturday. Want to go?
Don This Saturday? The game's at three, isn't it?
Greg No, at three thirty.
Don Well, it doesn't really make any difference. I can't go anyway. I have to visit a friend in the hospital.
Greg That's too bad. Anyone I know?
Don I don't think so. A friend from college. Saturday afternoon's the only time I can go see him. But thanks for the invitation.
Greg Sure. Maybe another time.

Kathleen Hello?
Greg Kathleen?
Kathleen Uh-huh. Greg?
Greg Yeah. Hi. How's it going? How's the actor?
Kathleen Terrific. I'm in a new play. It's opening this Saturday.
Greg This Saturday, huh? Then I guess you can't go to the football game with me Saturday afternoon.
Kathleen No, I can't, and I'd really like to go, too. You know I love sports, especially football. But we've got final rehearsal that afternoon. I'm sorry.
Greg Me too. Well, good luck on the play.
Kathleen Don't ever say that to an actor! You're supposed to say "Break a leg."
Greg Really? Well, O.K. Break a leg.
Kathleen Thanks.

Laura's Mom Hello?
Greg Hello, Mrs. Bravo. This is Greg Van Zandt. Is Laura there?
Laura's Mom No, she isn't home right now, Greg. Can I give her a message?
Greg No, thanks. I'll call her again later.
Laura's Mom All right, Greg. Good-bye.
Greg Bye.

Greg Hello?
Greg's Father Hi, son.
Greg Dad! How are you? How's Mom?
Greg's Father We're both fine. What are you doing?
Greg I've got tickets for the football game this Saturday, and I'm trying to get somebody to go with me. No luck so far.
Greg's Father The Patriots' game?
Greg Yeah.
Greg's Father I know someone who'd like to go.
Greg Really? Who?
Greg's Father Ahem.
Greg Why didn't I think of that? Dad, would you like to go to the game with me?
Greg's Father You bet I would. It would be just like old times—father and son at a football game.
Greg Great! I'll pick you up at three. See you then.

UNIT 14

Lesson 82 (p. 113)

1
1. **Man** Is this hers?
2. **Woman** No, it's ours.
3. **Man** I think that's mine. It has my name on it.
4. **Woman** Our coats are here. Where are theirs?
5. **Man** I think this is his.
6. **Woman** Well, *I* think it's hers.
7. **Man** Excuse me, is this yours?
8. **Woman** Yes, it is. No, I'm sorry, it's his.

Lesson 85 (p. 117)

1
1. **Woman** Where can I get some good food?
2. **Man** Is that yours or mine?
3. **Man** Would you like something to drink?
4. **Woman** What do you do?
5. **Man** Is this my umbrella?
6. **Woman** How did you like that job?
   Man It was hard work.
   Woman How was the pay?

2 **Mr. Bryan** I always get up at six, and I always have breakfast at six thirty. I usually have cereal, juice, and coffee. I never eat eggs for breakfast.

I sometimes drive to work, but I usually take the train.

I always eat lunch at my desk. I never go home for lunch.

I often eat at six, sometimes later. Dinner is my big meal of the day.

3
1. Where does he work?
2. Where did he work before?
3. How did she like it?
4. What do you eat for breakfast?
5. When does she get home from work?
6. Why does he say that?
7. Where did she go for vacation?
8. How do I look?

WORKBOOK ANSWER KEY

Lesson 1

2. M-O-L-N-A-R
3. Oh, hello, Scott.
4. Fine, thanks.

5. I'm Mark Molnar.
6. Nice to meet you, too.

Lesson 2

2. **A** Hello. My name's Randy Booth.
   B I'm Hector Mendez. It's nice to meet you.

3. **A** Hello. My name's Al Bergen.
   B Hello, Al. I'm Lucy Shaw.
   A It's nice to meet you, Lucy.

4. **A** Hello, I'm Erik Reid. I'm your new neighbor.
   B I'm Lisa Crosby. I live upstairs.

Lesson 3

1 2. **A** you   3. **A** you   4. **A** are
       B am   **B** am   **B** not

2 2. b   3. a   4. b   5. a

Lesson 4

1. 2, 3, 1
   B I'm fine, thank you. And you, Mrs. Harris?
   A Good, thanks.

2. 3, 1, 4, 2
   A Hi, Harry.
   B Hi, Pete. How are you?
   A O.K. How are you?
   B Oh, not bad.

3. 4, 2, 1, 3
   A Hello, Mr. Oshima.
   B Hello, Ms. Jacobs. How are you today?
   A Fine, thank you. How are you?
   B Good, thank you.

Lesson 5

1 1. that's, first, Mr.
   A S-M-I-T-H?
   B Yes, that's right.
   A Could you spell your first name, please?
   B S-Y-L-V-E-S-T-E-R.
   A Thank you, Mr. Smith. Sign here, please.

2. Are, am, last, Ms.
   A Are you Elena Lopes?
   B Yes, I am.
   A I'm sorry, could you spell your last name, please?
   B L-O-P-E-S.
   A Sign here, please.
   B O.K.
   A Thank you, Ms. Lopes.

2 | Across | Down |
| --- | --- |
| 1. neighbor | 1. name |
| 7. please | 2. right |
| 8. live | 3. Could |
| 10. meet | 4. Are |
| 12. last | 5. Yes |
| 14. upstairs | 6. spell |
| 16. Hello | 9. you |
| 17. to | 10. Mrs. |
| 18. not | 11. first |
| | 13. too |
| | 15. thanks |
| | 16. How |

Lesson 6

1 2. Anderson   5. Klein   8. Young
   3. Lopez   6. Stewart   9. Smyth
   4. Hough   7. Cook   10. Brown

2 2. Johnson   4. hello   6. upstairs
   3. Carolyn   5. neighbor

3 **Joe Wilson** Nelson
   Liz Nelson am
   Joe Wilson Wilson, upstairs
   Liz Nelson meet
   Joe Wilson too

Lesson 7

Answers will vary.

Lesson 8

1 2. a   **A** I'm sorry.
            B That's O.K.

   3. b   **A** Is this 555-1037?
            B No, it isn't.

   4. b   **A** Is Susan there?
            B Yes, she is.

2 2. I'd like the number of Jill Ito, please.
   3. Hello, Mr. Ito. Is Jill there?
   4. Hello, Jill? This is Ted.

Lesson 9

1 **B** Hello, is this Bill?
   A No, it isn't. This is Carlos.
   B Hi, Carlos. This is Jean. Is Bill there?
   A No, he isn't here right now. He's at work.

② 2. **Caller** is
Mrs. Hill she, She's

3. **Caller** there
Mrs. Hill here, He's

4. **Caller** this, Is
Mrs. Hill is, minute

③ 2. No, she isn't. 4. Yes, she is.
3. No, it isn't. 5. No, it isn't.

④ 2. **A** you 3. **B** this 4. **B** is
B am **A** it's **A** it

Lesson 10

① 2. nine 5. six 7. eight 9. three
3. nine 6. seven 8. seven 10. seven
4. zero

② 2. a 3. a 4. b

Lesson 11

① 1. **Man** I, you
Ray Thank
Man welcome

2. **Ray** I'd, of
Operator Could, name
Operator number
Ray Thank

3. **Ray** is, there
Woman have
Ray this
Woman isn't
Ray sorry
Woman That's

4. **Ray** Hello, there
Woman she
Ray This
Linda How
Ray are

② Could you spell your last name?
What's your telephone number?

③ Answers will vary.

④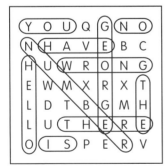

A Hello, is
B No, you, the wrong number.

⑤ 2. . 5. . 7. . 9. .
3. ? 6. ? 8. ? 10. ?
4. ?

Lesson 12

① 1. **B** Mary Quinn, Q-U-I-N-N
B Mary

2. **A** Bill

② 1. 555-3094 2. 555-8695

③ 2. **A** up 3. **A** up 4. **A** up
B down **B** down **B** up
A up **A** down **A** down
B down

Lesson 13

Answers will vary.

U N I T 3

Lesson 14

① 2. d 3. e 4. a 5. c

② 2. a **A** Where are you from?
B I'm from Seoul.

3. a **A** Do you want some coffee?
B Yes, please.

4. b **A** Good-bye, Song. Nice meeting you.
B Nice meeting you, too.

Lesson 15

① 2. Canada 9. Thailand
3. Germany 10. Kenya
4. the Soviet Union 11. Morocco
5. Japan 12. Brazil
6. Taiwan 13. Chile
7. Australia 14. Colombia
8. Indonesia

② 2. **A** Where are you from?
B 'm from England.

3. **A** Where are you from?
B 'm from the United States.

4. **A** Where are you from?
B 're from Japan.

5. **A** Where are you from?
B 'm from Mexico.
's from Ghana.

③ 2. Canada 4. Brazil 6. Korea
3. England 5. Japan

④ 2. The Cashes aren't in Munich. They're in Berlin.
3. Nina and Carol aren't sisters. They're friends.
4. Peter isn't from Russia. He's from Germany.
5. Nina isn't from Germany. She's from the United States.
6. The Cashes aren't from Canada. They're from the United States.

Lesson 16

1 1. 3, 1, 2
    B Fine. How are you, Susan?
    A Good.

    2. 3, 2, 1
    A Eva, this is my friend Frank from school.
    B Nice to meet you, Frank.
    C Nice to meet you, too, Eva.

    3. 2, 4, 1, 3
    A Do you want some coffee?
    B Yes, please.
    A Cream and sugar?
    B No, thanks.

2 2. **Jean** this, Janet
    Janet Hi
    David Nice

    3. **Jean** want
    Janet thank

    4. **David** from
    David I'm

    5. **Janet** Good-bye
    David meeting

Lesson 17

1 2. ninety   5. ninety-nine   8. fifty-two
    3. eighty-three   6. fifteen   9. thirty-three
    4. ninety-three   7. forty-four   10. thirty-five

2 POSSIBLE ANSWERS
What's your address?
Could you spell *Rockefeller*, please?
What's the number?
What's your telephone number?

3 2. 14   4. 230   6. 80
    3. 19   5. 50

Lesson 18

1 2. c   4. a   6. c   8. a
    3. c   5. b   7. c

2 2. Yes, please.   7. No, they aren't.
    3. No, thank you.   8. They're from Brazil.
    4. No, I don't. Sorry.   9. No, we're from Chile.
    5. Yes. Here you are.   10. Bye. Nice meeting
    6. They're fine.   you.

3 2. T   4. F   6. F
    3. T   5. T

Lesson 19

Here I am in New Orleans. The people are very friendly, and New Orleans is beautiful. My old friend Louise Tate lives here. She's on Barracks Street—only about fifteen minutes from my hotel. New Orleans is a very interesting city.
    I'll write again soon.
            Love,
            Cindy

Ms. Deborah Elliott
323 Woodson Avenue
Sacramento, California
95821

UNIT 4

Lesson 20

2. **C** No, it's not. It's on the corner of State and Fifth.

3. **B** I think it's that way. Or is it that way? I'm not sure.

4. **B** Go straight ahead for two blocks, and it's on your right.

Lesson 21

1 2. b   4. a   6. c
    3. b   5. b

2 2. across from the park.
    3. on State Street next to the State Street Hotel.
    4. on Second between State and Norwood.
    5. on the corner of Third and Main.

3 Main, Fourth, Fifth
right, one, right, two, left, Capital Theater

4 2. **A** Andrew Bloom's   5. **A** the Romanos'
      B on the third   **B** on the first

    3. **A** the Nutts'   6. **A** Georgia Dawson's
      B on the fourth   **B** on the second

    4. **A** Rosa Sanchez's
      B on the eighth

Lesson 22

1. **B** straight, left, Avenue, block, turn, right, next to

2. **B** Second, between, corner, right, ahead, one, right, Fred's Restaurant
    A across from

3. **B** left, one, on, the, corner, at

Lesson 23

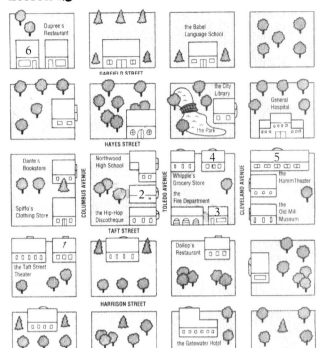

Lesson 24

1 2. b   4. b   6. a
   3. a   5. a

2 2. b   4. b   6. b   8. b
   3. a   5. a   7. a

3 2. a   3. b   4. a

Lesson 25

Answers will vary.

Review of units 1-4

1 1. **Gary** 's
       Clerk 'm
       Gary 's

   2. **Oscar** are
      Gary am
      Oscar 's, 'm
      Gary 's
      Oscar 's

   3. **Oscar** are
      Gary 'm
      Oscar is
      Gary is, are, Are
      Oscar 'm, 'm

   4. **Oscar** are
      Gary Is
      Oscar isn't, 's

2 POSSIBLE ANSWERS
   1. Is Stanley there?
      Is this 555-9358?
      I'm sorry.

   2. Is this Dean Bartlett?
      Is Dean there?
      Thank you.

3 POSSIBLE ANSWERS
   1. across from the post office. Go straight ahead on Third Avenue to Duke Street. Take a right on Duke and go one block to Second Avenue. Turn left on Second. The bank is on the right between Yale and Duke.

   2. on the corner of Penn Street and Second Avenue. Take Third Avenue to Penn Street. Turn right on Penn and go one block. The bookstore is on the right.

   3. next to the theater. Go straight ahead on Third Avenue to Yale Street. Take a right on Yale. It's on the left.

U N I T   5

Lesson 26

   2. I'm a biologist.
   3. On Leonardo Street.
   4. No, I don't. I live with my family.

Lesson 27

1 2. Dominique is a secretary.
      Secretaries work in offices.
      Dominique works in an office.
      She works at the Kline and Gross Law Office.

   3. Paitoon is a banker.
      Bankers work in banks.
      Paitoon works in a bank.
      He works at the National Bank of Thailand.

   4. Rose is a waitress.
      Waitresses work in restaurants.
      Rose works in a restaurant.
      She works at Lucky Sam's Restaurant.

2 1. At Baldwin High School.
      Where do you work?

   2. At Smith's Garage.
      I'm a mechanic.
      Are you a waitress?

Lesson 28

1 1. **A** on   2. **A** on   3. **B** in
      B on   **A** on   **A** in
                     B At   **B** on, in

2 1. **B** Johnson   2. **A** do
      A Where   **B** doctor
      B eleven, bank   **A** work
                           B Hospital

Lesson 29

1 POSSIBLE ANSWERS
   1. **A** Where do you work?
      A What do you do there?
      B How about you? What do you do?

2. **A** Do you live on Albany Street?
   A Where on Baker Street?
   B How about you? Where do you live?

3. **A** Are you married?
   B How about you? Are you married?
   B Do you live alone?

2 Answers will vary.

3
2. c	4. b	6. a
3. c	5. c	

Lesson 30

1 2. b   3. b   4. b

2 Part 1
2. False   3. It doesn't say.

Part 2
4. False   6. True   8. False
5. True   7. True   9. True

Lesson 31

Answers will vary.

U N I T 6

Lesson 32

1. 4, 3, 2, 1
   B It's the month, day, and year you were born.
   A Thanks.
   B You're welcome.

2. 4, 2, 1, 3
   A Where is Lisa from?
   B She's from Taipei.
   A Does she speak Chinese?
   B Yes, she does.

3. 4, 2, 1, 3
   A These are my parents, and this is my brother, David.
   B Who's that?
   A That's my cousin Dan.
   B He's very good-looking.

Lesson 33

1
February 19, 1984
March 15, l985
April 30, 1969
May 11, 1976
June 13, 1972
July 22, 1980
August 20, 1961
September 24, 1933
October 17, 1919
November 12, 1973
December 31, 1946

2 1. **A** What day is today?

2. **B** What's the date next Friday?
   B What year were you born?

3 2. twelfth   4. twenty-first   6. fifteenth
3. thirtieth   5. twenty-seventh

Lesson 34

1. is Ellen's cousin.
   is Ellen's uncle.
   is Ellen's aunt.
   is Ellen's grandmother.

2. is Bill's sister.
   is Bill's nephew.
   is Bill's father.
   is Bill's niece.
   is Bill's wife.

3. is Mary's daughter.
   is Mary's son.
   is Mary's granddaughter.
   is Mary's husband.
   is Mary's grandson.

Lesson 35

1 1. **Molly Torres**

She's a lab technician and she works at Prescott Memorial Hospital. Her husband teaches history at Elmwood High School.

2. **Peter Bates**

He has a sister named Anna, and he lives with his parents and sister. They live in the Gardenview Apartments. He goes to Elmwood High School, and he has a job, too. He works at Gordon's Restaurant.

2 1. **Molly Torres**
Where does she work?
What does she do?
What does her husband do?
Where does he teach?

2. **Peter Bates**
Does Peter live alone?
Does he go to school?
Does he have a job?
Does he have any brothers or sisters?

3 SAMPLE ANSWERS
2. Do you have a job?   4. Do you live alone?
3. Do you go to school?

Lesson 36

1. What's today's date?

2. Do you speak
   How do you say
   Could you spell that, please?

3. What does, mean
   Could you speak a little slower, please?
   Thank you.

Lesson 37

1
2. b	4. c	6. b	8. b	10. a
3. b	5. b	7. c	9. c	

2
213 6th Street
Dallas, Texas
87501
(505) 555-9037
June 23, 1972
Japanese

Lesson 38

Answers will vary.

U N I T 7

Lesson 39

1. Who's calling, please?
   I'm sorry, Mr. Day. Mr. Drysdale is in a meeting.
   May I take a message?
   I'll give him the message.

2. What are you going to do this weekend?
   We're going to visit my parents.
   You too. See you Monday.

Lesson 40

1 POSSIBLE ANSWERS
1. Could you ask her to call me?

2. Yes. May I speak to Lisa Davies, please?
   Yes. Could you ask her to call me?
   (*Student's last name*)
   Yes, she does. OR No, she doesn't. It's
   (*student's phone number*).
   Thank you. Good-bye.

2 I'm sorry, Mr. Mustard is in a meeting right now.
   May I take a message?
   Could you spell your last name, please?
   Does Mr. Mustard have your number?
   I'll give him the message.

3 No, she isn't. Can I take a message?
   What's your number?
   O.K. I'll tell her.

4 2. b   4. a   6. b   8. b
   3. a   5. b   7. a

5 1. **B** it   2. **A** them   3. **A** you
   B them, me   **A** him
   A them   **B** him, me
   A me
   A him

6 2. them   4. her   6. me   8. her
   3. it   5. him   7. him

Lesson 41

1 1. **B** go, have, about   3. **A** are, to, on
   A visit, play   **B** going, work
   B do   **A** mechanic
   B am

2. **A** What, going
   B watch, easy
   A have, go
   A night

2 **Mark** I'm going to watch TV. How about you?
   Ginny I'm going to visit my parents.
   Mark Have a nice evening.
   Ginny Thanks. You too. See you tomorrow.

3 Answers will vary.

Lesson 42

1 2. b   4. a   6. a   8. a
   3. a   5. a   7. b

2 **CALLER** George Greene
   PHONE NUMBER 555-4371
   MESSAGE Call Mr. Greene at his office.

   CALLER Catherine Barr
   PHONE NUMBER 555-9283
   MESSAGE Call Ms. Barr at home this
   evening.

3 1. b, d, e   2. a, c, d

Lesson 43

TO Marcia Brady
CALLER Danai Aswin
PHONE NUMBER 555-4017
MESSAGE Mr. Aswin isn't going to be in
class tonight. You can call him
at home.

Review of units 5-7

1 He lives in California now. He lives with his sister
and her husband in an apartment near Los Angeles.
He's very busy. He teaches Spanish at Pacific State
University and he goes to English classes at night.

Midori is from Toronto. Her grandparents still live
in Tokyo and every summer she visits them. She
speaks English and Japanese, but she doesn't write
Japanese very well. She's a biologist at the Ecotech
Company. She works in a laboratory and does
research.

2 POSSIBLE ANSWERS
Pedro
2. Where does he live now?
3. Does he live alone?
4. What does he do?
5. Where does he teach?
6. What does he do at night?

Midori
1. Where's Midori from?
2. What does she do in the summer?
3. What does she do there?
4. Where do they live?
5. Does she speak Japanese?
6. What does she do?
7. Where does she work?

U N I T 8

Lesson 44

1. What's wrong?
   What color is it?
   Just one moment...Is this it?
   On the floor over there.

2. Excuse me. Is there a pay phone on this floor?
   And which way are the elevators?
   Thanks.

Lesson 45

1 2. Those are   4. Those are   6. Those are
3. That's a   5. That's

2 2. That's a terrific sweater.
3. Those are nice sweaters.
4. That's a great jacket.
5. That's an interesting necklace.
6. Those are terrific shoes.

3 2. a **A** That's a beautiful ring.
      B Thank you. It was a gift.

3. b **A** You look good in yellow.
      B Thanks. It's my favorite color.

4. b **A** What color is Kevin's jacket?
      B Green.

4 2. It's   4. They're   6. They
3. His   5. Those

5 2. shirt   4. gloves   6. socks
3. skirt   5. shoes

6 1. gold   3. green   5. black
2. blue   4. gray   6. brown

Lesson 46

1 2. **A** Oh, no! I don't have my coat.
      B It's over there in the closet.
      A Oh, great!

3. **A** Oh, no! I don't have my key.
   B It's over there on the desk.
   A Oh, great!

4. **A** Oh, no! I don't have my shoes.
   B They're over there under the chair.
   A Oh, great!

5. **A** Oh, no! I don't have my traveler's checks.
   B They're over there on the sofa.
   A Oh, great!

2 **Tom** my, our, Our, their, his, her
Bill your

Lesson 47

1 2. a **A** Is there a drinking fountain on this floor?
      B No, there isn't.

3. a **A** Which way is the vice-president's office?
      B It's over there.

4. a **A** Is there a cafeteria in this building?
      B Yes. There's one upstairs.

2 2. the cafeteria   4. the restroom
3. the public telephones   5. the parking garage

Lesson 48

1 1. was, was
      A What was wrong?
      B My son was sick.

2. was, wasn't, were
   B It wasn't very good.
   A That's too bad. Who was there?
   B My classmates were there.

3. were, was, was
   B They were in my wallet.
   A Where was your wallet?
   B It was in my car.

2 2. a   3. a   4. b

Lesson 49

1 2. a pay phone   9. the coffee table
3. the Lost and Found 10. our credit cards
4. his favorite color 11. under the sofa
5. blue and white socks 12. drinking fountains
6. her earrings   13. the accountant's office
7. my briefcase   14. their traveler's checks
8. a beautiful dress

2 2. credit card   5. isn't   8. weren't
3. on   6. left
4. is   7. her

3 2. scarf   5. keys   8. watch
3. glasses   6. wallet
4. briefcase 7. credit card

Lesson 50

Answers will vary.

UNIT 9

Lesson 51

1. 3, 2, 4
   B We're sightseeing here in San Francisco.
   A How's the weather?
   B It's beautiful.

2. 2, 4, 1, 3
   A Are you having a good time?
   B Yes, I'm having a wonderful time.
   A I am too. I love San Francisco.
   B I do too.

3. 3, 2, 4, 1
   A What do you want to do now?
   B Let's go to a movie.
   A What time is it?
   B It's 7:00. The movie is at 8:00.

Lesson 52

1 2. 's going   4. 're having
3. 're walking 5. 's dancing

2 2. **A** What's Hiroko doing?
      B She's going to a movie.

3. **A** What are Antonia and Arthur doing?
   B They're walking to the Savoy Jazz Club.

4. **A** What are Mae Ling and Ashok doing?
   B They're having dinner at the Oyster Palace.

5. **A** What's Boris doing?
   B He's dancing with his girlfriend.

Lesson 53

1 2. **A** Is she having a good time?
   B No, she isn't.
   A How's the weather?
   B It's raining.

3. **A** Are they having a good time?
   B No, they aren't.
   A How's the weather?
   B It's cold.

4. **A** Are they having a good time?
   B Yes, they are.
   A How's the weather?
   B It's snowing.

5. **A** Is she having a good time?
   B No, she isn't.
   A How's the weather?
   B It's cloudy.

2 2. e   3. a   4. c   5. f   6. d

Lesson 54

1 2. **B** Let's go to a museum.
   A That's a good idea. Let's go to the Art Museum.

3. **B** Let's go for a walk in the park.
   A That's a good idea. It's a nice day.

4. **B** Let's go dancing.
   A Dancing? I'm too tired. Let's go to a movie instead.

2 **B** the   **B** the   **B** a
   A The   **A** an   **A** The

3 **Conversation 1**
   2. Mexican   3. seven   4. 7:00   5. 7:30

   Conversation 2
   1. three   2. closed   3. is   4. 9:00   5. 6:30

4 2. It's open from ten to five thirty every day.
   3. It's open from 9:00 p.m. to 2:00 a.m., Tuesday to Sunday.
   4. It's open from noon to midnight every day.

Lesson 55

1 2. **A** What
   B *Good-bye, My Love.*

3. **A** What's
   B *Attack from Mars* and *Space Adventure.*

4. **A** Who
   B Tex Montana.

2 2. d   **A** Let's go to see *Good-bye, My Love.*
           B I don't really like love stories.

3. e   **A** Joe Lombardo's Band is at the Galaxy Ballroom.
        B I don't really like to dance.

4. a   **A** Do you want to see *Western Blues* tonight?
        B It's too far.

5. c   **A** Let's go see *Attack from Mars.*
        B I don't really like science fiction movies.

Lesson 56

1 2. b   4. b   6. c   8. a
   3. a   5. a   7. b

2 **Conversation 1**   **Conversation 3**
   2. F   1. F   2. T

   Conversation 2   **Conversation 4**
   1. F   2. T   1. F   2. F

3 2. it isn't.   6. we aren't.   10. they do.
   3. he doesn't.   7. I don't.   11. it is.
   4. I am.   8. she isn't.   12. I'm not.
   5. it does.   9. they don't.

Lesson 57

1 1. The name of the movie is *Good-bye, My Love.*
   2. It's playing at the Surf Theater.
   3. Gabriel Maxim and Renee Marchand are starring in it.
   4. Yes, they are.
   5. It's interesting.
   6. The shows are at seven thirty and nine thirty, and there's a special midnight show on Saturdays.

2 Answers will vary.

U N I T   1 0

Lesson 58

A Great. That's my favorite food.
A OK. You buy the meat and I'll get the vegetables.

A I'd like a head of lettuce.
A Yes. Do you have any potatoes?
B How much are they?
B O.K. I'll take one bag, please.

Lesson 59

1 1. apple   4. melon   7. grapes   10. pineapple
   2. onion   5. tomato   8. garlic
   3. orange   6. pepper   9. lettuce

2 2. chicken   4. beef   6. onions
   3. apples   5. cheese

3 2. these   3. this   4. this   5. those   6. that

4 **A** that   **A** that   **A** that
   B These   **B** These   **B** this, that

⑤ POSSIBLE ANSWERS

2. These bananas are fresh.
3. This fruit stand has rotten grapes.
4. Those apples look good.

Lesson 60

①
2. How much are oranges?
3. How much is chicken?
4. How much are pork chops?
5. How much are potatoes?
6. How much is salmon?
7. How much is steak?
8. How much is lettuce?

②
2. some	4. any, some	6. any
3. some	5. any	7. some, some

③
B I'm sorry. I don't have any onions, but I have some fresh garlic.
A No, I don't like garlic. Do you have any tomatoes?
B Yes. I have some nice tomatoes for 89¢ a pound.
A I'll take two pounds. And do you have any grapes?
B I have some nice red grapes and some green grapes.
A O.K. I'll take some red grapes.

④ 2. a   3. a   4. b   5. c

⑤
2. b **A** Do you have any bananas?
      B Yes, we do.

3. b **A** I'd like two tomatoes, please.
      B I'm all out of tomatoes.

4. a **A** Anything else?
      B Yes, I'd like some potatoes.

5. a **A** How much are the apples?
      B They're sixty-nine cents a pound.

6. a **A** I'm sorry. I'm all out of bananas.
      B Well, how about some grapes?

7. b **A** I'd like some fruit.
      B I have some nice apples.

Lesson 61

①
B peaches, I'll, those, How much are they?
A for, How many would you like?
B six
A those, thirty-nine cents a pound
B a pound
A I'll take
B Some onions? Carrots? Tomatoes? Peppers? They're
A I don't need anything else.

②
	[ɪ]	[i]
2.	this	
3.		these
		green
	spinach	
4.	list	
	it's	

Lesson 62

① salad, peas, carrots, potatoes, beets, green beans

② Answers will vary.

UNIT 11

Lesson 63

2. b **A** How was your weekend?
      B It was pretty boring, actually.

3. c **A** What did you think of the movie?
      B I didn't like it very much.

4. a **A** We got ice cream after the movie.
      B I know. I saw you there.

Lesson 64

① 2. did   3. had   4. lost   5. watched

②
2. They watched TV yesterday afternoon.
3. They had dinner in a restaurant last night.
4. She did her homework in the afternoon.
5. He lost his wallet on Saturday.

③
Linda went	**Linda** it, how
Mitch How	**Mitch** worked, had
Linda saw	**Linda** to, was
Mitch was	**Mitch** It, had

④ 5, 1, 3, 7, 2, 6, 4

⑤ We saw *Rainy Day Blues*. Saturday afternoon I went shopping for clothes. I got a new jacket. Saturday night I had dinner with my roommate. On Sunday I was pretty tired. I relaxed at home and went to bed early.

Lesson 65

①
2. did she do on Monday night?
3. did she see in Nashville?
4. did she return to Boston?
5. did Mrs. Wilcox and Jenny have dinner?
6. did she take the day off?
7. did she play tennis on Saturday?

②
1. did you do
2. Where did you go
3. What time did she return
4. How was your
5. What did they see
6. Who did he visit

③ 2. b   3. a   4. a   5. b   6. a

④ Answers will vary.

Lesson 66

① 6, 4, 2, 5, 3

② to the   to, at the, to
in the   to

③ Answers will vary.

Lesson 67

1   **Conversation 1: Tom and Bill**
2. T   3. F   4. T   5. T

     Conversation 2: Lindsay and Maria
1. F   2. F   3. T   4. F   5. F

2
1. **B** television   3. **A** yesterday

2. **B** hospital   **B** afternoon
     A secretary   4. **A** library
     B biologist   **B** Sometimes

Lesson 68

1   3, 2

2   Answers will vary.

Review of units 8-11

1   POSSIBLE ANSWERS
2. Where are the restrooms?
3. Is there a drinking fountain on this floor?
4. Is there a Lost and Found near here?

2
Judy Not too bad. How are you?
  Pat I'm fine. What are you doing today?
Judy I'm watching a tennis game on TV.
  Pat How's the weather there in Miami?
Judy It's warm and sunny.
  Pat You're lucky. It's cold here in London.

3   POSSIBLE ANSWERS
2. Those oranges look good, and they're only five for a dollar.
3. Those red apples look fresh, and they're only twenty-five cents each.
4. That watermelon looks good, and it's two ninety-nine.
5. These yellow apples look ripe, and they're only six for a dollar.

4   Yes. They're five for a dollar.
Anything else?

5   Where's it playing?
What time does it start?
Hmm. The midnight show is too late. Let's go to the 10:00 show.

UNIT 12

Lesson 69

2. b   **A** Do you live in the city?
      B No. I live in the country.

3. a   **A** Do you like the city?
      B Yes. It's never boring.

4. b   **A** What are you reading?
      B A new book by Robert Bloom.

5. b   **A** What kind of music do you like?
      B Most kinds.

Lesson 70

1
1. Do you work near here?
And do you live in the city?
How do you get to work?

2. Awful day.
Do you live here in the city?
Do you like it?

2
2. John drives to work. It takes about twenty minutes.
3. Sharon takes the bus to work. It takes about an/one hour.
4. Rob walks to work. It takes about ten minutes.

3
1. There aren't any trees or flowers.
There aren't many good restaurants.
It's noisy.
It's dirty.
There isn't a museum.

2. It's safe.
There are trees and flowers.
It's quiet.
There are a lot of good restaurants.
There's a museum.
It's clean.

4   a, d, b

5   2. +   3. +   4. −

6   2. d   3. a   4. b

7   there, They're, they're, They're, There, their

Lesson 71

1
2. **A** What kind of books do you like?
   B Mystery novels.

3. **A** What kind of music do you like?
   B Rock music.

4. **A** What kind of books do you like?
   B Science fiction.

2   POSSIBLE ANSWERS
2. Maria doesn't like science fiction, but Alex does.
3. Maria likes romance novels, but Alex doesn't.
4. Maria doesn't like historical novels, and Alex doesn't either.

3
2. Maria and Alex like jazz, and I do too (but I don't).
3. Maria and Alex like rock, and I do too (but I don't).
4. Maria and Alex don't like rap, but I do (and I don't either).

4
2. I am too.   4. I am too.   6. I do too.
3. I don't either.   5. I'm not either.

5
A *no article*   **A** *the*
B *no article*, *the*   **B** *no article*, *the*
A *the*

Lesson 72

1
2. AGREE   5. DISAGREE   8. DISAGREE
3. AGREE   6. DISAGREE   9. DISAGREE
4. DISAGREE   7. AGREE   10. DISAGREE

2 1. up   3. up   5. up   7. down
    2. up   4. down   6. down   8. down

3 **DOWN**   **ACROSS**
    1. singer   4. live   6. either   9. Nice
    2. Why   5. get   7. favorite
    3. great   8. country

Lesson 73

1 POSSIBLE ANSWERS
1. The weather is terrific.
2. Yes, there are. There are great old buildings from the 1920s and 1930s.
3. You can go to the beach, and you can walk around the city and sightsee.
4. You can go to clubs and cafes.

2 Answers will vary.

UNIT 13

Lesson 74

1 2. b   3. a   4. d

2 2. **A** We have tickets for the soccer game. Would you like to join us?
    B I'd love to. When is it?

   3. **A** How's Alex doing?
    B Fine. He lives in the country now.

   4. **A** Do you want to go to a baseball game on Saturday?
    B I can't on Saturday. I have to work.

Lesson 75

1 Could you help me with it?
Could you close the door?
Could you call back in an hour?

2 1. **A** them   3. **A** us   5. **A** her
    B them   **B** you   **B** her, it

  2. **B** it, them, 4. **A** them, him
    you   **B** him

Lesson 76

1 **Sam** 's visiting
Chu is she having
Sam says
Chu Does she go
Sam goes
Chu are going, Do you want
Chu eat
Sam have

2 2. us   3. me   4. them 5. her 6. him

3 7, 4, 3, 5, 2, 1, 6

  B Oh, how's she doing?
  A She's doing great. She's working at the hospital now.
  B Really? When did she finish medical school?
  A Last month.

B That's great. Say hello to her for me, O.K.?
A Yeah, I will. Good-bye.

4 working, job, works, to, doesn't, On, relaxes

5 Answers will vary.

Lesson 77

1 2. They've got a terrific new car.
3. We've got an invitation to a party on Friday night.
4. I've got an extra ticket for the concert.

2 2. I'd love to, but I've got to babysit for my neighbors.
3. I can't today. I have to go to the dentist.
4. I'd like to, but I have to help my father.

3 **George** on   **Sue** In
    Sue on   **George** on, at
    Sue on

4 POSSIBLE ANSWERS
When is it?
What time on Saturday?
Where is it?

Lesson 78

1 2. in   4. on   6. in   8. on
    3. at   5. in   7. in   9. in, at

2 2. REFUSES   4. ACCEPTS
    3. ACCEPTS   5. ACCEPTS

3 2. b   4. c   6. b   8. c
    3. b   5. a   7. a

4 He goes to the game with his father.

Lesson 79

1   November 29, 1994

Dear Barry,

  I'm having a dinner party at my apartment next Friday. My friends from Mexico are going to be there. My sister and her new boyfriend will be there also. There's going to be music and dancing after dinner. Bring a friend and come at about seven o'clock.

              Love,
              Margaret

2 Answers will vary.

UNIT 14

Lesson 80

1. Where did you work before?
   How was that?

2. There's a coffee shop across the street.
   Could you bring me a cup of coffee?

3. To stay or to go?
Something to drink?
Anything else?

Lesson 81

1
1. **Hal** You, them   3. **Grandma** my
    Kay I, them   **Grandpa** they, hers

2. **Hal** they   4. **Grandma** my, they
    Kay yours   **Kay** You, yours,
    Hal they, mine   his, mine

2
B No. Mine's right here. Maybe it's hers.
A Excuse me, is this your umbrella?
C Yes, it is. Thanks a lot.

Lesson 82

1
2. ours   4. theirs   6. hers   8. his
3. mine   5. his   7. yours

2
1, 8, 3, 2, 5, 4, 7, 6

A What do you do?
B I'm a police officer.
A How do you like your job?
B I like it a lot, but it's dangerous.
A Where did you work before?
B I worked in a hospital before.
A How did you like it?
B Well, the people were really nice, but it wasn't too interesting.

3 Answers will vary.

Lesson 83

1
2. b   3. f   4. a   5. e   6. c

2
POSSIBLE ANSWERS
2. **B** Well, there's a department store next to the post office.
   A Where's the post office?
   B It's on Marcos Avenue.
   A Can I get you anything?
   B Yes. Could you get me some socks?
   A Sure.

3. **B** There's a drugstore next to the coffee shop.
   A Where's the coffee shop?
   B It's on Main Street.
   A Can I get you anything?
   B Yes. Could you get me some aspirin?
   A Sure.

Lesson 84

1
POSSIBLE ANSWERS
2. **A** Does he often walk to work?
   B Yes. He usually walks to work, but sometimes he takes the bus.

3. **A** Do they ever drive to work?
   B No. They never drive to work. They always ride their bicycles.

4. **A** Docs she ever leave the house late?
   B No. She never leaves the house late. She always gets to work on time.

5. **A** Does Gina usually buy her lunch at the school cafeteria?
   B Yes. She usually buys her lunch at the school cafeteria, but sometimes she goes to her grandmother's house for lunch.

2
SAMPLE ANSWERS
1. I usually eat lunch at home.
2. Sometimes I eat with my sister.
3. I always eat a sandwich.

3
What would you like?
Is that to stay or to go?
Something to drink?
Anything else?

4 Answers will vary.

Lesson 85

1
2. b   3. a   4. b   5. a   6. b

2
always, breakfast, 6:30
usually, coffee
never, eggs
sometimes, usually, train
always, lunch
never, home, lunch
often, sometimes
meal

3
1. does   3. did   5. does   7. did
2. did   4. do   6. does   8. do

Lesson 86

1
2. ?   4. F   6. T   8. ?
3. T   5. F   7. F

2 Answers will vary.

Review of units 12-14

1
1. **B** to, has, at, is, is
   A doesn't
   B worked, wasn't, either

2. **A** There, his, Do, at
   B On, go, for, their
   A too, a
   B There, to

2
POSSIBLE ANSWERS
Are you enjoying your job?
Do you work on weekends?
What do you do on weekends?

3 Answers will vary.

4 Answers will vary.

5 Answers will vary.